3rd edition

RESEARCH METHODOLOGY

a step-by-step guide for beginners

Ranjit Kumar

Los Angeles | London | New Delhi
Singapore | Washington DC

SAGE Publications Ltd
1 Oliver's Yard
55 City Road
London EC1Y 1SP

SAGE Publications Inc.
2455 Teller Road
Thousand Oaks, California 91320

SAGE Publications India Pvt Ltd
B 1/I 1 Mohan Cooperative Industrial Area
Mathura Road
New Delhi 110 044

SAGE Publications Asia-Pacific Pte Ltd
33 Pekin Street #02-01
Far East Square
Singapore 048763

Library of Congress Control Number available

British Library Cataloguing in Publication data

A catalogue record for this book is available from the British Library

ISBN 978-1-84920-300-5
ISBN 978-1-84920-301-2 (pbk)

Typeset by C&M Digitals (P) Ltd, Chennai, India
Printed and bound in Great Britain by TJ International Ltd, Padstow, Cornwall
Printed on paper from sustainable resources

To my daughter, Parul

Contents

Figures

Tables

Preface

This book is based upon my experiences in research as a student, practitioner and teacher. The difficulties I faced in understanding research as a student, my discoveries about what was applicable and inapplicable in the field as a practitioner, and my development of the ability effectively to communicate difficult concepts in simple language without sacrificing technicality and accuracy as a teacher have become the basis of this book.

Research methodology is taught as a supporting subject in several ways in many academic disciplines such as health, education, psychology, social work, nursing, public health, library studies and marketing research. The core philosophical base for this book comes from my conviction that, although these disciplines vary in content, their broad approach to a research enquiry is similar. This book, therefore, is addressed to these academic disciplines.

It is true that some disciplines place greater emphasis on quantitative research and some on qualitative research. My own approach to research is a combination of both. Firstly, it is the objective that should decide whether a study be carried out adopting a qualitative or a quantitative approach. Secondly, in real life most research is a combination of both methods. Though they differ in the philosophy that underpins their mode of enquiry, to a great extent their broad approach to enquiry is similar. The quantitative research process is reasonably well structured whereas the qualitative one is fairly unstructured, and these are their respective strengths as well as weaknesses. I strongly believe that both are important to portray a complete picture. In addition, there are aspects of quantitative research that are qualitative in nature. It depends upon how a piece of information has been collected and analysed. Therefore I feel very strongly that a good researcher needs to have both types of skill. I follow a qualitative–quantitative–qualitative approach to an enquiry. This book, therefore, has been written to provide theoretical information in an operational manner about methods, procedures and techniques that are used in both approaches.

Research as a subject is taught at different levels. The book is designed specifically for students who are newcomers to research and who may have a psychological barrier with regard to the subject. I have therefore not assumed any previous knowledge on the part of the reader; I have omitted detailed discussion of aspects that may be inappropriate for beginners; I have used many flow charts and examples to communicate concepts; and areas covered in the book follow a 'simple to complex' approach in terms of their discussion and coverage.

The structure of this book, which is based on the model developed during my teaching career, is designed to be practical. The theoretical knowledge that constitutes research methodology is therefore organised around the operational steps that form this research process for both quantitative and qualitative research. All the information needed to take a particular step, during the actual research journey, is provided in one place. The needed information is organised in chapters and each chapter is devoted to a particular aspect of that step (see Figure 2.3). For example, 'Formulating a research problem' is the first operational step in the research process. For formulating a 'good' research problem, in my opinion, you need to know how to review the literature, formulate a research problem, deal with variables and their measurement, and construct hypotheses. Hence, under this step, there are four chapters. The information they provide will enable you to formulate a problem that is researchable. These chapters are titled: 'Reviewing the literature', 'Formulating a research problem', 'Identifying variables' and 'Constructing hypotheses'. Similarly, for the operational step, step III, 'Constructing an instrument for data collection', the chapters titled 'Selecting a method of data collection', 'Collecting data using attitudinal scales' and 'Establishing the validity and reliability of a research instrument' will provide sufficient information for you to develop an instrument for data collection for your study. For every aspect at each step, a smorgasbord of methods, models, techniques and procedures is provided for both quantitative and qualitative studies in order for you to build your knowledge base in research methodology and also to help you to select the most appropriate ones when undertaking your own research.

It is my belief that a sound knowledge of research methodology is essential for undertaking a valid study. To answer your research questions, up to Step V, 'Writing a research proposal', knowledge of research methods is crucial as this enables you to develop a conceptual framework which is sound and has merits for undertaking your research endeavour with confidence. Having completed the preparatory work, the steps that follow are more practical in nature, the quality of which entirely depends upon the soundness of the methodology you proposed in your research proposal. Statistics and computers play a significant role in research but their application is mainly after the data has been collected. To me, statistics are useful in confirming or contradicting conclusions drawn from simply looking at analysed data, in providing an indication of the magnitude of the relationship between two or more variables under study, in helping to establish causality, and in ascertaining the level of confidence that can be placed in your findings. A computer's application is primarily in data analysis, the calculation of statistics, word processing and the graphic presentation of data. It saves time and makes it easier for you to undertake these activities; however, you need to learn this additional skill. This book does not include statistics or information about computers.

The third edition of the book incorporates some of the suggestions made by the reviewers, colleagues and students on the first and second editions. There are some major changes in the third edition:

- I have taken a very bold step in breaking down, where possible, the wall between qualitative and quantitative research by describing both methodologies parallel to one another within a common framework. A lot more information on qualitative research has been added and integrated with the current eight-step research model. Now, almost each chapter has a new section that is specifically devoted to information related to qualitative research pertaining to the main theme of the chapter. For example, Chapter 9, 'Selecting a method of data collection', now has a section 'Methods of data collection in qualitative research' that specifically discusses the major methods of data collection in qualitative studies. Similarly, Chapter 8, 'Selecting a study design', has a section 'Study designs in qualitative research' that is devoted to the designs dominantly used in qualitative research. As far as possible each chapter also has information on other aspects of qualitative research along with the existing quantitative body of knowledge.

- More in-depth field examples, based upon actual experiences, have been incorporated to explain procedures and methods.
- Exercises, a part of the Appendix, have now been thoroughly revised with the expectation that those who are developing a research project can operationalise the theoretical knowledge in an actual situation to evaluate the application of theory to practice in addition to developing their research project.
- A glossary of technical terms is a new addition to this edition. This will provide students with readily available definitions and meanings of technical terms in one place.
- Title pages dividing chapters and operational steps have now been redesigned to provide greater clarity as well as informing students in advance what they are expected to learn in a chapter. Also, each chapter has a list of keywords that students are likely to encounter in the chapter.
- In places the language has been changed to enhance flow, understanding and ease of reading.

I am grateful to a number of people who have helped me in the writing of this book. First of all, to my students, who have taught me how to teach research methods. The basic structure of this book is an outcome of the feedback I have received from them over the years. How, and at what stage of the research process, a concept or a procedure should be taught, I have learnt from my students. I thankfully acknowledge their contribution to this book.

I am extremely grateful to a friend and colleague, Dr Norma Watson, whose efforts in editing the first edition were of immense help. The book would not have come to its present stage without her unconditional help.

I also thank Professor Denis Ladbrook, a friend and colleague, for his continuous encouragement and support.

Ranjit Kumar

CHAPTER 1
Research: A Way of Thinking

In this chapter you will learn about:

- Some of the reasons for doing research
- How research can be used to gather evidence to inform your practice
- The applications of research
- Characteristics and requirements of the research process
- Types of research from the perspective of applications, objectives and enquiry modes
- Research paradigms

Keywords: *applied research, controlled, correlational research, descriptive research, empirical, explanatory research, exploratory research, evidence-based practice, interpretive paradigm, positivistic paradigm, pure research, qualitative research, quantitative research, reliability, research, structured and unstructured enquiries, systematic, validity.*

Research: an integral part of your practice

Research is undertaken within most professions. More than a set of skills, research is a way of thinking: examining critically the various aspects of your day-to-day professional work; understanding and formulating guiding principles that govern a particular procedure; and developing and testing new theories that contribute to the advancement of your practice and profession. It is a habit of questioning what you do, and a systematic examination of clinical observations to explain and find answers for what you perceive, with a view to instituting appropriate changes for a more effective professional service. Let us take some disciplines as examples.

Suppose you are working in the field of health. You may be a front-line service provider, supervisor or health administrator/planner. You may be in a hospital or working as an outreach community health worker. You may be a nurse, doctor, occupational therapist, physiotherapist, social worker or other paramedic. In any of these positions, some of the following questions may come to your mind or someone else may ask you for their answers:

- How many patients do I see every day?
- What are some of the most common conditions prevalent among my patients?
- What are the causes of these conditions?
- Why do some people have a particular condition whereas others do not?
- What are the health needs of the community?
- What are the benefits of this programme to the community?
- How do I demonstrate the effectiveness of my service?
- Why do some people use the service while others do not?
- What do people think about the service?
- How satisfied are patients with the service?
- How effective is the service?
- How can the service be improved?

You can add many other questions to this list. At times it may be possible to ignore these questions because of the level at which you work, at other times you may make an effort to find answers on your own initiative, or, sometimes, you may be required to obtain answers for effective administration and planning.

Let us take another discipline: business studies. Assume you work in the area of marketing. Again, you can work at different levels: as a salesperson, sales manager or sales promotion executive. The list of questions that may come to your mind can be endless. The types of questions and the need to find answers to them will vary with the level at which you work in the organisation. You may just want to find out the monthly fluctuation in the sales of a particular product, or you may be asked to develop an R&D strategic plan to compete for a greater share of the market for the products produced by your company. The list of questions that may come to mind could be endless. For example:

- What is the best strategy to promote the sale of a particular product?
- How many salespersons do I need?
- What is the effect of a particular advertising campaign on the sale of this product?
- How satisfied are the consumers with this product?
- How much are consumers prepared to spend on this product?
- What do consumers like or dislike about this product?
- What type of packaging do consumers prefer for this product?

- What training do the salespersons need to promote the sale of this product?
- What are the attributes of a good salesperson?

To take a different example, let us assume that you work as a psychologist, counsellor or social worker. While engaging in the helping process you may ask yourself (or someone else may ask you) the following questions:

- What are my clients' most common presenting problems?
- What are their most common underlying problems?
- What is the socioeconomic background of my clients?
- Why am I successful in certain cases and not in others?
- What resources are available in the community to help a client with a particular need?
- What intervention strategies are appropriate for this problem?
- How satisfied are my clients with my services?

As a supervisor, administrator or manager of an agency, again different questions relating to effectiveness and efficiency of a service may come to your mind. For example:

- How many people are coming to my agency?
- What are the socioeconomic–demographic characteristics of my clients?
- How many cases in a day can a worker effectively handle?
- Why do some people use the service while others do not?
- How effective is the service?
- What are the most common needs of clients who come to this agency?
- What are the strengths and weaknesses of the service?
- How satisfied are the clients with the service?
- How can I improve this service for my clients?

As a professional you might be interested in finding answers to theoretical questions, such as:

- Which is the most effective intervention for a particular problem?
- What causes X or what are the effects of Y?
- What is the relationship between two phenomena?
- How do I measure the self-esteem of my clients?
- How do I ascertain the validity of my questionnaire?
- What is the pattern of programme adoption in the community?
- Which is the best way of finding out community attitudes towards an issue?
- Which is the best way to find out the effectiveness of a particular treatment?
- How can I select an unbiased sample?
- What is the best way to find out about the level of marriage satisfaction among my clients?

In this age of consumerism you cannot afford to ignore the consumers of a service. Consumers have the right to ask questions about the quality and effectiveness of the service they are receiving and you, as the service provider, have an obligation to answer their questions. Some of the questions that a consumer may ask are:

- How effective is the service that I am receiving?
- Am I getting value for money?
- How well trained are the service providers?

Most professions that are in the human service industry would lend themselves to the questions raised above and you as a service provider should be well prepared to answer them. Research is one of the ways to help you answer such questions objectively.

Research: a way to gather evidence for your practice

Evidence-based practice (EBP) is the delivery of services based upon research evidence about their effectiveness; the service provider's clinical judgement as to the suitability and appropriateness of the service for a client; and the client's own preference as to the acceptance of the service. EBP is fast becoming a service delivery norm among many professions. Though its origin is credited to medical practice, EBP has become an important part of many other professions such as nursing, allied health services, mental health, community health, social work, psychology and teaching. It is now being promoted as an acceptable and scientific method for policy formulation and practice assessment.

The concept of EBP encourages professionals and other decision-makers to use evidence regarding the effectiveness of an intervention in conjunction with the characteristics and circumstance of a client and their own professional judgement to determine the appropriateness of an intervention when providing a service to a client. In this age of accountability, you as a professional must be accountable to your clients as well as your profession. It is as a part of this accountability that you need to demonstrate the effectiveness of the service(s) you provide.

Research is one of the ways of collecting accurate, sound and reliable information about the effectiveness of your interventions, thereby providing you with evidence of its effectiveness. As service providers and professionals, we use techniques and procedures developed by research methodologists to consolidate, improve, develop, refine and advance clinical aspects of our practice to serve our clients better.

Applications of research

Very little research in the field is pure in nature. That is, very few people do research in research methodology per se. Most research is applied research, which has wide application in many disciplines. Every profession uses research methods in varying amounts in many areas. They use the methods and procedures developed by research methodologists in order to increase understanding in their own profession and to advance the professional knowledge base. It is through the application of research methodology that they strengthen and advance their own profession. Examine your own field. You will find that its professional practice follows procedures and practices tested and developed by others over a long period of time. It is in this testing process that you need research skills, the developments of which fall in the category of pure research. As a matter of fact, the validity of your findings entirely depends upon the soundness of the research methods and procedures adopted by you.

Within any profession, where you directly or indirectly provide a service, such as health (nursing, occupational therapy, physiotherapy, community health, health promotion and public health), education, psychology or social work, the application of research can be viewed from four different perspectives:

1 the service provider;
2 the service administrator, manager and/or planner;
3 the service consumer; and
4 the professional.

These perspectives are summarised in Figure 1.1. Though it is impossible to list all the issues in every discipline, this framework can be applied to most disciplines and situations in the humanities and the social sciences. You should be able to use this to identify, from the viewpoint of the above perspectives, the possible issues in your own academic field where research techniques can be used to find answers.

Research: what does it mean?

There are several ways of obtaining answers to your professional questions. These methods range from the fairly informal, based upon clinical impressions, to the strictly scientific, adhering to the conventional expectations of scientific procedures. Research is one of the ways to find answers to your questions. When you say that you are undertaking a research study to find out answers to a question, you are implying that the process being applied:

1 is being undertaken within a framework of a set of philosophies;
2 uses procedures, methods and techniques that have been tested for their validity and reliability;
3 is designed to be unbiased and objective.

Your philosophical orientation may stem from one of the several paradigms and approaches in research – positivist, interpretive, phenomenology, action or participatory, feminist, qualitative, quantitative – and the academic discipline in which you have been trained. The concept of 'validity' can be applied to any aspect of the research process. It ensures that in a research study correct procedures have been applied to find answers to a question. 'Reliability' refers to the quality of a measurement procedure that provides repeatability and accuracy. 'Unbiased and objective' means that you have taken each step in an unbiased manner and drawn each conclusion to the best of your ability and without introducing your own vested interest. The author makes a distinction between **bias** and **subjectivity**. Subjectivity is an integral part of your way of thinking that is 'conditioned' by your

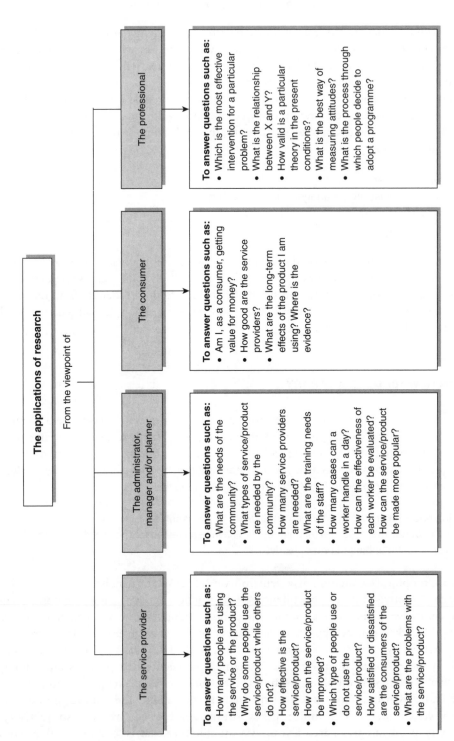

FIGURE 1.1   *The applications of research*

educational background, discipline, philosophy, experience and skills. For example, a psychologist may look at a piece of information differently from the way in which an anthropologist or a historian looks at it. Bias, on the other hand, is a deliberate attempt to either conceal or highlight something. Adherence to the three criteria mentioned above enables the process to be called 'research'. Therefore, when you say you are undertaking a research study to find the answer to a question, this implies that the method(s) you are adopting fulfils these expectations (discussed later in the chapter).

However, the degree to which these criteria are expected to be fulfilled varies from discipline to discipline and so the meaning of 'research' differs from one academic discipline to another. For example, the expectations of the research process are markedly different between the physical and the social sciences. In the physical sciences a research endeavour is expected to be strictly controlled at each step, whereas in the social sciences rigid control cannot be enforced and sometimes is not even demanded.

Within the social sciences the level of control required also varies markedly from one discipline to another, as social scientists differ over the need for the research process to meet the above expectations. Despite these differences among disciplines, their broad approach to enquiry is similar. The research model, the basis of this book, is based upon this broad approach.

As beginners in research you should understand that research is not all technical, complex, statistics and computers. It can be a very simple activity designed to provide answers to very simple questions relating to day-to-day activities. On the other hand, research procedures can also be employed to formulate intricate theories or laws that govern our lives. The difference between research and non-research activity is, as mentioned, in the way we find answers to our research questions. For a process to be called research, it is important that it meets certain requirements and possesses certain characteristics. To identify these requirements and characteristics let us examine some definitions of research:

> The word *research* is composed of two syllables, *re* and *search*. The dictionary defines the former as a prefix meaning again, anew or over again and the latter as a verb meaning to examine closely and carefully, to test and try, or to probe. Together they form a noun describing a careful, systematic, patient study and investigation in some field of knowledge, undertaken to establish facts or principles. (Grinnell 1993: 4)

Grinnell further adds: 'research is a structured inquiry that utilises acceptable scientific methodology to solve problems and creates new knowledge that is generally applicable.' (1993: 4)

Lundberg (1942) draws a parallel between the social research process, which is considered scientific, and the process that we use in our daily lives. According to him:

> Scientific methods consist of systematic observation, classification and interpretation of data. Now, obviously, this process is one in which nearly all people engage in the course of their daily lives. The main difference between our day-to-day generalisations and the conclusions usually recognised as scientific method lies in the degree of formality, rigorousness, verifiability and general validity of the latter. (Lundberg 1942: 5)

Burns (1997: 2) defines research as 'a systematic investigation to find answers to a problem'.

According to Kerlinger (1986: 10), 'scientific research is a systematic, controlled empirical and critical investigation of propositions about the presumed relationships about various phenomena'. Bulmer (1977: 5) states: 'Nevertheless sociological research, as research, is primarily committed to establishing systematic, reliable and valid knowledge about the social world.'

The research process: characteristics and requirements

From these definitions it is clear that research is a process for collecting, analysing and interpreting information to answer questions. But to qualify as research, the process must have certain characteristics: it must, as far as possible, be controlled, rigorous, systematic, valid and verifiable, empirical and critical.

Let us briefly examine these characteristics to understand what they mean:

- **Controlled** – In real life there are many factors that affect an outcome. A particular event is seldom the result of a one-to-one relationship. Some relationships are more complex than others. Most outcomes are a sequel to the interplay of a multiplicity of relationships and interacting factors. In a study of cause-and-effect relationships it is important to be able to link the effect(s) with the cause(s) and vice versa. In the study of causation, the establishment of this linkage is essential; however, in practice, particularly in the social sciences, it is extremely difficult – and often impossible – to make the link.

The concept of control implies that, in exploring causality in relation to two variables, you set up your study in a way that minimises the effects of other factors affecting the relationship. This can be achieved to a large extent in the physical sciences, as most of the research is done in a laboratory. However, in the social sciences it is extremely difficult as research is carried out on issues relating to human beings living in society, where such controls are impossible. Therefore, in the social sciences, as you cannot control external factors, you attempt to quantify their impact.

- **Rigorous** – You must be scrupulous in ensuring that the procedures followed to find answers to questions are relevant, appropriate and justified. Again, the degree of rigour varies markedly between the physical and the social sciences and within the social sciences.
- **Systematic** – This implies that the procedures adopted to undertake an investigation follow a certain logical sequence. The different steps cannot be taken in a haphazard way. Some procedures must follow others.
- **Valid and verifiable** – This concept implies that whatever you conclude on the basis of your findings is correct and can be verified by you and others.
- **Empirical** – This means that any conclusions drawn are based upon hard evidence gathered from information collected from real-life experiences or observations.

- **Critical** – Critical scrutiny of the procedures used and the methods employed is crucial to a research enquiry. The process of investigation must be foolproof and free from any drawbacks. The process adopted and the procedures used must be able to withstand critical scrutiny.

For a process to be called research, it is imperative that it has the above characteristics.

FIGURE 1.2   *Types of research*

Types of research

Types of research can be looked at from three different perspectives (Figure 1.2):

1 *applications* of the findings of the research study;
2 *objectives* of the study;
3 *mode of enquiry* used in conducting the study.

The classification of the types of a study on the basis of these perspectives is *not* mutually exclusive: that is, a research study classified from the viewpoint of 'application' can also be classified from the perspectives of 'objectives' and 'enquiry mode' employed. For example, a research project may be classified as pure or applied research (from the perspective of application), as descriptive, correlational, explanatory or exploratory (from the perspective of objectives) and as qualitative or quantitative (from the perspective of the enquiry mode employed).

Types of research: application perspective

If you examine a research endeavour from the perspective of its application, there are two broad categories: **pure research** and **applied research**. In the social sciences, according to Bailey (1978: 17):

> Pure research involves developing and testing theories and hypotheses that are intellectually challenging to the researcher but may or may not have practical application at the present time or in the future. Thus such work often involves the testing of hypotheses containing very abstract and specialised concepts.

Pure research is also concerned with the development, examination, verification and refinement of research methods, procedures, techniques and tools that form the body of research methodology. Examples of pure research include developing a sampling technique that can be applied to a particular situation; developing a methodology to assess the validity of a procedure; developing an instrument, say, to measure the stress level in people; and finding the best way of measuring people's attitudes. The knowledge produced through pure research is sought in order to add to the existing body of knowledge of research methods.

Most of the research in the social sciences is applied. In other words, the research techniques, procedures and methods that form the body of research methodology are applied to the collection of information about various aspects of a situation, issue, problem or phenomenon so that the information gathered can be used in other ways – such as for policy formulation, administration and the enhancement of understanding of a phenomenon.

Types of research: objectives perspective

If you examine a research study from the perspective of its objectives, broadly a research endeavour can be classified as descriptive, correlational, explanatory or exploratory.

A research study classified as a **descriptive study** attempts to describe systematically a situation, problem, phenomenon, service or programme, or provides information about, say, the living conditions of a community, or describes attitudes towards an issue. For example, it may attempt to describe the types of service provided by an organisation, the administrative structure of an organisation, the living conditions of Aboriginal people in the outback, the needs of a community, what it means to go through a divorce, how a child feels living in a house with domestic violence, or the attitudes of employees towards management. The main purpose of such studies is to describe what is prevalent with respect to the issue/problem under study.

The main emphasis in a **correlational study** is to discover or establish the existence of a relationship/association/interdependence between two or more aspects of a situation. What is the impact of an advertising campaign on the sale of a product? What is the relationship between stressful living and the incidence of heart attack? What is the relationship between fertility and mortality? What is the relationship between technology and unemployment? What is the effect of a health service on the control of a disease, or the home environment on educational achievement? These studies examine whether there is a relationship between two or more aspects of a situation or phenomenon and, therefore, are called correlational studies.

Explanatory research attempts to clarify why and how there is a relationship between two aspects of a situation or phenomenon. This type of research attempts to explain, for example, why stressful living results in heart attacks; why a decline in mortality is followed by a fertility decline; or how the home environment affects children's level of academic achievement.

The fourth type of research, from the viewpoint of the objectives of a study, is called **exploratory research**. This is when a study is undertaken with the objective either to explore an area where little is known or to investigate the possibilities of undertaking a particular research study. When a study is carried out to determine its feasibility it is also called a **feasibility study** or a **pilot study**. It is usually carried out when a researcher wants to explore areas about which s/he has little or no knowledge. A small-scale study is undertaken to decide if it is worth carrying out a detailed investigation. On the basis of the assessment made during the exploratory study, a full study may eventuate. Exploratory studies are also conducted to develop, refine and/or test measurement tools and procedures. Table 1.1 shows the types of research study from the viewpoint of objectives.

Although, theoretically, a research study can be classified in one of the above objectives–perspective categories, in practice, most studies are a combination of the first three; that is, they contain elements of descriptive, correlational and explanatory research. In this book the guidelines suggested for writing a research report encourage you to integrate these aspects.

Types of research: mode of enquiry perspective

The third perspective in our typology of research concerns the process you adopt to find answers to your research questions. Broadly, there are two approaches to enquiry:

1 the *structured* approach;
2 the *unstructured* approach.

In the structured approach everything that forms the research process – objectives, design, sample, and the questions that you plan to ask of respondents – is predetermined. The unstructured approach, by contrast, allows flexibility in all these aspects of the process. The structured approach is more appropriate to determine the *extent* of a problem, issue or phenomenon,

TABLE 1.1 *Types of research studies from the perspective of objectives*

Examples	Aim	Main theme	Type of research
• Socioeconomic characteristics of residents of a community • Attitudes of students towards quality of teaching • Types of service provided by an agency • Needs of a community • Sale of a product • Attitudes of nurses towards death and dying • Attitudes of workers towards management • Number of people living in a community • Problems faced by new immigrants • Extent of occupational mobility among immigrants • Consumers' likes and dislikes with regard to a product • Effects of living in a house with domestic violence • Strategies put in place by a company to increase productivity of workers	**To describe what is prevalent regarding:** • a group of people • a community • a phenomenon • a situation • a programme • an outcome	**To describe what is prevalent**	**Descriptive research**
• Impact of a programme • Relationship between stressful living and incidence of heart attacks • Impact of technology on employment • Impact of maternal and child health services on infant mortality • Effectiveness of a marriage counselling service on extent of marital problems • Impact of an advertising campaign on sale of a product • Impact of incentives on productivity of workers • Effectiveness of an immunisation programme in controlling infectious disease	**To establish or explore:** • a relationship • an association or • an interdependence	**To ascertain if there is a relationship**	**Correlational research**
• Why does stressful living result in heart attacks? • How does technology create unemployment/employment? • How do maternal and child health services affect infant mortality? • Why do some people have a positive attitude towards an issue while others do not? • Why does a particular intervention work for some people and not for others? • Why do some people use a product while others do not? • Why do some people migrate to another country while others do not? • Why do some people adopt a programme while others do not?	**To explain:** • *why* a relationship, association or interdependence exists • *why* a particular event occurs	**To explain why the relationship is formed**	**Explanatory research**

whereas the unstructured approach is predominantly used to explore its *nature*, in other words, variation/diversity per se in a phenomenon, issue, problem or attitude towards an issue. For example, if you want to research the different perspectives of an issue, the problems experienced by people living in a community or the different views people hold towards an issue, then these are better explored using unstructured enquiries. On the other hand, to find out how many people have a particular perspective, how many people have a particular problem, or how many people hold a particular view, you need to have a structured approach to enquiry. Before undertaking a structured enquiry, in the author's opinion, an unstructured enquiry must be undertaken to ascertain the diversity in a phenomenon which can then be quantified through the structured enquiry. Both approaches have their place in research. Both have their strengths and weaknesses. Therefore, you should not 'lock' yourself solely into a structured or unstructured approach.

The structured approach to enquiry is usually classified as **quantitative research** and unstructured as **qualitative research**. Other distinctions between quantitative and qualitative research are outlined in Table 2.1 in Chapter 2. The choice between quantitative and qualitative approaches (or structured or unstructured) should depend upon:

- **Aim of your enquiry** – exploration, confirmation or quantification.
- **Use of the findings** – policy formulation or process understanding.

The distinction between quantitative and qualitative research, in addition to the structured/unstructured process of enquiry, is also dependent upon some other considerations which are briefly presented in Table 2.1.

A study is classified as qualitative if the purpose of the study is primarily to describe a situation, phenomenon, problem or event; if the information is gathered through the use of variables measured on nominal or ordinal scales (qualitative measurement scales); and if the analysis is done *to establish the variation* in the situation, phenomenon or problem *without quantifying it*. The description of an observed situation, the historical enumeration of events, an account of the different opinions people have about an issue, and a description of the living conditions of a community are examples of qualitative research.

On the other hand, the study is classified as quantitative if you want to *quantify the variation* in a phenomenon, situation, problem or issue; if information is gathered using predominantly quantitative variables; and if the analysis is geared to ascertain the *magnitude of the variation*. Examples of quantitative aspects of a research study are: How many people have a particular problem? How many people hold a particular attitude?

The use of statistics is *not* an integral part of a quantitative study. The main function of statistics is to act as a test to confirm or contradict the conclusions that you have drawn on the basis of your understanding of analysed data. Statistics, among other things, help you to quantify the magnitude of an association or relationship, provide an indication of the confidence you can place in your findings and help you to isolate the effect of different variables.

It is strongly recommended that you do not 'lock yourself' into becoming either solely a quantitative or solely a qualitative researcher. It is true that there are disciplines that lend themselves predominantly either to qualitative or to quantitative research. For example, such disciplines as anthropology, history and sociology are more inclined towards qualitative research, whereas psychology, epidemiology, education, economics, public health and marketing are more inclined towards quantitative research. However, this does not mean that an economist or a psychologist never uses the qualitative approach, or that an anthropologist never uses quantitative information. There is increasing recognition by most disciplines in the social sciences that both types of research are important for a good research study. The research problem itself should determine whether the study is carried out using quantitative or qualitative methodologies.

As both qualitative and quantitative approaches have their strengths and weaknesses, and advantages and disadvantages, 'neither one is markedly superior to the other in all respects' (Ackroyd & Hughes 1992: 30). The measurement and analysis of the variables about which information is obtained in a research study are dependent upon the purpose of the study. In many studies you need to combine both qualitative and quantitative approaches. For example, suppose you want to find out the types of service available to victims of domestic violence in a city and the extent of their utilisation. Types of service is the qualitative aspect of the study as finding out about them entails description of the services. The extent of utilisation of the services is the quantitative aspect as it involves estimating the number of people who use the services and calculating other indicators that reflect the extent of utilisation.

Paradigms of research

There are two main paradigms that form the basis of research in the social sciences. It is beyond the scope of this book to go into any detail about these. The crucial question that divides the two is whether the methodology of the physical sciences can be applied to the study of social phenomena. The paradigm that is rooted in the physical sciences is called the systematic, scientific or positivist approach. The opposite paradigm has come to be known as the qualitative, ethnographic, ecological or naturalistic approach. The advocates of the two opposing sides have developed their own values, terminology, methods and techniques to understand social phenomena. However, since the mid-1960s there has been a growing recognition that both paradigms have their place. It is the purpose for which a research activity is undertaken that should determine the mode of enquiry, hence the paradigm. To indiscriminately apply one approach to all the research problems can be misleading and inappropriate.

A positivist paradigm lends itself to both quantitative and qualitative research. However, the author makes a distinction between qualitative data on the one hand and qualitative research on the other as the first is confined to the measurement of variables and the second to a use of methodology.

The author believes that no matter what paradigm the researcher works within, s/he should adhere to certain values regarding the control of bias, and the maintenance of objectivity in terms of both the research process itself and the conclusions drawn. It is the application of these values to the process of information gathering, analysis and interpretation that enables it to be called a research process.

Summary

There are several ways of collecting and understanding information and finding answers to your questions – research is one way. The difference between research and other ways of obtaining answers to your questions is that in a process that is classified as research, you work within a framework of a set of philosophies, use methods that have been tested for validity and reliability, and attempt to be unbiased and objective.

Research has many applications. You need to have research skills to be an effective service provider, administrator/manager or planner. As a professional who has a responsibility to enhance professional knowledge, research skills are essential.

The typology of research can be looked at from three perspectives: application, objectives and the enquiry process. From the point of view of the application of research, there is applied and pure research. Most of the research undertaken in the social sciences is applied, the findings being designed either for use in understanding a phenomenon/issue or to bring change in a programme/situation. Pure research is academic in nature and is undertaken in order to gain knowledge about phenomena that may or may not have applications in the near future, and to develop new techniques and procedures that form the body of research methodology. A research study can be carried out with four objectives: to describe a situation, phenomenon, problem or issue (descriptive research); to establish or explore a relationship between two or more variables (correlational research); to explain why certain things happen the way they do (explanatory research); and to examine the feasibility of conducting a study or exploring a subject area where nothing or little is known (exploratory research). From the point of view of the mode of enquiry, there are two types of research: quantitative (structured approach) and qualitative (unstructured approach). The main objective of a qualitative study is to describe the variation and diversity in a phenomenon, situation or attitude with a very flexible approach so as to identify as much variation and diversity as possible, whereas quantitative research, in addition, helps you to quantify the variation and diversity. There are many who strongly advocate a combined approach to social enquiries.

These are the two paradigms that form the basis of social science research. Though these may provide values, terminology, methods and techniques for you to apply to your research, it is the purpose of research rather than the paradigm that should determine the mode of enquiry.

For You to Think About

▸ Refamiliarise yourself with the keywords listed at the beginning of this chapter and if you are uncertain about the meaning or application of any of them revisit these in the chapter before moving on.

▸ Consider how you would go about convincing a service provider that evidence-based research might benefit them.

▸ Identify two or three research questions, related to your own academic field or professional area, that could be answered by undertaking each of the following types of research:

   ▸ descriptive research;
   ▸ correlational research;
   ▸ explanatory research;
   ▸ exploratory research.

▸ Consider how both unstructured and structured approaches to research could be applied to improve practice in your own professional area.

▸ Critically examine your own research philosophy in relation to the two research paradigms.

CHAPTER 2
The Research Process: A Quick Glance

In this chapter you will learn about:

- The eight-step model for carrying out research

PHASE I *DECIDING WHAT* TO RESEARCH

- Step I *Formulating* a research problem

PHASE II *PLANNING* A RESEARCH STUDY

- Step II *Conceptualising* a research design
- Step III *Constructing* an instrument for data collection
- Step IV *Selecting* a sample
- Step V *Writing* a research proposal

PHASE III *CONDUCTING* A RESEARCH STUDY

- Step VI *Collecting* data
- Step VII *Processing* and *displaying* data
- Step VIII *Writing* a research report

Keywords: *data, data display, data processing, empiricism, hypotheses, interview schedule, non-probability sample, primary data, probability sample, qualitative research, questionnaire, rationalism, reliability, research design, research instrument, research objectives, research problem, research proposal, sample, sample size, sampling design, secondary data, study design, unstructured interview, validity, variables.*

But much advantage will occur if men of science become their own epistemologists, and show to the world by critical exposition in non-technical terms the results and methods of their constructive work, that more than mere instinct is involved in it: the community has indeed a right to expect as much as this. (Poincaré 1952: xii)

The research process: an eight-step model

Research methodology is taught as a supporting subject in several ways in many academic disciplines at various levels by people committed to a variety of research paradigms. Though paradigms vary in their contents and substance, their broad approach to enquiry, in the author's opinion, is similar. Such ideas have also been expressed by Festinger and Katz, who in the fore-word of their book *Research Methods in Behavioral Sciences* say that, 'Although the basic logic of scientific methodology is the same in all fields, its specific techniques and approaches will vary, depending upon the subject matter' (1966: vi). Therefore, the model developed here is generic in nature and can be applied to a number of disciplines in the social sciences. It is based upon a practical and step-by-step approach to a research enquiry and each step provides a smorgasbord of methods, models and procedures.

Suppose you want to go out for a drive. Before you start, you must decide where you want to go and then which route to take. If you know the route, you do not need to consult a street directory, but, if you do not know the route, then you need to use one. Your problem is compounded if there is more than one route. You need to decide which one to take. The research process is very similar to undertaking a journey. As with your drive, for a research journey there are also two important decisions to make. The first is to decide *what you want to find out about* or, in other words, what **research questions** you want to find answers to. Having decided upon your research questions or **research problems**, you then need to decide *how to go about finding their answers*. The path to finding answers to your research questions constitutes research methodology. Just as there are posts along the way as you travel to your destination, so there are practical steps through which you must pass in your research journey in order to find the answers to your research questions (Figure 2.1). The sequence of these steps is not fixed and with experience you can change it. At each operational step in the research process you are required to choose from a multiplicity of methods, procedures and models of research methodology which will help you best achieve your **research objectives**. This is where your knowledge base of research methodology plays a crucial role.

The aim of this book is to provide you with knowledge that will enable you to select the most appropriate methods and procedures. The strength of this book lies in anchoring the theoretical knowledge of the steps that you need to go through on your research journey. At each operational step, the book aims to provide, at a beginner's level, knowledge of methods and procedures used by both qualitative and quantitative researchers, though there is an inclination towards the quantitative way of thinking.

Quantitative and qualitative research methodologies differ both in their underpinning philosophy and, to some extent, in the methods, models and procedures used. Though the research process is broadly the same in both, quantitative and qualitative research are

FIGURE 2.1   *The research journey – touch each post and select methods and procedures appropriate for your journey*

differentiated in terms of the methods of data collection, the procedures adopted for data processing and analysis, and the style of communication of the findings. For example, if your research problem lends itself to a qualitative mode of enquiry, you are more likely to use the *unstructured interview* or *observation* as your method of data collection. When analysing data in qualitative research, you go through the process of identifying themes and describing what you have found out during your interviews or observation rather than subjecting your data to statistical procedures. Table 2.1 summarises the differences between qualitative and quantitative research.

Since, at a number of steps of the research process, the choice of methods and procedures is influenced by the quantitative/qualitative distinction, the methods and procedures discussed in some of the chapters in this book are dealt with under separate headings for qualitative and quantitative research; however, the author has tried to keep this distinction to a minimum as the model is applicable to both. Also note that this book is for beginners, it does not cover extensively the applicability and use of each method, model and procedure. In addition, the author has elaborated more on methods, models and procedures associated with quantitative research as compared with those linked with qualitative research. For a deeper understanding of a method or procedure relating to either, you may wish to consult other books identified in the text or in the Bibliography.

TABLE 2.1 *Differences between qualitative and quantitative research*

Difference with respect to:	Quantitative research	Qualitative research
Underpinning philosophy	Rationalism: 'That human beings achieve knowledge because of their capacity to reason' (Bernard 1994: 2)	Empiricism: 'The only knowledge that human beings acquire is from sensory experiences' (Bernard 1994: 2)
Approach to enquiry	Structured/rigid/predetermined methodology	Unstructured/flexible/open methodology
Main purpose of investigation	To quantify extent of variation in a phenomenon, situation, issue, etc.	To describe variation in a phenomenon, situation, issue, etc.
Measurement of variables	Emphasis on some form of either measurement or classification of variables	Emphasis on description of variables
Sample size	Emphasis on greater sample size	Fewer cases
Focus of enquiry	Narrows focus in terms of extent of enquiry, but assembles required information from a greater number of respondents	Covers multiple issues but assembles required information from fewer respondents
Dominant research value	Reliability and objectivity (value-free)	Authenticity but does not claim to be value-free
Dominant research topic	Explains prevalence, incidence, extent, nature of issues, opinions and attitude; discovers regularities and formulates theories	Explores experiences, meanings, perceptions and feelings
Analysis of data	Subjects variables to frequency distributions, cross-tabulations or other statistical procedures	Subjects responses, narratives or observational data to identification of themes and describes these
Communication of findings	Organisation more analytical in nature, drawing inferences and conclusions, and testing magnitude and strength of a relationship	Organisation more descriptive and narrative in nature

Figure 2.2 shows the proposed model. The tasks identified in *arrows* are the operational steps you need to follow in order to conduct a study, quantitative or qualitative. Topics identified in *rectangles* are the required theoretical knowledge needed to carry out these steps. The tasks identified in *circles* are the intermediary steps that you need to complete to go from one step to another. It is important for a beginner to work through these steps in the proposed sequence, though, as already stated, with experience you do not need to follow the sequence.

In this book the theoretical knowledge required is written around each operational step and follows the same sequential progression as is needed when actually undertaking a research investigation. For each operational step, the required theoretical knowledge is further organised, in different chapters, around the operational step to which, in the author's opinion, it is

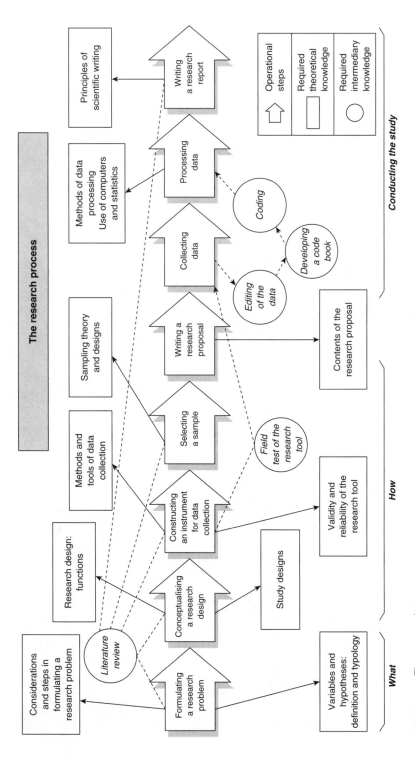

FIGURE 2.2 *The research process*

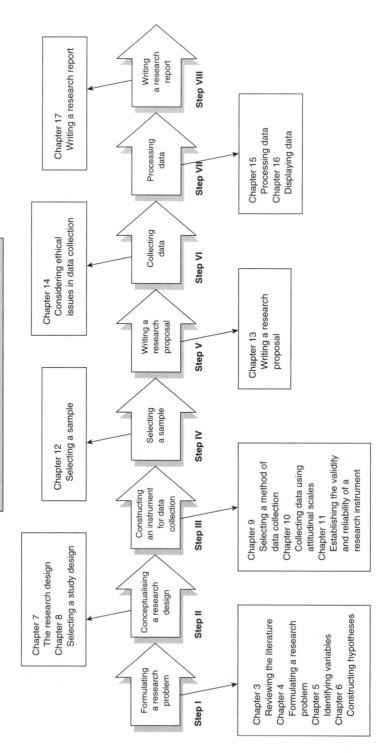

FIGURE 2.3   *The chapters in the book in relation to the operational steps*

most logically related (Figure 2.3). Again, for a beginner, it is important to study this diagram to relate the theoretical knowledge to the operational steps.

The following sections of this chapter provide a quick glance at the whole process to acquaint you with the various tasks you need to undertake to carry out your study, thus giving you some idea of what the research journey involves.

Phase I: deciding what to research

Step I: formulating a research problem

Formulating a research problem is the first and most important step in the research process. A research problem identifies your destination: it should tell you, your research supervisor and your readers *what* you intend to research. The more specific and clearer you are the better, as everything that follows in the research process – study design, measurement procedures, sampling strategy, frame of analysis and the style of writing of your dissertation or report – is greatly influenced by the way in which you formulate your research problem. Hence, you should examine it thoroughly, carefully and critically. The main function of formulating a research problem is to decide *what* you want to find out *about*. Chapter 4 deals in detail with various aspects of formulating a research problem.

It is extremely important to evaluate the research problem in the light of the financial resources at your disposal, the time available, and your own and your research supervisor's expertise and knowledge in the field of study. It is equally important to identify any gaps in your knowledge of relevant disciplines, such as statistics required for analysis. Also, ask yourself whether you have sufficient knowledge about computers and software if you plan to use them.

Phase II: planning a research study

Step II: conceptualising a research design

An extremely important feature of research is the use of appropriate methods. Research involves systematic, controlled, valid and rigorous exploration and description of what is not known and establishment of associations and causation that permit the accurate prediction of outcomes under a given set of conditions. It also involves identifying gaps in knowledge, verification of what is already known and identification of past errors and limitations. The strength of *what* you find largely rests on *how* it was found.

The main function of a research design is to explain *how* you will find answers to your research questions. The research design sets out the specific details of your enquiry. A research design should include the following: the study design per se and the logistical arrangements that you propose to undertake, the measurement procedures, the sampling strategy, the frame of analysis and the time-frame. (You should not be confused between study design and research design. Note that the study design is one part of the research design. It is the design of the study itself, whereas the research design also includes other parts which constitute the research process.)

For any investigation, the selection of an appropriate **research design** is crucial in enabling you to arrive at valid findings, comparisons and conclusions. A faulty design results in misleading findings and is therefore tantamount to wasting human and financial resources. In scientific circles, the strength of an empirical investigation is primarily evaluated in the light of the research design adopted. When selecting a research design it is important to ensure that it is *valid*, *workable* and *manageable*. Chapter 7 provides details about the research design most commonly used in quantitative and qualitative research.

There is an enormous variety of study designs and you need to be acquainted with some of the most common ones. Chapter 8 explains some of these designs. Select or develop the design that is most suited to your study. You must have strong reasons for selecting a particular design; you must be able to justify your selection; and you should be aware of its strengths, weaknesses and limitations. In addition, you will need to explain the logistical details needed to implement the suggested design.

Step III: constructing an instrument for data collection

Anything that becomes a means of collecting information for your study is called a 'research tool' or a 'research instrument', for example observation forms, interview schedules, questionnaires and interview guides.

The construction of a research instrument is the first 'practical' step in carrying out a study. You will need to decide how you are going to collect data for the proposed study and then construct a research instrument for data collection. Chapter 9 details the various methods of data collection for qualitative and quantitative studies and the process of developing a research instrument.

If you are planning to collect data specifically for your study (primary data), you need either to construct a research instrument or to select one that has already been constructed. Chapter 10 deals with methods for collecting data using attitudinal scales. The concepts of validity and reliability in relation to a research instrument are discussed in Chapter 11.

If you are using secondary data (information already collected for other purposes), you will need to identify what information is needed and then develop a form to extract the required data. In order to determine what information is required, you need to go through the same process as for primary data, described above.

Field testing (or pre-testing) a research tool is an integral part of instrument construction. As a rule, the pre-test of a research instrument should not be carried out on the sample of your study population but on a similar population which you are not proposing to study. This is covered in greater detail in Chapter 9.

If you are planning to use a computer for data analysis, you may wish to provide space for coding the data on the research instrument. This is explained in Chapter 15.

Step IV: selecting a sample

The accuracy of your findings largely depends upon the way you select your sample. The basic objective of any sampling design is to minimise, within the limitation of cost, the gap between the values obtained from your sample and those prevalent in the study population.

The underlying premise in sampling is that a relatively small number of units, if selected in a manner that they genuinely represent the study population, can provide – with a sufficiently high degree of probability – a fairly true reflection of the sampling population that is being studied.

When selecting a sample you should attempt to achieve two key aims of sampling the avoidance of bias in the selection of a sample; and the attainment of maximum precision for a given outlay of resources.

There are three categories of sampling design (Chapter 12): random/probability sampling designs, non-random/non-probability sampling designs and 'mixed' sampling design.

There are several sampling strategies within the first two categories. You need to be acquainted with these sampling designs – the strengths and weaknesses of each and the situations in which they can or cannot be applied – in order to select the one most appropriate for your study. The type of sampling strategy you use will influence your ability to make generalisations from the sample findings about the study population, and the type of statistical tests you can apply to the data.

Step V: writing a research proposal

Having done all the preparatory work, the next step is to put everything together in a way that provides adequate information about your research study, for your research supervisor and others. This overall plan, called a research proposal, tells a reader about your research problem and how you are planning to investigate. Broadly, a research proposal's main function is to detail the operational plan for obtaining answers to your research questions. In doing so it ensures – and reassures the readers of – the validity of the methodology to obtain answers accurately and objectively.

Universities and other institutions may have differing requirements regarding the style and content of a research proposal, but the majority of institutions would require most of what is set out here. Requirements may also vary within an institution, from discipline to discipline or from supervisor to supervisor. However, the guidelines set out in Chapter 13 provide a framework which will be acceptable to most.

A research proposal must tell you, your research supervisor and a reviewer the following information about your study:

- *what* you are proposing to do;
- *how* you plan to proceed;
- *why* you selected the proposed strategy.

Therefore it should contain the following information about your study (Chapter 13):

- a statement of the *objectives* of the study;
- a list of *hypotheses*, if you are testing any;
- the *study design* you are proposing to use;
- the *setting* for your study;
- the research *instrument(s)* you are planning to use;
- information on *sample size* and *sampling design*;
- information on *data processing* procedures;
- an outline of the proposed *chapters* for the report;
- the study's *problems* and *limitations*; and
- the proposed *time-frame*.

Phase III: conducting a research study

Step VI: collecting data

Having formulated a research problem, developed a study design, constructed a research instrument and selected a sample, you then collect the data from which you will draw inferences and conclusions for your study.

Many methods could be used to gather the required information. As a part of the research design, you decided upon the procedure you wanted to adopt to collect your data. In this phase *you actually collect the data*. For example, depending upon your plans, you might commence interviews, mail out a questionnaire, conduct nominal/focus group discussions or make observations. Collecting data through any one of the methods may involve some ethical issues, which are discussed in Chapter 14.

Step VII: processing and displaying data

The way you analyse the information you collected largely depends upon two things: the type of information (descriptive, quantitative, qualitative or attitudinal); and the way you want to communicate your findings to your readers.

Chapter 15 describes different ways of analysing quantitative and qualitative data and Chapter 16 details various methods of displaying analysed data.

In addition to the qualitative–quantitative distinction, it is important for data analysis that you consider whether the data is to be analysed manually or by a computer.

If your study is purely descriptive, you can write your dissertation/report on the basis of your field notes, manually analyse the contents of your notes (content analysis), or use a computer program such as NUD★IST N6, NVivio or Ethnograph for this purpose.

If you want quantitative analysis, it is also necessary to decide upon the type of analysis required (i.e. frequency distribution, cross-tabulations or other statistical procedures, such as regression analysis, factor analysis and analysis of variance) and how it should be presented. You will also need to identify the variables to be subjected to these statistical procedures.

Step VIII: writing a research report

There are two broad categories of reports: quantitative and qualitative. As mentioned earlier, the distinction is more academic than real as in most studies you need to combine quantitative and qualitative skills. Nevertheless, there are some solely qualitative and some solely quantitative studies.

Writing the report is the last and, for many, the most difficult step of the research process. This report informs the world what you have done, what you have discovered and what conclusions you have drawn from your findings. If you are clear about the whole process, you will also be clear about the way you want to write your report. Your report should be written in an academic style and be divided into different chapters and/or sections based upon the main themes of your study. Chapter 17 suggests some of the ways of writing a research report.

Summary

This chapter has provided an overview of the research process, which has been broken down into eight steps, the details of which are covered in the remainder of this book. At each step the research model provides a smorgasbord of methods, models, techniques and procedures so you can select the one most appropriate for your study. It is like a buffet party with eight tables, each with different dishes made from similar ingredients. You go to all eight tables and select the dish that you like the most from each table. The main difference between the model and this example is that in the model you select what is most appropriate for your study and not what you like the most. For a beginner it is important to go through all the steps, although perhaps not in the same sequence. With experience you can take a number of shortcuts.

The eight steps cover the total spectrum of a research endeavour, from problem formulation through to writing a research report. The steps are operational in nature, following a logical sequence, and detailing the various methods and procedures in a simple step-by-step manner.

For You to Think About

▸ Refamiliarise yourself with the keywords listed at the beginning of this chapter and if you are uncertain about the meaning or application of any of them revisit these in the chapter before moving on.

▸ Reflecting on the differences between quantitative and qualitative research (as outlined in Table 2.1), determine which approach you are more inclined to follow. To what extent does this reflect your own underpinning philosophy?

▸ Use the information provided in Table 2.1 to map the main differences between quantitative and qualitative research at each step in the eight-step model.

This operational step includes four chapters:

- Chapter 3: Reviewing the literature
- Chapter 4: Formulating a research problem
- Chapter 5: Identifying variables
- Chapter 6: Constructing hypotheses

STEP I

Formulating a Research Problem

CHAPTER 3
Reviewing the Literature

In this chapter you will learn about:

- The functions of the literature review in research
- How to carry out a literature search
- How to review the selected literature
- How to develop theoretical and conceptual frameworks
- How to write a literature review

Keywords: *catalogue, conceptual framework, contextualise, Internet, knowledge base, literature review, search engines, summary of literature, thematic writing, theoretical framework.*

The place of the literature review in research

One of the essential preliminary tasks when you undertake a research study is to go through the existing literature in order to acquaint yourself with the available body of knowledge in your area of interest. Reviewing the literature can be time consuming, daunting and frustrating, but it is also rewarding. The **literature review** is an integral part of the research process and makes a valuable contribution to almost every operational step. It has value even before the first step; that is, when you are merely thinking about a research question that you may want to find answers to through your research journey. In the initial stages of research it helps you to establish the theoretical roots of your study, clarify your ideas and develop your research methodology. Later in the process, the literature review serves to enhance and consolidate your own knowledge base and helps you to integrate your findings with the existing body of knowledge. Since an important responsibility in research is to compare your findings with those of others, it is here that the literature review plays an extremely important role. During the write-up of your report it helps you to integrate your findings with existing knowledge – that is, to either support or contradict earlier research. The higher the academic level of your research, the more important a thorough integration of your findings with existing literature becomes.

In summary, a literature review has the following functions:

- It provides a theoretical background to your study.
- It helps you establish the links between what you are proposing to examine and what has already been studied.
- It enables you to show how your findings have contributed to the existing body of knowledge in your profession. It helps you to integrate your research findings into the existing body of knowledge.

In relation to your own study, the literature review can help in four ways. It can:

1 bring clarity and focus to your research problem;
2 improve your research methodology;
3 broaden your knowledge base in your research area; and
4 contextualise your findings.

Bringing clarity and focus to your research problem

The literature review involves a paradox. On the one hand, you cannot effectively undertake a literature search without some idea of the problem you wish to investigate. On the other hand, the literature review can play an extremely important role in shaping your research problem because the process of reviewing the literature helps you to understand the subject area better and thus helps you to conceptualise your research problem clearly and precisely and makes it more relevant and pertinent to your field of enquiry. When reviewing the literature you learn what aspects of your subject area have been examined by others, what they have found out about these aspects, what gaps they have identified and what suggestions they have made for further research. All these will help you gain a greater insight into your own research questions and provide you with clarity and focus which are central to a relevant and valid study. In addition, it will help you to focus your study on areas where there are gaps in the existing body of knowledge, thereby enhancing its relevance.

Improving your research methodology

Going through the literature acquaints you with the methodologies that have been used by others to find answers to research questions similar to the one you are investigating. A literature review tells you if others have used procedures and methods similar to the ones that you are proposing, which procedures and methods have worked well for them and what problems they have faced with them. By becoming aware of any problems and pitfalls, you will be better positioned to select a methodology that is capable of providing valid answers to your research question. This will increase your confidence in the methodology you plan to use and will equip you to defend its use.

Broadening your knowledge base in your research area

The most important function of the literature review is to ensure you read widely around the subject area in which you intend to conduct your research study. It is important that you know what other researchers have found in regard to the same or similar questions, what theories have been put forward and what gaps exist in the relevant body of knowledge. When you undertake a research project for a higher degree (e.g. an MA or a PhD) you are expected to be an expert in your area of research. A thorough literature review helps you to fulfil this expectation. Another important reason for doing a literature review is that it helps you to understand how the findings of your study fit into the existing body of knowledge (Martin 1985: 30).

Enabling you to contextualise your findings

Obtaining answers to your research questions is comparatively easy: the difficult part is examining how your findings fit into the existing body of knowledge. How do answers to your research questions compare with what others have found? What contribution have you been able to make to the existing body of knowledge? How are your findings different from those of others? Undertaking a literature review will enable you to compare your findings with those of others and answer these questions. It is important to place your findings in the context of what is already known in your field of enquiry.

How to review the literature

If you do not have a specific research problem, you should review the literature in your broad area of interest with the aim of gradually narrowing it down to what you want to find out about. After that the literature review should be focused around your research problem. There is a danger in reviewing the literature without having a reasonably specific idea of what you want to study. It can condition your thinking about your study and the methodology you might use, resulting in a less innovative choice of research problem and methodology than otherwise would have been the case. Hence, you should try broadly to conceptualise your research problem before undertaking your major literature review.

There are four steps involved in conducting a literature review:

1 Searching for the existing literature in your area of study.
2 Reviewing the selected literature.
3 Developing a theoretical framework.
4 Developing a conceptual framework.

The skills required for these tasks are different. Developing theoretical and conceptual frameworks is more difficult than the other tasks.

Searching for the existing literature

To search effectively for the literature in your field of enquiry, it is imperative that you have at least some idea of the broad subject area and of the problem you wish to investigate, in order to set parameters for your search. Next, compile a bibliography for this broad area. There are three sources that you can use to prepare a bibliography:

(a) books;
(b) journals;
(c) the Internet.

Books

Though books are a central part of any bibliography, they have their disadvantages as well as advantages. The main advantage is that the material published in books is usually important and of good quality, and the findings are 'integrated with other research to form a coherent body of knowledge' (Martin 1985: 33). The main disadvantage is that the material is not completely up to date, as it can take a few years between the completion of a work and its publication in the form of a book.

The best way to search for a book is to look at your library catalogues. When librarians catalogue a book they also assign to it subject headings that are usually based on *Library of Congress Subject Headings*. If you are not sure, ask your librarian to help you find the best subject heading for your area. This can save you a lot of time. Publications such as *Book Review Index* can help you to locate books of interest.

Use the *subject catalogue* or *keywords* option to search for books in your area of interest. Narrow the subject area searched by selecting the appropriate keywords. Look through these titles carefully and identify the books you think are likely to be of interest to you. If you think the titles seem appropriate to your topic, print them out (if this facility is available), as this will save you time, or note them down on a piece of paper. Be aware that sometimes a title does not provide enough information to help you decide if a book is going to be of use so you may have to examine its contents too.

When you have selected 10–15 books that you think are appropriate for your topic, examine the bibliography of each one. It will save time if you photocopy their bibliographies. Go through these bibliographies carefully to identify the books common to several of them. If a book has been referenced by a number of authors, you should include it in your reading list. Prepare a final list of books that you consider essential reading.

Having prepared your reading list, locate these books in your library or borrow them from other sources. Examine their contents to double-check that they really are relevant to your topic. If you find that a book is not relevant to your research, delete it from your reading list. If you find that something in a book's contents is relevant to your topic, make an annotated bibliography. An annotated bibliography contains a brief abstract of the aspects covered in a book and your own notes of its relevance. Be careful to keep track of your references. To do this you can prepare your own card index or use a computer program such as Endnotes or Pro-Cite.

Journals

You need to go through the journals relating to your research in a similar manner. Journals provide you with the most up-to-date information, even though there is often a gap of two to three years between the completion of a research project and its publication in a journal. You should select as many journals as you possibly can, though the number of journals available depends upon the field of study – certain fields have more journals than others. As with books, you need to prepare a list of the journals you want to examine for identifying the literature relevant to your study. This can be done in a number of ways. You can:

- locate the hard copies of the journals that are appropriate to your study;
- look at citation or abstract indices to identify and/or read the abstracts of such articles;
- search electronic databases.

If you have been able to identify any useful journals and articles, prepare a list of those you want to examine, by journal. Select one of these journals and, starting with the latest issue, examine its contents page to see if there is an article of relevance to your research topic. If you feel that a particular article is of interest to you, read its abstract. If you think you are likely to use it, depending upon your financial resources, either photocopy it, or prepare a summary and record its reference for later use.

There are several sources designed to make your search for journals easier and these can save you enormous time. They are:

- indices of journals (e.g. *Humanities Index*);
- abstracts of articles (e.g. *ERIC*);
- citation indices (e.g. *Social Sciences Citation Index*).

Each of these indexing, abstracting and citation services is available in print, or accessible through the Internet.

In most libraries, information on books, journals and abstracts is stored on computers. In each case the information is classified by subject, author and title. You may also have the keywords option (author/keyword; title/keyword; subject/keyword; expert/keyword; or just keywords). What system you use depends upon what is available in your library and what you are familiar with.

There are specially prepared electronic databases in a number of disciplines. These can also be helpful in preparing a bibliography. For example, most libraries carry the electronic databases shown in Table 3.1.

Select the database most appropriate to your area of study to see if there are any useful references. Of course, any computer database search is restricted to those journals and articles that

TABLE 3.1   *Some commonly used electronic databases in public health, sociology, education and business studies*

Electronic database	Description	Printed equivalent
ABI/INFORM	Abstracted Business Information contains references to business information worldwide. It covers subjects such as accounting, banking, data processing, economics, finance, health care, insurance, law, management, marketing, personnel, product development, public administration, real estate, taxation and telecommunications	None
ERIC	ERIC is a database of educational material collected by the Education Resources Information Center of the US Department of Education. It covers subjects such as adult career or vocational education, counselling and personnel services, educational management, primary and early childhood education, handicapped and gifted children, higher education, information resources, language and linguistics, reading and communication, rural education, science, mathematics and environment education, social science education, teacher education, secondary education, evaluation and urban education	*CIJE: Current Index to Journals in Education*
HEALTHROM	HEALTHROM provides references and some full-text publications on the environment, health, HIV/AIDS and communicable diseases, Aboriginal health, clinical medicine, nutrition, alcohol and drug addiction	None
MEDLINE	MEDLINE contains references to material in the biomedical sciences, including medicine, pharmacology, nursing, dentistry, allied health professions, public health, behavioural sciences, physiotherapy, occupational therapy, medical technology, hospital administration, and basic sciences such as anatomy and physiology	*Index Medicus*
CINAHL	CINAHL (Cumulative Indices to Nursing and Allied Health Literature) provides access to virtually all English-language nursing journals and primary journals from 13 allied health disciplines including health education, medical records, occupational therapy, physical therapy and radiologic technology	Cumulative indices to nursing and allied health literature

are already on the database. You should also talk to your research supervisor and other available experts to find out about any additional relevant literature to include in your reading list.

The Internet

In almost every academic discipline and professional field, the Internet has become an important tool for finding published literature. Through an Internet search you can identify published material in books, journals and other sources with immense ease and speed.

An Internet search is carried out through search engines, of which there are many, though the most commonly used are *Google* and *Yahoo*. Searching through the Internet is very similar to the search for books and articles in a library using an electronic catalogue, as it is based on the use of keywords. An Internet search basically identifies all material in the database of a search engine that contains the keywords you specify, either individually or in combination. It is important that you choose words or combinations of words that other people are likely to use.

According to Gilbert (2008: 73), 'Most search facilities use Boolean logic, which allows three types of basic search "AND", "OR" and "NOT".' With practice you will become more efficient and effective in using keywords in combination with AND, OR and NOT, and so learn to narrow your search to help you identify the most relevant references.

Reviewing the selected literature

Now that you have identified several books and articles as useful, the next step is to start reading them critically to pull together themes and issues that are of relevance to your study. Unless you have a theoretical framework of themes in mind to start with, use separate sheets of paper for each theme or issue you identify as you go through selected books and articles. The following example details the process.

> The author recently examined, as part of an evaluation study, the extent of practice of the concept of 'community responsiveness' in the delivery of health services in Western Australia by health service providers. Before evaluating the extent of its use, pertinent literature relating to 'community responsiveness in health' was identified and reviewed. Through this review, many themes emerged, which became the basis of developing the theoretical framework for the study. Out of all of this, the following themes were selected to construct the theoretical framework for the evaluation study:
>
> - Community responsiveness: what does it mean?
> - Philosophies underpinning community responsiveness.
>
> *(Continued)*

(Continued)

- Historical development of the concept in Australia.
- The extent of use in health planning?
- Strategies developed to achieve community responsiveness.
- Indicators of success or failure.
- Seeking community participation.
- Difficulties in implementing community responsiveness.
- Attitude of stakeholders towards the concept of community responsiveness.

Once you develop a rough framework, slot the findings from the material so far reviewed into these themes, using a separate sheet of paper for each theme of the framework so far developed. As you read further, go on slotting the information where it logically belongs under the themes so far developed. Keep in mind that you may need to add more themes as you go along. While going through the literature you should carefully and critically examine it with respect to the following aspects:

- Note whether the knowledge relevant to your theoretical framework has been confirmed beyond doubt.
- Note the theories put forward, the criticisms of these and their basis, the methodologies adopted (study design, sample size and its characteristics, measurement procedures, etc.) and the criticisms of them.
- Examine to what extent the findings can be generalised to other situations.
- Notice where there are significant differences of opinion among researchers and give your opinion about the validity of these differences.
- Ascertain the areas in which little or nothing is known – the gaps that exist in the body of knowledge.

Developing a theoretical framework

Examining the literature can be a never-ending task, but as you have limited time it is important to set parameters by reviewing the literature in relation to some main themes pertinent to your research topic. As you start reading the literature, you will soon discover that the problem you wish to investigate has its roots in a number of theories that have been developed from different perspectives. The information obtained from different books and journals now needs to be sorted under the main themes and theories, highlighting agreements and disagreements among the authors and identifying the unanswered questions or gaps. You will also realise that the literature deals with a number of aspects that have a direct or indirect bearing on your research topic. Use these aspects as a basis for developing your theoretical framework. Your review of the literature should sort out the information, as mentioned earlier, within this framework. Unless you review the literature in relation to this framework, you will not be able to develop a focus in your literature search: that is, your theoretical framework provides you with a guide as you read. This brings us to the paradox mentioned previously: until you go through the literature you cannot develop a theoretical framework, and until you have developed a theoretical framework you cannot effectively review the literature. The solution is to read some of the literature and then attempt to develop a framework, even a loose one, within which you can organise the rest of the literature you read. As you read more about the area, you are likely to change the framework. However, without it, you will get bogged down in a great deal of unnecessary reading and note-taking that may not be relevant to your study.

Literature pertinent to your study may deal with two types of information:

1 universal;
2 more specific (i.e. local trends or a specific programme).

In writing about such information you should start with the general information, gradually narrowing it down to the specific.

Look at the example in Figure 3.1a and 3.1b

If you want to study the relationship between mortality and fertility, you should review the literature about:

- *fertility* – trends, theories, some of the indices and critiques of them, factors affecting fertility, methods of controlling fertility, factors affecting acceptance of contraceptives, and so on;
- *mortality* – factors affecting mortality, mortality indices and their sensitivity in measuring change in mortality levels of a population, trends in mortality, and so on; and, most importantly,
- *the relationship between fertility and mortality* – theories that have been put forward to explain the relationship, implications of the relationship.

Out of this literature review you need to develop the theoretical framework for your study. Primarily this should revolve around theories that have been put forward about the relationship between mortality and fertility. You will discover that a number of theories have been proposed to explain this relationship. For example, it has been explained from economic, religious, medical and psychological perspectives. Within each perspective several theories have been put forward: 'insurance theory', 'fear of non-survival', 'replacement theory', 'price theory', 'utility theory', 'extra' or 'hoarding theory' and 'risk theory'.

Your literature review should be written under the following headings, with most of the review involving the examination of the relationships between fertility and mortality:

- fertility theories;
- the theory of demographic transition;
- trends in fertility (global, and then narrow it to national and local levels);
- methods of contraception (their acceptance and effectiveness);
- factors affecting mortality;
- trends in mortality (and their implications);
- measurement of mortality indices (their sensitivity);
- *relationships between fertility and mortality* (different theories such as 'insurance', 'fear of non-survival', 'replacement', 'price', 'utility', 'risk' and 'hoarding').

FIGURE 3.1a *Developing a theoretical framework – the relationship between mortality and fertility*

Note: *Preliminary discussions with some stakeholders revealed that not much was known to them about community responsiveness and therefore it was proposed that the study be carried out in two phases: preparatory phase and actual evaluation phase. The main aim of the preparatory phase was to ascertain the understanding of the concept, identify the strategies that are being or can be used, and developing a set of indicators for measuring its success or failure. This framework became the basis of the first phase of the study.*

The review of literature was written around the following theoretical framework which, of course, emerged from the literature review itself.

Community responsiveness: What do the stakeholders (service providers, service managers and the consumers) understand by community responsiveness, why it is needed, and what purpose does it serve?
Historical and philosophical perspectives: Start of the concept, an historical overview of its emergence, philosophical perspective that underpins the concept.
Implementation strategies: What strategies have been used to achieve community responsiveness in the service delivery area?
Attitude of the stakeholders: What are the attitudes of service providers, service managers and consumers of the services towards community responsiveness?
Evaluation of community responsiveness: What indicators can be used to determine the impact of these strategies, what should determine the success or failure of the implementation of the strategies and who and how should it be determined?

FIGURE 3.1b *Theoretical framework for the study 'community responsiveness in health'*

Developing a conceptual framework

The conceptual framework is the basis of your research problem. It stems from the theoretical framework and usually focuses on the section(s) which become the basis of your study. Whereas the theoretical framework consists of the theories or issues in which your study is embedded, the conceptual framework describes the aspects you selected from the theoretical framework to become the basis of your enquiry. For instance, in the example cited in Figure 3.1a, the theoretical framework includes all the theories that have been put forward to explain the relationship between fertility and mortality. However, out of these, you may be planning to test only one, say the fear of non-survival. Similarly, in Figure 3.1b, the conceptual framework is focused on indicators to measure the success or failure of the strategies to enhance community responsiveness. Hence the conceptual framework grows out of the theoretical framework and relates to the specific research problem.

Writing about the literature reviewed

Now, all that remains to be done is to write about the literature you have reviewed. As mentioned in the beginning of this chapter, two of the broad functions of a literature review are (1) to provide a theoretical background to your study and (2) to enable you to contextualise your findings in relation to the existing body of knowledge in addition to refining your methodology. The content of your literature review should reflect these two purposes. In order to fulfil the first purpose, you should identify and describe various theories relevant to your field; and specify gaps in existing knowledge in the area, recent advances in the area of study, current trends and so on. In order to comply with the second function you should integrate the results from your study with specific and relevant findings from the existing literature by comparing the two for confirmation or contradiction. Note that at this stage you can only accomplish the first function of the literature review, to provide a theoretical background to your study. For the second function, the contextualisation of the findings, you have to wait till you are at the research report writing stage.

While reading the literature for theoretical background of your study, you will realise that certain themes have emerged. List the main ones, converting them into subheadings. Some people write up the entire literature review in one section, entitled 'Review of the literature', 'Summary of literature' or 'The literature review', without subheadings, but the author strongly suggests that you write your literature review under subheadings based upon the main themes that you have discovered and which form the basis of your theoretical framework. These subheadings should be precise, descriptive of the theme in question and follow a logical progression. Now, under each subheading, record the main findings with respect to the theme in question (thematic writing), highlighting the reasons for and against an argument if they exist, and identifying gaps and issues. Figure 3.2 shows the subheadings used to describe the themes in a literature review conducted by the author for a study entitled 'Intercountry adoption in Western Australia'.

Intercountry adoption in Western Australia

(A profile of adoptive families)

The literature was reviewed under the following themes:

- Introduction (*introductory remarks about adoption*)
- History and philosophy of adoption
- Reasons for adoption
- Trends in adoption (*global and national*)
- Intercountry adoption
- History of intercountry adoption in Western Australia
- Trends in intercountry adoption in Western Australia
- The Adoption Act in Western Australia
- The adoption process in Western Australia
- Problems and issues in adoption
- Gaps in the literature (*in this case it was a lack of information about those parents who had adopted children from other countries that became the basis of the study*)

FIGURE 3.2   *Sample of outline of a literature review*

The second broad function of the literature review – contextualising the findings of your study – requires you to compare very systematically your findings with those made by others. Quote from these studies to show how your findings contradict, confirm or add to them. It places your findings in the context of what others have found out providing complete reference in an acceptable format. This function is undertaken, as mentioned earlier, when writing about your findings, that is after analysis of your data.

Summary

Reviewing the literature is a continuous process. It begins before a research problem is final-ised and continues until the report is finished. There is a paradox in the literature review: you cannot undertake an effective literature review unless you have formulated a research problem, yet your literature search plays an extremely important role in helping you to for-mulate your research problem. The literature review brings clarity and focus to your research problem, improves your research methodology and broadens your knowledge base.

Reviewing the literature involves a number of steps: searching for existing literature in your area of study; reviewing the selected literature; using it to develop a theoretical frame-work from which your study emerges and also using it to develop a conceptual framework which will become the basis of your investigation. The main sources for identifying literature are books, journals and the Internet. There are several sources which can provide informa-tion about locating relevant journals.

The literature review serves two important function: (1) it provides theoretical back-ground to your study, and (2) it helps you to contextualise your findings by comparing them with what others have found out in relation to the area of enquiry. At this stage of the research process, only the first function can be fulfilled. You can only take steps to achieve the second function when you have analysed your data and are in the process of writing about your findings.

Your writing about the literature reviewed should be thematic in nature, that is based on main themes; the sequence of these themes in the write-up should follow a logical progres-sion; various arguments should be substantiated with specific quotations and citations from the literature and should adhere to an acceptable academic referencing style.

For You to Think About

▸ Refamiliarise yourself with the keywords listed at the beginning of this chapter and if you are uncertain about the meaning or application of any of them revisit these in the chapter before moving on.
▸ Undertake a keyword search for a theme or issue that interests you using (a) an Internet search engine, such as Google Scholar, and (b) a library search facility. Compare the results.
▸ Choose two or three research reports from your search and scan through the summaries noting the theories put forward, the methodologies adopted and any recommendations for further study. Do these reports point to a consensus or differences of opinion in the field?
▸ Develop a theoretical framework for the theme or issue you selected.

CHAPTER 4
Formulating a Research Problem

In this chapter you will learn about:

- The importance of formulating a research problem
- Sources of research problems
- Considerations in selecting a research problem
- Specific issues to consider when formulating a research problem in qualitative research
- Steps in formulating a research problem
- How to formulate research objectives
- The importance of establishing operational definitions

Keywords: *concepts, dissect, operational definition, qualitative research, quantitative research, research objectives, research problem, study area, study population, subject area, validity, variable, working definition.*

The central aim of this chapter is to detail the process of formulating a research problem, even though the specific process that you are likely to adopt depends upon:

- your expertise in research methodology;
- your knowledge of the subject area;
- your understanding of the issues to be examined;
- the extent to which the focus of your study is predetermined.

If you are not very familiar with the research process and/or do not have a very specific idea about what is to be researched, you need to follow every step detailed in this chapter.

However, more experienced researchers can take a number of shortcuts. The process outlined here assumes that you have neither the required knowledge of the process of formulating a research problem nor a specific idea about what is to be researched. If you have a specific idea for the basis of your enquiry, you do not need to go through this chapter. However, you should make sure that your idea is researchable as not all problems lend themselves to research methodologies.

The research problem

Broadly speaking, any question that you want answered and any assumption or assertion that you want to challenge or investigate can become a research problem or a research topic for your study. However, it is important to remember that not all questions can be transformed into research problems and some may prove to be extremely difficult to study. According to Powers, Meenaghan and Twoomey (1985: 38), 'Potential research questions may occur to us on a regular basis, but the process of formulating them in a meaningful way is not at all an easy task.' As a newcomer it might seem easy to formulate a problem but it requires considerable knowledge of both the **subject area** and research methodology. Once you examine a question more closely you will soon realise the complexity of formulating an idea into a problem which is researchable. 'First identifying and then specifying a research problem might seem like research tasks that ought to be easy and quickly accomplished. However, such is often not the case' (Yegidis & Weinback 1991: 35).

It is essential for the problem you formulate to be able to withstand scrutiny in terms of the procedures required to be undertaken. Hence you should spend considerable time in thinking it through.

The importance of formulating a research problem

The formulation of a research problem is the first and most important step of the research process. It is like the identification of a destination before undertaking a journey. In the absence of a destination, it is impossible to identify the shortest – or indeed any – route. Similarly, in the absence of a clear research problem, a clear and economical plan is impossible. To use another analogy, a research problem is like the foundation of a building. The type and design of the building are dependent upon the foundation. If the foundation is well designed and strong you can expect the building to be also. The research problem serves as the foundation of a research study: if it is well formulated, you can expect a good study to follow. According to Kerlinger:

> If one wants to solve a problem, one must generally know what the problem is. It can be said that a large part of the problem lies in knowing what one is trying to do. (1986: 17)

You must have a clear idea with regard to what it is that you want to find out *about* and not what you think you must find.

A research problem may take a number of forms, from the very simple to the very complex. The way you formulate a problem determines almost every step that follows: the type of study design that can be used; the type of sampling strategy that can be employed; the research instrument that can be used or developed; and the type of analysis that can be undertaken. Suppose your broad area of interest is depression. Further suppose you want to conduct a research study regarding services available to patients with depression living in a community. If your focus is to find out the types of service available to patients with depression, the study will dominantly be descriptive and qualitative in nature. These types of studies fall in the category of qualitative research and are carried out using qualitative research methodologies. On the other hand, if you want to find out the extent of use of these services, that is the number of people using them, it will dominantly use quantitative methodologies even though it is descriptive in nature describing the number of people using a service. If your focus is to determine the extent of use in relation to the personal attributes of the patients, the study will be classified as correlational (and quantitative). The methodology used will be different than the one used in the case of a descriptive study. Similarly, if your aim is to find out the effectiveness of these services, the study will again be classified as correlational and the study design used, methods of collecting data and its analysis will be a part of the quantitative methodology. Hence, it is important for you to understand that the way you formulate a research problem determines all the subsequent steps that you have to follow during your research journey.

The formulation of a problem is like the 'input' to a study, and the 'output' – the quality of the contents of the research report and the validity of the associations or causation established – is entirely dependent upon it. Hence the famous saying about computers, 'garbage in, garbage out', is equally applicable to a research problem.

Initially, you may become more confused but this is normal and a sign of progression. *Remember: confusion is often but a first step towards clarity.* Take time over formulating your problem, for the clearer you are about your research problem/question, the easier it will be for you later on. *Remember, this is the most crucial step.*

Sources of research problems

This section is of particular relevance if you have not yet selected a research topic and do not know where to start. If you have already selected your topic or question, go to the next section.

Most research in the humanities revolves around four Ps:

- people;
- problems;
- programmes;
- phenomena.

In fact, a closer look at any academic or occupational field will show that most research revolves around these four Ps. The emphasis on a particular 'P' may vary from study to study but generally, in practice, most research studies are based upon at least a combination of two Ps. You may select a group of individuals (a group of individuals – or a community as such – 'people'), to examine the existence of certain issues or problems relating to their lives, to ascertain their attitude towards an issue ('problem'), to establish the existence of a regularity ('phenomenon') or to evaluate the effectiveness of an intervention ('programme'). Your focus may be the study of an issue, an association or a phenomenon per se; for example, the relationship between unemployment and street crime, smoking and cancer, or fertility and mortality, which is done on the basis of information collected from individuals, groups, communities or organisations. The emphasis in these studies is on exploring, discovering or establishing associations or causation. Similarly, you can study different aspects of a programme: its effectiveness, its structure, the need for it, consumers' satisfaction with it, and so on. In order to ascertain these you collect information from people.

Every research study has two aspects: the *people* provide you with the 'study population', whereas the other three Ps furnish the 'subject areas'. Your study population – individuals, groups and communities – is the *people* from whom the information is collected. Your subject area is a *problem, programme* or *phenomenon* about which the information is collected. This is outlined further in Table 4.1, which shows the aspects of a research problem.

TABLE 4.1   *Aspects of a research problem*

Aspects of a study	About	Study of	
Study population	People	Individuals, organisations, groups, communities	They provide you with the required information or you collect information from or about them
Subject area	Problem	Issues, situations, associations, needs, population composition, profiles, etc.	Information that you need to collect to find answers to your service research questions
	Programme	Contents, structure, outcomes, attributes, satisfaction, consumers, providers, etc.	
	Phenomenon	Cause and effect, relationships, the study of a phenomenon itself, etc.	

You can study a problem, a programme or a phenomenon in any academic field or from any professional perspective. For example, you can measure the effectiveness of a programme in the field of health, education, social work, industrial management, public health, nursing, health promotion or welfare, or you can look at a problem from a health, business or welfare perspective. Similarly you can gauge consumers' opinions about any aspect of a programme in the above fields.

Examine your own academic discipline or professional field in the context of the four Ps in order to identify anything that looks interesting. For example, if you are a student in the health field there are an enormous number of issues, situations and associations within each subfield of health that you could examine. Issues relating to the spread of a disease, drug rehabilitation, an immunisation programme, the effectiveness of a treatment, the extent of consumers' satisfaction or issues concerning a particular health programme can all provide you with a range of research problems. Similarly, in education there are several issues: students' satisfaction with a teacher, attributes of a good teacher, the impact of the home environment on the educational achievement of students, and the supervisory needs of postgraduate students in higher education. Any other academic or occupational field can similarly be dissected into subfields and examined for a potential research problem. Most fields lend themselves to the above categorisation even though specific problems and programmes vary markedly from field to field.

The concept of 4Ps is applicable to both quantitative and qualitative research though the main difference at this stage is the extent of their specificity, dissection, precision and focus. In qualitative research these attributes are deliberately kept very loose so that you can explore more as you go along, in case you find something of relevance. You do not bind yourself with constraints that would put limits on your ability to explore. There is a separate section on 'Formulating a research problem in qualitative research' later in the chapter, which provides further guidance on the process.

Considerations in selecting a research problem

When selecting a research problem/topic there are a number of considerations to keep in mind which will help to ensure that your study will be manageable and that you remain motivated. These considerations are:

- **Interest** – Interest should be the most important consideration in selecting a research problem. A research endeavour is usually time consuming, and involves hard work and possibly unforeseen problems. If you select a topic which does not greatly interest you, it could become extremely difficult to sustain the required motivation and put in enough time and energy to complete it.
- **Magnitude** – You should have sufficient knowledge about the research process to be able to visualise the work involved in completing the proposed study. Narrow the topic down to something manageable, specific and clear. It is extremely important to select a topic that you can manage within the time and with the resources at your disposal. Even if you are undertaking a descriptive study, you need to consider its magnitude carefully.
- **Measurement of concepts** – If you are using a concept in your study (in quantitative studies), make sure you are clear about its indicators and their measurement. For example, if you plan to measure the effectiveness of a health promotion programme, you must be clear as to what determines effectiveness and how it will be measured. Do not use concepts in your research problem that you are not sure how to measure. This does not mean you cannot develop a measurement procedure as the study progresses. While most of the developmental work will be done during your study, it is imperative that you are reasonably clear about the measurement of these concepts at this stage.

- **Level of expertise** – Make sure you have an adequate level of expertise for the task you are proposing. Allow for the fact that you will learn during the study and may receive help from your research supervisor and others, but remember that you need to do most of the work yourself.
- **Relevance** – Select a topic that is of relevance to you as a professional. Ensure that your study adds to the existing body of knowledge, bridges current gaps or is useful in policy formulation. This will help you to sustain interest in the study.
- **Availability of data** – If your topic entails collection of information from secondary sources (office records, client records, census or other already-published reports, etc.) make sure that this data is available and in the format you want before finalising your topic.
- **Ethical issues** – Another important consideration in formulating a research problem is the ethical issues involved. In the course of conducting a research study, the study population may be adversely affected by some of the questions (directly or indirectly); deprived of an intervention; expected to share sensitive and private information; or expected to be simply experimental 'guinea pigs'. How ethical issues can affect the study population and how ethical problems can be overcome should be thoroughly examined at the problem-formulation stage.

Steps in formulating a research problem

The formulation of a research problem is the most crucial part of the research journey as the quality and relevance of your research project entirely depends upon it. As mentioned earlier, every step that constitutes the *how* part of the research journey (Figure 2.1) depends upon the way you formulated your research problem. Despite the importance of this step, there is very little available by way of specific guidance in other books. This task is largely left either to the teachers of research methodology or to students to learn for themselves. One of the strengths of this book is that it offers a beginner a very specific set of step-by-step guidelines in one place despite the fear of being labelled as prescriptive.

The process of formulating a research problem consists of a number of steps. Working through these steps presupposes a reasonable level of knowledge in the broad subject area within which the study is to be undertaken and the research methodology itself. A brief review of the relevant literature helps enormously in broadening this knowledge base. Without such knowledge it is difficult to 'dissect' a subject area clearly and adequately.

If you do not know what specific research topic, idea, questions or issue you want to research (which is not uncommon among students), first go through the following steps:

Step 1   **Identify a broad field or subject area of *interest* to you.** Ask yourself, 'What is it that really interests me as a professional?' In the author's opinion, it is a good idea to think about the field in which you would like to work after graduation. This will help you to find an interesting topic, and one which may be of use to you in the future. For example, if you are a social work student, inclined to work in the area of youth welfare, refugees or domestic violence after graduation, you might take to research in one of these areas. Or if you are studying marketing you might be interested in researching consumer behaviour. Or, as a student of public health, intending to work with patients who have HIV/AIDS,

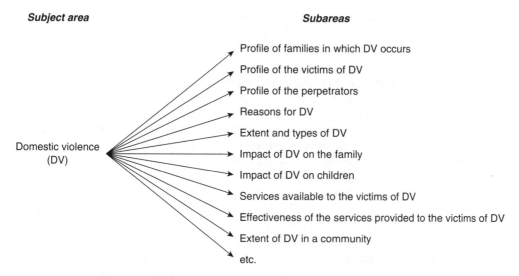

FIGURE 4.1   *Dissecting the subject area of domestic violence into subareas*

you might like to conduct research on a subject area relating to HIV/AIDS. As far as the research journey goes, these are the broad research areas. It is imperative that you identify one of interest to you before undertaking your research journey.

Step 2   **Dissect the broad area into subareas.** At the onset, you will realise that all the broad areas mentioned above – youth welfare, refugees, domestic violence, consumer behaviour and HIV/AIDS – have many aspects. For example, there are many aspects and issues in the area of domestic violence, illustrated in Figure 4.1.

Similarly, you can select any subject area from other fields such as community health or consumer research and go through this dissection process. In preparing this list of subareas you should also consult others who have some knowledge of the area and the literature in your subject area. Once you have developed an exhaustive list of the subareas from various sources, you proceed to the next stage where you select what will become the basis of your enquiry.

Step 3   **Select what is of most interest to you.** It is neither advisable nor feasible to study all subareas. Out of this list, select issues or subareas about which you are passionate. This is because your interest should be the most important determinant for selection, even though there are other considerations which have been discussed in the previous section, 'Considerations in selecting a research problem'. One way to decide what interests you most is to start with the process of elimination. Go through your list and delete all those subareas in which you are not very interested. You will find that towards the end of this process, it will become very difficult for you to delete anything further. You need to continue until you are left with something that is *manageable* considering the time available to you, your level of expertise and other resources needed to undertake the study. Once you are confident that you have selected an issue you are passionate about and can manage, you are ready to go to the next step.

Step 4   **Raise research questions.** At this step ask yourself, 'What is it that I want to find out about in this subarea?' Make a list of whatever questions come to your mind relating to your chosen subarea and if you think there are too many to be manageable, go through the process of elimination, as you did in Step 3.

Step 5   **Formulate objectives.** Both your main objectives and your subobjectives now need to be formulated, which grow out of your research questions. The main difference between objectives and research questions is the way in which they are written. Research questions are obviously that – questions. Objectives transform these questions into behavioural aims by using action-oriented words such as 'to find out', 'to determine', 'to ascertain' and 'to examine'. Some researchers prefer to reverse the process; that is, they start from objectives and formulate research questions from them. Some researchers are satisfied only with research questions, and do not formulate objectives at all. If you prefer to have only research questions or only objectives, this is fine, but keep in mind the requirements of your institution for research proposals. For guidance on formulating objectives, see the later section.

Step 6   **Assess your objectives.** Now examine your objectives to ascertain the feasibility of achieving them through your research endeavour. Consider them in the light of the time, resources (financial and human) and technical expertise at your disposal.

Step 7   **Double-check.** Go back and give final consideration to whether or not you are sufficiently interested in the study, and have adequate resources to undertake it. Ask yourself, 'Am I really enthusiastic about this study?' and 'Do I really have enough resources to undertake it?' Answer these questions thoughtfully and realistically. If your answer to one of them is 'no', reassess your objectives.

Figures 4.2 to 4.4 operationalise Steps 1–7 with examples from different academic disciplines (health, social work/social sciences and community development).

The formulation of research objectives

Objectives are the goals you set out to attain in your study. Since these objectives inform a reader of what you want to achieve through the study, it is extremely important to word them clearly and specifically.

Objectives should be listed under two headings:

- main objectives;
- subobjectives.

The main objective is an overall statement of the thrust of your study. It is also a statement of the main associations and relationships that you seek to discover or establish. The subobjectives are the specific aspects of the topic that you want to investigate within the main framework of your study.

Example 1: Suppose you want to conduct a study in the area of alcoholism. In formulating your research problem take the following steps.

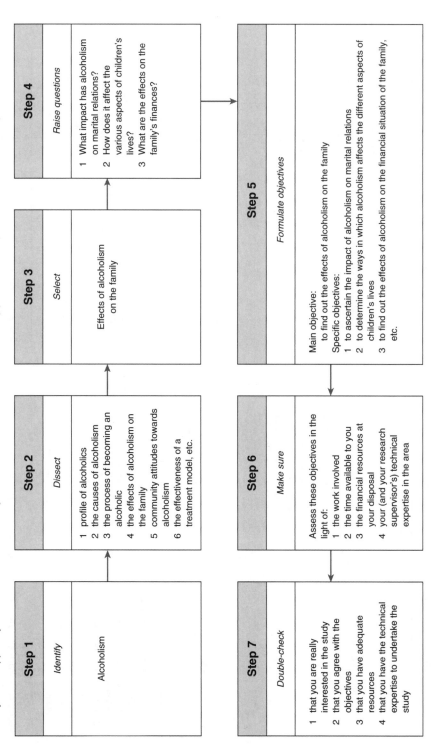

FIGURE 4.2   *Steps in formulating a research problem – alcoholism*

Example 2: Suppose you want to study the relationship between fertility and mortality. Follow these steps.

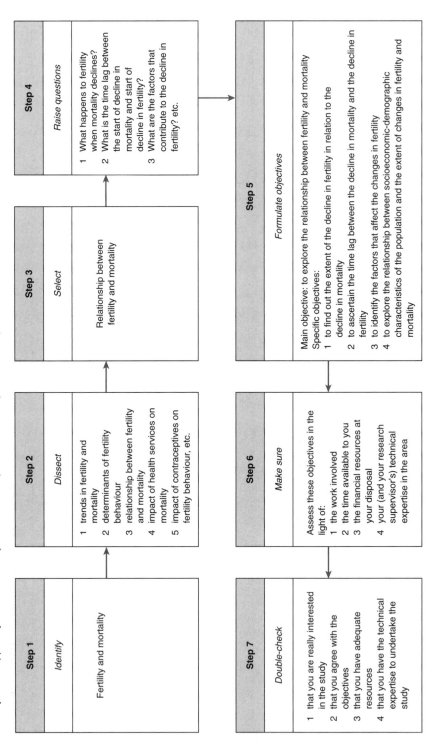

FIGURE 4.3 *Formulating a research problem – the relationship between fertility and mortality*

Example 3: Suppose you want to conduct a study in the area of health. Follow these steps.

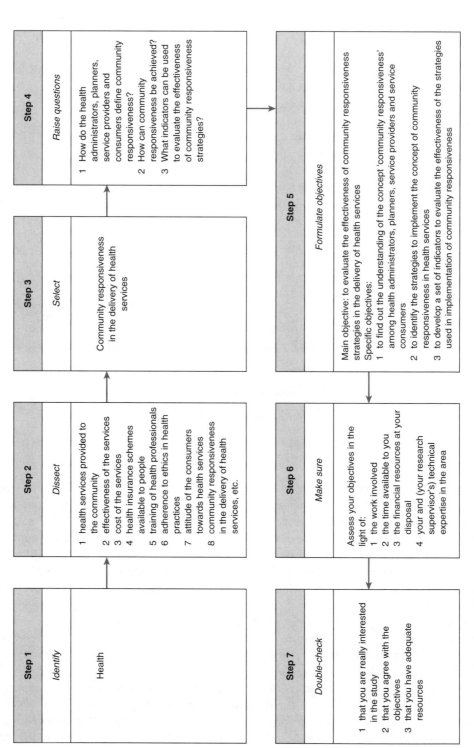

FIGURE 4.4 *Narrowing a research problem – health*

Subobjectives should be numerically listed. They should be worded clearly and unambiguously. Make sure that each subobjective contains only one aspect of the study. Use action–oriented words or verbs when writing your objectives. The objectives should start with words such as 'to determine', 'to find out', 'to ascertain', 'to measure' and 'to explore'.

The way the main objectives and subobjectives are worded determines how your research is classified (e.g. descriptive, correlational or experimental). In other words, the wording of your objectives determines the type of research design you need to adopt to achieve them. Hence, be careful about the way you word your objectives.

Irrespective of the type of research, the objectives should be expressed in such a way that the wording clearly, completely and specifically communicates to your readers your intention. There is no place for ambiguity, non-specificity or incompleteness, either in the wording of your objectives or in the ideas they communicate. Figure 4.5 displays the characteristics of the wording of objectives in relation to the type of research study.

FIGURE 4.5 *Characteristics of objectives*

If your study is primarily descriptive, your main objective should clearly describe the major focus of your study, even mentioning the organisation and its location unless these are to be kept confidential (e.g. to describe the types of treatment programme provided by [name of the organisation] to alcoholics in [name of the place] *or* to find out the opinion of the community about the health services provided by [name of the health centre/department] in [name of the place]). Identification of the organisation and its location is important as the services may be peculiar to the place and the organisation and may not represent the services provided by others to similar populations.

If your study is correlational in nature, in addition to the first three characteristics shown in Figure 4.5, the wording of the main objective should also include the main variables being correlated (e.g. to ascertain the *impact of migration* on *family roles* or to compare the effectiveness of *different teaching methods* on the *comprehension of students*).

If the overall thrust of your study is to test a hypothesis, the wording of the main objectives should also indicate the direction of the relationship being tested (e.g. to ascertain if an *increase in youth unemployment* will *increase the incidence of street crime*, or to demonstrate that the provision of maternal and child health services to Aboriginal people in rural Australia will *reduce infant mortality*).

The study population

So far we have focused on only one aspect of a study, the *research problem*. But every study in social sciences has a second aspect, the **study population**, from whom the required information to find answers to your research questions is obtained. As you narrow the research problem, similarly you need to decide very specifically and clearly who constitutes your study population, in order to select the appropriate respondents.

Suppose you have designed a study to ascertain the needs of young people living in a community. In terms of the study population, one of the first questions you need to answer is: 'Who do I consider to be a young person?' You need to decide, in measurable terms, which age group your respondents should come from. Is it those between 15 and 18, 15 and 20 or 15 and 25 years of age? Or you may be interested in some other age group. You need to decide this before undertaking your research journey. Having decided the age group that constitutes your 'young person', the next question you need to consider is whether you want to select young people of either gender or confine the study to one only. In addition, there is another dimension to consider: that is, what constitutes the community? Which geographical area(s) or ethnic background should I select my respondents from?

Let us take another example. Suppose you want to find out the settlement process of immigrants. As a part of identifying your study population, you need to decide who would you consider an immigrant. Is it a person who immigrated 5, 10, 15 or 20 years ago? You also need to consider the countries from where the immigrants come. Will you select your respondents irrespective of the country of origin or select only those who have come from a specific country(ies)? In a way you need to narrow your definition of the study population as you have done with your research problem. These issues are discussed in greater depth under 'Establishing operational definitions' following this section.

In quantitative research, you need to narrow both the research problem and the study population and make them as specific as possible so that you and your readers are clear about them. In qualitative research, reflecting the 'exploratory' philosophical base of the approach, both the study population and the research problem should remain loose and flexible to ensure the freedom necessary to obtain varied and rich data if a situation emerges.

Establishing operational definitions

In defining the problem you may use certain words or items that are difficult to measure and/or the understanding of which may vary from respondent to respondent. In a research study it is important to develop, define or establish a set of rules, indicators or yardsticks in order to establish clearly the meaning of such words/items. It is sometimes also important to define clearly the study population from which you need to obtain the required information. When you define concepts that you plan to use either in your research problem and/or in identifying the study population in a measurable form, they are called **working definitions** or **operational definitions**. You must understand that these working definitions that you develop are only for the purpose of your study and could be quite different to legal definitions, or those used by others. As the understanding of concepts can vary markedly from person to person, your working definitions will inform your readers what exactly you mean by the concepts that you have used in your study. The following example studies help to explain this. The main objectives are:

1 To find out the number of *children* living below the *poverty line* in Australia.
2 To ascertain the impact of immigration on *family roles* among *immigrants*.
3 To measure the *effectiveness* of a retraining programme designed to help *young people*.

Although these objectives clearly state the main thrust of the studies, they are not specific in terms of the main variables to be studied and the study populations. You cannot count the number of children living below the poverty line until you decide what constitutes the poverty line and how to determine it; you cannot find out the impact of immigration on family roles unless you identify which roles constitute family roles; and you cannot measure effectiveness until you define what effectiveness is. On the other hand, it is equally important to decide exactly what you mean by 'children', 'immigrants' or 'young'. Up to what age will you consider a person to be a child (i.e. 5, 10, 15 or 18)? Who would you consider young? A person 15 years of age, 20, 25 or 30? Who would you consider to be an immigrant? A person who immigrated 40, 20 or 5 years ago? In addition, are you going to consider immigrants from every country or only a few? In many cases you need to develop operational definitions for the variables and concepts you are studying and for the population that becomes the source of the information for your study. Table 4.2 lists the concepts and the population groups to be operationalised for the above examples.

TABLE 4.2   *Operationalisation of concepts and the study populations*

Study	Concept to be studied		Population to be studied	
	Concepts	**Issues**	**Study populations**	**Issues**
1	Poverty line	What constitutes 'poverty line'?	Children	Who would you consider a child?
2	Family roles	What constitutes 'family roles'?	Immigrants	Who would you consider an immigrant?
3	Effectiveness	What constitutes 'effectiveness'?	The young	Who would you consider a young person?
You must:	Operationalise the concepts: define in practical, observable and measurable terms 'poverty line', 'family roles' and 'effectiveness'		Operationalise the study population: define in identifiable terms 'children', 'immigrants' and 'young'	

In a research study you need to define these clearly in order to avoid ambiguity and confusion. This is achieved through the process of developing operational/working definitions. You need to develop operational definitions for the major concepts you are using in your study and develop a framework for the study population enabling you to select appropriate respondents.

Operational definitions may differ from day-to-day meanings as well as dictionary or legal definitions. These meanings may not be helpful in identifying either your study population or the concepts you are studying. Though in daily life you often use words such as 'children', 'youth' and 'immigrant' loosely, you need to be more specific when using them in a research study. You should work through your own definitions.

Operational definitions give an operational meaning to the study population and the concepts used. It is only through making your procedures explicit that you can validly describe, explain, verify and test. It is important to remember that there are no rules for deciding if an operational definition is valid. Your arguments must convince others about the appropriateness of your definitions.

Formulating a research problem in qualitative research

The difference in qualitative and quantitative studies starts with the way you formulate your research problem. In quantitative research you strive to be as specific as possible, attempt to narrow the magnitude of your study and develop a framework within which you confine your search. On the other hand, in qualitative research, this specificity in scope, methods and framework is almost completely ignored. You strive to maintain flexibility, openness and freedom to include any new ideas or exclude any aspect that you initially included but later consider not to be relevant. At the initial stage you only identify the main thrust of your study and some specific aspects which *you want to find out about*. Qualitative research primarily employs inductive reasoning. In contrast to quantitative research, where a research problem is stated before data collection, in qualitative research the problem is reformulated several times after you have begun the data collection. The research problem as well as data collection strategies are reformulated as necessary throughout data collection either to acquire the 'totality' of a phenomenon or to select certain aspects for greater in-depth study.

This flexibility and freedom, though providing you with certain advantages, can also create problems in terms of comparability of the information gathered. It is possible that your areas of search may become markedly different during the preliminary and final stages of data gathering. During the initial developmental phase, many researchers produce a framework of 'reminders' (a conceptual framework of enquiry) to ensure that key issues/aspects are covered during discussions with the respondents. As the study progresses, if needs be, issues or themes are added to this framework. This is not a list of questions but reminders that are only used if for some reason the interaction with respondents lacks discussion.

Let us take an example to detail the process of formulation of a research problem in qualitative research:

Once I supervised a student who was interested in attention-deficit hyperactivity disorder (ADHD). She wanted to find out, as she put it, 'What does it means to have a child with ADHD in the family?' Of course my first question to her was, 'What do you mean by "what does it mean"?' She paused for a while and then said, 'it means what it means'. I asked her to treat me as one of her respondents and ask the question. She asked me, 'What does it mean to have a child with ADHD?' to which my answer was, 'I do not understand your question. Could you please explain to me the meaning of "what does it mean"?' She found it difficult to explain and immediately realised the problem with the question. What she thought was very clear to her became quite difficult to explain. It took her a while to explain to me what she had in mind. During the discussion that followed, though she could explain some of the things she had in mind, she realised that she could not go to a respondent with her initial question.

The student knew a family who had a child with ADHD from which her interest in the topic had probably stemmed. I suggested that she have a talk with the mother. She did, and, to her surprise, the mother asked her the same question that I had.

I advised her to read some literature on ADHD and also have informal talks with two families who have a child with ADHD. We decided to select one single mother family and the other where the father and the mother both take responsibility for the child. She was advised to record all the issues and aspects that reflected her understanding of 'what does it mean', relating to bringing up a child with ADHD in the family. After going through the above, she developed a list three and a half pages long of the aspects and issues that, according to her, reflected her understanding of 'what does it mean'. She did not construct any specific questions around these aspects or issues. They served as background for her to raise with potential respondents in case respondents did not come up with issues or aspects for discussion in terms of 'What does it mean to have a child with ADHD in the family?'

This list brought immense clarification to her thinking about 'what does it mean' and served as the basis of her interviews with the families. A number of times during the supervisory sessions she had mentioned that she would not have been able to do much without the conceptual framework. You should not confuse it with the interview guide. The list is a conceptual construction of the thoughts that serve as background and become the basis of discussions in case there is insufficient dialogue with your potential respondents.

Summary

The formulation of a research problem is the most important step in the research process. It is the foundation, in terms of design, on which you build the whole study. Any defects in it will adversely affect the validity and reliability of your study.

There are no specific guidelines but the model suggested in this chapter could serve as a useful framework for the beginner. The seven-step model helps you to narrow your broad area of interest to enable you to decide what specifically you want to study. It is operational in nature and follows a logical sequence that takes the beginner through the complexities of formulating a research problem in a simple and easy-to-understand manner.

It is important to articulate the objectives of your study clearly. Objectives should be specific and free from ambiguity, and each one should relate to only one aspect of the study. They should be under two headings: main objective and subobjectives. Use action-oriented words when writing your objectives.

Formulation of a research problem in qualitative research follows a different path. You do not predetermine the exact nature and extent of the research problem you propose to find answers to. You continue to modify it as you start finding out more about it. However, it will help you if you develop a conceptual framework of the different aspects of a problem to serve as a backdrop for issues to be discussed with potential respondents.

Developing operational definitions for the concepts that you propose to study is extremely important. This enhances clarity about the issues you are trying to find out about and about the study population you plan to gather information from. It is important that you operationalise both the main variables you are proposing to study and the study population.

For You to Think About

▸ Refamiliarise yourself with the keywords listed at the beginning of this chapter and if you are uncertain about the meaning or application of any of them revisit these in the chapter before moving on.
▸ Identify two or three potential research questions, related to your own academic field or professional area, that would fall under each of the four Ps (as outlined in Table 4.1):

  ▸ people;
  ▸ problems;
  ▸ programs;
  ▸ phenomena.

▸ For each of these hypothetical research questions, identify which concepts and study populations would need to be operationally defined. Consider what problems might occur if this was not done.
▸ Select a broad subject area of interest to you and 'dissect' it into subareas.

CHAPTER 5
Identifying Variables

In this chapter you will learn about:

- What variables and concepts are and how they are different
- How to turn concepts into operational variables
- Types of variables from the viewpoint of:
  - Causation
  - The study design
  - The unit of measurement
- Types of measurement scales:
  - The nominal or classificatory scale
  - The ordinal or ranking scale
  - The interval scale
  - The ratio scale

Keywords: *active variables, attribute variables, categorical variables, causation, constant variables, continuous variables, dependent variables, dichotomous, extraneous variables, independent variables, interval scale, intervening variables, measurement scales, nominal scale, ordinal scale, polytomous, ratio scale, unit of measurement.*

If it exists, it can be measured. (Babbie 1989: 105)

In the process of formulating a research problem, in the case of quantitative research, there are two important considerations: the use of concepts and the construction of hypotheses. In the previous chapter, we established that concepts are highly subjective as an understanding of them varies from person to person. It follows, therefore, that as such they may not be measurable. In a research study it is important that the concepts used should be operationalised in measurable terms so that the extent of variation in respondents' understanding is reduced if not eliminated. Using techniques to operationalise concepts, and knowledge about variables, plays an important role in reducing this variability and 'fine tuning' your research problem.

What is a variable?

Whether we accept it or not, we all make value judgements constantly in our daily lives: 'This food is *excellent*'; 'I could not sleep *well* last night'; 'I do not *like* this'; and 'I think this is *wonderful*'. These are all judgements based upon our *own* preferences, indicators or assessment. Because these explain feelings or preferences, the basis on which they are made may vary markedly from person to person. There is no uniform yardstick with which to measure them. A particular food may be judged 'excellent' by one person but 'awful' by another, and something else could be wonderful to one person but ugly to another. When people express these feelings or preferences, they do so on the basis of certain criteria in their minds, or in relation to their expectations. If you were to question them you will discover that their judgement is based upon indicators and/or expectations that lead them to conclude and express a particular opinion.

Let us consider this in a professional context:

- 'This programme is *effective*.'
- 'This programme is *not effective*.'
- 'We are providing a *quality* service to our clients.'
- 'This is a *waste of time*.'
- 'In this institution women are *discriminated* against.'
- 'There is no *accountability* in this office.'
- 'This product is not doing *well*.'

These are not preferences per se; these are judgements that require a sound basis on which to proclaim. For example, if you want to find out if a programme is effective, if a service is of quality or if there is discrimination, you need to be careful that such judgements have a rational and sound basis. This warrants the use of a measuring mechanism and it is in the process of measurement that knowledge about variables plays an important role.

An image, perception or concept that is capable of measurement – hence capable of taking on different values – is called a **variable**. In other words, a concept that can be measured is called a variable. According to Kerlinger, 'A variable is a property that takes on different values. Putting it redundantly, a variable is something that varies … A variable is a symbol to which numerals or values are attached' (1986: 27). Black and Champion define a variable as 'rational units of analysis that can assume any one of a number of designated sets of values' (1976: 34). A concept that can be measured on any one of the four types of measurement **scale**, which have varying degrees of precision in measurement, is called a variable (measurement scales are discussed later in this chapter).

However, there are some who believe that scientific methods are incapable of measuring feelings, preferences, values and sentiments. In the author's opinion most of these things can be measured, though there are situations where such feelings or judgements cannot be directly measured but can be measured indirectly through appropriate indicators. These feelings and judgements are based upon observable behaviours in real life, though the extent to which the behaviours reflect their judgements may vary from person to person. Cohen and Nagel express their opinion in the following words:

> There are, indeed, a great many writers who believe that scientific method is inherently inapplicable to such judgements as estimation or value, as 'This is beautiful', 'This is good' or 'This ought to be done' … all judgements of the latter type express nothing but feelings, tastes or individual preferences, such judgements cannot be said to be true or false (except as descriptions of the personal feelings of the one who utters them) … Almost all human discourse would become meaningless if we took the view that every moral or aesthetic judgement is no more true or false than any other. (1966: 352)

The difference between a concept and a variable

Measurability is the main difference between a **concept** and a variable. Concepts are mental images or perceptions and therefore their meanings vary markedly from individual to individual, whereas variables are measurable, though, of course, with varying degrees of accuracy. A concept cannot be measured whereas a variable can be subjected to measurement by crude/ refined or subjective/objective units of measurement. Concepts are subjective impressions which, if measured as such would cause problems in comparing responses obtained from different respondents. According to Young:

> Each collaborator must have the same understanding of the concepts if the collaborative data are to be similarly classified and the findings pooled and tested, or reproduced. Classification and comparison demand uniform and precise definitions of categories expressed in concepts. (1966: 18)

It is therefore important for the concepts to be converted into variables (either directly or through a set of indicators) as they can be subjected to measurement, even though the degree of precision with which they can be measured markedly varies from one measurement scale to another (*nominal*, *ordinal*, *interval* and *ratio*). Table 5.1 gives examples of concepts and variables to illustrate the differences between them.

TABLE 5.1 *Examples of concepts and variables*

Concepts	Variables
• Effectiveness • Satisfaction • Impact • Excellent • High achiever • Self-esteem • Rich • Domestic violence • Extent and pattern of alcohol consumption • etc.	• Gender (male/female) • Attitude • Age (*x* years, *y* months) • Income ($ ___ per year) • Weight (___ kg) • Height (___ cm) • Religion (Catholic, Protestant, Jew, Muslim) • etc.
– Subjective impression – No uniformity as to its understanding among different people – As such cannot be measured	– Measurable though the degree of precision varies from scale to scale and from variable to variable (e.g. attitude – subjective, income – objective)

Converting concepts into variables

If you are using a concept in your study, you need to consider its operationalisation – that is, how it will be measured. In most cases, to operationalise a concept you first need to go through the process of identifying indicators – a set of criteria reflective of the concept – which can then be converted into variables. The choice of indicators for a concept might vary with the researcher but those selected must have a logical link with the concept. Some concepts, such as 'rich' (in terms of wealth), can easily be converted into indicators and then variables. For example, to decide objectively if a person is 'rich', one first needs to decide upon the indicators of wealth. Assume that we decide upon income and assets as the indicators. Income is also a variable since it can be measured in dollars; therefore, you do not need to convert this into a variable. Although the assets owned by an individual are indicators of his/her 'richness', they still belong to the category of concepts. You need to look further at the indicators of assets. For example, house, boat, car and investments are indicators of assets. Converting the value of each one into dollars will give the total value of the assets owned by a person. Next, fix a level, based upon available information on income distribution and an average level of assets owned by members of a community, which acts as the basis for classification. Then analyse the information on income and the total value of the assets to make a decision about whether the person should be classified as 'rich'. The operationalisation of other concepts, such as the 'effectiveness' or 'impact' of a programme, may prove more difficult. Table 5.2 shows some examples that will help you to understand the process of converting concepts into variables.

One of the main differences between quantitative and qualitative research studies is in the area of variables. In qualitative research, as it usually involves studying perceptions, beliefs, or feelings, you do not make any attempt to establish uniformity in them across respondents

TABLE 5.2 Converting concepts into variables

Concepts → Indicators → Variables

Concepts	Indicators	Variables	
		Variables	
		Variables	Decision level (working definitions)
Rich	1 Income 2 Assets	1 Income per year 2 Total value of: home(s); boat; car(s); investments	1 if > $100 000 2 if > $250 000
High academic achievement	1 Average marks obtained in examinations 2 Average marks obtained in practical work 3 Aggregate marks 4 etc.	1 Percentage of marks 2 Percentage of marks 3 Percentage of marks	1 if > 75% 2 if > 75% 3 if > 80%
Effectiveness (of a health programme)	1 Number of patients 2 Changes in morbidity (a) Changes in the extent of morbidity (b) Changes in the *pattern* of morbidity 3 Changes in mortality (a) Changes in the *Crude Death Rate (CDR)* (b) Changes in the *Age-Specific Death Rate (ASDR)* 4 Changes in nutritional status (a) Changes in *weight* (b) Changes in *illness episodes* (c) Changes in *morbidity*	1 number of patients serviced in a month/year 2 (a) Changes in morbidity rate (number of illness or episodes per 1000 pop.) (b) Changes in morbidity typology 3 1 Changes in CDR 2 Changes in ASDR 4 1 Changes in weight 2 Illness episodes in a year 3 Changes in morbidity type	Whether the difference in before-and-after levels is statistically significant Point-prevalence increase or decrease in each variable as decided by the researcher or other experts

and hence measurements and variables do not carry much significance. On the other hand, in quantitative studies, as the emphasis is on exploring commonalities in the study population, measurements and variables play an important role.

Types of variable

A variable can be classified in a number of ways. The classification developed here results from looking at variables in three different ways (see Figure 5.1):

- the causal relationship;
- the study design;
- the unit of measurement.

From the viewpoint of causal relationship

In studies that attempt to investigate a causal relationship or association, four sets of variables may operate (see Figure 5.2):

1 *change* variables, which are responsible for bringing about change in a phenomenon, situation or circumstance;
2 *outcome* variables, which are the effects, impacts or consequences of a change variable;
3 variables which *affect or influence* the link between cause-and-effect variables;
4 *connecting* or *linking* variables, which in certain situations are necessary to complete the relationship between cause-and-effect variables.

In research terminology, change variables are called **independent variables**, outcome/effect variables are called **dependent variables**, the unmeasured variables affecting the cause-and-effect relationship are called **extraneous variables** and the variables that link a cause-and-effect relationship are called **intervening variables**. Hence:

1 **Independent variable** – the cause supposed to be responsible for bringing about change(s) in a phenomenon or situation.
2 **Dependent variable** – the outcome or change(s) brought about by introduction of an independent variable.
3 **Extraneous variable** – several other factors operating in a real-life situation may affect changes in the dependent variable. These factors, not measured in the study, may increase or decrease the magnitude or strength of the relationship between independent and dependent variables.
4 **Intervening variable** – sometimes called the confounding variable (Grinnell 1988: 203), it links the independent and dependent variables. In certain situations the relationship between an independent and a dependent variable cannot be established without the intervention of another variable. The cause, or independent, variable will have the assumed effect only in the presence of an intervening variable.

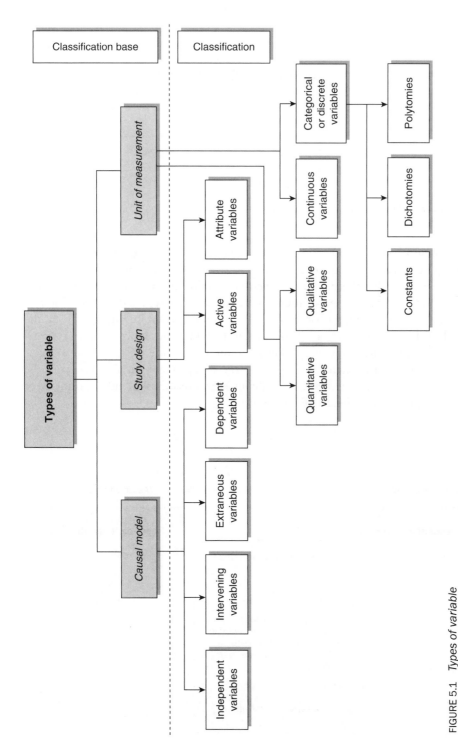

FIGURE 5.1 *Types of variable*

Note: Classification across a classification base is not mutually exclusive but classification within a classification base is. Within a study an independent variable can be an active variable, or a quantitative or a qualitative variable and it can also be a continuous or a categorical variable but it cannot be a dependent, an extraneous or an intervening variable.

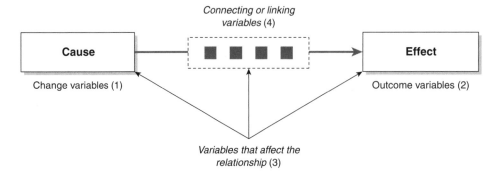

FIGURE 5.2   *Types of variable in a causal relationship*

To explain these variables let us consider some examples. Suppose you want to study the relationship between smoking and cancer. You assume that smoking is a cause of cancer. Studies have shown that there are many factors affecting this relationship, such as the number of cigarettes or the amount of tobacco smoked every day; the duration of smoking; the age of the smoker; dietary habits; and the amount of exercise undertaken by the individual. All of these factors may affect the extent to which smoking might cause cancer. These variables may either increase or decrease the magnitude of the relationship.

In the above example the extent of smoking is the independent variable, cancer is the dependent variable and all the variables that might affect this relationship, either positively or negatively, are extraneous variables. See Figure 5.3.

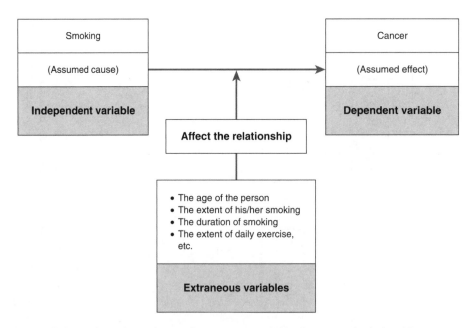

FIGURE 5.3   *Independent, dependent and extraneous variables in a causal relationship*

Let us take another example. Suppose you want to study the effects of a marriage counselling service on marital problems among clients of an agency providing such a service. Figure 5.4 shows the sets of variables that may operate in studying the relationship between counselling and marriage problems.

FIGURE 5.4   *Sets of variables in counselling and marriage problems*

In studying the relationship between a counselling service and marriage problems, it is assumed that the counselling service will influence the extent of marital problems. Hence, in the study of the above relationship, the type of counselling service is the independent variable and the extent of marriage problems is the dependent variable. The magnitude or strength of this relationship can be affected, positively or negatively, by a number of other factors that are not the focus of the study. These extraneous variables might be the birth of a child; improvement in a couple's economic situation; the couple's motivation to change the situation; the involvement of another person; self-realisation; and pressure from relatives and friends. Extraneous variables that work both ways can increase or decrease the strength of the relationship.

The example in Figure 5.5 should help you to understand intervening variables. Suppose you want to study the relationship between fertility and mortality. Your aim is to explore what happens to fertility when mortality declines. The history of demographic transition has shown that a reduction in the fertility level follows a decline in the mortality level, though the time taken to attain the same level of reduction in fertility varied markedly from

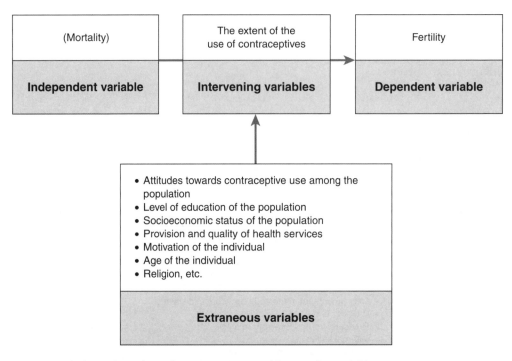

FIGURE 5.5   *Independent, dependent, extraneous and intervening variables*

country to country. As such, there is no direct relationship between fertility and mortality. With the reduction in mortality, fertility will decline only if people attempt to limit their family size. History has shown that for a multiplicity of reasons (the discussion of which is beyond the scope of this book) people have used one method or another to control their fertility, resulting in lower fertility levels. It is thus the intervention of contraceptive methods that completes the relationship: the greater the use of contraceptives, the greater the decline in the fertility level and the sooner the adoption of contraceptive methods by people, the sooner the decline. The extent of the use of contraceptives is also affected by a number of other factors, for example attitudes towards contraception, level of education, socioeconomic status and age, religion, and provision and quality of health services. These are classified as extraneous variables.

In the above example, decline in mortality is assumed to be the cause of a reduction in fertility, hence the mortality level is the independent variable and fertility is the dependent variable. But this relationship will be completed only if another variable intervenes – that is, the use of contraceptives. A reduction in mortality (especially child mortality) increases family size, and an increase in family size creates a number of social, economic and psychological pressures on families, which in turn create attitudes favourable to a smaller family size. This change in attitudes is eventually operationalised in behaviour through the adoption of contraceptives. If people do not adopt methods of contraception, a change in mortality levels

Study intervention	Study population
• Different teaching models • Experimental intervention • Programme service, etc.	• Age • Gender • Level of motivation • Attitudes • Religion, etc.
Active variables	**Attribute variables**
A researcher can manipulate, control or measure	*A researcher cannot manipulate, control or measure*

FIGURE 5.6 *Active and attribute variables*

will not be reflected in fertility levels. The population explosion in developing countries is primarily due to lack of acceptance of contraceptives. The extent of the use of contraceptives determines the level of the decline in fertility. The extent of contraceptive adoption by a population is dependent upon a number of factors. As mentioned earlier, in this causal model, the fertility level is the dependent variable, the extent of contraceptive use is the intervening variable, the mortality level is the independent variable, and the unmeasured variables such as attitudes, education, age, religion, the quality of services, and so on, are all extraneous variables. Without the intervening variable the relationship between the independent and dependent variables will not be complete.

From the viewpoint of the study design

A study that examines association or causation may be a controlled/contrived experiment, a quasi-experiment or an *ex post facto* or non-experimental study. In controlled experiments the independent (cause) variable may be introduced or manipulated either by the researcher or by someone else who is providing the service. In these situations there are two sets of variables (see Figure 5.6):

- **Active variables** – those variables that can be manipulated, changed or controlled.
- **Attribute variables** – those variables that cannot be manipulated, changed or controlled, and that reflect the characteristics of the study population, for example age, gender, education and income.

Suppose a study is designed to measure the relative effectiveness of three teaching models (Model A, Model B and Model C). The structure and contents of these models could vary and any model might be tested on any population group. The contents, structure and testability of a model on a population group may also vary from researcher to researcher. On the other hand, a researcher does not have any control over characteristics of the student population such as their age, gender or motivation to study. These characteristics of the study population are called attribute variables. However, a researcher does have the ability to control and/or change the teaching models. S/he can decide what constitutes a teaching model and on which group of the student population it should be tested (if randomisation is not used).

From the viewpoint of the unit of measurement

From the viewpoint of the unit of measurement, there are two ways of categorising variables:

- whether the unit of measurement is categorical (as in nominal and ordinal scales) or continuous in nature (as in interval and ratio scales);
- whether it is qualitative (as in nominal and ordinal scales) or quantitative in nature (as in interval and ratio scales).

On the whole there is very little difference between categorical and qualitative, and between continuous and quantitative, variables. The slight difference between them is explained below.

Categorical variables are measured on nominal or ordinal measurement scales, whereas for **continuous variables** the measurements are made on either an interval or a ratio scale. There are three types of categorical variables:

- **constant variable** – has only one category or value, for example taxi, tree and water;
- **dichotomous variable** – has only two categories, as in male/female, yes/no, good/bad, head/tail, up/down and rich/poor;
- **polytomous variable** – can be divided into more than two categories, for example religion (Christian, Muslim, Hindu); political parties (Labor, Liberal, Democrat); and attitudes (strongly favourable, favourable, uncertain, unfavourable, strongly unfavourable).

Continuous variables, on the other hand, have continuity in their measurement, for example age, income and attitude score. They can take any value on the scale on which they are measured. Age can be measured in years, months and days. Similarly, income can be measured in dollars and cents.

In many ways qualitative variables are similar to categorical variables as both use either nominal or ordinal measurement scales. However, there are some differences. For example, it is possible to develop categories on the basis of measurements made on a continuous scale, such as measuring the income of a population in dollars and cents and then developing categories such as 'low', 'middle' and 'high' income. The measurement of income in dollars and cents is classified as the measurement of a continuous variable, whereas its subjective measurement in categories such as 'low', 'middle' and 'high' groups is a qualitative variable.

Although this distinction exists, for most practical purposes there is no real difference between categorical and qualitative variables or between continuous and quantitative variables. Table 5.3 shows similarities and differences among the various types of variable.

TABLE 5.3 *Categorical/continuous and quantitative/qualitative variables*

Categorical			Continuous	Qualitative	Quantitative
Constant	**Dichotomous**	**Polytomous**	**Continuous**	**Qualitative**	**Quantitative**

• water	• yes/no	Attitudes
		  • strongly
		    favourable
		  • favourable
		  • uncertain
		  • strongly
		    unfavourable
		Political
		parties
		  • Labor
		  • Liberal
		  • Democrat
		Age*
		  • old
		  • child
		  • young
		Income^
		  • high
		  • middle
		  • low
			Income ($)
			
			Age (years)
			
			Weight (kg)
				Gender
				  • female
				  • male
				Educational
				level
				  • high
				  • average
				  • low
				Age*
				  • old
				  • young
				  • child
				Income
				  • high
				  • middle
				  • low
				Temperature+
				  • hot
				  • cold
					Educational
					level
					___ no. of
					years
					completed
					Age:*
					___
					years/months
					
					Income^
					___ $ per
					year
					
					Temperature+
					
					___ °C or °F

• tree	• good/bad				
• taxi	• rich/poor				
	• day/night				
	• male/ female				
	• hot/cold*				

* Can be classified in qualitative categories, e.g. old, young, child; or quantitatively on a continuous scale, e.g. in years, months and days.
∧ Can be measured quantitatively in dollars and cents as well as qualitatively in categories such as high, middle and low.
+ Similarly, temperature can be measured quantitatively in degrees on different scales (Celsius, Fahrenheit) or in qualitative categories such as hot and cold.

For a beginner it is important to understand that the way a variable is measured determines the type of analysis that can be performed, the statistical procedures that can be applied to the data, the way the data can be interpreted and the findings that can be communicated. You may not realise in the beginning that the style of your report is entirely dependent upon the way the different variables have been measured – that is, the way a question has been asked and its response recorded. The way you measure the variables in your study determines whether a study is 'qualitative' or 'quantitative' in nature. It is therefore important to know about the measurement scales for variables.

Types of measurement scale

The frame into which we wish to make everything fit is one of our own construction; but we do not construct it at random, we construct it by measurement so to speak; and that is why we can fit the facts into it without altering their essential qualities. (Poincaré 1952: xxv)

Measurement is central to any enquiry. In addition to the ideology and philosophy that underpin each mode of enquiry, the most significant difference between qualitative and quantitative research studies is in the types of measurement used in collecting information from the respondents. Qualitative research mostly uses descriptive statements to seek answers to the research questions, whereas in quantitative research these answers are usually sought on one of the measurement scales (nominal, ordinal, interval or ratio). If a piece of information is not collected using one of the scales at the time of data collection, it is transformed into variables by using these measurement scales at the time of analysis. Measurement on these scales could be either in the form of qualitative categories or through a precise unit of measurement. Those scales which have a unit of measurement (interval and ratio) are considered to be more refined, objective and accurate. On the other hand, nominal and ordinal scales are considered subjective and hence not as accurate as they do not have a unit of measurement per se. The greater the refinement in the unit of measurement of a variable, the greater the confidence placed in the findings by others, other things being equal. One of the main differences between the physical and the social sciences is the units of measurement used and the degree of importance attached to them. In the physical sciences measurements have to be absolutely accurate and precise, whereas in the social sciences they may vary from the very subjective to the very quantifiable. Within the social sciences the emphasis on precision in measurement varies markedly from one discipline to another. An anthropologist normally uses very 'subjective' units of measurement, whereas an economist or an epidemiologist emphasises 'objective' measurement.

There are two main classification systems in the social sciences for measuring different types of variable. One was developed by S. S. Stevens (in 1946) and the other by Duncan (in 1984). According to Smith (1991: 72), 'Duncan (1984) has enumerated, in increasing order of interest to scientists, five types of measurement: nominal classification, ordinal scaling, cardinal scaling, ratio scaling, and probability scaling'. Duncan writes about Stevens's classification as follows:

> The theory of scale types proposed in 1946 by S S Stevens focused on nominal, ordinal, interval, and ratio scales of measurement. Some of his examples of these types – notably those concerning psychological test scores – are misleading. (1984: viii)

However, Bailey considers that 'S S Stevens constructed a widely adopted classification of levels of measurement' (1978: 52). As this book is written for the beginner and as Stevens's classification is simpler, it is this that is used for discussion in this chapter. Stevens has classified the different types of measurement scale into four categories:

- nominal or classificatory scale;
- ordinal or ranking scale;
- interval scale;
- ratio scale.

Table 5.4 summarises the characteristics of the four scales.

TABLE 5.4 *Characteristics and examples of the four measurement scales*

Measurement scale	Examples	Characteristics of the scale
Nominal or classificatory	A Tree, house, taxi, etc. B Gender: male/female Attitude: Favourable/unfavourable C Political parties • Labor • Liberal • Democrat • Green Psychiatric disorders • Schizophrenic • Paranoid • Manic-depressive, etc. Religions • Christian • Islam • Hindu, etc.	Each subgroup has a characteristic/property which is common to all classified within that subgroup
Ordinal or ranking	Income • above average • average • below average Socioeconomic status • upper • middle • low Attitudes • strongly favourable • favourable • uncertain • unfavourable • strongly unfavourable Attitudinal scale (Likert scale – these are numerical categories) • 0–30 • 31–40 • 41–50, etc.	It has the characteristics of a nominal scale, e.g. individuals, groups, characteristics classified under a subgroup have a common characteristic PLUS Subgroups have a relationship to one another. They are arranged in ascending or descending order
Interval	Temperature: • Celsius → 0°C • Fahrenheit → 32°F Attitudinal scale (Thurstone scale): • 10–20 • 21–30 • 31–40 • 41–50, etc.	It has all the characteristics of an ordinal scale (which also includes a nominal scale) PLUS It has a unit of measurement with an arbitrary starting and terminating point
	Height: cm Income: $ Age: years/months Weight: kg Attitudinal score: Guttman scale	It has all the properties of an interval scale PLUS It has a fixed starting point, e.g. a zero point

The nominal or classificatory scale

A nominal scale enables the classification of individuals, objects or responses based on a common/ shared property or characteristic. These people, objects or responses are divided into a number of subgroups in such a way that each member of the subgroup has a common characteristic. A variable measured on a nominal scale may have one, two or more subcategories depending upon the extent of variation. For example, 'water' and 'taxi' have only one subgroup, whereas the variable 'gender' can be classified into two subcategories: male and female. Political parties in Australia can similarly be classified into four main subcategories: Labor, Liberal, Democrats and Greens. Those who identify themselves, either by membership or belief, as belonging to the Labor Party are classified as 'Labor', those identifying with the Liberals are classified as 'Liberal', and so on. The name chosen for a subcategory is notional, but for effective communication it is best to choose something that describes the characteristic of the subcategory.

Classification by means of a nominal scale ensures that individuals, objects or responses within the same subgroup have a common characteristic or property as the basis of classification. The sequence in which subgroups are listed makes no difference as there is no relationship among subgroups.

The ordinal or ranking scale

An ordinal scale has all the properties of a nominal scale – categorising individuals, objects, responses or a property into subgroups on the basis of a common characteristic – but also ranks the subgroups in a certain order. They are arranged in either ascending or descending order according to the extent that a subcategory reflects the magnitude of variation in the variable. For example, income can be measured either quantitatively (in dollars and cents) or qualitatively, using subcategories: 'above average', 'average' and 'below average'. (These categories can also be developed on the basis of quantitative measures, for example below $10 000 = below average, $10 000–$25 000 = average and above $25 000 = above average.) The subcategory 'above average' indicates that people so grouped have more income than people in the 'average' category, and people in the 'average' category have more income than those in the 'below average' category. These subcategories of income are related to one another in terms of the magnitude of people's income, but the magnitude itself is not quantifiable, and hence the difference between 'above average' and 'average' or between 'average' and 'below average' subcategories cannot be ascertained. The same is true for other variables such as socioeconomic status and attitudes measured on an ordinal scale.

Therefore, an ordinal scale has all the properties/characteristics of a nominal scale, in addition to its own. Subcategories are arranged in order of the magnitude of the property/characteristic. Also, the 'distance' between the subcategories is not equal as there is no quantitative unit of measurement.

The interval scale

An interval scale has all the characteristics of an ordinal scale; that is, individuals or responses belonging to a subcategory have a common characteristic and the subcategories are arranged in an ascending or descending order. In addition, an interval scale uses a unit of measurement that enables the individuals or responses to be placed at equally spaced intervals in relation to the spread of the variable. This scale has a starting and a terminating point and is divided into equally spaced units/intervals. The starting and terminating points and the number of units/intervals between them are arbitrary and vary from scale to scale.

Celsius and Fahrenheit scales are examples of an interval scale. In the Celsius system the starting point (considered as the freezing point) is 0°C and the terminating point (considered as the boiling point) is 100°C. The gap between the freezing and boiling points is divided into 100 equally spaced intervals, known as degrees. In the Fahrenheit system the freezing point is 32°F and the boiling point is 212°F, and the gap between the two points is divided into 180 equally spaced intervals. Each degree or interval is a measurement of temperature – the higher the degree, the higher the temperature. As the starting and terminating points are arbitrary, they are not absolute; that is, you cannot say that 60°C is twice as hot as 30°C or 30°F is three times hotter than 10°F. This means that while no mathematical operation can be performed on the readings, it can be performed on the differences between readings. For example, if the difference in temperature between two objects, A and B, is 15°C and the difference in temperature between two other objects, C and D, is 45°C, you can say that the difference in temperature between C and D is three times greater than that between A and B. An attitude towards an issue measured on the Thurstone scale is similar. However, the Likert scale does not measure the absolute intensity of the attitude but simply measures it in relation to another person.

The interval scale is relative; that is, it plots the position of individuals or responses in relation to one another with respect to the magnitude of the measurement variable. Hence, an interval scale has all the properties of an ordinal scale, and it has a unit of measurement with an arbitrary starting and terminating point.

The ratio scale

A ratio scale has all the properties of nominal, ordinal and interval scales and it also has a starting point fixed at zero. Therefore, it is an absolute scale – the difference between the intervals is always measured from a zero point. This means the ratio scale can be used for mathematical operations. The measurement of income, age, height and weight are examples of this scale. A person who is 40 years of age is twice as old as a 20-year-old. A person earning $60 000 per year earns three times the salary of a person earning $20 000.

Summary

The understanding and interpretation of a concept or a perception may vary from respondent to respondent, hence its measurement may not be consistent. A variable has some basis of classification and hence there is far less inconsistency in its meaning and understanding. Concepts are mental perceptions whereas variables are measurable either subjectively or objectively on one of the measurement scales. When you convert a concept into a variable you classify it on the basis of measurement into categories, thereby minimising the inherent variability in understanding. When you are unable to measure a concept directly, you need first to convert it into indicators and then into variables.

The way the required information is collected in quantitative and qualitative research is the most significant difference between them. Qualitative research mostly uses descriptive or narrative statements as the 'units of measurement' whereas quantitative research places greater emphasis of measuring responses on one of the four measurement scales. Though qualitative research places emphasis on descriptive statements in data collection, at the time of analysis, these statements are classified into categories on the basis of the main themes they communicate.

Knowledge of the different types of variables and the way they are measured plays a crucial role in quantitative research. Variables are important in bringing clarity and specificity to the conceptualisation of a research problem, to the formulation of hypotheses and to the development of a research instrument. They affect how the data can be analysed, what statistical tests can be applied to the data, what interpretations can be made, how the data can be presented and what conclusions can be drawn. The way you ask a question determines its categorisation on a measurement scale, which in turn affects how the data can be analysed, what statistical tests can be applied to the data, what interpretations can be made, how the data can be presented and what conclusions can be drawn. Also, the way a variable is measured at the data collection stage to a great extent determines whether a study is considered to be predominantly 'qualitative' or 'quantitative' in nature.

It is important for a beginner to understand the different ways in which a variable can be measured and the implications of this for the study. A variable can be classified from three perspectives that are not mutually exclusive: causal relationship, design of the study and unit of measurement. From the perspective of causality a variable can be classified into one of four categories: independent, dependent, extraneous and intervening. From the viewpoint of study design, there are two categories of variable: active and attribute. If we examine a variable from the perspective of the unit of measurement, it can be classified into categorical and continuous or qualitative and quantitative.

There are four measurement scales used in the social sciences: nominal, ordinal, interval and ratio. Any concept that can be measured on these scales is called a variable. Measurement scales enable highly subjective responses, as well as responses that can be measured with extreme precision, to be categorised. The choice of measuring a variable on a measurement scale is dependent upon the purpose of your study and the way you want to communicate the findings to readers.

For You to Think About

▸ Refamiliarise yourself with the keywords listed at the beginning of this chapter and if you are uncertain about the meaning or application of any of them revisit these in the chapter before moving on.

▸ Imagine that you have been asked to evaluate your lecturer. Determine which aspects of teaching you would consider important and develop a set of indicators that might reflect these.

▸ Self-esteem is a difficult concept to operationalise. Think about how you might go about developing a set of indicators to determine variance in the level of self-esteem in a group of individuals.

▸ Critically examine the typology of variables developed in this chapter. What changes would you like to propose?

CHAPTER 6
Constructing Hypotheses

In this chapter you will learn about:

- The definition of a hypothesis
- The functions of a hypothesis in your research
- How hypotheses are tested
- How to formulate a hypothesis
- Different types of hypotheses and their applications
- How errors in the testing of a hypothesis can occur
- The use of hypotheses in qualitative research

Keywords: *alternate hypotheses, hunch, hypothesis, hypothesis of point-prevalence, null hypothesis, operationalisable, research hypothesis, Type I error, Type II error, unidimensional, valid.*

Almost every great step [in the history of science] has been made by the 'anticipation of nature', that is, by the invention of hypotheses which, though verifiable, often had very little foundation to start with. (T. H. Huxley cited in Cohen & Nagel 1966: 197)

The definition of a hypothesis

The second important consideration in the formulation of a research problem in quantitative research is the construction of a **hypothesis**. Hypotheses bring clarity, specificity and focus to a research problem, but are not essential for a study. You can conduct a valid investigation without constructing a single formal hypothesis. On the other hand, within the context of a research study, you can construct as many hypotheses as you consider to be appropriate. Some believe that one must formulate a hypothesis to undertake an investigation; however, the author does not hold this opinion. Hypotheses primarily arise from a set of 'hunches' that are tested through a study and one can conduct a perfectly valid study without having these hunches or speculations. However, in epidemiological studies, to narrow the field of investigation, it is important to formulate hypotheses.

The importance of hypotheses lies in their ability to bring direction, specificity and focus to a research study. They tell a researcher what specific information to collect, and thereby provide greater focus.

Let us imagine you are at the races and you place a bet. You bet on a hunch that a particular horse will win. You will only know if your hunch was right after the race. Take another example. Suppose you have a hunch that there are more smokers than non-smokers in your class. To test your hunch, you ask either all or just some of the class if they are smokers. You can then conclude whether your hunch was right or wrong.

Now let us take a slightly different example. Suppose you work in the area of public health. Your clinical impression is that a higher rate of a particular condition prevails among people coming from a specific population subgroup. You want to find out the probable cause of this condition. There could be many causes. To explore every conceivable possibility would require an enormous amount of time and resources. Hence, to narrow the choice, based on your knowledge of the field, you could identify what you assume to be the most probable cause. You could then design a study to collect the information needed to verify your hunch. If on verification you were able to conclude that the assumed cause was the real cause of the condition, your assumption would have been right.

In these examples, you started with a superficial hunch or assumption. In one case (horse racing) you waited for the event to take place and in the other two instances you designed a study to assess the validity of your assumption, and only after careful investigation did you arrive at a conclusion about the validity of your assumptions.

Hypotheses are based upon similar logic. As a researcher you *do not know* about a phenomenon, a situation, the prevalence of a condition in a population or about the outcome of a programme, but you *do have a hunch* to form the basis of certain *assumptions or guesses*. You test these, mostly one by one, by collecting information that will enable you to conclude if your hunch was right. The verification process can have one of three outcomes. Your hunch may prove to be: right, partially right or wrong. Without this process of verification, you cannot conclude anything about the validity of your assumption.

Hence, a hypothesis is a hunch, assumption, suspicion, assertion or an idea about a phenomenon, relationship or situation, the reality or truth of which you do not know. A researcher calls these assumptions, assertions, statements or hunches hypotheses and they become the basis of an enquiry. In most studies the hypothesis will be based upon either previous studies or your own or someone else's observations.

There are many definitions of a hypothesis. According to Kerlinger, 'A hypothesis is a conjectural statement of the relationship between two or more variables' (1986: 17). *Webster's Third New International Dictionary* (1976) defines a hypothesis as:

a proposition, condition, or principle which is assumed, perhaps without belief, in order to draw out its logical consequences and by this method to test its accord with facts which are known or may be determined.

Black and Champion define a hypothesis as 'a tentative statement about something, the validity of which is usually unknown' (1976: 126). In another definition, Bailey defines a hypothesis as:

a proposition that is stated in a testable form and that predicts a particular relationship between two (or more) variables. In other words, if we think that a relationship exists, we first state it as a hypothesis and then test the hypothesis in the field. (1978: 35)

According to Grinnell:

A hypothesis is written in such a way that it can be proven or disproven by valid and reliable data – it is in order to obtain these data that we perform our study. (1988: 200)

From the above definitions it is apparent that a hypothesis has certain characteristics:

1 It is a tentative proposition.
2 Its validity is unknown.
3 In most cases, it specifies a relationship between two or more variables.

The functions of a hypothesis

While some researchers believe that to conduct a study requires a hypothesis, having a hypothesis is not essential as already mentioned. However, a hypothesis is important in terms of bringing clarity to the research problem. Specifically, a hypothesis serves the following functions:

- The formulation of a hypothesis provides a study with focus. It tells you what specific aspects of a research problem to investigate.
- A hypothesis tells you what data to collect and what not to collect, thereby providing focus to the study.
- As it provides a focus, the construction of a hypothesis enhances objectivity in a study.
- A hypothesis may enable you to add to the formulation of theory. It enables you to conclude specifically what is true or what is false.

The testing of a hypothesis

To test a hypothesis you need to go through a process that comprises three phases: (1) constructing a hypothesis; (2) gathering appropriate evidence; and (3) analysing evidence to draw

FIGURE 6.1   *The process of testing a hypothesis*

conclusions as to its validity. Figure 6.1 shows this process diagrammatically. It is only after analysing the evidence that you can conclude whether your hunch or hypothesis was true or false. When concluding about a hypothesis, conventionally, you specifically make a statement about the correctness or otherwise of a hypothesis in the form of 'the hypothesis is true' or 'the hypothesis is false'. It is therefore imperative that you formulate your hypotheses clearly, precisely and in a form that is testable. In arriving at a conclusion about the validity of your hypothesis, the way you collect your evidence is of central importance and it is therefore essential that your study design, sample, data collection method(s), data analysis and conclusions, and communication of the conclusions be valid, appropriate and free from any bias.

The characteristics of a hypothesis

There are a number of considerations to keep in mind when constructing a hypothesis, as they are important for valid verification. The wording of a hypothesis therefore must have certain attributes that make it easier for you to ascertain its validity. These attributes are:

- **A hypothesis should be simple, specific and conceptually clear.** There is no place for ambiguity in the construction of a hypothesis, as ambiguity will make the verification of your hypothesis almost impossible. It should be 'unidimensional' – that is, it should test only one relationship or hunch at a time. To be able to develop a good hypothesis you must be familiar with the subject area (the literature review is of immense help). The more insight you have into a problem, the easier it is to construct a hypothesis. For example:

  The average age of the male students in this class is higher than that of the female students.

  The above hypothesis is clear, specific and easy to test. It tells you what you are attempting to compare (average age of this class), which population groups are being compared (female and male students), and what you want to establish (higher average age of the male students).
  Let us take another example:

  Suicide rates vary inversely with social cohesion. (Black & Champion 1976: 126)

This hypothesis is clear and specific, but a lot more difficult to test. There are three aspects of this hypothesis: 'suicide rates'; 'vary inversely', which stipulates the direction of the relationship; and 'social cohesion'. To find out the suicide rates and to establish whether the relationship is inverse or otherwise are comparatively easy, but to ascertain social cohesion is a lot more difficult. What determines social cohesion? How can it be measured? This problem makes it more difficult to test this hypothesis.

- **A hypothesis should be capable of verification.** Methods and techniques must be available for data collection and analysis. There is no point in formulating a hypothesis if it cannot be subjected to verification because there are no techniques to verify it. However, this does not necessarily mean that you should not formulate a hypothesis for which there are no methods of verification. You might, in the process of doing your research, develop new techniques to verify it.
- **A hypothesis should be related to the existing body of knowledge.** It is important that your hypothesis emerges from the existing body of knowledge, and that it adds to it, as this is an important function of research. This can only be achieved if the hypothesis has its roots in the existing body of knowledge.
- **A hypothesis should be operationalisable.** This means that it can be expressed in terms that can be measured. If it cannot be measured, it cannot be tested and, hence, no conclusions can be drawn.

Types of hypothesis

Theoretically there should be only one type of hypothesis, that is the research hypothesis – the basis of your investigation. However, because of the conventions in scientific enquiries and because of the wording used in the construction of a hypothesis, hypotheses can be classified into several types. Broadly, there are two categories of hypothesis:

1 research hypotheses;
2 alternate hypotheses.

The formulation of an **alternate hypothesis** is a convention in scientific circles. Its main function is to explicitly specify the relationship that will be considered as true in case the research hypothesis proves to be wrong. In a way, an alternate hypothesis is the opposite of the research hypothesis. Conventionally, a null hypothesis, or hypothesis of no difference, is formulated as an alternate hypothesis.

Let us take an example. Suppose you want to test the effect that different combinations of maternal and child health services (MCH) and nutritional supplements (NS) have on the infant mortality rate. To test this, a two-by-two factorial experimental design is adopted (see Figure 6.2).

There are several ways of formulating a hypothesis. For example:

1 There will be no difference in the level of infant mortality among the different treatment modalities.
2 The MCH and NS treatment groups will register a greater decline in infant mortality than the only MCH treatment group, the only NS treatment group or the control group.

Maternal and child health services (MCH)		
	Yes	No
Yes	MCH + NS	NS
No	MCH	Control

Nutritional supplements (NS)

FIGURE 6.2   *Two-by-two factorial experiment to study the relationship between MCH, NS and infant mortality*

3   Infant mortality in the MCH treatment group will reach a level of 30/1000 over five years.
4   Decline in the infant mortality rate will be three times greater in the MCH treatment group than in the NS group only over five years.

Let us take another example. Suppose you want to study the smoking pattern in a community in relation to gender differentials. The following hypotheses could be constructed:

1   There is no significant difference in the proportion of male and female smokers in the study population.
2   A greater proportion of females than males are smokers in the study population.
3   A total of 60 per cent of females and 30 per cent of males in the study population are smokers.
4   There are twice as many female smokers as male smokers in the study population.

In both sets of examples, the way the first hypothesis has been formulated indicates that there is no difference either in the extent of the impact of different treatment modalities on the infant mortality rate or in the proportion of male and female smokers. When you construct a hypothesis stipulating that there is no difference between two situations, groups, outcomes, or the prevalence of a condition or phenomenon, this is called a **null hypothesis** and is usually written as H0.

The second hypothesis in each example implies that there is a difference either in the extent of the impact of different treatment modalities on infant mortality or in the proportion of male and female smokers among the population, though the extent of the difference is not specified. A hypothesis in which a researcher stipulates that there will be a difference but does not specify its magnitude is called a **hypothesis of difference**.

FIGURE 6.3 *Types of hypothesis*

A researcher may have enough knowledge about the smoking behaviour of the community or the treatment programme and its likely outcomes to speculate almost the exact prevalence of the situation or the outcome of a treatment programme in quantitative units. Examine the third hypothesis in both sets of examples: the level of infant mortality is 30/1000 and the proportion of female and male smokers is 60 and 30 per cent respectively. This type of hypothesis is known as a **hypothesis of point-prevalence**.

The fourth hypothesis in both sets of examples speculates a relationship between the impact of different combinations of MCH and NS programmes on the dependent variable (infant mortality) or the relationship between the prevalence of a phenomenon (smoking) among different populations (male and female). This type of hypothesis stipulates the extent of the relationship in terms of the effect of different treatment groups on the dependent variable ('three times greater in the MCH treatment group than in the NS group only over five years') or the prevalence of a phenomenon in different population groups ('twice as many female as male smokers'). This type of hypothesis is called a **hypothesis of association**.

Note that in Figure 6.3 the null hypothesis is also classified as a hypothesis of no difference under 'Research hypothesis'. Any type of hypothesis, including a null hypothesis, can become the basis of an enquiry. When a null hypothesis becomes the basis of an investigation, it becomes a research hypothesis.

Errors in testing a hypothesis

As already mentioned, a hypothesis is an assumption that may prove to be either correct or incorrect. It is possible to arrive at an incorrect conclusion about a hypothesis for a variety of reasons. Incorrect conclusions about the validity of a hypothesis may be drawn if:

When all null hypothesis is actually:

FIGURE 6.4   *Type I and Type II errors in testing a hypothesis*

- the study design selected is faulty;
- the sampling procedure adopted is faulty;
- the method of data collection is inaccurate;
- the analysis is wrong;
- the statistical procedures applied are inappropriate; or
- the conclusions drawn are incorrect.

Any, some or all of these aspects of the research process could be responsible for the inadvertent introduction of error in your study, making conclusions misleading. Hence, in the testing of a hypothesis there is always the possibility of errors attributable to the reasons identified above. Figure 6.4 shows the types of error that can result in the testing of a hypothesis.

Hence, in drawing conclusions about a hypothesis, two types of error can occur:

- *Rejection* of a null hypothesis when it is true. This is known as a **Type I error**.
- *Acceptance* of a null hypothesis when it is false. This is known as a **Type II error**.

Hypotheses in qualitative research

One of the differences in qualitative and quantitative research is around the importance attached to and the extent of use of hypotheses when undertaking a study. As qualitative studies are characterised by an emphasis on describing, understanding and exploring phenomena using categorical and subjective measurement procedures, construction of hypotheses is neither advocated nor practised. In addition, as the degree of specificity needed to test a hypothesis is deliberately not adhered to in qualitative research, the testing of a hypothesis becomes difficult and meaningless. This does not mean that you cannot construct hypotheses in qualitative research; the non-specificity of the problem as well as methods and procedures make the convention of hypotheses formulation far less practicable and advisable. Even within quantitative studies the importance attached to and the practice of formulating hypotheses vary markedly from one academic discipline to another. Fro example, hypotheses are most prevalent in epidemiological research and research relating to the establishment of causality of a phenomenon, where it becomes important to narrow the list of probable causes so that a specific cause-and-effect relationship can be studied. In the social sciences formulation of hypotheses is mostly dependent on the researcher and the academic discipline, whereas within an academic discipline it varies markedly between the quantitative and qualitative research paradigms.

Summary

Hypotheses, though important, are not essential for a study. A perfectly valid study can be conducted without constructing a single hypothesis. Hypotheses are important for bringing clarity, specificity and focus to a research study.

A hypothesis is a speculative statement that is subjected to verification through a research study. In formulating a hypothesis it is important to ensure that it is simple, specific and conceptually clear; able to be verified; rooted in an existing body of knowledge; and able to be operationalised.

There are two broad types of hypothesis: a research hypothesis and an alternate hypothesis. A research hypothesis can be further classified, based upon the way it is formulated, as a null hypothesis, a hypothesis of difference, a hypothesis of point-prevalence and a hypothesis of association.

One of the main differences in qualitative and quantitative research is the extent to which hypotheses are used and the importance attached to them. In qualitative research, because of the purpose of an investigation and methods used to obtain information, hypotheses are not used and almost no importance is given to them. However, in quantitative research, their use is far more prevalent though it varies markedly from one academic discipline to another and from researcher to researcher. On the whole it can be said that if the aim of a study is to explore where very little is known, hypotheses are usually not formulated; however, if a study aims to test an assertion by way of causality or association, validate the prevalence of something or establish its existence, hypotheses can be constructed.

The testing of a hypothesis becomes meaningless if any one of the aspects of your study – design, sampling procedure, method of data collection, analysis of data, statistical procedures applied or conclusions drawn – is faulty or inappropriate. This can result in erroneous verification of a hypothesis: Type I error occurs where you reject a null hypothesis when it is true and should not have been rejected; and Type II error is introduced where you accept a null hypothesis when it is false and should not have been accepted.

For You to Think About

▸ *Refamiliarise yourself with the keywords listed at the beginning of this chapter and if you are uncertain about the meaning or application of any of them revisit these in the chapter before moving on.*

▸ *To what extent do you think that the use of hypotheses is relevant to social research?*

▸ *Formulate two or three hypotheses that relate to your own areas of interest and consider the factors that might affect their validity.*

This operational step includes two chapters:

- Chapter 7: The research design
- Chapter 8: Selecting a study design

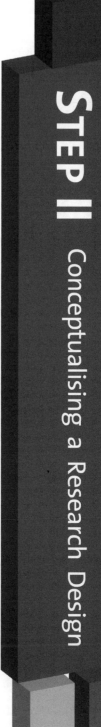

STEP II

Conceptualising a Research Design

CHAPTER 7
The Research Design

In this chapter you will learn about:

- What research design means
- The important functions of research design
- Issues to consider when designing your own research
- The theory of causality and the research design

Keywords: *chance variables, control group, experimental group, extraneous variables, independent variable, matching, 'maxmincon' principle, random error, randomisation, research design, study design, treatment group.*

If you are clear about your research problem, your achievement is worth praising. You have crossed one of the most important and difficult sections of your research journey. Having decided *what* you want to study, you now need to determine *how* you are going to conduct your study. There are a number of questions that need to be answered before you can proceed with your journey. What procedures will you adopt to obtain answers to research questions? How will you carry out the tasks needed to complete the different components of the research process? What should you do and what should you not do in the process of undertaking the study? Basically, answers to these questions constitute the core of a research design.

What is a research design?

> A research design is a plan, structure and strategy of investigation so conceived as to obtain answers to research questions or problems. The plan is the complete scheme or programme of the research. It includes an outline of what the investigator will do from writing the hypotheses and their operational implications to the final analysis of data. (Kerlinger 1986: 279)

> A traditional research design is a blueprint or detailed plan for how a research study is to be completed—operationalizing variables so they can be measured, selecting a sample of interest to study, collecting data to be used as a basis for testing hypotheses, and analysing the results. (Thyer 1993: 94)

A research design is a procedural plan that is adopted by the researcher to answer questions validly, objectively, accurately and economically. According to Selltiz, Deutsch and Cook, 'A research design is the arrangement of conditions for collection and analysis of data in a manner that aims to combine relevance to the research purpose with economy in procedure' (1962: 50). Through a research design you decide for yourself and communicate to others your decisions regarding what study design you propose to use, how you are going to collect information from your respondents, how you are going to select your respondents, how the information you are going to collect is to be analysed and how you are going to communicate your findings. In addition, you will need to detail in your research design the rationale and justification for each decision that shapes your answers to the 'how' of the research journey. In presenting your rationale and justification you need to support them critically from the literature reviewed. You also need to assure yourself and others that the path you have proposed will yield valid and reliable results.

The functions of a research design

The above definitions suggest that a research design has two main functions. The first relates to the identification and/or development of procedures and logistical arrangements required to undertake a study, and the second emphasises the importance of quality in these procedures to ensure their validity, objectivity and accuracy. Hence, through a research design you:

- conceptualise an operational plan to undertake the various procedures and tasks required to complete your study;
- ensure that these procedures are adequate to obtain valid, objective and accurate answers to the research questions. Kerlinger calls this function the **control of variance** (1986: 280).

Let us take the first of these functions. The research design should detail for you, your supervisor and other readers all the procedures you plan to use and the tasks you are going to perform to obtain answers to your research questions. One of the most important requirements of a research design is to specify everything clearly so a reader will understand what procedures to follow and how to follow them. A research design, therefore, should do the following:

- Name the study design per se – that is, 'cross-sectional', 'before-and-after', 'comparative', 'control experiment' or 'random control'.
- Provide detailed information about the following aspects of the study:
  - Who will constitute the study population?
  - How will the study population be identified?
  - Will a sample or the whole population be selected?
  - If a sample is selected, how will it be contacted?
  - How will consent be sought?
  - What method of data collection will be used and why?
  - In the case of a questionnaire, where will the responses be returned?
  - How should respondents contact you if they have queries?
  - In the case of interviews, where will they be conducted?
  - How will ethical issues be taken care of?

Chapter 8 describes some of the commonly used study designs. The rest of the topics that constitute a research design are covered in the subsequent chapters.

The theory of causality and the research design

Now let's turn to the second function of the research design – ensuring that the procedures undertaken are adequate to obtain valid, objective and accurate answers to the research questions. To ensure this, it is important that you select a study design that helps you to isolate, eliminate or quantify the effects of different sets of variable influencing the independent variable. To help explain this, we look at a few examples.

Suppose you want to find out the effectiveness of a marriage counselling service provided by an agency – that is, the extent to which the service has been able to resolve the marital problems of its clients. In studying such relationships you must understand that in real life there are many outside factors that can influence the outcome of your intervention. For example, during visits to your agency for counselling, your client may get a better job. If some of the marital problems came about because of economic hardship, and if the problem of money is now solved, it may be a factor in reducing the marital problems. On the other hand, if a client loses his/her job, the increase in the economic problems may either intensify or lessen the marital problems; that is, for some couples a perceived financial threat may increase marital problems, whereas, for others, it may create more closeness between partners. In some situations, an improvement in a marriage may have very little to do with the counselling received, coming about almost entirely because of a change in economic circumstances. Other events such as the birth of a child to a couple or a couple's independent 'self-realisation', independently arrived at, may also affect the extent and nature of marital problems. Figure 7.1 lists other possible factors under the category of extraneous variables. This does not exhaust the list by any means.

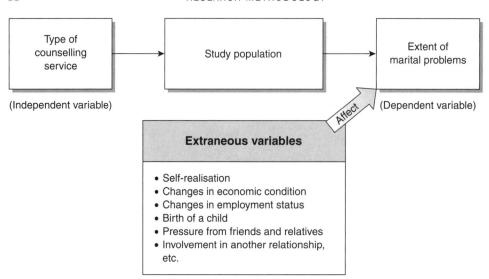

FIGURE 7.1   *Factors affecting the relationship between a counselling service and the extent of marital problems*

Continuing the example of marriage and counselling, there are sets of factors that can affect the relationship between counselling and marriage problems, and each is a defined category of variables:

1   Counselling per se.
2   All the factors other than counselling that affect the marital problems.
3   The outcome – that is, the change or otherwise in the extent of the marital problems.
4   Sometimes, the variation in response to questions about marital problems can be accounted for by the mood of respondents or ambiguity in the questions. Some respondents may either overestimate or underestimate their marital problems because of their state of mind at the time. Or some respondents, in spite of being in exactly the same situation, may respond to non-specific or ambiguous questions differently, according to how they interpret the question.

As already explained in Chapter 5, any variable that is responsible for bringing about a change is called an *independent variable*. In this example, the counselling is an independent variable. When you study a cause-and-effect relationship, usually you study the impact of only one independent variable. Occasionally you may study the impact of two independent variables, or (very rarely) more than two, but these study designs are more complex.

For this example *counselling* was the assumed cause of change in the *extent of marital problems*; hence, the extent of marital problems is the *dependent variable*, as the change in the degree of marital problems was dependent upon counselling.

All other factors that affect the relationship between marital problems and counselling are called *extraneous variables*. In the social sciences, extraneous variables operate in every study and cannot be eliminated. However, they can be controlled to some extent. (Some of the methods for controlling them are described later in this chapter.) Nevertheless, it is possible to find out the impact attributable to extraneous variables. This is done with the introduction of a **control group** in the study design. The sole function of a control group is to quantify the impact of extraneous variables on the dependent variable(s).

Changes in the dependent variable, because of the respondent's state of mood or ambiguity in the research instrument, are called **random variables** or **chance variables.** The error thus introduced is called the *chance* or *random error.* In most cases the net effect of chance variables is considered to be negligible as respondents who overreport tend to cancel out those who underreport. The same applies to responses to ambiguous questions in a research instrument.

Hence in any causal relationship, changes in the dependent variable may be attributed to three types of variable:

Let us take another example. Suppose you want to study the impact of different teaching models on the level of comprehension of students for which you adopt a comparative study design. In this study, the change in the level of comprehension, in addition to the teaching models, can be attributed to a number of other factors, some of which are shown in Figure 7.2:

[change in level of comprehension] =

[change attributable to the teaching model] ±
[change attributable to extraneous variables] ±
[change attributable to chance variables]

In fact, in any study that attempts to establish a causal relationship, you will discover that there are three sets of variables operating to bring about a change in the dependent variable. This can be expressed as an equation:

[change in the outcome variable] =

[change because of the chance variable] ±
[change because of extraneous variables] ±
[change because of chance or random variables]

or in other words:

[change in the dependent variable] =

[change attributable to the independent variable] ±
[change attributable to extraneous variables] ±
[change attributable to chance variables]

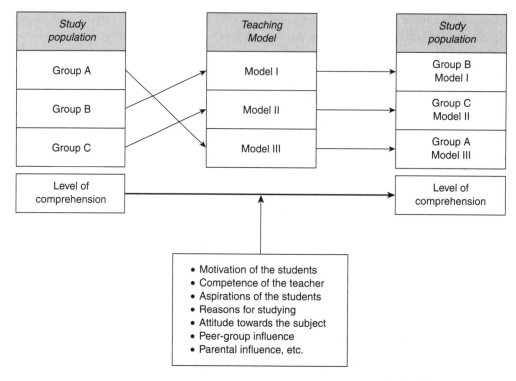

FIGURE 7.2   *The relationship between teaching models and comprehension*

or in technical terms:

[total variance] =

    [variance attributable to the independent variable] ±
    [variance attributable to extraneous variables] ±
    [random or chance variance]

It can also be expressed graphically (Figure 7.3).

As the total change measures the combined effect of all three components it is difficult to isolate the individual impact of each of them (see Figure 7.3). Since your aim as a researcher is to determine the change that can be attributed to the independent variable, you need to design your study to ensure that the independent variable has the *maximum* opportunity to have its full effect on the dependent variable, while the effects that are attributed to extraneous and chance variables are minimised (if possible) or quantified or eliminated. This is what Kerlinger (1986: 286) calls the 'maxmincon' principle of variance.

One of the most important questions is: how do we minimise the effect attributable to extraneous and chance variables? The answer is that in most situations we cannot;

FIGURE 7.3   *The proportion attributable to the three components may vary markedly*

however, it can be quantified. The sole purpose of having a control group, as mentioned earlier, is to measure the change that is a result of extraneous variables. The effect of chance variables is often assumed to be none or negligible. As discussed, chance varia- tion comes primarily from two sources: respondents and the research instrument. It is assumed that if some respondents affect the dependent variable positively, others will affect it negatively. For example, if some respondents are extremely positive in their atti- tude towards an issue, being very liberal or positively biased, there are bound to be others who are extremely negative (being very conservative or negatively biased). Hence, they tend to cancel each other out so the net effect is assumed to be zero. However, if in a study population most individuals are either negatively or positively biased, a systematic error in the findings will be introduced. Similarly, if a research instrument is not reliable (i.e. it is not measuring correctly what it is supposed to measure), a systematic bias may be introduced into the study.

In the physical sciences a researcher can control extraneous variables as experiments are usually done in a laboratory. By contrast, in the social sciences, the laboratory is society, over which the researcher lacks control. Since no researcher has control over extraneous vari- ables, their effect, as mentioned, in most situations cannot be minimised. The best option is to quantify their impact through the use of a control group, though the introduction of a control group creates the problem of ensuring that the extraneous variables have a similar effect on both control and experimental groups. In some situations their impact can be eliminated (this is possible only where one or two variables have a marked impact on the dependent variable). There are two methods used to ensure that extraneous variables have a similar effect on control and experimental groups and two methods for eliminating extraneous variables:

FIGURE 7.4 *Building into the design*

1 **Ensure that extraneous variables have a similar impact on control and experimental groups.** It is assumed that if two groups are comparable, the extent to which the extraneous variables will affect the dependent variable will be similar in both groups. The following two methods ensure that the control and experimental groups are comparable with one another:

   (a) **Randomisation** – Ensures that the two groups are comparable with respect to the variable(s). It is assumed that if the groups are comparable, the extent to which extraneous variables are going to affect the dependent variable is the same in each group.

   (b) **Matching** – Another way of ensuring that the two groups are comparable so that the effect of extraneous variables will be the same in both groups (discussed in Chapter 8).

2 **Eliminate extraneous variable(s).** Sometimes it is possible to eliminate the extraneous variable or to build it into the study design. This is usually done when there is strong evidence that the extraneous variable has a high correlation with the dependent variable, or when you want to isolate the impact of the extraneous variable. There are two methods used to achieve this:

   (a) **Build the affecting variable into the design of the study** – To explain this concept let us take an example. Suppose you want to study the impact of maternal health services on the infant mortality of a population. It can be assumed that the nutritional status of children also has a marked effect on infant mortality. To study the impact of maternal health services per se, you adopt a two-by-two factorial design as explained in Figure 7.4. In this way you can study the impact of the extraneous variables separately and interactively with the independent variable.

   (b) **Eliminate the variable** – To understand this, let us take another example. Suppose you want to study the impact of a health education programme on the attitudes towards, and beliefs about, the causation and treatment of a certain illness among non-indigenous Australians and indigenous Australians living in a particular community. As attitudes and beliefs vary markedly from culture to culture, studying non-indigenous Australians and indigenous Australians as one group will not provide an accurate picture. In such studies it is appropriate to eliminate the cultural variation in the study population by selecting and studying the populations separately or by constructing culture-specific cohorts at the time of analysis.

Summary

In this chapter you have learnt about the functions of a research design. A research design serves two important functions: (1) to detail the procedures for undertaking a study; and (2) to ensure that, in the case of causality, the independent variable has the maximum opportunity to have its effect on the dependent variable while the effect of extraneous and chance variables is minimised. In terms of the first function, a research design should outline the logistical details of the whole process of the research journey. You need to spell out in detail what type of study design per se you are proposing to use and why, who are going to be your respondents and how they will be selected, from how many you are proposing to get the needed information, how the information will be collected by you and how you are going to analyse the information. For each aspect you need to provide your rationale and justification and as far as possible support them from the literature reviewed.

Through the second function, 'Control of variance', when establishing association or causality, it ensures your supervisor and readers that you have set up your study in such a way that your independent variable has the maximum chance of affecting the dependent variable and that the effects of extraneous and chance variables are minimised, quantified and/or controlled (the 'maxmincon' principle of variance).

A study without a control group measures the total change (change attributable to independent variable ± extraneous variables ± chance variables) in a phenomenon or situation. The purpose of introducing a control group is to quantify the impact of extraneous and chance variables.

The study design is a part of the research design. It is the design of the study per se, whereas the research design also includes other details related to the carrying out of the study.

For You to Think About

▸ *Refamiliarise yourself with the keywords listed at the beginning of this chapter and if you are uncertain about the meaning or application of any of them revisit these in the chapter before moving on.*
▸ *What are the main functions of a research design? Why is it important to have a research design before undertaking a study?*
▸ *Provide examples from your own area of study to illustrate the main variables in terms of causality (you may find it useful to refer back to Chapter 5).*
▸ *Identify one or two examples from an area that interests you to demonstrate how the 'maxmincon' principle of variance can be applied.*

CHAPTER 8
Selecting a Study Design

In this chapter you will learn about:

- The differences between quantitative and qualitative study designs
- Common study designs in quantitative research and when to use them
- Common study design in qualitative research and when to use them
- The strengths and weaknesses of different study designs

Keywords: *action research, after-only design, before-and-after study design, blind studies, case studies, cohort studies, control studies, cross-sectional study design, double-blind studies, experimental study design, feminist research, focus studies, longitudinal studies, non-experimental studies, panel studies, prospective study design, quasi-experimental studies, reflective journal, retrospective studies, semi-experimental studies, trend studies.*

Differences between quantitative and qualitative study designs

In this chapter we will discuss some of the most commonly used study designs in both quantitative and qualitative research. Overall, there are many more study designs in quantitative research than in qualitative research. Quantitative study designs are specific, well structured, have been tested for their validity and reliability, and can be explicitly defined and recognised. Study designs in qualitative research either do not have these attributes or have them to a lesser degree. They are less specific and precise, and do not have the same structural depth.

Differences in philosophical perspectives in each paradigm combined with the aims of a study, to a large extent, determine the focus, approach and mode of enquiry which, in turn, determine the structural aspects of a **study design**. The main focus in qualitative research is to understand, explain, explore, discover and clarify situations, feelings, perceptions, attitudes, values, beliefs and experiences of a group of people. The study designs are therefore often based on deductive rather than inductive logic, are flexible and emergent in nature, and are often non-linear and non-sequential in their operationalisation. The study designs mainly entail the selection of people from whom the information, through an open frame of enquiry, is explored and gathered. The parameters of the scope of a study, and information gathering methods and processes, are often flexible and evolving; hence, most qualitative designs are not as structured and sequential as quantitative ones. On the other hand, in quantitative research, the measurement and classification requirements of the information that is gathered demand that study designs are more structured, rigid, fixed and predetermined in their use to ensure accuracy in measurement and classification.

In qualitative studies the distinction between study designs and methods of data collection is far less clear. Quantitative study designs have more clarity and distinction between designs and methods of data collection. In qualitative research there is an overlap between the two. Some designs are basically methods of data collection. For example, in-depth interviewing is a design as well as a method of data collection and so are oral history and participant observation.

One of the most distinguishing features of qualitative research is the adherence to the concept of respondent concordance whereby you as a researcher make every effort to seek agreement of your respondents with your interpretation, presentation of the situations, experiences, perceptions and conclusions. In quantitative research respondent concordance does not occupy an important place. Sometimes it is assumed to be achieved by circulating or sharing the findings with those who participated in the study.

The 'power-gap' between the researcher and the study population in qualitative research is far smaller than in quantitative research because of the informality in structure and situation in which data is collected.

In quantitative research enough detail about a study design is provided for it to be replicated for verification and reassurance. In qualitative research little attention is paid to study designs or the other structural aspects of a study, hence the replication of a study design becomes almost impossible. This leads to the inability of the designs to produce findings that can be replicated. Findings through quantitative study designs can be replicated and retested whereas this cannot be easily done by using qualitative study designs.

Another difference in the designs in qualitative and quantitative studies is the possibility of introducing researcher bias. Because of flexibility and lack of control it is more difficult to check researcher bias in qualitative studies.

Study designs in each paradigm are appropriate for finding different things. Study designs in qualitative research are more appropriate for exploring the variation and diversity in any aspect of social life, whereas in quantitative research they are more suited to finding out the extent of this variation and diversity. If your interest is in studying values, beliefs, understandings, perceptions, meanings, etc., qualitative study designs are more appropriate as they provide immense flexibility. On the other hand, if your focus is to measure the magnitude of that variation, 'how many people have a particular value, belief, etc.?', the quantitative designs are more appropriate. For good quantitative research it is important that you combine quantitative skills with qualitative ones when ascertaining the nature and extent of diversity and variation in a phenomenon. In the author's opinion, the qualitative–quantitative–qualitative approach to research is comprehensive and worth consideration. This involves starting with qualitative methods to determine the spread of diversity, using quantitative methods to quantify the spread and then going back to qualitative to explain the observed patterns. As already stated, the author does not recommend your locking yourself into either the qualitative or quantitative paradigm and, though you may have your preference, it is the purpose that should determine the choice between quantitative and qualitative study designs. If you already know (from previous studies or practice knowledge) the nature of diversity in any area of interest to you, knowledge about its extent can be determined only by using quantitative methods. In most cases where you want to explore both, you need to use methods that fall in the domain of both paradigms.

Study designs in quantitative research

Some of the commonly used designs in quantitative studies can be classified by examining them from three different perspectives:

1 the number of contacts with the study population;
2 the reference period of the study;
3 the nature of the investigation.

Every study design can be classified from each one of these perspectives. These perspectives are arbitrary bases of classification; hence, the terminology used to describe them is not universal. However, the names of the designs within each classification base are universally used. Note that the designs within each category are mutually exclusive; that is, if a particular study is cross-sectional in nature it cannot be at the same time a before-and-after or a **longitudinal study**, but it can be a non-experimental or experimental study, as well as a **retrospective study** or a **prospective study**. See Figure 8.1.

Another section has been added to the three sections listed above titled 'Others – some commonly used study designs'. This section includes some commonly used designs which are based on a certain philosophy or methodology, and which have acquired their own names.

Study designs based on the number of contacts

Based on the number of contacts with the study population, designs can be classified into three groups:

1 cross-sectional studies;
2 before-and-after studies;
3 longitudinal studies.

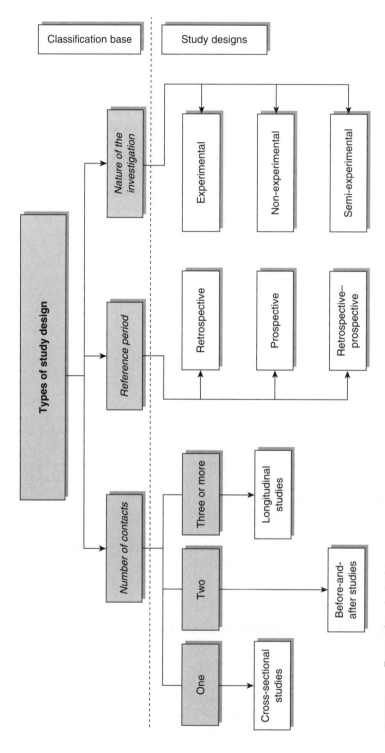

FIGURE 8.1 Types of study design

The cross-sectional study design

Cross-sectional studies, also known as one-shot or status studies, are the most commonly used design in the social sciences. This design is best suited to studies aimed at finding out the prevalence of a phenomenon, situation, problem, attitude or issue, by taking a cross-section of the population. They are useful in obtaining an overall 'picture' as it stands at the time of the study. They are 'designed to study some phenomenon by taking a cross-section of it at one time' (Babbie 1989: 89). Such studies are cross-sectional with regard to both the study population and the time of investigation.

A cross-sectional study is extremely simple in design. You decide what you want to find out about, identify the study population, select a sample (if you need to) and contact your respondents to find out the required information. For example, a cross-sectional design would be the most appropriate for a study of the following topics:

- The attitude of the study population towards uranium mining in Australia.
- The socioeconomic–demographic characteristics of immigrants in Western Australia.
- The incidence of HIV-positive cases in Australia.
- The reasons for homelessness among young people.
- The quality assurance of a service provided by an organisation.
- The impact of unemployment on street crime (this could also be a before-and-after study).
- The relationship between the home environment and the academic performance of a child at school.
- The attitude of the community towards equity issues.
- The extent of unemployment in a city.
- Consumer satisfaction with a product.
- The effectiveness of random breath testing in preventing road accidents (this could also be a before-and-after study).
- The health needs of a community.
- The attitudes of students towards the facilities available in their library.

As these studies involve only one contact with the study population, they are comparatively cheap to undertake and easy to analyse. However, their biggest disadvantage is that they cannot measure change. To measure change it is necessary to have at least two data collection points – that is, at least two cross-sectional studies, at two points in time, on the same population.

The before-and-after study design

The main advantage of the before-and-after design (also known as the pre-test/post-test design) is that it can measure change in a situation, phenomenon, issue, problem or attitude. It is the most appropriate design for measuring the impact or effectiveness of a programme. A before-and-after design can be described as two sets of cross-sectional data collection points on the same population to find out the change in the phenomenon or variable(s) between two points in time. The change is measured by comparing the difference in the phenomenon or variable(s) before and after the intervention (see Figure 8.2).

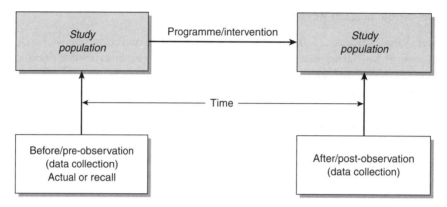

FIGURE 8.2   *Before-and-after (pre-test/post-test) study design*

A before-and-after study is carried out by adopting the same process as a cross-sectional study except that it comprises two cross-sectional data sets, the second being undertaken after a certain period. Depending upon how it is set up, a before-and-after study may be either an experiment or a non-experiment. It is one of the most commonly used designs in evaluation studies. The difference between the two sets of data collection points with respect to the dependent variable is considered to be the impact of the programme. The following are examples of topics that can be studied using this design:

- The impact of administrative restructuring on the quality of services provided by an organisation.
- The effectiveness of a marriage counselling service.
- The impact of sex education on sexual behaviour among schoolchildren.
- The effect of a drug awareness programme on the knowledge about, and use of, drugs among young people.
- The impact of incentives on the productivity of employees in an organisation.
- The impact of increased funding on the quality of teaching in universities.
- The impact of maternal and child health services on the infant mortality rate.
- The effect of random breath testing on road accidents.
- The effect of an advertisement on the sale of a product.

The main advantage of before-and-after design is its ability to measure change in a phenomenon or to assess the impact of an intervention. However, there can be disadvantages which may not occur, individually or collectively, in every study. The prevalence of a particular disadvantage(s) is dependent upon the nature of the investigation, the study population and the method of data collection. These disadvantages include the following:

- As two sets of data must be collected, involving two contacts with the study population, the study is more expensive and more difficult to implement. It also requires a longer time to complete, particularly if you are using an experimental design, as you will need to wait until your intervention is completed before you collect the second set of data.

- In some cases the time lapse between the two contacts may result in attrition in the study population. It is possible that some of those who participated in the pre-test may move out of the area or withdraw from the experiment for other reasons.
- One of the main limitations of this design, in its simplest form, is that as it measures *total change*, you cannot ascertain whether independent or extraneous variables are responsible for producing change in the dependent variable. Also, it is not possible to quantify the contribution of independent and extraneous variables separately.
- If the study population is very young and if there is a significant time lapse between the before-and-after sets of data collection, changes in the study population may be because it is maturing. This is particularly true when you are studying young children. The effect of this maturation, if it is significantly correlated with the dependent variable, is reflected at the 'after' observation and is known as the *maturation effect*.
- Sometimes the instrument itself educates the respondents. This is known as the *reactive effect* of the instrument. For example, suppose you want to ascertain the impact of a programme designed to create awareness of drugs in a population. To do this, you design a questionnaire listing various drugs and asking respondents to indicate whether they have heard of them. At the pre-test stage a respondent, while answering questions that include the names of the various drugs, is being made aware of them, and this will be reflected in his/her responses at the post-test stage. Thus, the research instrument itself has educated the study population and, hence, has affected the dependent variable. Another example of this effect is a study designed to measure the impact of a family planning education programme on respondents' awareness of contraceptive methods. Most studies designed to measure the impact of a programme on participants' awareness face the difficulty that a change in the level of awareness, to some extent, may be because of this reactive effect.
- Another disadvantage that may occur when you use a research instrument twice to gauge the attitude of a population towards an issue is a possible shift in attitude between the two points of data collection. Sometimes people who place themselves at the extreme positions of a measurement scale at the pre-test stage may, for a number of reasons, shift towards the mean at the post-test stage (see Figure 8.3). They might feel that they have been too negative or too positive at the pre-test stage. Therefore, the mere expression of

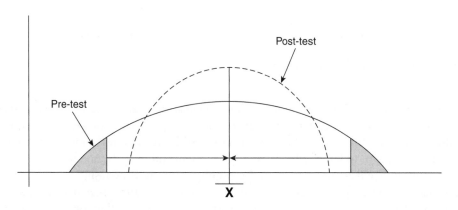

FIGURE 8.3 *The regression effect*

an attitude in response to a questionnaire or interview has caused them to think about and alter their attitude at the time of the post-test. This type of effect is known as the *regression effect*.

The longitudinal study design

The before-and–after study design is appropriate for measuring the extent of change in a phenomenon, situation, problem, attitude, and so on, but is less helpful for studying the pattern of change. To determine the pattern of change in relation to time, a longitudinal design is used; for example, when you wish to study the proportion of people adopting a programme over a period. Longitudinal studies are also useful when you need to collect factual information on a continuing basis. You may want to ascertain the trends in the demand for labour, immigration, changes in the incidence of a disease or in the mortality, morbidity and fertility patterns of a population.

In longitudinal studies the study population is visited a number of times at regular intervals, usually over a long period, to collect the required information (see Figure 8.4). These intervals are not fixed so their length may vary from study to study. Intervals might be as short as a week or longer than a year. Irrespective of the size of the interval, the type of information gathered each time is identical. Although the data collected is from the same study population, it may or may not be from the same respondents. A longitudinal study can be seen as a series of repetitive cross-sectional studies.

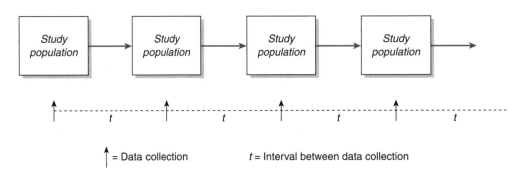

FIGURE 8.4   *The longitudinal study design*

Longitudinal studies have many of the same disadvantages as before-and–after studies, in some instances to an even greater degree. In addition, longitudinal studies can suffer from the **conditioning effect**. This describes a situation where, if the same respondents are contacted frequently, they begin to know what is expected of them and may respond to questions without thought, or they may lose interest in the enquiry, with the same result.

The main advantage of a longitudinal study is that it allows the researcher to measure the pattern of change and obtain factual information, requiring collection on a regular or continuing basis, thus enhancing its accuracy.

Study designs based on the reference period

The *reference period* refers to the time-frame in which a study is exploring a phenomenon, situation, event or problem. Studies are categorised from this perspective as:

- retrospective;
- prospective;
- retrospective–prospective.

The retrospective study design

Retrospective studies investigate a phenomenon, situation, problem or issue that has happened in the past. They are usually conducted either on the basis of the data available for that period or on the basis of respondents' recall of the situation (Figure 8.5a). For example, studies conducted on the following topics are classified as retrospective studies:

- The living conditions of Aboriginal and Torres Strait Islander peoples in Australia in the early twentieth century.
- The utilisation of land before the Second World War in Western Australia.
- A historical analysis of migratory movements in Eastern Europe between 1915 and 1945.
- The relationship between levels of unemployment and street crime.

The prospective study design

Prospective studies refer to the likely prevalence of a phenomenon, situation, problem, attitude or outcome in the future (Figure 8.5b). Such studies attempt to establish the outcome of an event or what is likely to happen. Experiments are usually classified as prospective studies as the researcher must wait for an intervention to register its effect on the study population. The following are classified as prospective studies:

- To determine, under field conditions, the impact of maternal and child health services on the level of infant mortality.
- To establish the effects of a counselling service on the extent of marital problems.
- To determine the impact of random breath testing on the prevention of road accidents.
- To find out the effect of parental involvement on the level of academic achievement of their children.
- To measure the effects of a change in migration policy on the extent of immigration in Australia.

The retrospective–prospective study design

Retrospective–prospective studies focus on past trends in a phenomenon and study it into the future. Part of the data is collected retrospectively from the existing records before the intervention is introduced and then the study population is followed to ascertain the impact of the intervention (Figure 8.5c).

(a)

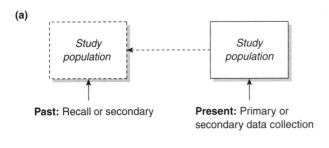

Past: Recall or secondary

Present: Primary or
secondary data collection

(b)

Present: Data collection –
primary or secondary

Future: Data collection –
primary

(c)

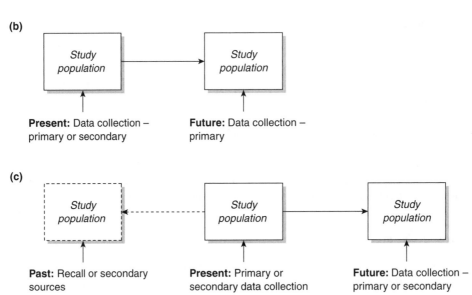

Past: Recall or secondary
sources

Present: Primary or
secondary data collection

Future: Data collection –
primary or secondary

FIGURE 8.5   *(a) Retrospective study design; (b) prospective study design; (c) retrospective–prospective
study design.*

A study is classified under this category when you measure the impact of an intervention
without having a control group. In fact, most before-and-after studies, if carried out without having a control – where the baseline is constructed from the same population before
introducing the intervention – will be classified as retrospective–prospective studies. Trend
studies, which become the basis of projections, fall into this category too. Some examples of
retrospective–prospective studies are:

- The effect of random breath testing on road accidents.
- The impact of incentives on the productivity of the employees of an organisation.
- The impact of maternal and child health services on the infant mortality rate.
- The effect of an advertisement on the sale of a product.

Study designs based on the nature of the investigation

On the basis of the nature of the investigation, study designs in quantitative research can be classified as:

- experimental;
- non-experimental;
- quasi- or semi-experimental.

To understand the differences, let us consider some examples. Suppose you want to test the following: the impact of a particular teaching method on the level of comprehension of students; the effectiveness of a programme such as random breath testing on the level of road accidents; or the usefulness of a drug such as azidothymidine (AZT) in treating people who are HIV-positive; or imagine any similar situation in your own academic or professional field. In such situations there is assumed to be a *cause-and-effect* relationship. There are two ways of studying this relationship. The first involves the researcher (or someone else) introducing the intervention that is assumed to be the 'cause' of change, and waiting until it has produced – or has been given sufficient time to produce – the change. The second consists of the researcher observing a phenomenon and attempting to establish what caused it. In this instance the researcher starts from the effect(s) or outcome(s) and attempts to determine causation. If a relationship is studied in the first way, starting from the cause to establish the effects, it is classified as an **experimental study**. If the second path is followed – that is, starting from the effects to trace the cause – it is classified as a **non-experimental study** (see Figure 8.6).

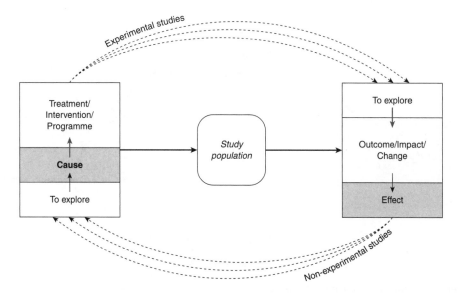

FIGURE 8.6 *Experimental and non-experimental studies*

In the former case the independent variable can be 'observed', introduced, controlled or manipulated by the researcher or someone else, whereas in the latter this cannot happen as the assumed cause has already occurred. Instead, the researcher retrospectively links the cause(s) to the outcome(s). A **semi-experimental study** or **quasi-experimental study** has the properties of both experimental and non-experimental studies; part of the study may be non-experimental and the other part experimental.

An experimental study can be carried out in either a 'controlled' or a 'natural' environment. For an experiment in a controlled environment, the researcher (or someone else) introduces the intervention or stimulus to study its effects. The study population is in a 'controlled' situation such as a room. For an experiment in a 'natural' environment, the study population is exposed to an intervention in its own environment.

Experimental studies can be further classified on the basis of whether or not the study population is randomly assigned to different treatment groups. One of the biggest problems in comparable designs (those in which you compare two or more groups) is a lack of certainty that the different groups are in fact comparable in every respect except the treatment. The process of randomisation is designed to ensure that the groups are comparable. In a **random design**, the study population, the experimental treatments or both are not predetermined but randomly assigned (see Figure 8.7). Random assignment in experiments means that any individual or unit of a study population group has an *equal* and *independent* chance of becoming part of an experimental or control group or, in the case of multiple treatment modalities, any treatment has an equal and independent chance of being assigned to any of the population groups. It is important to note that the concept of randomisation can be applied to any of the experimental designs we discuss.

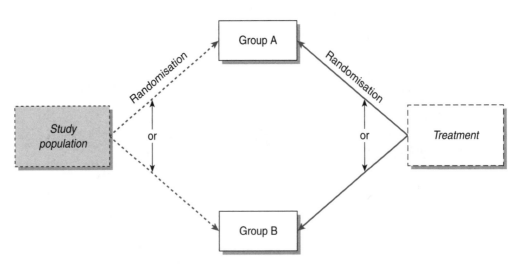

FIGURE 8.7 *Randomisation in experiments*

Experimental study designs

There are so many types of experimental design that not all of them can be considered within the scope of this book. This section, therefore, is confined to describing those most commonly used in the social sciences, the humanities, public health, marketing, education, epidemiology, social work, and so on. These designs have been categorised as:

- the after-only experimental design;
- the before-and-after experimental design;
- the control group design;
- the double-control design;
- the comparative design;
- the 'matched control' experimental design;
- the placebo design.

The after-only experimental design

In an after-only design the researcher knows that a population is being, or has been, exposed to an intervention and wishes to study its impact on the population. In this design, information on baseline (pre-test or before observation) is usually 'constructed' on the basis of respondents' recall of the situation before the intervention, or from information available in existing records – secondary sources (Figure 8.8). The change in the dependent variable is measured by the difference between the 'before' (baseline) and 'after' data sets. Technically, this is a very faulty design for measuring the impact of an intervention as there are no proper baseline data

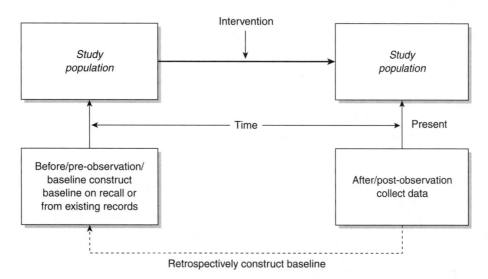

FIGURE 8.8 *The after-only design*

to compare the 'after' observation with. Therefore, one of the major problems of this design is that the two sets of data are not strictly comparable. For example, some of the changes in the dependent variable may be attributable to the difference in the way the two sets of data were compiled. Another problem with this design is that it measures total change, including change attributable to extraneous variables; hence, it cannot identify the net effect of an intervention. However, this design is widely used in impact assessment studies, as in real life many programmes operate without the benefit of a planned evaluation at the programme planning stage (though this is fast changing) in which case it is just not possible to follow the sequence strictly – collection of baseline information, implementation of the programme and then programme evaluation. An evaluator therefore has no choice but to adopt this design.

In practice, the adequacy of this design depends on having reasonably accurate data available about the prevalence of a phenomenon before the intervention is introduced. This might be the case for situations such as the impact of random breath testing on road accidents, the impact of a health programme on the mortality of a population, the impact of an advertisement on the sale of a product, the impact of a decline in mortality on the fertility of a population, or the impact of a change in immigration policy on the extent of immigration. In these situations it is expected that accurate records are kept about the phenomenon under study and so it may be easier to determine whether any change in trends is primarily because of the introduction of the intervention or change in the policy.

The before-and-after experimental design

The before-and-after design overcomes the problem of retrospectively constructing the 'before' observation by establishing it before the intervention is introduced to the study population (see Figure 8.2). Then, when the programme has been completely implemented or is assumed to have had its effect on the population, the 'after' observation is carried out to ascertain the impact attributable to the intervention (see Figure 8.9).

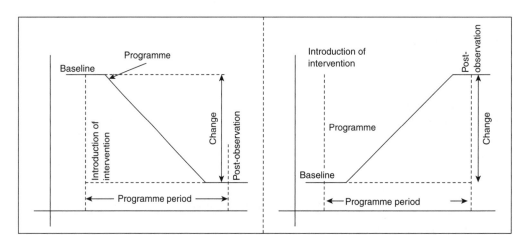

FIGURE 8.9   *Measurement of change through a before-and-after design*

The before-and-after design takes care of only one problem of the after-only design – that is, the comparability of the before-and-after observations. It still does not enable one to conclude that any change – in whole or in part – can be attributed to the programme intervention. To overcome this, a 'control' group is used. Before-and-after designs may also suffer from the problems identified earlier in this chapter in the discussion of before-and-after study designs. The impact of the intervention in before-and-after design is calculated as follows:

[change in dependent variable] =

　　[status of the dependent variable at the 'after' observation] –
　　[status of the dependent variable at the 'before' observation]

The control group design

In a study utilising the control group design the researcher selects two population groups instead of one: a **control group** and an **experimental group** (Figure 8.10). These groups are expected to be comparable as far as possible in every respect except for the intervention (that is assumed to be the cause responsible for bringing about the change). The experimental group either receives or is exposed to the intervention, whereas the control group is not. Firstly, the 'before' observations are made on both groups at the same time. The experimental group is then exposed to the intervention. When it is assumed that the intervention has had an impact, an 'after' observation is made on both groups. Any difference in the 'before' and 'after' observations between the groups regarding the dependent variable(s) is attributed to the intervention.

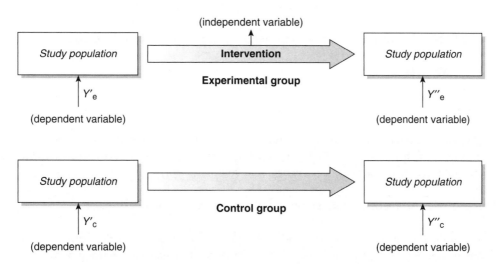

FIGURE 8.10　*The control experimental design*

In the experimental group, total change in the dependent variable (Y_e) can be calculated as follows:

$$Y_e = (Y''_e - Y'_e)$$

where

Y''_e = 'after' observation on the experimental group
Y'_e = 'before' observation on the experimental group

In other words,

$(Y''_e - Y'_e)$ = (impact of programme intervention) $\pm$ (impact of extraneous variables) $\pm$ (impact of chance variables)

In the control group, total change in the dependent variable (Y_c) can be calculated as follows:

$$Y_c = (Y''_c - Y'_c)$$

where

Y''_c = post-test observation on the control group
Y'_c = pre-test observation on the control group

In other words,

$(Y''_c - Y'_c)$ = (impact of extraneous variables) $\pm$ (impact of chance variables)

The difference between the control and experimental groups can be calculated as

$$(Y''_e - Y'_e) - (Y''_c - Y'_c),$$

which is

{(impact of programme intervention) $\pm$ (impact of extraneous variables in experimental groups) $\pm$ (impact of chance variables in experimental groups)} − {(impact of extraneous variables in control group) $\pm$ (impact of chance variables in control group)}

Using simple arithmetic operations, this equals the impact of the intervention.

Therefore, the impact of any intervention is equal to the difference in the 'before' and 'after' observations in the dependent variable between the experimental and control groups.

It is important to remember that the chief objective of the control group is to quantify the impact of extraneous variables. This helps you to ascertain the impact of the intervention only.

The double-control design

Although the **control design** helps you to quantify the impact that can be attributed to extraneous variables, it does not separate out other effects that may be due to the research instrument (such as the reactive effect) or respondents (such as the maturation or regression effects, or placebo effect). When you need to identify and separate out these effects, a double-control design is required.

In **double-control studies**, you have two control groups instead of one. To quantify, say, the reactive effect of an instrument, you exclude one of the control groups from the 'before' observation (Figure 8.11).

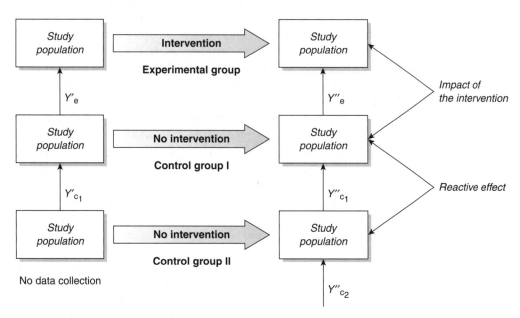

FIGURE 8.11   *Double-control designs*

You can calculate the different effects as follows:

$(Y''_e - Y'_e)$ = (impact of programme intervention) $\pm$ (impact of extraneous variables) $\pm$ (reactive effect) $\pm$ (random effect)

$(Y''_{c1} - Y'_{c1})$ = (impact of extraneous variables) $\pm$ (reactive effect) $\pm$ (random effect)

$(Y''_{c2} - Y'_{c1})$ = (impact of extraneous variables) $\pm$ (random effect)

(Note that $(Y''_{c2} - Y'_{c1})$ and not $(Y''_{c2} - Y'_{c2})$ as there is no 'before' observation for the second control group.)

$(Y''_e - Y'_e) - (Y''_{c1} - Y'_{c1}) =$ impact of programme intervention
$(Y''_{c1} - Y'_{c1}) - (Y'_{c2} - Y'_{c1}) =$ reactive effect

The net effect of the programme intervention can be calculated in the same manner as for the control group designs as explained earlier.

The comparative design

Sometimes you seek to compare the effectiveness of different treatment modalities and in such situations a comparative design is appropriate.

With a comparative design, as with most other designs, a study can be carried out either as an experiment or as a non-experiment. In the comparative experimental design, the study population is divided into the same number of groups as the number of treatments to be tested. For each group the baseline with respect to the dependent variable is established. The different treatment models are then introduced to the different groups. After a certain period, when it is assumed that the treatment models have had their effect, the 'after' observation is carried out to ascertain any change in the dependent variable. The degree of change in the dependent variable in the different population groups is then compared to establish the relative effectiveness of the various interventions.

In the non-experimental form of comparative design, groups already receiving different interventions are identified, and only the post-observation with respect to the dependent variable is conducted. The pre-test data set is constructed either by asking the study population in each group to recall the required information relating to the period before the introduction of the treatment, or by extracting such information from existing records. Sometimes a pre-test observation is not constructed at all, on the assumption that if the groups are comparable the baseline must be identical. As each group is assumed to have the same baseline, the difference in the post-test observation is assumed to be because of the intervention.

To illustrate this, imagine you want to compare the effectiveness of three teaching models (A, B and C) on the level of comprehension of students in a class (Figure 8.12). To undertake the study, you divide the class into three groups (X, Y and Z), through randomisation, to ensure their comparability. Before exposing these groups to the teaching models, you first establish the baseline for each group's level of comprehension of the chosen subject. You then expose each group to a different teaching model to teach the chosen subject. Afterwards, you again measure the groups' levels of comprehension of the material. Suppose X_a is the average level of comprehension of group X before the material is taught, and X_a' is this group's average level of comprehension after the material is taught. The change in the level of comprehension, $X_a' - X_a$ is therefore attributed to model A. Similarly, changes in group Y and Z, $Y_b' - Y_b$ and $Z_c' - Z_c$, are attributed to teaching models B and C respectively. The changes in the average level of comprehension for the three groups are then compared to establish which

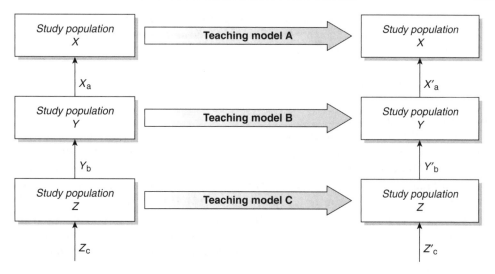

FIGURE 8.12   *Comparative experimental design*

teaching model is the most effective. (Note that extraneous variables will affect the level of comprehension in all groups equally, as they have been formed randomly.)

It is also possible to set up this study as a non-experimental one, simply by exposing each group to one of the three teaching models, following up with an 'after' observation. The difference in the levels of comprehension is attributed to the difference in the teaching models as it is assumed that the three groups are comparable with respect to their original level of comprehension of the topic.

The matched control experimental design

Comparative groups are usually formed on the basis of their overall comparability with respect to a relevant characteristic in the study population, such as socioeconomic status, the prevalence of a certain condition or the extent of a problem in the study population. In matched studies, comparability is determined on an individual-by-individual basis. Two individuals from the study population who are almost identical with respect to a selected characteristic and/or condition, such as age, gender or type of illness, are matched and then each is allocated to a separate group (the matching is usually done on an easily identifiable characteristic). In the case of a matched control experiment, once the two groups are formed, you as a researcher decide through randomisation or otherwise which group is to be considered control, and which experimental.

The matched design can pose a number of challenges:

- Matching increases in difficulty when carried out on more than one variable.
- Matching on variables that are hard to measure, such as attitude or opinion, is extremely difficult.

- Sometimes it is hard to know which variable to choose as a basis for matching. You may be able to base your decision upon previous findings or you may have to undertake a preliminary study to determine your choice of variable.

Matched groups are most commonly used in the testing of new drugs.

The 'placebo' design

A patient's belief that s/he is receiving treatment can play an important role in his/her recovery from an illness even if treatment is ineffective. This psychological effect is known as the **placebo effect**. A placebo design attempts to determine the extent of this effect. A **placebo study** involves two or three groups, depending on whether or not the researcher wants to have a control group (Figure 8.13). If the researcher decides to have a control group, the first group receives the treatment, the second receives the placebo treatment and the third – the control group – receives nothing. The decision as to which group will be the treatment, the placebo or the control group can also be made through randomisation.

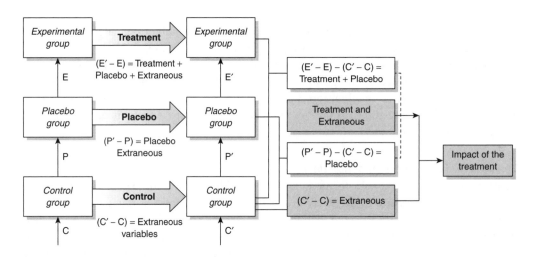

FIGURE 8.13   *The placebo design*

Other designs commonly used in quantitative research

There are some research designs that may be classified in the typology described above but, because of their uniqueness and prevalence, have acquired their own names. They are therefore described separately below.

The cross-over comparative experimental design

The denial of treatment to the control group is considered unethical by some professionals. In addition, the denial of treatment may be unacceptable to some individuals in the control group, which could result in them dropping out of the experiment and/or going elsewhere to receive treatment. The former increases 'experimental mortality' and the latter may contaminate the study. The **cross-over comparative experimental design** makes it possible to measure the impact of a treatment without denying treatment to any group, though this design has its own problems.

In the cross-over design, also called the ABAB design (Grinnell 1993: 104), two groups are formed, the intervention is introduced to one of them and, after a certain period, the impact of this intervention is measured. Then the interventions are 'crossed over'; that is, the experimental group becomes the control and vice versa, sometimes repeatedly over the period of the study (Figure 8.14). However, in this design, population groups do not constitute experimental or control groups but only segments upon which experimental and control observations are conducted.

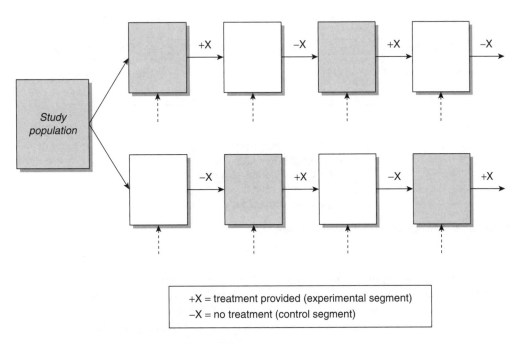

FIGURE 8.14   *The cross-over experimental design*

One of the main disadvantages of this design is discontinuity in treatment. The main question is: what impact would intervention have produced had it not been provided in segments?

The replicated cross-sectional design

In practice one usually examines programmes already in existence and ones in which clients are at different stages of an intervention. Evaluating the effectiveness of such programmes within a conventional experimental design is impossible because a baseline cannot be established as the intervention has already been introduced. In this situation, the usual method of selecting a group of people who were recently recruited to the programme and following them through until the intervention has been completed may take a long time. In such situations, it is possible to choose clients who are at different phases of the programme to form the basis of your study (Figure 8.15).

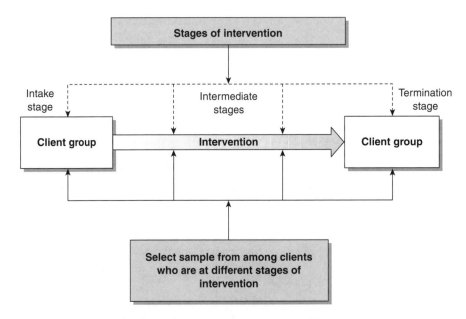

FIGURE 8.15   *The replicated cross-sectional design*

This design is based upon the assumption that participants at different stages of a programme are similar in terms of their socioeconomic–demographic characteristics and the problem for which they are seeking intervention. Assessment of the effectiveness of an intervention is done by taking a sample of clients at different stages of the intervention. The difference in the dependent variable among clients at intake and termination stage is considered to be the impact of the intervention.

Trend studies

If you want to map change over a period, a **trend study** is the most appropriate method of investigation. Trend analysis enables you to find out what has happened in the past, what is happening now and what is likely to happen in the future in a population group. This design involves selecting a number of data observation points in the past, together with a picture of the present or immediate past with respect to the phenomenon under study, and then making certain assumptions as to future trends. In a way you are collecting cross-sectional observations about the trend being observed at different points in time over past–present–future. From these cross-sectional observations you draw conclusions about the pattern of change.

Trend studies are useful in making forecasting by extrapolating present and past trends thus making a valuable contribution to planning. Trends regarding the phenomenon under study can be correlated with other characteristics of the study population. For example, you may want to examine the changes in political preference of a study population in relation to age, gender, income or ethnicity. This design can also be classified as retrospective–prospective study on the basis of the reference period classification system developed earlier in this chapter.

Cohort studies

Cohort studies are based upon the existence of a common characteristic such as year of birth, graduation or marriage, within a subgroup of a population. Suppose you want to study the employment pattern of a batch of accountants who graduated from a university in 1975, or study the fertility behaviour of women who were married in 1930. To study the accountants' career paths you would contact all the accountants who graduated from the university in 1975 to find out their employment histories. Similarly, you would investigate the fertility history of those women who married in 1930. Both of these studies could be carried out either as cross-sectional or longitudinal designs. If you adopt a cross-sectional design you gather the required information in one go, but if you choose the longitudinal design you collect the required information at different points in time over the study period. Both these designs have their strengths and weaknesses. In the case of a longitudinal design, it is not important for the required information to be collected from the same respondents; however, it is important that all the respondents belong to the cohort being studied; that is, in the above examples they must have graduated in 1975 or married in 1930.

Panel studies

Panel studies are similar to trend and cohort studies except that in addition to being longitudinal they are also prospective in nature and the information is always collected from the same respondents. (In trend and cohort studies the information can be collected in a cross-sectional manner and the observation points can be retrospectively constructed.) Suppose you want to study the changes in the pattern of expenditure on household items in a community. To do this, you would select a few families to find out the amount they spend every fortnight on household items. You would keep collecting the same information from the same families over a period of time to ascertain the changes in the expenditure pattern. Similarly, a panel study design could be used to study the morbidity pattern in a community.

Blind studies

The concept of a **blind study** can be used with comparable and placebo experimental designs and is applied to studies measuring the effectiveness of a drug. In a blind study, the study population does not know whether it is getting real or fake treatment or which treatment modality. The main objective of designing a blind study is to isolate the placebo effect.

Double-blind studies

The concept of a **double-blind study** is very similar to that of a blind study except that it also tries to eliminate researcher bias by concealing the identity of the experimental and placebo groups from the researcher. In other words, in a double-blind study neither the researcher nor the study participants know who is receiving real and who is receiving fake treatment or which treatment model they are receiving.

Study designs in qualitative research

This section provides a brief description of some of the commonly used designs in qualitative research. For an in-depth understanding you are advised to consult books on qualitative research.

Case study

The **case study,** though dominantly a qualitative study design, is also prevalent in quantitative research. A case could be an individual, a group, a community, an instance, an episode, an event, a subgroup of a population, a town or a city. To be called a case study it is important to treat the total study population as one entity.

In a case study design the 'case' you select becomes the basis of a thorough, holistic and in-depth exploration of the aspect(s) that you want to find out about. It is an approach 'in which a particular instance or a few carefully selected cases are studied intensively' (Gilbert 2008: 36). According to Burns (1997: 364), 'to qualify as a case study, *it must be a bounded system,* an entity in itself. A case study should focus on a bounded subject/unit that is either very representative or extremely atypical.' A case study according to Grinnell (1981: 302), 'is characterized by a very flexible and open-ended technique of data collection and analysis'.

The case study design is based upon the assumption that the case being studied is atypical of cases of a certain type and therefore a single case can provide insight into the events and situations prevalent in a group from where the case has been drawn. According to Burns (1997: 365), 'In a case study the focus of attention is the case in its idiosyncratic complexity, not on the whole population of cases.' In selecting a case therefore you usually use purposive, judgemental or information-oriented sampling techniques.

It is a very useful design when exploring an area where little is known or where you want to have a holistic understanding of the situation, phenomenon, episode, site, group or community. This design is of immense relevance when the focus of a study is on extensively exploring and understanding rather than confirming and quantifying. It provides an overview and in-depth understanding of a case(s), process and interactional dynamics within a unit of study but cannot claim to make any generalisations to a population beyond cases similar to the one studied.

In this design your attempt is not to select a random sample but a case that can provide you with as much information as possible to understand the case in its totality. When studying an episode or an instance, you attempt to gather information from all available sources so as to understand it in its entirety. If the focus of your study is a group or community you should spend sufficient time building a trustworthy rapport with its members before collecting any information about them.

Though you can use a single method, the use of multiple methods to collect data is an important aspect of a case study, namely in-depth interviewing, obtaining information from secondary records, gathering data through observations, collecting information through focus groups and group interviews, etc. However, it is important that at the time of analysis you continue to consider the case as a single entity.

Oral history

Oral history is more a method of data collection than a study design; however, in qualitative research, this has become an approach to study perceptions, experiences and accounts of an event or gathering historical knowledge as viewed by individuals. It is a picture of something in someone's own words. Oral history is a process of obtaining, recording, presenting and interpreting historical or current information, based upon personal experiences and opinions of some members of a study group or unit. These opinions or experiences could be based upon eye-witness evidence or information passed on from other sources such as older people, ancestors, folklore, stories. According to Ritchie (2003: 19), 'Memory is the core of oral history, from which meaning can be extracted and preserved. Simply put, oral history collects memories and personal commentaries of historical significance through recorded interviews.' According to Burns (1997: 368), 'these are usually first person narratives that the researcher collects using extensive interviewing of a single individual'.

In terms of design it is quite simple. You first decide what types of account, experience, perception or historical event you want to find out about. Then you need to identify the individuals or sources (which could be difficult and time consuming) that can best provide you with the needed information. You then collect information from them to be analysed and interpreted.

Focus groups/group interviews

Focus groups are a form of strategy in qualitative research in which attitudes, opinions or perceptions towards an issue, product, service or programme are explored through a free and open discussion between members of a group and the researcher. Both focus groups and **group interviews** are facilitated group discussions in which a researcher raises issues or asks questions that stimulate discussion among members of the group. Because of its low cost, it is a popular method for finding information in almost every professional area and academic field. Social, political and behavioural scientists, market research and product testing agencies, and urban and town planning experts often use this design for a variety of situations. For example, in marketing research this design is widely used to find out consumers' opinion of and feedback on a product, their opinions on the quality of the product, its acceptance and appeal, price and packaging, how to improve the quality and increase the sale of the product, etc. Focus groups are also prevalent in formative and summative evaluations and for developing social programmes and services. It is also a useful tool in social and urban planning for identifying issues, options, development strategies, and future planning and development directions.

In its design it is very simple. You as a researcher select a group of people who you think are best equipped to discuss what you want to explore. The group could comprise individuals drawn from a group of highly trained professionals or average residents of a community depending upon the objectives of the focus group. In the formation of a focus group the size of the group is an important consideration. It should be neither too large nor too small as this can impede upon the extent and quality of the discussion. Approximately eight to ten people are the optimal number for such discussion groups. You also need to identify carefully the issues for discussion providing every opportunity for additional relevant ones to emerge. As a researcher you also need to decide, in consultation with the group, the process of recording the discussion. This may include fixing the times that the group can meet to extensively discussing the issues and arriving at agreements on them. Your records of the discussions then become the basis of analysis for findings and conclusions. The main difference between a focus group and a group interview is in the degree of specificity with respect to the issues to be discussed. The issues discussed in focus groups are more specific and focused than in group interviews and they are largely predetermined by the researcher. In a group interview you let the group members discuss whatever they want. However, your role as a researcher is to bring them back to the issues of interest as identified by the group.

Compared with other designs this is less expensive and needs far less time to complete. The information generated can be detailed and rich and can be used to explore a vast variety of issues. However, the disadvantage is that if the discussion is not carefully directed it may reflect the opinion of those who have a tendency to dominate a group. This design is very useful for exploring the diversity in opinions on different issues but will not help you if you want to find out the extent or magnitude of this diversity.

Participant observation

Participant observation is another strategy for gathering information about a social interaction or a phenomenon in qualitative studies. This is usually done by developing a close interaction with members of a group or 'living' in the situation which is being studied. Though predominantly a qualitative research design, it is also used in quantitative research, depending upon how the information has been generated and recorded. In qualitative research, an observation is always recorded in a descriptive format whereas in quantitative research it is recorded either in categories or on a scale. It can also be a combination of both – some categorisation and some description or categorisation accompanied by a descriptive explanation. You can also change a descriptive recording into a categorical one through analysis and classification. In addition to the observation itself, where you as an observer generate information, the information can also be collected through other methods such as informal interviewing, in-depth interviewing, group discussions, previous documents, oral histories. Use of multiple methods will enhance the richness of the information collected by participant observation.

In its design it is simple. You as a researcher get involved in the activities of the group, create a rapport with group members and then, having sought their consent, keenly observe the situation, interaction, site or phenomenon. You make detailed notes of what you observe in a format that best suits you as well as the situation. You can also collect information using other methods of data collection, if need be. You analyse records of your observations and data collected by other means to draw inferences and conclusions.

The main advantage of participant observation is that as you spend sufficient time with the group or in the situation, you gain much deeper, richer and more accurate information, but the main disadvantage is that, if you are not very careful, you can introduce your own bias.

Holistic research

The holistic approach to research is once again more a philosophy than a study design. The design is based upon the philosophy that as a multiplicity of factors interacts in our lives, we cannot understand a phenomenon from just one or two perspectives. To understand a situation or phenomenon you need to look at it in its totality – that is, holistically from every perspective.

You can use any design when exploring a situation from different perspectives and the use of multiple methods is prevalent and desirable.

Community discussion forums

Community discussion forums are designed to find opinions, attitudes and/or ideas of a community with regard to community issues and problems. It is one of the very popular ways of seeking a community's participation in deciding about issues of concern to members of the community. Such forums are also used for a variety of other reasons such as developing town planning options and community health programmes for a community, seeking participation of its members in resolving issues relating to traffic management, infrastructure development and determining future directions for the area, informing communities of new initiatives.

Community forums are very similar to group discussions except that these are on a bigger scale in terms of number of participants. Also, in group discussions you may select the participants, but for community forums there is self-selection of the participants as they are open to everyone with an interest in the issues or concerns. The researcher usually uses local media to inform the residents of a local community about the forums.

This is a useful design to find out the spread of issues, concerns, etc., at a community level. It is economical and quick but there are some disadvantages. For example, it is possible that a few people with a vested interest can dominate the discussion in a forum and it is equally possible that on occasions there may be very low attendance. Such situations may result in the discussion not reflecting the community attitudes.

Reflective journal log

Basically, this design entails keeping a **reflective journal log** of your thoughts as a researcher whenever you notice anything, talk to someone, participate in an activity or observe something that helps you understand or add to whatever you are trying to find out about. These reflective records then become the basis of your findings and conclusions. You can have a reflective journal as the only method of data collection or it can be used in combination with other methods such as interviewing, group interviews, or secondary sources.

Other commonly used philosophy-guided designs

There are a number of other approaches to research that have acquired recognition, in terms of design and name, in the research literature. While not designs per se, they do enhance a particular philosophical perspective in social research. These are: action research, feminist research, participatory research and collaborative enquiry. Strictly speaking, a piece of research within each of these could be either quantitative or qualitative, though by many they are considered dominantly as qualitative designs. The need to place them in a separate category stems from their prominence and possible use in each paradigm. These designs are more philosophy guided than methods based. For example, action research is guided by the philosophy that a piece of research should be followed by some form of appropriate action to achieve betterment in life or service, and feminist research is influenced by the philosophy that opposes and challenges the dominant male bias in social science research; it seems to believe that issues relating to women are best understood and researched by women alone. For participatory research and collaborative enquiry, the involvement of research participants or the community in the research process is the underlying philosophy. One of the important aspects of all these 'designs' is that they attempt to involve research participants in the research process. The research findings are then used to depict the current situation with respect to certain issues or problems and help to form a sound basis for strategy development to deal with them.

Action research

As the name suggests, **action research** comprises two components: *action* and *research* (see Figure 8.16). Research is a means to action, either to improve your practice or to take action to deal with a problem or an issue. Since action research is guided by the desire to take action, strictly speaking it is not a design per se. Most action research is concerned with improving the quality of service. It is carried out to identify areas of concern, develop and test alternatives, and experiment with new approaches.

FIGURE 8.16 *Action research design*

Action research seems to follow two traditions. The British tradition tends to view action research as a means of improvement and advancement of practice (Carr & Kemmis 1986), whereas in the US tradition it is aimed at systematic collection of data that provides the basis for social change (Bogdan & Biklen 1992).

Action research, in common with **participatory research** and **collaborative enquiry**, is based upon a philosophy of community development that seeks the involvement of community members. Involvement and participation of a community, in the total process from problem identification to implementation of solutions, are the two salient features of all three approaches (action research, participatory research and collaborative enquiry). In all three, data is collected through a research process, and changes are achieved through action. This action is taken either by officials of an institution or the community itself in the case of action research, or by members of a community in the case of collaborative or participatory research.

There are two focuses of action research:

1 An existing programme or intervention is studied in order to identify possible areas of improvement in terms of enhanced efficacy and/or efficiency. The findings become the basis of bringing about changes.
2 A professional identifies an unattended problem or unexplained issue in the community or among a client group and research evidence is gathered to justify the introduction of a new service or intervention. Research techniques establish the prevalence of the problem or the importance of an issue so that appropriate action can be taken to deal with it.

Feminist research

Feminist research is characterised by its feminist theory philosophical base that underpins all enquiries and feminist concerns act as the guiding framework. Feminist research differs from traditional research in three ways:

1 Its main focus is the experiences and viewpoints of women. It uses research methods aimed at exploring these.
2 It actively tries to remove or reduce the power imbalance between the researcher and respondents.
3 The goal of feminist research is changing the social inequality between men and women. In fact, feminist research may be classified as action research in the area of gender inequality, using research techniques to create awareness of women's issues and concerns, and to foster action promoting equality between sexes.

Any study design could be used in feminist research.

Participatory and collaborative research enquiry

As already mentioned, to the author's mind, these are not designs per se but signify a philosophical perspective that advocates the active involvement of research participants in the research process. Participatory research is based upon the principle of minimising the 'gap' between the researcher and the research participants and increased community involvement and participation to enhance the relevance of the research findings to their needs. It is assumed that such involvement will increase the possibility of the community accepting the research findings and, if need be, its willingness and involvement in solving the problems and issues that confront it. You can undertake a quantitative or qualitative study in these enquiries but the main emphasis is on people's engagement, collaboration and participation in the research process. In a way these designs are based on the community development model where engagement of a community by way of consultation and participation in planning and execution of research tasks is imperative. In these designs you are not merely a researcher but also a community organiser seeking active participation of the community.

As a researcher you work at two different aspects: (1) community organisation and (2) research. Through community organisation you seek a community's involvement and participation in planning and execution of the research tasks and share research findings with its members. In terms of research, your main responsibility is to develop, in consultation with the community, the research tasks and procedures. Consultation with research participants is a continuous and integral part of these designs.

Summary

In this chapter various study designs in both quantitative and qualitative research have been examined. For each study design, details have been provided on the situations in which the design is appropriate to use, its strengths and weaknesses, and the process you adopt in its operationalisation.

In quantitative research the various study designs have been examined from three perspectives. The terminology used to describe these perspectives is that of the author but the names of the study designs are universally used. The different study designs across each category are mutually exclusive but not so within a category.

The three perspectives are the number of contacts, the reference period and the nature of the investigation. The first comprises cross-sectional studies, before-and-after studies and longitudinal studies. The second categorises the studies as retrospective, prospective and retrospective–prospective. The third perspective classifies studies as experimental, non-experimental and semi-experimental studies.

Qualitative study designs are not as specific, precise and well defined as designs in quantitative research. Also, there is a degree of overlap between study designs and methods of data collection. Some designs can easily be considered as methods of data collection. Some of the commonly used designs in qualitative research are: case study design, oral history, focus group studies, participant observation, community discussion forums and reflective journal log.

Four additional approaches to research have been described: action research, feminist research, and participatory and collaborative enquiries. Though these cannot really be considered designs in themselves, they have acquired their own identity. Both action and feminist research can be carried out either quantitatively or qualitatively, but participatory and collaborative enquiries are usually qualitative in nature.

For You to Think About

▸ Refamiliarise yourself with the keywords listed at the beginning of this chapter and if you are uncertain about the meaning or application of any of them revisit these in the chapter before moving on.
▸ Identify two or three situations relating to your own area of interest where you think qualitative study designs might be more beneficial and consider why this might be the case.
▸ Take an example from your own academic field or professional area where an experimental-control or placebo group might be used and explore the ethical issues relating to this.

This operational step includes three chapters:

- Chapter 9: Selecting a method of data collection
- Chapter 10: Collecting data using attitudinal scales
- Chapter 11: Establishing the validity and reliability of a research instrument

STEP III Constructing an Instrument for Data Collection

CHAPTER 9
Selecting a Method of Data Collection

In this chapter you will learn about:

- Differences in methods of data collection in quantitative and qualitative research
- Major approaches to information gathering
- Collecting data using primary sources

  - Observation
  - The interview
  - The questionnaire

- Methods of data collection in qualitative research
- Collecting data using secondary sources

Keywords: *closed questions, content analysis, double-barrelled questions, elevation effect, error of central tendency, focus group, halo effect, Hawthorne effect, interview schedule, leading questions, non-participant observation, open-ended questions, oral history, participant observation, primary data, primary sources, questionnaire, secondary data, secondary sources, structured interview, unstructured interview.*

Differences in the methods of data collection in quantitative and qualitative research

Most methods of data collection can be used in both qualitative and quantitative research. The distinction is mainly due to the restrictions imposed on flexibility, structure, sequential order, depth and freedom that a researcher has in their use during the research process. Quantitative methods favour these restrictions whereas qualitative ones advocate against them. The classification of a method into the quantitative or qualitative category depends upon your answers to the following questions:

- What philosophical epistemology is underpinning your approach to research enquiry?
- How was the information collected? Was it through a structured or unstructured/flexible format of data collection?
- Were the questions or issues discussed during data collection predetermined or developed during data collection?
- How was the information you gathered recorded? Was it in a descriptive, narrative, categorical, quantitative form or on a scale?
- How was the information analysed? Was it a descriptive, categorical or numerical analysis?
- How do you propose to communicate the findings? Do you want to write in a descriptive or analytical manner?

For example, if an observation is recorded in a narrative or descriptive format, it becomes qualitative information, but if it is recorded in categorical form or on a scale, it will be classified as quantitative information. Similarly for data collected through interviews. An unstructured interview, recorded in a descriptive or narrative form, becomes a qualitative method, but in a structured interview, if the information is recorded in response categories or if the categories are developed and quantified out of descriptive responses, it is a quantitative method. Descriptive responses obtained in reply to open-ended questions are all qualitative but if the responses are in numerals they will be considered quantitative. If you develop categories and quantify the categorisation as a part of the analysis of descriptive responses to an open-ended question, it becomes a quantitative analysis. Data generated by focus groups, oral histories, narratives, group interviews is always qualitative in nature.

Major approaches to information gathering

There are two major approaches to gathering information about a situation, person, problem or phenomenon. When you undertake a research study, in most situations, you need to collect the required information; however, sometimes the information required is already available and need only be extracted. Based upon these broad approaches to information gathering, data can be categorised as:

- **primary data**;
- **secondary data**.

FIGURE 9.1 *Methods of data collection*

Information gathered using the first approach is said to be collected from **primary sources**, whereas the sources used in the second approach are called **secondary sources**. Examples of primary sources include finding out first-hand the attitudes of a community towards health services, ascertaining the health needs of a community, evaluating a social programme, determining the job satisfaction of the employees of an organisation, and ascertaining the quality of service provided by a worker are examples of information collected from primary sources. On the other hand, the use of census data to obtain information on the age–sex structure of a population, the use of hospital records to find out the morbidity and mortality patterns of a community, the use of an organisation's records to ascertain its activities, and the collection of data from sources such as articles, journals, magazines, books and periodicals to obtain historical and other types of information, are all classified as secondary sources. In summary, primary sources provide first-hand information and secondary sources provide second-hand data. Figure 9.1 shows the various methods of data collection.

None of the methods of data collection provides 100 per cent accurate and reliable information. The quality of the data gathered is dependent upon a number of other factors, which we will identify as we discuss each method. Your skill as a researcher lies in your ability to take care of the factors that could affect the quality of your data. One of the main differences between experienced and amateur researchers lies in their understanding of, and ability to control, these factors. It is therefore important for a beginner to be aware of them.

Collecting data using primary sources

Several methods can be used to collect primary data. The choice of a method depends upon the purpose of the study, the resources available and the skills of the researcher. There are times when the method most appropriate to achieve the objectives of a study cannot be used because of constraints such as a lack of resources and/or required skills. In such situations you should be aware of the problems that these limitations impose on the quality of the data.

In selecting a method of data collection, the socioeconomic–demographic characteristics of the study population play an important role: you should know as much as possible about characteristics such as educational level, age structure, socioeconomic status and ethnic background. If possible, it is helpful to know the study population's interest in, and attitude towards, participation in the study. Some populations, for a number of reasons, may not feel either at ease with a particular method of data collection (such as being interviewed) or comfortable with expressing opinions in a questionnaire. Furthermore, people with little education may respond differently to certain methods of data collection compared with people with more education.

Another important determinant of the quality of your data is the way the purpose and relevance of the study are explained to potential respondents. Whatever method of data collection is used, make sure that respondents clearly understand the purpose and relevance of the study. This is particularly important when you use a questionnaire to collect data, because in an interview situation you can answer a respondent's questions but in a questionnaire you will not have this opportunity.

In the following sections each method of data collection is discussed from the point of view of its applicability and suitability to a situation, and the problems and limitations associated with it.

Observation

Observation is one way to collect primary data. Observation is a purposeful, systematic and selective way of watching and listening to an interaction or phenomenon as it takes place. There are many situations in which observation is the most appropriate method of data collection; for example, when you want to learn about the interaction in a group, study the dietary patterns of a population, ascertain the functions performed by a worker, or study the behaviour or personality traits of an individual. It is also appropriate in situations where full and/ or accurate information cannot be elicited by questioning, because respondents either are not co-operative or are unaware of the answers because it is difficult for them to detach themselves from the interaction. In summary, when you are more interested in the behaviour than in the perceptions of individuals, or when subjects are so involved in the interaction that they are unable to provide objective information about it, observation is the best approach to collect the required information.

Types of observation

There are two types of observation:

1 participant observation;
2 non-participant observation.

Participant observation is when you, as a researcher, participate in the activities of the group being observed in the same manner as its members, with or without their knowing that they are being observed. For example, you might want to examine the reactions of the general population towards people in wheelchairs. You can study their reactions by sitting in a wheelchair yourself. Or you might want to study the life of prisoners and pretend to be a prisoner in order to do this.

Non-participant observation, on the other hand, is when you, as a researcher, do not get involved in the activities of the group but remain a passive observer, watching and listening to its activities and drawing conclusions from this. For example, you might want to study the functions carried out by nurses in a hospital. As an observer, you could watch, follow and record the activities as they are performed. After making a number of observations, conclusions could be drawn about the functions nurses carry out in the hospital. Any occupational group in any setting can be observed in the same manner.

Problems with using observation as a method of data collection

The use of observation as a method of data collection may suffer from a number of problems, which is not to suggest that all or any of these necessarily prevail in every situation. But as a beginner you should be aware of these potential problems:

- When individuals or groups become aware that they are being observed, they may change their behaviour. Depending upon the situation, this change could be positive or negative – it may increase or decrease, for example, their productivity – and may occur for a number of reasons. When a change in the behaviour of persons or groups is attributed to their being observed it is known as the **Hawthorne effect**. The use of observation in such a situation may introduce distortion: what is observed may not represent their normal behaviour.
- There is always the possibility of observer bias. If an observer is not impartial, s/he can easily introduce bias and there is no easy way to verify the observations and the inferences drawn from them.
- The interpretations drawn from observations may vary from observer to observer.
- There is the possibility of incomplete observation and/or recording, which varies with the method of recording. An observer may watch keenly but at the expense of detailed recording. The opposite problem may occur when the observer takes detailed notes but in doing so misses some of the interaction.

Situations in which observations can be made

Observations can be made under two conditions:

1 natural;
2 controlled.

Observing a group in its natural operation rather than intervening in its activities is classified as observation under natural conditions. Introducing a stimulus to the group for it to react to and observing the reaction is called controlled observation.

Recording observations

There are many ways of recording observations. The selection of a method of recording depends upon the purpose of the observation. The way an observation is recorded also determines whether it is a quantitative or qualitative study. Narrative and descriptive recording is mainly used in qualitative research but if you are doing a quantitative study you would record an observation in categorical form or on a numerical scale. Keep in mind that each method of recording an observation has its advantages and disadvantages:

- **Narrative recording** – In this form of recording the researcher records a description of the interaction in his/her own words. Such a type of recording clearly falls in the domain of qualitative research. Usually, a researcher makes brief notes while observing the interaction and then soon after completing the observation makes detailed notes in narrative form. In addition, some researchers may interpret the interaction and draw conclusions from it. The biggest advantage of narrative recording is that it provides a deeper insight into the interaction. However, a disadvantage is that an observer may be biased in his/her observation and, therefore, the interpretations and conclusions drawn from the observation may also be biased. In addition, interpretations and conclusions drawn are bound to be subjective reflecting the researcher's perspectives. Also, if a researcher's attention is on observing, s/he might forget to record an important piece of interaction and, obviously, in the process of recording, part of the interaction may be missed. Hence, there is always the possibility of incomplete recording and/or observation. In addition, when there are different observers the comparability of narrative recording can be a problem.
- **Using scales** – At times some observers may prefer to develop a scale in order to rate various aspects of the interaction or phenomenon. The recording is done on a scale developed by the observer/researcher. A scale may be one-, two- or three-directional, depending upon the purpose of the observation. For example, in the scale in Figure 9.2 – designed to record the nature of the interaction within a group – there are three directions: positive, negative and neutral.

  The main advantage of using scales in recording observation is that you do not need to spend time on taking detailed notes and can thus concentrate on observation. On the other hand, the problems with using a scale are that it does not provide specific and in-depth information about the interaction. In addition, it may suffer from any of the following errors:

  - Unless the observer is extremely confident of his/her ability to assess an interaction, s/he may tend to avoid the extreme positions on the scale, using mostly the central part. The error that this tendency creates is called the **error of central tendency**.
  - Some observers may prefer certain sections of the scale in the same way that some teachers are strict markers and others are not. When observers have a tendency to use a particular part of the scale in recording an interaction, this phenomenon is known as the **elevation effect**.

A study of the nature of interaction in a group

Aspects of interaction	Positive	Neutral	Negative

Aspects of interaction   ←——— Positive   Neutral   Negative ———→

Participation   5 4 3 2 1 0 1 2 3 4 5

Rapport   5 4 3 2 1 0 1 2 3 4 5

Confidence   5 4 3 2 1 0 1 2 3 4 5

Aggressiveness   5 4 3 2 1 0 1 2 3 4 5

Withdrawnness   5 4 3 2 1 0 1 2 3 4 5

Friendliness   5 4 3 2 1 0 1 2 3 4 5

Aloofness   5 4 3 2 1 0 1 2 3 4 5

FIGURE 9.2   *A three-directional rating scale*

- Another type of error that may be introduced is when the way an observer rates an individual on one aspect of the interaction influences the way s/he rates that individual on another aspect of the interaction. Again something similar to this can happen in teaching when a teacher's assessment of the performance of a student in one subject may influence his/her rating of that student's performance in another. This type of effect is known as the **halo effect**.

- **Categorical recording** – Sometimes an observer may decide to record his/her observation using categories. The type and number of categories depend upon the type of interaction and the observer's choice about how to classify the observation. For example, passive/active (two categories); introvert/extrovert (two categories); always/sometimes/never (three categories); strongly agree/agree/uncertain/disagree/strongly disagree (five categories). The use of categories to record an observation may suffer from the same problems as those associated with scales.

- **Recording on electronic devices** – Observation can also be recorded on videotape or other electronic devices and then analysed. The advantage of recording an interaction in this way is that the observer can see it a number of times before interpreting an interaction or drawing any conclusions from it and can also invite other professionals to view the interaction in order to arrive at more objective conclusions. However, one of the disadvantages is that some people may feel uncomfortable or may behave differently before a camera. Therefore the interaction may not be a true reflection of the situation.

The choice of a particular method for recording your observation is dependent upon the purpose of the observation, the complexity of the interaction and the type of population being observed. It is important to consider these factors before deciding upon the method for recording your observation.

The interview

Interviewing is a commonly used method of collecting information from people. In many walks of life we collect information through different forms of interaction with others. There are many definitions of interviews. According to Monette et al. (1986: 156), 'an interview involves an interviewer reading questions to respondents and recording their answers'. According to Burns (1997: 329), 'an interview is a verbal interchange, often face to face, though the telephone may be used, in which an interviewer tries to elicit information, beliefs or opinions from another person'. Any person-to-person interaction, either face to face or otherwise, between two or more individuals with a specific purpose in mind is called an interview.

When interviewing a respondent, you, as a researcher, have the freedom to decide the format and content of questions to be asked of your respondents, select the wording of your questions, decide the way you want to ask them and choose the order in which they are to be asked. This process of asking questions can be either very flexible, where you as the interviewer have the freedom to think about and formulate questions as they come to your mind around the issue being investigated, or inflexible, where you have to keep strictly to the questions decided beforehand – including their wording, sequence and the manner in which they are asked. Interviews are classified into different categories according to this degree of flexibility as in Figure 9.3.

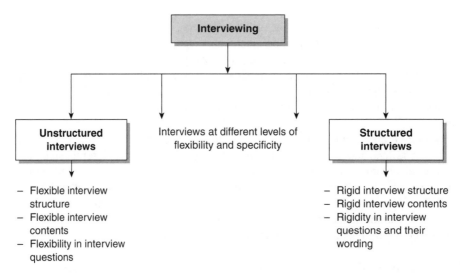

FIGURE 9.3 *Types of interview*

Unstructured Interviews

The strength of *unstructured interviews* is the almost complete freedom they provide in terms of content and structure. You are free to order these in whatever sequence you wish. You also have complete freedom in terms of the wording you use and the way you explain questions to your respondents. You may formulate questions and raise issues on the spur of the moment, depending upon what occurs to you in the context of the discussion.

Unstructured interviews are prevalent in both quantitative and qualitative research. The difference is in how information obtained through them in response to your questions is likely to be used. In quantitative research you develop response categorisations from responses which are then coded and quantified. In qualitative research the responses are used as descriptors, often in verbatim form, and can be integrated with your arguments, flow of writing and sequence of logic. As unstructured interviews are dominantly used in qualitative research, they are described in greater detail under 'Methods of data collection in qualitative research' later in this chapter.

Structured interviews

In a *structured interview* the researcher asks a predetermined set of questions, using the same wording and order of questions as specified in the interview schedule. An **interview schedule** is a written list of questions, open ended or closed, prepared for use by an interviewer in a person-to-person interaction (this may be face to face, by telephone or by other electronic media). Note that an interview schedule is a research tool/instrument for collecting data, whereas interviewing is a method of data collection.

One of the main advantages of the structured interview is that it provides uniform information, which assures the comparability of data. Structured interviewing requires fewer interviewing skills than does unstructured interviewing.

The questionnaire

A **questionnaire** is a written list of questions, the answers to which are recorded by respondents. In a questionnaire respondents read the questions, interpret what is expected and then write down the answers. The only difference between an interview schedule and a questionnaire is that in the former it is the interviewer who asks the questions (and if necessary, explains them) and records the respondent's replies on an interview schedule, and in the latter replies are recorded by the respondents themselves. This distinction is important in accounting for the respective strengths and weaknesses of the two methods.

In the case of a questionnaire, as there is no one to explain the meaning of questions to respondents, it is important that the questions are clear and easy to understand. Also, the layout of a questionnaire should be such that it is easy to read and pleasant to the eye, and the sequence of questions should be easy to follow. A questionnaire should be developed in an interactive style. This means respondents should feel as if someone is talking

Where to go? A study of occupational mobility among immigrants

The questionnaire opened with the following interactive statement:

Personal circumstances, and educational and occupational background, to a great extent determine the occupational mobility of an individual. This is especially true for immigrants. We would therefore like to ask you some questions about you and your family background. Knowledge of these factors is also important for assessing the representativeness of those who participated in the study and to understand the extent, nature and reasons of occupational mobility in relation to your background. We would appreciate your answering these questions as the information you provide will be very useful to us. We would like to emphasise that your responses are extremely valuable to us and we would greatly appreciate your answering all questions. However, if you feel that you do not want to answer a particular question, we will gladly accept your decision. We can assure you that your responses will be completely anonymous and will not be used for any other purpose.

Before asking questions about family background, the following interactive statement was inserted in the questionnaire:

Now, we would like to ask some questions about your family. Your family circumstances can affect your choice of an occupation after immigration. Again, we assure you of the complete anonymity of your responses.

Before ascertaining respondents' experiences with respect to recognition of their qualifications in Australia, the following interactive statement prepared them to be at ease with the area of inquiry:

Recognition of educational and professional qualifications, in addition to other factors, plays a major role in determining an individual's occupational mobility in a new country. In this section we would like to ask your opinion about the process of getting your qualifications recognised. We would also like to know how satisfied or dissatisfied you are with the outcome. If you are dissatisfied, we would like to know your reasons as this information may help decision makers to improve the process. Again, we assure you that your answers will be completely confidential. However, if you still feel that you do not want to answer a particular question, please feel free to omit it.

FIGURE 9.4   *Example 1*

to them. In a questionnaire, a sensitive question or a question that respondents may feel hesitant about answering should be prefaced by an interactive statement explaining the relevance of the question. It is a good idea to use a different font for these statements to distinguish them from the actual questions. Examples in Figures 9.4 and 9.5 taken from two surveys recently carried out by the author with the help of two students explain some of the above points.

Ways of administering a questionnaire

A questionnaire can be administered in different ways.

Occupational redeployment – a study of occupational redeployment among state government employees

The following interactive statement was inserted in the questionnaire before questions asking about the socioeconomic–demographic background of respondents:

In order to gain an understanding of the situation of employees who have experienced occupational redeployment in state government departments during the last three years, we would like to ask some questions about your background. Your answers will help us to determine the types of occupation where redeployment has occurred and the backgrounds of the employees who have been affected by it. Please do not feel obliged to answer a question if you do not wish to, though we assure you that any information you provide will be treated with strict confidentiality.

Questions about occupational history were prefaced by the following statement:

We would like to ask some questions about your work history. The answers to these questions will enable us to compare the type of work you have been doing since entering the workforce with the job you have been assigned after redeployment. This will help us to establish the nature and extent of change in your job before and after redeployment. Again, there is no obligation to answer a question if you do not want to. However, answers to these questions are extremely important to us. We assure you of the anonymity of the information you provide.

Before asking questions about the impact of redeployment, the following interactive statement was incorporated into the questionnaire:

The following questions ask you to express your opinion about different aspects of your job after and before redeployment. Your answers will help us to gauge the impact of redeployment on different aspects of your work and family situation. We would appreciate your honest opinions. Be assured that your responses will be completely anonymous.

FIGURE 9.5   *Example 2*

- **The mailed questionnaire** – The most common approach to collecting information is to send the questionnaire to prospective respondents by mail. Obviously this approach presupposes that you have access to their addresses. Usually it is a good idea to send a prepaid, self-addressed envelope with the questionnaire as this might increase the response rate. A mailed questionnaire *must* be accompanied by a covering letter (see below for details). One of the major problems with this method is the low response rate. In the case of an extremely low response rate, the findings have very limited applicability to the population studied.
- **Collective administration** – One of the best ways of administering a questionnaire is to obtain a captive audience such as students in a classroom, people attending a function, participants in a programme or people assembled in one place. This ensures a very high response rate as you will find few people refuse to participate in your study. Also, as you have personal contact with the study population, you can explain the purpose, relevance and

importance of the study and can clarify any questions that respondents may have. The author's advice is that if you have a captive audience for your study, don't miss the opportunity – it is the quickest way of collecting data, ensures a very high response rate and saves you money on postage.

- **Administration in a public place** – Sometimes you can administer a questionnaire in a public place such as a shopping centre, health centre, hospital, school or pub. Of course this depends upon the type of study population you are looking for and where it is likely to be found. Usually the purpose of the study is explained to potential respondents as they approach and their participation in the study is requested. Apart from being slightly more time consuming, this method has all the advantages of administering a questionnaire collectively.

Choosing between an interview and a questionnaire

The choice between a questionnaire and an interview schedule is important and should be considered thoroughly as the strengths and weaknesses of the two methods can affect the validity of the findings. The nature of the investigation and the socioeconomic–demographic characteristics of the study population are central in this choice. The selection between an interview schedule and a questionnaire should be based upon the following criteria:

- **The nature of the investigation** – If the study is about issues that respondents may feel reluctant to discuss with an investigator, a questionnaire may be the better choice as it ensures anonymity. This may be the case with studies on drug use, sexuality, indulgence in criminal activities and personal finances. However, there are situations where better information about sensitive issues can be obtained by interviewing respondents. It depends on the type of study population and the skills of the interviewer.
- **The geographical distribution of the study population** – If potential respondents are scattered over a wide geographical area, you have no choice but to use a questionnaire, as interviewing in these circumstances would be extremely expensive.
- **The type of study population** – If the study population is illiterate, very young or very old, or handicapped, there may be no option but to interview respondents.

Advantages of a questionnaire

A questionnaire has several advantages:

- **It is less expensive.** As you do not interview respondents, you save time, and human and financial resources. The use of a questionnaire, therefore, is comparatively convenient and inexpensive. Particularly when it is administered collectively to a study population, it is an extremely inexpensive method of data collection.
- **It offers greater anonymity.** As there is no face-to-face interaction between respondents and interviewer, this method provides greater anonymity. In some situations where sensitive questions are asked it helps to increase the likelihood of obtaining accurate information.

Disadvantages of a questionnaire

Although a questionnaire has several disadvantages, it is important to note that not all data collection using this method has these disadvantages. The prevalence of a disadvantage depends on a number of factors, but you need to be aware of them to understand their possible bearing on the quality of the data. These are:

- **Application is limited.** One main disadvantage is that application is limited to a study population that can read and write. It cannot be used on a population that is illiterate, very young, very old or handicapped.
- **Response rate is low.** Questionnaires are notorious for their low response rates; that is, people fail to return them. If you plan to use a questionnaire, keep in mind that because not everyone will return their questionnaire, your sample size will in effect be reduced. The response rate depends upon a number of factors: the interest of the sample in the topic of the study; the layout and length of the questionnaire; the quality of the letter explaining the purpose and relevance of the study; and the methodology used to deliver the questionnaire. You should consider yourself lucky to obtain a 50 per cent response rate and sometimes it may be as low as 20 per cent. However, as mentioned, the response rate is not a problem when a questionnaire is administered in a collective situation.
- **There is a self-selecting bias.** Not everyone who receives a questionnaire returns it, so there is a self-selecting bias. Those who return their questionnaire may have attitudes, attributes or motivations that are different from those who do not. Hence, if the response rate is very low, the findings may not be representative of the total study population.
- **Opportunity to clarify issues is lacking.** If, for any reason, respondents do not understand some questions, there is almost no opportunity for them to have the meaning clarified unless they get in touch with you – the researcher (which does not happen often). If different respondents interpret questions differently, this will affect the quality of the information provided.
- **Spontaneous responses are not allowed for.** Mailed questionnaires are inappropriate when spontaneous responses are required, as a questionnaire gives respondents time to reflect before answering.
- **The response to a question may be influenced by the response to other questions.** As respondents can read all the questions before answering (which usually happens), the way they answer a particular question may be affected by their knowledge of other questions.
- **It is possible to consult others.** With mailed questionnaires respondents may consult other people before responding. In situations where an investigator wants to find out only the study population's opinions, this method may be inappropriate, though requesting respondents to express their own opinion may help.
- **A response cannot be supplemented with other information.** An interview can sometimes be supplemented with information from other methods of data collection such as observation. However, a questionnaire lacks this advantage.

Advantages of the interview

- **The interview is more appropriate for complex situations.** It is the most appropriate approach for studying complex and sensitive areas as the interviewer has the opportunity to prepare a respondent before asking sensitive questions and to explain complex ones to respondents in person.

- **It is useful for collecting in-depth information.** In an interview situation it is possible for an investigator to obtain in-depth information by probing. Hence, in situations where in-depth information is required, interviewing is the preferred method of data collection.
- **Information can be supplemented.** An interviewer is able to supplement information obtained from responses with those gained from observation of non-verbal reactions.
- **Questions can be explained.** It is less likely that a question will be misunderstood as the interviewer can either repeat a question or put it in a form that is understood by the respondent.
- **Interviewing has a wider application.** An interview can be used with almost any type of population: children, the handicapped, illiterate or very old.

Disadvantages of the interview

- **Interviewing is time consuming and expensive.** This is especially so when potential respondents are scattered over a wide geographical area. However, if you have a situation such as an office, a hospital or an agency where potential respondents come to obtain a service, interviewing them in that setting may be less expensive and less time consuming.
- **The quality of data depends upon the quality of the interaction.** In an interview the quality of interaction between an interviewer and interviewee is likely to affect the quality of the information obtained. Also, because the interaction in each interview is unique, the quality of the responses obtained from different interviews may vary significantly.
- **The quality of data depends upon the quality of the interviewer.** In an interview situation the quality of the data generated is affected by the experience, skills and commitment of the interviewer.
- **The quality of data may vary when many interviewers are used.** Use of multiple interviewers may magnify the problems identified in the two previous points.
- **The researcher may introduce his/her bias.** Researcher bias in the framing of questions and the interpretation of responses is always possible. If the interviews are conducted by a person or persons, paid or voluntary, other than the researcher, it is also possible that they may exhibit bias in the way they interpret responses, select response categories or choose words to summarise respondents' expressed opinions.

Contents of the covering letter

It is essential that you write a covering letter with your mailed questionnaire. It should very briefly:

- introduce you and the institution you are representing;
- describe in two or three sentences the main objectives of the study;
- explain the relevance of the study;
- convey any general instructions;
- indicate that participation in the study is voluntary – if recipients do not want to respond to the questionnaire, they have the right not to;

- assure respondents of the anonymity of the information provided by them;
- provide a contact number in case they have any questions;
- give a return address for the questionnaire and a deadline for its return;
- thank them for their participation in the study.

Forms of question

The form and wording of questions used in an interview or a questionnaire are extremely important in a research instrument as they have an effect on the type and quality of information obtained from a respondent. The wording and structure of questions should therefore be appropriate, relevant and free from any of the problems discussed in the section titled 'Formulating effective questions' later in this chapter. Before this, let us discuss the two forms of questions, open ended and closed, which are both commonly used in social sciences research.

In an **open-ended question** the possible responses are *not* given. In the case of a questionnaire, the respondent writes down the answers in his/her words, but in the case of an interview schedule the investigator records the answers either verbatim or in a summary. In a **closed question** the possible answers are set out in the questionnaire or schedule and the respondent or the investigator ticks the category that best describes the respondent's answer. It is usually wise to provide a category 'Other/please explain' to accommodate any response not listed. The questions in Figure 9.6 are classified as closed questions. The same questions could be asked as open-ended questions, as shown in Figure 9.7.

When deciding whether to use open-ended or closed questions to obtain information about a variable, visualise how you plan to use the information generated. This is important because the way you frame your questions determines the unit of measurement which could be used to classify the responses. The unit of measurement in turn dictates what statistical procedures can be applied to the data and the way the information can be analysed and displayed.

Let us take, as an example, the question about the variable: 'income'. In closed questions income can be qualitatively recorded in categories such as 'above average/average/below average', or quantitatively in categories such as 'under $10 000/$10 000–$19 999/...'. Your choice of qualitative and quantitative categories affects the unit of measurement for income (qualitative uses the ordinal scale and quantitative the ratio scale of measurement), which in turn will affect the application of statistical procedures. For example, you cannot calculate the average income of a person from the responses to question C(a) in Figure 9.6; nor can you calculate the median or modal category of income. But from the responses to question C, you can accurately calculate modal category of income. However, the average and the median income cannot be accurately calculated (such calculations are usually made under certain assumptions). From the responses to question C in Figure 9.7, where the income for a respondent is recorded in exact dollars, the different descriptors of income can be calculated very accurately. In addition, information on income can be displayed in any form. You can calculate the average, median or mode. The same is true for any other information obtained in response to open-ended and closed questions.

A. Please indicate your age by placing a tick in the appropriate category.

Under 15 ☐

15–19 years ☐

20–24 years ☐

B. How would you describe your current marital status?

Married ☐

Single ☐

De facto ☐

Divorced ☐

Separated ☐

C. What is your average annual income?

Under $10 000 ☐

$10 000–$19 999 ☐

$20 000–$29 999 ☐

$30 000–$39 999 ☐

$40 000+ ☐

OR

C(a). How would you categorise your average annual income?

Above average ☐

Average ☐

Below average ☐

D. What, in your opinion, are the qualities of a good administrator?

Able to make decisions ☐

Fast decision maker ☐

Able to listen ☐

Impartial ☐

Skilled in interpersonal communication ☐

Other, please specify

_____

_____

FIGURE 9.6   *Examples of closed questions*

In closed questions, having developed categories, you cannot change them; hence, you should be very certain about your categories when developing them. If you ask an open-ended question, you can develop any number of categories at the time of analysis.

Both open-ended and closed questions have their advantages and disadvantages in different situations. To some extent, their advantages and disadvantages depend upon whether they

A. What is your current age? _____ years

B. How would you describe your current marital status? _____

C. What is your average annual income? $ _____

D. What, in your opinion, are the qualities of a good administrator?

    1 ————————

    2 ————————

    3 ————————

    4 ————————

    5 ————————

FIGURE 9.7   *Examples of open-ended questions*

are being used in an interview or in a questionnaire and on whether they are being used to seek information about facts or opinions. As a rule, closed questions are extremely useful for eliciting factual information and open-ended questions for seeking opinions, attitudes and perceptions. The choice of open-ended or closed questions should be made according to the purpose for which a piece of information is to be used, the type of study population from which information is going to be obtained, the proposed format for communicating the findings and the socioeconomic background of the readership.

Advantages and disadvantages of open-ended questions

- Open-ended questions provide in-depth information if used in an interview by an experienced interviewer. In a questionnaire, open-ended questions can provide a wealth of information provided respondents feel comfortable about expressing their opinions and are fluent in the language used. On the other hand, analysis of open-ended questions is more difficult. The researcher usually needs to go through another process – **content analysis** – in order to classify the data.
- In a questionnaire, open-ended questions provide respondents with the opportunity to express themselves freely, resulting in a greater variety of information. Thus respondents are not 'conditioned' by having to select answers from a list. The disadvantage of free choice is that, in a questionnaire, some respondents may not be able to express themselves, and so information can be lost.
- As open-ended questions allow respondents to express themselves freely, they virtually eliminate the possibility of investigator bias (investigator bias is introduced through the response pattern presented to respondents). On the other hand, there is a greater chance of interviewer bias in open-ended questions.

Advantages and disadvantages of closed questions

- One of the main disadvantages of closed questions is that the information obtained through them lacks depth and variety.

- There is a greater possibility of investigator bias because the researcher may list only the response patterns that s/he is interested in or those that come to mind. Even if the category of 'other' is offered, most people will usually select from the given responses, and so the findings may still reflect researcher bias.
- In a questionnaire, the given response pattern for a question could condition the thinking of respondents, and so the answers provided may not truly reflect respondents' opinions. Rather, they may reflect the extent of agreement or disagreement with the researcher's opinion or analysis of a situation.
- The ease of answering a ready-made list of responses may create a tendency among some respondents and interviewers to tick a category or categories without thinking through the issue.
- Closed questions, because they provide 'ready-made' categories within which respondents reply to the questions asked by the researcher, help to ensure that the information needed by the researcher is obtained and the responses are also easier to analyse.

Formulating effective questions

The wording and tone of your questions are important because the information and its quality largely depend upon these factors. It is therefore important to be careful about the way you formulate questions. The following are some considerations to keep in mind when formulating questions:

- **Always use simple and everyday language.** Your respondents may not be highly educated, and even if they are they still may not know some of the 'simple' technical jargon that you are used to. Particularly in a questionnaire, take extra care to use words that your respondents will understand as you will have no opportunity to explain questions to them. A pre-test should show you what is and what is not understood by your respondents. For example:

  Is anyone in your family a *dipsomaniac*? (Bailey 1978: 100)

  In this question many respondents, even some who are well educated, will not understand 'dipsomaniac' and, hence, they either do not answer or answer the question without understanding.
- **Do not use ambiguous questions.** An **ambiguous question** is one that contains more than one meaning and that can be interpreted differently by different respondents. This will result in different answers, making it difficult, if not impossible, to draw any valid conclusions from the information. The following questions highlight the problem:

  Is your work made difficult because you are expecting a baby? (Moser & Kalton 1989: 323)   Yes ☐   No ☐

  In the survey all women were asked this question. Those women who were not pregnant ticked 'No', meaning no they were not pregnant, and those who were pregnant and who ticked 'No' meant pregnancy had not made their work difficult. The question has other ambiguities as well: it does not specify the type of work and the stage of pregnancy.

  Are you satisfied with your canteen? (Moser & Kalton 1989: 319)

This question is also ambiguous as it does not ask respondents to indicate the aspects of the canteen with which they may be satisfied or dissatisfied. Is it with the service, the prices, the physical facilities, the attitude of the staff or the quality of the meals? Respondents may have any one of these aspects in mind when they answer the question. Or the question should have been worded differently like, 'Are you, on the whole, satisfied with your canteen?'

- **Do not ask double-barrelled questions.** A **double-barrelled question** is a question within a question. The main problem with this type of question is that one does not know which particular question a respondent has answered. Some respondents may answer both parts of the question and others may answer only one of them.

    How often and how much time do you spend on each visit?

This question was asked in a survey in Western Australia to ascertain the need for child-minding services in one of the hospitals. The question has two parts: how often do you visit and how much time is spent on each visit? In this type of question some respondents may answer the first part, whereas others may answer the second part and some may answer both parts. Incidentally, this question is also ambiguous in that it does not specify 'how often' in terms of a period of time. Is it in a week, a fortnight, a month or a year?

    Does your department have a special recruitment policy for racial minorities and women? (Bailey 1978: 97)

This question is double barrelled in that it asks respondents to indicate whether their office has a special recruitment policy for two population groups: racial minorities and women. A 'yes' response does not necessarily mean that the office has a special recruitment policy for both groups.

- **Do not ask leading questions.** A **leading question** is one which, by its contents, structure or wording, leads a respondent to answer in a certain direction. Such questions are judgemental and lead respondents to answer either positively or negatively.

    Unemployment is increasing, isn't it?

    Smoking is bad, isn't it?

The first problem is that these are not questions but statements. Because the statements suggest that 'unemployment is increasing' and 'smoking is bad', respondents may feel that to disagree with them is to be in the wrong, especially if they feel that the researcher is an authority and that if s/he is saying that 'unemployment is increasing' or 'smoking is bad', it must be so. The feeling that there is a 'right' answer can 'force' people to respond in a way that is contrary to their true position.

- **Do not ask questions that are based on presumptions.** In such questions the researcher assumes that respondents fit into a particular category and seeks information based upon that assumption.

    How many cigarettes do you smoke in a day? (Moser & Kalton 1989: 325)

    What contraceptives do you use?

Both these questions were asked without ascertaining whether or not respondents were smokers or sexually active. In situations like this it is important to ascertain first whether or not a respondent fits into the category about which you are enquiring.

Constructing a research instrument in quantitative research

The construction of a research instrument or tool is an extremely important aspect of a research project because anything you say by way of findings or conclusions is based upon the type of information you collect, and the data you collect is entirely dependent upon the questions that you ask of your respondents. The famous saying about computers – 'garbage in, garbage out' – is also applicable to data collection. The research tool provides the input to a study and therefore the quality and validity of the output, the findings, are solely dependent upon it.

In spite of its immense importance, to the author's knowledge, no specific guidelines for beginners on how to construct a research tool exist. Students are left to learn for themselves under the guidance of their research supervisor. The guidelines suggested below outline a broad approach, especially for beginners. The underlying principle is to ensure the validity of your instrument by making sure that *your questions relate to the objectives of your study*. Therefore, clearly defined objectives play an extremely important role as each question in the instrument must stem from the objectives, research questions and/or hypotheses of the study. It is suggested that a beginner should adopt the following procedure:

Step I   If you have not already done so, clearly define and individually list all the specific objectives, research questions or hypotheses, if any, to be tested.

Step II   For each objective, research question or hypothesis, list all the associated questions that you want to answer through your study.

Step III Take each question that you identified in Step II and list the information required to answer it.

Step IV   Formulate question(s) that you want to ask of your respondents to obtain the required information.

In the above process you may find that the same piece of information is required for a number of questions. In such a situation the question should be asked once only. To understand this process, see Table 9.1 for which we have already developed a set of objectives in Figure 4.4 in Chapter 4.

Asking personal and sensitive questions

In the social sciences, sometimes one needs to ask questions that are of a personal nature. Some respondents may find this offensive. It is important to be aware of this as it may affect the quality of information or even result in an interview being terminated or questionnaires not being returned. Researchers have used a number of approaches to deal with this problem but it is difficult to say which approach is best. According to Bradburn and Sudman:

> no data collection method is superior to other methods for all types of threatening questions. If one accepts the results at face value, each of the data gathering methods is best under certain conditions. (1979: 12–13)

TABLE 9.1 *Guidelines for constructing a research instrument (quantitative research): a study to evaluate community responsiveness in a health programme*

Objectives/research questions/hypotheses → Step I	Main and associated research questions → Step II	Information required → Step III	Questions Step IV
1 To find out the understanding of the concept 'community responsiveness' among health administrators, planners, service providers and consumers of health services	What is community responsiveness? What does it mean when people use the term 'community responsiveness'?	1 Perception of community responsiveness	Q1.1 When you use the term 'community responsiveness', what do you mean by it? Q1.2 What comes to your mind when you use the term 'community responsiveness' in the delivery of health services? Q1.3 What, in your opinion, are the characteristics of 'community responsiveness'? Q1.4 What, in your opinion, is the difference between 'community development and community responsiveness'?
2 To identify the strategies needed to foster community responsiveness in the delivery of health services	What are the differences in the perception of community responsiveness among health administrators, planners, service providers and consumers of health services?	2 Occupational status, i.e. health administrator, planner, service provider or consumer	Q2.1 What would you categorise your job as? • Health administrator/planner • Service provider • Health consumer
3 To develop a set of indicators to evaluate the effectiveness of strategies to foster community responsiveness		3 Age, gender, education	Q3.1 How old are you? _____ Q3.2 Are you _____ female _____ male? Q3.3 What is the highest level of educational achievement you have attained?

In terms of the best technique for asking sensitive or threatening questions, there appears to be two opposite opinions, based on the manner in which the question is asked:

1 a direct manner;
2 an indirect manner.

The advantage with the first approach is that one can be sure that an affirmative answer is accurate. Those who advocate the second approach believe that direct questioning is likely to offend respondents and hence they are unlikely to answer even the non-sensitive questions. Some ways of asking personal questions in an indirect manner are as follows:

* by showing drawings or cartoons;
* by asking a respondent to complete a sentence;
* by asking a respondent to sort cards containing statements;
* by using random devices.

To describe these methods in detail is beyond the scope of this book.

The order of questions

The order of questions in a questionnaire or in an interview schedule is important as it affects the quality of information, and the interest and even willingness of a respondent to participate in a study. Again, there are two categories of opinion as to the best way to order questions. The first is that questions should be asked in a random order and the second is that they should follow a logical progression based upon the objectives of the study. The author believes that the latter procedure is better as it gradually leads respondents into the themes of the study, starting with simple themes and progressing to complex ones. This approach sustains the interest of respondents and gradually stimulates them to answer the questions. However, the random approach is useful in situations where a researcher wants respondents to express their agreement or disagreement with different aspects of an issue. In this case a logical listing of statements or questions may 'condition' a respondent to the opinions expressed by the researcher through the statements.

Pre-testing a research instrument

Having constructed your research instrument, whether an interview schedule or a questionnaire, it is important that you test it out before using it for actual data collection. Pre-testing a research instrument entails a critical examination of the understanding of each question and its meaning as understood by a respondent. A pre-test should be carried out under actual field conditions on a group of people similar to your study population. The purpose is not to collect data but to identify problems that the potential respondents might have in either understanding or interpreting a question. Your aim is to identify if there are problems in understanding the way a question has been worded, the appropriateness of the meaning it communicates, whether different respondents interpret a question differently, and to establish whether their interpretation is different to what you were trying to convey. If there are problems you need to re-examine the wording to make it clearer and unambiguous.

Prerequisites for data collection

Before you start obtaining information from potential respondents it is imperative that you make sure of their:

- **motivation to share the required information** – It is essential for respondents to be willing to share information with you. You should make every effort to motivate them by explaining clearly and in simple terms the objectives and relevance of the study, either at the time of the interview or in the covering letter accompanying the questionnaire and/or through interactive statements in the questionnaire.
- **clear understanding of the questions** – Respondents must understand what is expected of them in the questions. If respondents do not understand a question clearly, the response given may be either wrong or irrelevant, or make no sense.
- **possession of the required information** – The third prerequisite is that respondents must have the information sought. This is of particular importance when you are seeking factual or technical information. If respondents do not have the required information, they cannot provide it.

Methods of data collection in qualitative research

To draw a clear distinction between quantitative and qualitative methods of data collection is both difficult and inappropriate because of the overlap between them. The difference between them mainly lies in the manner in which a method is applied in an actual data collection situation. Use of these methods in quantitative research demands standardisation of questions to be asked of the respondents, a rigid adherence to their structure and order, an adoption of a process that is tested and predetermined, and making sure of the validity and reliability of the process as well as the questions. However, the methods of data collection in qualitative research follow a convention which is almost opposite to quantitative research. The wording, order and format of these questions are neither predetermined nor standardised. Qualitative methods are characterised by flexibility and freedom in terms of structure and order given to the researcher.

As mentioned in the previous chapter, most qualitative study designs are method based: that is, the method of data collection seems to determine the design. In some situations it becomes difficult to separate a study design from the method of data collection. For example, in-depth interviewing, narratives and oral history are both designs and methods of data collection. This may confuse some but here they are detailed as methods and not designs.

There are three main methods of data collection in qualitative research:

1 unstructured interviews;
2 participant observation;
3 secondary sources.

Participant observation has been adequately covered earlier in this chapter and secondary sources will be covered in a later section, so at this point we will focus on unstructured interviews, which are by far the most commonly used method of data collection in qualitative research.

Flexibility, freedom and spontaneity in contents and structure underpin an interaction in all types of unstructured interview. This interaction can be at a one-to-one (researcher and a respondent) or a group (researcher and a group of respondents) level. There are several types of unstructured interview that are prevalent in qualitative research, for example *in-depth interviewing*, *focus group interviewing*, *narratives* and *oral histories*. Below is a brief description of each of them. For a detailed understanding readers should consult the relevant references listed in the Bibliography.

In-depth interviews

The theoretical roots of **in-depth interviewing** are in what is known as the interpretive tradition. According to Taylor and Bogdan, in-depth interviewing is 'repeated face-to-face encounters between the researcher and informants directed towards understanding informants' perspectives on their lives, experiences, or situations as expressed in their own words' (1998: 77). This definition underlines two essential characteristics of in-depth interviewing: (1) it involves face-to-face, repeated interaction between the researcher and his/her informant(s); and (2) it seeks to understand the latter's perspectives. Because this method involves repeated contacts and hence an extended length of time spent with an informant, it is assumed that the rapport between researcher and informant will be enhanced, and that the corresponding understanding and confidence between the two will lead to in-depth and accurate information.

Focus group interviews

The only difference between a focus group interview and an in-depth interview is that the former is undertaken with a group and the latter with an individual. In a focus group interview, you explore the perceptions, experiences and understandings of a group of people who have some experience in common with regard to a situation or event. For example, you may explore with relevant groups such issues as domestic violence, physical disability or refugees.

In focus group interviews, broad discussion topics are developed beforehand, either by the researcher or by the group. These provide a broad frame for discussions which follow. The specific discussion points emerge as a part of the discussion. Members of a focus group express their opinions while discussing these issues.

You, as a researcher, need to ensure that whatever is expressed or discussed is recorded accurately. Use the method of recording that suits you the best. You may audiotape discussions, employ someone else to record them or record them yourself immediately after each session. If you are taking your own notes during discussions, you need to be careful not to lose something of importance because of your involvement in discussions. You can and should take your write-up on discussions back to your focus group for correction, verification and confirmation.

Narratives

The narrative technique of gathering information has even less structure than the focus group. **Narratives** have almost no predetermined contents except that the researcher seeks to hear a person's retelling of an incident or happening in his/her life. Essentially, the person tells his/her story about an incident or situation and you, as the researcher, listen passively. Occasionally, you encourage the individual by using active listening techniques; that is, you say words such as 'uh huh', 'mmmm', 'yeah', 'right' and nod as appropriate. Basically, you let the person talk freely and without interrupting.

Narratives are a very powerful method of data collection for situations which are sensitive in nature. For example, you may want to find out about the impact of child sexual abuse on people who have gone through such an experience. You, as a researcher, ask these people to narrate their experiences and how they have been affected. Narratives may have a therapeutic impact; that is, sometimes simply telling their story may help a person to feel more at ease with the event. Some therapists specialise in narrative therapy. But here, we are concerned with narratives as a method of data collection.

As with focus group interviews, you need to choose the recording system that suits you the best. Having completed narrative sessions you need to write your detailed notes and give them back to the respondent to check for accuracy.

Oral histories

Oral histories, like narratives, involve the use of both passive and active listening. Oral histories, however, are more commonly used for learning about a historical event or episode that took place in the past or for gaining information about a cultural, custom or story that has been passed from generation to generation. Narratives are more about a person's personal experiences whereas historical, social or cultural events are the subjects of oral histories.

Suppose you want to find out about the life after the Second World War in some regional town of Western Australia or about the living conditions of Aboriginal and Torres Strait Islander people in the 1960s. You would talk to persons who were alive during that period and ask them about life at that time.

Data collection through unstructured interviewing is extremely useful in situations where either in-depth information is needed or little is known about the area. The flexibility allowed to the interviewer in what s/he asks of a respondent is an asset as it can elicit extremely rich information. As it provides in-depth information, this technique is used by many researchers for constructing a structured research instrument. On the other hand, since an unstructured interview does not list specific questions to be asked of respondents, the comparability of questions asked and responses obtained may become a problem. As the researcher gains experience during the interviews, the questions asked of respondents change; hence, the type of information obtained from those who are interviewed at the beginning may be markedly different from that obtained from those interviewed towards the end. Also, this freedom can introduce investigator bias into the study. Using an interview guide as a means of data collection requires much more skill on the part of the researcher than does using a structured interview.

Constructing a research instrument in qualitative research

Data in qualitative research are not collected through a set of predetermined questions but by raising issues around different areas of enquiry. Hence there are no predetermined research tools, as such, in qualitative research. However, many people develop a loose list of issues that they want to discuss with respondents or to have ready in case what they want to discuss does not surface during the discussions. This loosely developed list of issues is called an **interview guide.** In the author's opinion, particularly for a newcomer, it is important to develop an interview guide to ensure desired coverage of the areas of enquiry and comparability of information across respondents. Note that in-depth interviewing is both a method of data collection and a study design in qualitative research and the interview guide is a research tool that is used to collect data in this design.

Recently the author conducted a study using in-depth interviewing and focus group methodologies to construct a conceptual service delivery model for providing child protection services through family consultation, involvement and engagement. The project was designed to develop a model that can be used by the field workers when dealing with a family on matters relating to child protection. The author conducted a number of in-depth interviews with some staff members working at different levels to gather ideas of the issues that service providers and managers thought to be important. On the basis of the information obtained from these in-depth interviews, a list of likely topics/issues was prepared. This list, the interview guide, became the basis of collecting the required information from individuals and focus groups in order to construct the conceptual model. Though this list was developed the focus groups were encouraged to raise any issue relating to the service delivery. The following topics/issues/questions formed the core of the interview guide for focus groups:

1 What do you understand by the concept of family engagement and involvement when deciding about a child?
2 What should be the extent and nature of the involvement?
3 How can it be achieved?

4 What do you think are the advantages of involving families in the decision making?
5 What in your opinion are its disadvantages?
6 What is your opinion about this concept?
7 What can a field worker do to involve a family?
8 How can the success or failure of this model be measured?
9 How will this model affect current services to children?

Note that these served as starting points for discussions. The group members were encouraged to discuss whatever they wanted to in relation to the perceived model. All one-to-one in-depth interviews and focus group discussions were recorded on audiotape and were analysed to identify major themes that emerged from these discussions.

Collecting data using secondary sources

So far we have discussed the primary sources of data collection where the required data was collected either by you or by someone else for the specific purpose you have in mind. There are occasions when your data have already been collected by someone else and you need only to extract the required information for the purpose of your study.

Both qualitative and quantitative research studies use secondary sources as a method of data collection. In qualitative research you usually extract descriptive (historical and current) and narrative information and in quantitative research the information extracted is categorical or numerical. The following section provides some of the many secondary sources grouped into categories:

- **Government or semi-government publications** – There are many government and semi-government organisations that collect data on a regular basis in a variety of areas and publish it for use by members of the public and interest groups. Some common examples are the census, vital statistics registration, labour force surveys, health reports, economic forecasts and demographic information.
- **Earlier research** – For some topics, an enormous number of research studies that have already been done by others can provide you with the required information.
- **Personal records** – Some people write historical and personal records (e.g. diaries) that may provide the information you need.
- **Mass media** – Reports published in newspapers, in magazines, on the Internet, and so on, may be another good source of data.

Problems with using data from secondary sources

When using data from secondary sources you need to be careful as there may be certain problems with the availability, format and quality of data. The extent of these problems varies from source to source. While using such data some issues you should keep in mind are:

- **Validity and reliability** – The validity of information may vary markedly from source to source. For example, information obtained from a census is likely to be more valid and reliable than that obtained from most personal diaries.
- **Personal bias** – The use of information from personal diaries, newspapers and magazines may have the problem of personal bias as these writers are likely to exhibit less rigorousness and objectivity than one would expect in research reports.
- **Availability of data** – It is common for beginning researchers to assume that the required data will be available, but you cannot and should not make this assumption. Therefore, it is important to make sure that the required data is available before you proceed further with your study.
- **Format** – Before deciding to use data from secondary sources it is equally important to ascertain that the data is available in the required format. For example, you might need to analyse age in the categories 23–33, 34–48, and so on, but, in your source, age may be categorised as 21–24, 25–29, and so on.

Summary

In this chapter you have learnt about the various methods of data collection. Information collected about a situation, phenomenon, issue or group of people can come from either primary sources or secondary sources.

Primary sources are those where you or someone else collects information from respondents for the specific purpose for which a study is undertaken. These include interviewing, observation and the use of questionnaires. All other sources, where the information required is already available, such as government publications, reports and previous research, are called secondary sources.

There is a considerable overlap in the methods of data collection between quantitative and qualitative research studies. The difference lies in the way the information is generated, recorded and analysed. In quantitative research the information, in most cases, is generated through a set of predetermined questions and either the responses are recorded in categorical format or the categories are developed out of the responses. The information obtained then goes through data processing and is subjected to a number of statistical procedures. In qualitative research the required information is generated through a series of questions which are not predetermined and pre-worded. In addition, the recording of information is in descriptive format and the dominant mode of analysis is content analysis to identify the main themes. Structured interviews, use of questionnaires and structured observations are the most common methods of data collection in quantitative research, whereas in qualitative research unstructured interviews (oral histories, in-depth interviews and narratives) and participant observation are the main methods of data collection from primary sources.

The choice of a particular method of collecting data depends upon the purpose of collecting information, the type of information being collected, the resources available to you, your skills in the use of a particular method of data collection and the socioeconomic–demographic characteristics of your study population. Each method has its own advantages and disadvantages and each is appropriate for certain situations. The choice of a particular method for collecting data is important in itself for ensuring the quality of the information but no method of data collection will guarantee 100 per cent accurate information. The quality of your information is dependent upon several methodological, situational and respondent-related factors and your ability as a researcher lies in either controlling or minimising the effect of these factors in the process of data collection.

The use of open-ended and closed questions is appropriate for different situations. Both of them have strengths and weaknesses and you should be aware of these so that you can use them appropriately.

The construction of a research instrument is the most important aspect of any research endeavour as it determines the nature and quality of the information. This is the input of your study and the output, the relevance and accuracy of your conclusions, is entirely dependent upon it. A research instrument in quantitative research must be developed in light of the objectives of your study. The method suggested in this chapter ensures that questions in an instrument have a direct link to your objectives. The wording of questions can pose several problems and you should keep them in mind while formulating your questions.

In qualitative research you do not develop a research instrument as such but it is advisable that you develop a conceptual framework of the likely areas you plan to cover, providing sufficient allowance for new ones to emerge when collecting data from your respondents.

For You to Think About

▸ Refamiliarise yourself with the keywords listed at the beginning of this chapter and if you are uncertain about the meaning or application of any of them revisit these in the chapter before moving on.

▸ Identify two or three examples from your own academic field where it may be better to use a questionnaire rather than interviewing, and vice versa.

▸ Identify three situations where it would be better to use open-ended questions and three where closed questions might be more useful.

▸ There is a considerable overlap in the methods of data collection between quantitative and qualitative research. In spite of that they are different. Make a list of a few of the factors that differentiate them.

CHAPTER 10
Collecting Data Using Attitudinal Scales

In this chapter you will learn about:

- What attitudinal scales are and how to use them
- The functions of attitudinal scales in quantitative research
- Difficulties in developing an attitudinal scale and how to overcome them
- Different types of attitudinal scales and when to use them
- The relationship between attitudinal and measurement scales
- Methods for exploring attitudes in qualitative research

Keywords: *attitudinal scales, attitudinal score, attitudinal value, attitudinal weight, cumulative scale, equal-appearing scale, Guttman scale, interval scale, Likert scale, negative statements, neutral items, non-discriminate items, numerical scale, ordinal scale, positive statements, ratio scale, summated rating scale, Thurstone scale.*

Measurement of attitudes in quantitative and qualitative research

There are a number of differences in the way attitudes are measured in quantitative and qualitative research. In quantitative research you are able to explore, measure, determine the intensity and combine attitudes to different aspects of an issue to arrive at one indicator that is reflective of the overall attitude. In qualitative research, you can only explore the spread of attitudes and establish the types of attitudes prevalent. In quantitative research you can ascertain the types of attitudes people have in a community, how many people have a particular attitude and what the intensity is of those attitudes. A number of techniques have been developed to measure attitudes and their intensity in quantitative research, but such techniques are lacking in qualitative research. This is mainly because in qualitative research you do not make an attempt to measure or quantify. The concept of attitudinal scales, therefore, is only prevalent in quantitative research.

Attitudinal scales in quantitative research

In quantitative research there are three scales which have been developed to 'measure' attitudes. Each of these scales is based upon different assumptions and follows different procedures in their construction. As a beginner in research methods it is important for you to understand these procedures and the assumptions behind them so that you can make appropriate and accurate interpretation of the findings. As you will see, it is not very easy to construct an attitudinal scale. Out of the three scales, the Likert scale is the easiest to construct and therefore is used far more.

Functions of attitudinal scales

If you want to find out the attitude of respondents towards an issue, you can ask either a closed or an open-ended question. For example, let us say that you want to ascertain the attitude of students in a class towards their lecturer and that you have asked them to respond to the following question: 'What is your attitude towards your lecturer?' If your question is open ended, it invites each respondent to describe the attitude that s/he holds towards the lecturer. If you have framed a closed question, with categories such as 'extremely positive', 'positive', 'uncertain', 'negative' and 'extremely negative', this guides the respondents to select a category that best describes their attitude. This type of questioning, whether framed descriptively or in a categorical form, elicits an overall attitude towards the lecturer. While ascertaining the overall attitude may be sufficient in some situations, in many others, where the purpose of attitudinal questioning is to develop strategies for improving a service or intervention, or to formulate policy, eliciting attitudes on various aspects of the issue under study is required.

But as you know, every issue, including that of the attitude of students towards their lecturers, has many aspects. For example, the attitude of the members of a community towards the provision of a particular service comprises their attitude towards the need for the service, its manner of delivery, its location, the physical facilities provided to users, the behaviour of the staff, the competence of the staff, the effectiveness and efficiency of the service, and so on. Similarly, other examples – such as the attitude of employees towards the management of their organisation, the attitude of employees towards occupational redeployment and redundancy, the attitude of nurses towards death and dying, the attitude of consumers towards a particular product, the attitude of students towards a lecturer, or the attitude of staff towards the strategic plan for their organisation – can be broken down in the same manner.

Respondents usually have different attitudes towards different aspects. Only when you ascertain the attitude of respondents to an issue by formulating a question for each aspect, using either open-ended or closed questions, do you find out their attitude towards each aspect. The main limitation of this method is that it is difficult to draw any conclusion about the overall attitude of a respondent from the responses. Take the earlier example, where you want to find out the attitude of students towards a lecturer. There are different aspects of teaching: the contents of lectures; the organisation of material; the lecturer's ability to communicate material; the presentation and style; knowledge of the subject; responsiveness; punctuality; and so on. Students may rate the lecturer differently on different aspects. That is, the lecturer might be considered extremely competent and knowledgeable in his/her subject but may not be considered a good communicator by a majority of students. Further, students may differ markedly in their opinion regarding any one aspect of a lecturer's teaching. Some might consider the lecturer to be a good communicator and others might not. The main problem is: how do we find out the 'overall' attitude of the students towards the lecturer? In other words, how do we combine the responses to different aspects of any issue to come up with one indicator that is reflective of an overall attitude? Attitudinal scales play an important role in overcoming this problem.

Attitudinal scales measure the intensity of respondents' attitudes towards the various aspects of a situation or issue and provide techniques to combine the attitudes towards different aspects into one overall indicator. This reduces the risk of an expression of opinion by respondents being influenced by their opinion on only one or two aspects of that situation or issue.

Difficulties in developing an attitudinal scale

In developing an attitudinal scale there are three problems:

1   Which aspects of a situation or issue should be included when seeking to measure an attitude? For instance, in the example cited above, what aspects of teaching should be included in a scale to find out the attitude of students towards their lecturer?
2   What procedure should be adopted for combining the different aspects to obtain an overall picture?
3   How can one ensure that a scale really is measuring what it is supposed to measure?

The first problem is extremely important as it largely determines the third problem: the extent to which the statements on different aspects are reflective of the main issue largely determines the validity of the scale. You can solve the third problem by ensuring that your statements on the various aspects have a logical link with the main issue under study – the greater the link, the higher the validity. The different types of attitudinal scale (Likert, Thurstone and Guttman) provide an answer to the second problem. They guide you as to the procedure for combining the attitudes towards various aspects of an issue, though the degree of difficulty in following the procedure for these scales varies from scale to scale.

Types of attitudinal scale

There are three major types of attitudinal scale:

1 the summated rating scale, also known as the Likert scale;
2 the equal-appearing interval scale or differential scale, also known as the Thurstone scale;
3 the cumulative scale, also known as the Guttman scale.

The summated rating or Likert scale

The **summated rating scale**, more commonly known as the **Likert scale**, is based upon the assumption that each statement/item on the scale has equal **attitudinal value**, 'importance' or 'weight' in terms of reflecting an attitude towards the issue in question. This assumption is also the main limitation of this scale as statements on a scale seldom have equal attitudinal value. For instance, in the examples in Figures 10.1 and 10.2, 'knowledge of subject' is not as important in terms of the degree to which it reflects the attitude of the students towards the lecturer as 'has published a great deal' or 'some students like, some do not', but, on the Likert scale, each is treated as having the same 'weight'. A student may not bother much about whether a lecturer has published a great deal, but may be more concerned about 'knowledge of the subject', 'communicates well' and 'knows how to teach'.

The lecturer:	Strongly agree	Agree	Uncertain	Disagree	Strongly disagree
1 Knows the subject well	▭	▭	▭	▭	▭
2 Is unenthusiastic about teaching	▭	▭	▭	▭	▭
3 Shows concern for students	▭	▭	▭	▭	▭
4 Makes unreasonable demands	▭	▭	▭	▭	▭
5 Has poor communication skills	▭	▭	▭	▭	▭
6 Knows how to teach	▭	▭	▭	▭	▭
7 Can explain difficult concepts in simple terms	▭	▭	▭	▭	▭
8 Is hard to approach	▭	▭	▭	▭	▭
9 Is liked by some students and not by others	▭	▭	▭	▭	▭
10 Is difficult to get along with	▭	▭	▭	▭	▭

FIGURE 10.1 *An example of a categorical scale*

It is important to remember that the Likert scale does not measure attitude per se. It does help to place different respondents in relation to each other in terms of the intensity of their attitude towards an issue: it shows the strength of one respondent's view in relation to that of another and not the absolute attitude.

The lecturer:

		7	6	5	4	3	2	1
1	Knows the subject well	7	6	5	4	3	2	1
2	Is enthusiastic about teaching	7	6	5	4	3	2	1
3	Shows no concern for students	7	6	5	4	3	2	1
4	Demands too much	7	6	5	4	3	2	1
5	Communicates well	7	6	5	4	3	2	1
6	Knows how to teach	7	6	5	4	3	2	1
7	Can explain difficult concepts in simple terms	7	6	5	4	3	2	1
8	Is seldom available to the students	7	6	5	4	3	2	1
9	Is liked by some students and not by others	7	6	5	4	3	2	1
10	Has published a great deal	7	6	5	4	3	2	1

FIGURE 10.2   *An example of a seven-point numerical scale*

1:   The lecturer

(a) knows the subject *extremely well*
(b) knows the subject *well*
(c) has an *average* knowledge of the subject
(d) *does not know* the subject
(e) has an *extremely poor knowledge* of the subject

FIGURE 10.3   *An example of a scale with statements reflecting varying degrees of an attitude*

Considerations in constructing a Likert scale

In developing a Likert scale, there are a number of things to consider. Firstly, decide whether the attitude to be measured is to be classified into one-, two- or three-directional categories (i.e. whether you want to determine positive, negative and neutral positions in the study population) with respect to their attitude towards the issue under study. Next, consider whether you want to use categories or a numerical scale. This should depend upon whether you think that your study population can express itself better on a numerical scale or in categories. The decision about the number of points or the number of categories on a categorical scale depends upon how finely you want to measure the intensity of the attitude in question and on the capacity of the population to make fine distinctions. Figure 10.1 shows a five-point categorical scale that is three directional and Figure 10.2 illustrates a seven-point numerical scale that is one directional. Sometimes you can also develop statements reflecting opinion about an issue in varying degrees (Figure 10.3). In this instance a respondent is asked to select the statement which best describes the opinion.

Procedure

Step 1   Assemble or construct statements that are reflective of the attitudes towards the main issue in question. Statements should be worded to reflect both positive and negative attitudes towards the issue; that is, they should be for, as well as against, the issue. (If your scale is one directional, you need only positive statements.) Make sure that all the statements have a logical link with the main issue. You also need to decide whether you want respondents to answer in categories or on a numerical scale.

Step 2   Administer the statements to a small group of people to test them.

Step 3   Analyse the responses by assigning a weighting – a numerical value – to the responses. Numerical values are assigned differently to positive and negative statements. For a positive statement the response indicating the most favourable attitude is to be given the highest score. For example, on a five-category or five-point scale, 5 is assigned to the response that indicates the most favourable attitude and 1 to the response which indicates the least favourable attitude. By contrast, a person who agrees strongly with a negative statement indicates that s/he does not have a favourable attitude; hence, the scoring is reversed, i.e. 1 is assigned to the response where a respondent strongly agrees with a negative statement and 5 to the response where s/he strongly disagrees with it.

Step 4   Calculate each respondent's attitudinal score by adding numerical values assigned in Step 3 to the responses s/he gave to each statement.

Step 5   Compare all respondents' scores for each item to identify non-discriminative items. Non-discriminative statements do not help you to distinguish respondents with respect to attitude as almost everyone responds to them in the same way.

Step 6   Eliminate non-discriminative items.

Step 7   Construct a questionnaire/interview schedule comprising the selected statements/items.

FIGURE 10.4   *The procedure for constructing a Likert scale*

The procedure for constructing a Likert scale

Figure 10.4 shows the procedure used in constructing a Likert scale.

Calculating attitudinal scores

Suppose you have developed a questionnaire/interview schedule to measure the attitudes of a class of students towards their lecturer using a scale with five categories.

In Figure 10.5, statement 1 is a positive statement; hence, if a respondent ticks 'strongly agree', s/he is assumed to have a more positive attitude on this item than a person who ticks 'agree'. The person who ticks 'agree' has a more positive attitude than a person who ticks 'uncertain', and so on. Therefore, a person who ticks 'strongly agree' has the most positive attitude compared with all of the others with different responses. Hence, the person is given the highest score, 5, as there are only five response categories. If there were four categories you could assign a score of 4. As a matter of fact, any score can be assigned as long as the intensity of the response pattern is reflected in the score and the highest score is assigned to the response with the highest intensity.

The lecturer:	SA	A	U	D	SD
1 Knows the subject well (+)	5	4	3	2	1
2 Is unenthusiastic about teaching (–)	1	2	3	4	5
3 Shows concern for students (+)	5	4	3	2	1
4 Makes unreasonable demands (–)	1	2	3	4	5
5 Has poor communication skill) (–)					
6 Knows how to teach (+)					
7 Can explain difficult concepts in simple terms (+)					
8 Is hard to approach (–)					
9 Is liked by some students and not by others (+/–)					
10 Is difficult to get along with (–)					
SA = strongly agree, A = agree, U = uncertain, D = disagree, SD = strongly disagree					

FIGURE 10.5   *Scoring positive and negative statements*

The lecturer:	SA	A	U	D	SD
1 Knows the subject well (+)	@				#
2 Is unenthusiastic about teaching (–)		#			@
3 Shows concern for students (+)			@		#
4 Makes unreasonable demands (–)		#			@
5 Communicates poorly (–)		#			@
6 Knows how to teach (+)			@	#	
7 Can explain difficult concepts in simple terms (+)	@	#			
8 Is hard to approach (–)			@#		
9 Is liked by some students and not by others (+/–)				@#	
10 Is difficult to get along with (–)			#		@
SA = strongly agree, A = agree, U = uncertain, D = disagree, SD = strongly disagree					

FIGURE 10.6   *Calculating an attitudinal score*

Statement 2 is a negative statement. In this case a person who ticks 'strongly disagree' has the most positive attitude on this item; hence, the highest score is assigned, 5. On the other hand, a respondent who ticks 'strongly agree' has the least positive attitude on the item and therefore is assigned the lowest score, 1. The same scoring system is followed for the other statements.

Note statement 9. There will always be some people who like a lecturer and some who do not; hence, this type of statement is neutral. There is no point in including such items in the scale but, here, for the purpose of this example, we have.

To illustrate how to calculate an individual's **attitudinal score**, let us take the example of two respondents who have ticked the different statements marked in our example by # and @ (see Figure 10.6).

Let us work out their attitudinal score:

Statement no.	1	2	3	4	5	6	7	8	9	10	
Respondent @ =	5 +	5 +	3 +	5 +	5 +	4 +	5 +	3 +	2 +	5	= 42
Respondent # =	1 +	2 +	1 +	2 +	2 +	2 +	4 +	3 +	2 +	3	= 20

The analysis shows that, overall, respondent @ has a 'more' positive attitude towards the lecturer than respondent #. You cannot say that the attitude of respondent @ is twice (42/20 = 2.10) as positive as that of respondent #. The attitudinal score only places respondents in a position relative to one another. Remember that the Likert scale does not measure the attitude per se, but helps you to rate a group of individuals in descending or ascending order with respect to their attitudes towards the issues in question.

The equal-appearing interval or Thurstone scale

Unlike the Likert scale, the **Thurstone scale** calculates a 'weight' or 'attitudinal value' for each statement. The weight (equivalent to the median value) for each statement is calculated on the basis of rating assigned by a group of judges. Each statement with which respondents express agreement (or to which they respond in the affirmative) is given an attitudinal score equivalent to the 'attitudinal value' of the statement. The procedure for constructing the Thurstone scale is as given in Figure 10.7.

Step 1   Assemble or construct statements reflective of attitudes towards the issue in question.
Step 2   Select a panel of judges who are experts in the field of the attitudes being explored.
Step 3   Send the statements to these judges with a request to rate each statement's importance in reflecting an attitude towards the issue being studied. Ask them to rate each statement on an 11-point scale.
Step 4   On the basis of the judges' ratings, calculate the median value of their ratings for each item.
Step 5   If the judges' ratings of any item are scattered over the scale, this indicates that, even among the experts, there is no agreement as to the degree to which that statement reflects an attitude towards the issue in question. Discard such statements.
Step 6   From the remaining statements select items that best reflect attitudes towards various aspects of the issue.
Step 7   Construct a questionnaire/interview schedule comprising the selected items.

FIGURE 10.7   *The procedure for constructing the Thurstone scale*

The main advantage of this scale is that, as the importance of each statement is determined by judges, it reflects the absolute rather than relative attitudes of respondents. The scale is thus able to indicate the intensity of people's attitudes and any change in this intensity should the study be replicated. On the other hand, the scale is difficult to construct, and a major criticism is that judges and respondents may assess the importance of a particular statement differently and, therefore, the respondents' attitudes might not be reflected.

The cumulative or Guttman scale

The **Guttman scale** is one of the most difficult scales to construct and therefore is rarely used. This scale does not have much relevance for beginners in research and so is not discussed in this book.

Attitudinal scales and measurement scales

Different **attitudinal scales** use different measurement scales. It is important to know which attitudinal scale belongs to which measurement scale as this will help you in the interpretation of respondents' scores. Table 10.1 shows attitudinal scales in relation to measurement scales.

TABLE 10.1   *The relationship between attitudinal and measurement scales*

Attitudinal scales	Measurement scales
Likert scale	Ordinal scale
Thurstone scale	Interval scale
Guttman scale	Ratio scale

Attitudes and qualitative research

As mentioned at the beginning of this chapter, in qualitative research you can only explore the spread of the attitudes. Whatever methods of data collection you use – in-depth interviewing, focus group, observation – you can explore the diversity in the attitudes but cannot find other aspects like: how many people have a particular attitude, the intensity of a particular attitude, or overall what the attitude of a person is. Qualitative methods are therefore best suited to explore the diversity in attitudes.

Summary

One of the significant differences between quantitative and qualitative research is in the availability of methods and procedures to measure attitudes. In quantitative research there are a number of methods that can be used to measure attitudes but qualitative research lacks methodology in this aspect primarily because its aim is to explain rather than to measure and quantify. Through qualitative research methodology you can find the diversity or spread of attitudes towards an issue but not their intensity and a combined overall indicator.

Attitudinal scales are used in quantitative research to measure attitudes towards an issue. Their strength lies in their ability to combine attitudes towards different aspects of an issue and to provide an indicator that is reflective of an overall attitude. However, there are problems in developing an attitudinal scale. You must decide which aspects should be included when measuring attitudes towards an issue, how the responses given by a respondent should be combined to ascertain the overall attitude, and how you can ensure that the scale developed really measures attitude towards the issue in question.

There are three types of scale that measure attitude: the Likert, Thurstone and Guttman scales. The Likert scale is most commonly used because it is easy to construct. The main assumption of the scale is that each statement is 'equally important'. The 'importance' of each item for the Thurstone scale is determined by a panel of judges.

For You to Think About

▸ Refamiliarise yourself with the keywords listed at the beginning of this chapter and if you are uncertain about the meaning or application of any of them revisit these in the chapter before moving on.
▸ Identify examples of how the Likert and Thurstone scales can be applied to research in your own academic field.
▸ Consider how you would go about developing a five-point Likert scale to measure the self-esteem of a group of university students, and the difficulties you might face in trying to do so.

CHAPTER 11
Establishing the Validity and Reliability of a Research Instrument

In this chapter you will learn about:

- The concept of validity
- Different types of validity in quantitative research
- The concept of reliability
- Factors affecting the reliability of a research instrument
- Methods of determining the reliability of an instrument in quantitative research
- Validity and reliability in qualitative research

Keywords: *concurrent validity, confirmability, construct validity, content validity, credibility, dependability, external consistency, face validity, internal consistency, reliability, transferability, validity.*

In the previous two chapters we discussed various methods of data collection in both quantitative and qualitative research. The questions asked of your respondents are the basis of your findings and conclusions. These questions constitute the 'input' for your conclusions (the 'output'). This input passes through a series of steps – the selection of a sample, the collection of information, the processing of data, the application of statistical procedures and the writing of a report – and the manner in which all of these are done can affect the accuracy and quality of your conclusions. Hence, it is important for you to attempt to establish the quality of your results. As a researcher you can also be asked by others to establish the appropriateness, quality and accuracy of the procedures you adopted for finding answers to your research questions. Broadly, this concept of appropriateness and accuracy as applied to a research process is called

validity. As inaccuracies can be introduced into a study at any stage, the concept of validity can be applied to the research process as a whole or to any of its steps: study design, sampling strategy, conclusions drawn, the statistical procedures applied or the measurement procedures used. Broadly, there are two perspectives on validity:

1 Is the research investigation providing answers to the research questions for which it was undertaken?
2 If so, is it providing these answers using appropriate methods and procedures?

In this chapter we will discuss the concept of validity as applied to measurement procedures or the research tools used to collect the required information from your respondents.

There are prominent differences between quantitative and qualitative research in relation to the concepts of validity and reliability. Because of the defined and established structures and methods of data collection in quantitative research, the concepts of validity and reliability and the methods to determine them are well developed. However, the same is not the case in qualitative research where it would be appropriate to say that these concepts cannot be rigorously applied in the same way as they are in quantitative research because of the flexibility, freedom and spontaneity given to a researcher in the methods and procedures of data collection. It becomes difficult to establish standardisation in the method(s) of data collection in qualitative research and, hence, their validity and reliability. Despite these difficulties there are some methods which have been proposed to establish validity and reliability in qualitative research which are detailed in this chapter.

The concept of validity

To examine the concept of validity, let us take a very simple example. Suppose you have designed a study to ascertain the health needs of a community. In doing so, you have developed an interview schedule. Further suppose that most of the questions in the interview schedule relate to the attitude of the study population towards the health services being provided to them. Note that your aim was to *find out about health needs* but the interview schedule is finding out what *attitudes respondents have to the health services*; thus, the instrument is not measuring what it was designed to measure. The author has come across many similar examples among students and less skilled researchers.

In terms of measurement procedures, therefore, validity is the ability of an instrument to measure what it is designed to measure: 'Validity is defined as the degree to which the researcher has measured what he has set out to measure' (Smith 1991: 106). According to Kerlinger, 'The commonest definition of validity is epitomised by the question: Are we measuring what we think we are measuring?' (1973: 457). Babbie writes, 'validity refers to the extent to which an empirical measure adequately reflects the real meaning of the concept under consideration' (1989: 133). These definitions raise two key questions:

• Who decides whether an instrument is measuring what it is supposed to measure?
• How can it be established that an instrument is measuring what it is supposed to measure?

Obviously the answer to the first question is the person who designed the study, the readership of the report and experts in the field. The second question is extremely important. On what basis do you (as a researcher), a reader as a consumer or an expert make this judgement? In the social sciences there appear to be two approaches to establishing the validity of a research instrument. These approaches are based upon either logic that underpins the construction of the research tool or statistical evidence that is gathered using information generated through the use of the instrument. Establishing validity through logic implies justification of each question in relation to the objectives of the study, whereas the statistical procedures provide hard evidence by way of calculating the coefficient of correlations between the questions and the outcome variables.

Establishing a logical link between the questions and the objectives is both simple and difficult. It is simple in the sense that you may find it easy to see a link for yourself, and difficult because your justification may lack the backing of experts and the statistical evidence to convince others. Establishing a logical link between questions and objectives is easier when the questions relate to tangible matters. For example, if you want to find out about age, income, height or weight, it is relatively easy to establish the validity of the questions, but to establish whether a set of questions is measuring, say, the effectiveness of a programme, the attitudes of a group of people towards an issue, or the extent of satisfaction of a group of consumers with the service provided by an organisation is more difficult. When a less tangible concept is involved, such as effectiveness, attitude or satisfaction, you need to ask several questions in order to cover different aspects of the concept and demonstrate that the questions asked are actually measuring it. Validity in such situations becomes more difficult to establish, and especially in qualitative research where you are mostly exploring feelings, experiences, perceptions, motivations or stories.

It is important to remember that the concept of validity is pertinent only to a particular instrument and it is an ideal state that you as a researcher aim to achieve.

Types of validity in quantitative research

There are three types of validity in quantitative research:

1 face and content validity;
2 concurrent and predictive validity;
3 construct validity.

Face and content validity

The judgement that an instrument is measuring what it is supposed to is primarily based upon the logical link between the questions and the objectives of the study. Hence, one of the main advantages of this type of validity is that it is easy to apply. Each question or item on the research instrument must have a logical link with an objective. Establishment of this link is called **face validity**. It is equally important that the items and questions cover the full range of the issue or attitude being measured. Assessment of the items of an instrument in this respect is called **content validity**. In addition, the coverage of the issue or attitude should be balanced; that is, each aspect should have similar and adequate representation in the questions or items. Content validity is also judged on the basis of the extent to which statements or questions represent the issue they are supposed to measure, as judged by you as a researcher, your readership and experts in the field. Although it is easy to present logical arguments to establish validity, there are certain problems:

- The judgement is based upon subjective logic; hence, no definite conclusions can be drawn. Different people may have different opinions about the face and content validity of an instrument.
- The extent to which questions reflect the objectives of a study may differ. If the researcher substitutes one question for another, the magnitude of the link may be altered. Hence, the validity or its extent may vary with the questions selected for an instrument.

Concurrent and predictive validity

'In situations where a scale is developed as an indicator of some observable criterion, the scale's validity can be investigated by seeing how good an indicator it is' (Moser & Kalton 1989: 356). Suppose you develop an instrument to determine the suitability of applicants for a profession. The instrument's validity might be determined by comparing it with another assessment, for example by a psychologist, or with a future observation of how well these applicants have done in the job. If both assessments are similar, the instrument used to make the assessment at the time of selection is assumed to have higher validity. These types of comparisons establish two types of validity: **predictive validity** and **concurrent validity**. Predictive validity is judged by the degree to which an instrument can forecast an outcome. Concurrent validity is judged by how well an instrument compares with a second assessment concurrently done: 'It is usually possible to express predictive validity in terms of the correlation coefficient between the predicted status and the criterion. Such a coefficient is called a validity coefficient' (Burns 1997: 220).

Construct validity

Construct validity is a more sophisticated technique for establishing the validity of an instrument. It is based upon statistical procedures. It is determined by ascertaining the contribution of each construct to the total variance observed in a phenomenon.

Suppose you are interested in carrying out a study to find the degree of job satisfaction among the employees of an organisation. You consider status, the nature of the job and remuneration as the three most important factors indicative of job satisfaction, and construct questions to ascertain the degree to which people consider each factor important for job satisfaction. After the pre-test or data analysis you use statistical procedures to establish the contribution of each construct (status, the nature of the job and remuneration) to the total variance (job satisfaction). The contribution of these factors to the total variance is an indication of the degree of validity of the instrument. The greater the variance attributable to the constructs, the higher the validity of the instrument.

One of the main disadvantages of construct validity is that you need to know about the required statistical procedures.

The concept of reliability

We use the word 'reliable' very often in our lives. When we say that a person is reliable, what do we mean? We infer that s/he is dependable, consistent, predictable, stable and honest.

The concept of **reliability** in relation to a research instrument has a similar meaning: if a research tool is consistent and stable, hence predictable and accurate, it is said to be reliable. The greater the degree of consistency and stability in an instrument, the greater its reliability. Therefore, 'a scale or test is reliable to the extent that repeat measurements made by it under constant conditions will give the same result' (Moser & Kalton 1989: 353).

The concept of reliability can be looked at from two sides:

1 How reliable is an instrument?
2 How unreliable is it?

The first question focuses on the ability of an instrument to produce consistent measurements. When you collect the same set of information more than once using the same instrument and get the same or similar results under the same or similar conditions, an instrument is considered to be reliable. The second question focuses on the degree of inconsistency in the measurements made by an instrument – that is, the extent of difference in the measurements when you collect the same set of information more than once, using the same instrument under the same or similar conditions. Hence, the degree of inconsistency in the different measurements is an indication of the extent of its inaccuracy. This 'error' is a reflection of an instrument's unreliability. Therefore, reliability is the degree of accuracy or precision in the measurements made by a research instrument. The lower the degree of 'error' in an instrument, the higher the reliability.

Let us take an example. Suppose you develop a questionnaire to ascertain the prevalence of domestic violence in a community. You administer this questionnaire and find that domestic violence is prevalent in, say, 5 per cent of households. If you follow this with another survey using the same questionnaire on the same population under the same conditions, and discover that the prevalence of domestic violence is, say, 15 per cent, the questionnaire has not given a comparable result, which may mean it is unreliable. The less the difference between the two sets of results, the higher the reliability of the instrument.

Factors affecting the reliability of a research instrument

In the social sciences it is impossible to have a research tool which is 100 per cent accurate, not only because a research instrument cannot be so, but also because it is impossible to control the factors affecting reliability. Some of these factors are:

- **The wording of questions** – A slight ambiguity in the wording of questions or statements can affect the reliability of a research instrument as respondents may interpret the questions differently at different times, resulting in different responses.
- **The physical setting** – In the case of an instrument being used in an interview, any change in the physical setting at the time of the repeat interview may affect the responses given by a respondent, which may affect reliability.
- **The respondent's mood** – A change in a respondent's mood when responding to questions or writing answers in a questionnaire can change and may affect the reliability of that instrument.
- **The interviewer's mood** – As the mood of a respondent could change from one interview to another so could the mood, motivation and interaction of the interviewer, which could affect the responses given by respondents thereby affecting the reliability of the research instrument.
- **The nature of interaction** – In an interview situation, the interaction between the interviewer and the interviewee can affect responses significantly. During the repeat interview the responses given may be different due to a change in interaction, which could affect reliability.
- **The regression effect of an instrument** – When a research instrument is used to measure attitudes towards an issue, some respondents, after having expressed their opinion, may feel that they have been either too negative or too positive towards the issue. The second time they may express their opinion differently, thereby affecting reliability.

Methods of determining the reliability of an instrument in quantitative research

There are a number of ways of determining the reliability of an instrument and these can be classified as either external or internal consistency procedures.

External consistency procedures

External consistency procedures compare findings from two independent processes of data collection with each other as a means of verifying the reliability of the measure. The two methods of doing this are as follows:

1 **Test/retest** - This is a commonly used method for establishing the reliability of a research tool. In the test/retest (repeatability test) an instrument is administered once, and then again, under the same or similar conditions. The ratio between the test and retest scores (or any other finding, for example the prevalence of domestic violence, a disease or incidence of an

illness) is an indication of the reliability of the instrument – the greater the value of the ratio, the higher the reliability of the instrument. As an equation,

(test score)/(retest) = 1

or

(test score) – (retest) = 0

A ratio of 1 shows 100 per cent reliability (no difference between test and retest) and any deviation from it indicates less reliability – the less the value of this ratio, the less the reliability of the instrument. Expressed in another way, zero difference between the test and retest scores is an indication of 100 per cent reliability. The greater the difference between scores or findings obtained from the two tests, the greater the unreliability of the instrument.

The main advantage of the test/retest procedure is that it permits the instrument to be compared with itself, thus avoiding the sort of problems that could arise with the use of another instrument.

The main disadvantage of this method is that a respondent may recall the responses that s/he gave in the first round, which in turn may affect the reliability of the instrument. Where an instrument is reactive in nature (when an instrument educates the respondent with respect to what the researcher is trying to find out) this method will not provide an accurate assessment of its reliability. One of the ways of overcoming this problem is to increase the time span between the two tests, but this may affect reliability for other reasons, such as the maturation of respondents and the impossibility of achieving conditions similar to those under which the questionnaire was first administered.

2 **Parallel forms of the same test** – In this procedure you construct two instruments that are intended to measure the same phenomenon. The two instruments are then administered to two similar populations. The results obtained from one test are compared with those obtained from the other. If they are similar, it is assumed that the instrument is reliable.

The main advantage of this procedure is that it does not suffer from the problem of recall found in the test/retest procedure. Also, a time lapse between the two tests is not required. A disadvantage is that you need to construct two instruments instead of one. Moreover, it is extremely difficult to construct two instruments that are comparable in their measurement of a phenomenon. It is equally difficult to achieve comparability in the two population groups and in the two conditions under which the tests are administered.

Internal consistency procedures

The idea behind internal consistency procedures is that items or questions measuring the same phenomenon, if they are reliable indicators, should produce similar results irrespective of their number in an instrument. Even if you randomly select a few items or questions out of the total pool to test the reliability of an instrument, each segment of questions thus constructed should reflect reliability more or less to the same extent. It is based upon the logic that if each item or question is an indicator of some aspect of a phenomenon, each segment constructed will still reflect different aspects of the phenomenon even though it is based upon fewer items/questions. Hence, even if we reduce the number of items or questions, as long as they reflect some aspect of a phenomenon, a lesser number of items can provide an indication of the reliability of an instrument. The internal consistency procedure is based upon this logic. The following method is commonly used for measuring the reliability of an instrument in this way:

- **The split-half technique** – This technique is designed to correlate half of the items with the other half and is appropriate for instruments that are designed to measure attitudes towards an issue or phenomenon. The questions or statements are divided in half in such a way that any two questions or statements intended to measure the same aspect fall into different halves. The scores obtained by administering the two halves are correlated. Reliability is calculated by using the product moment correlation (a statistical procedure) between scores obtained from the two halves. Because the product moment correlation is calculated on the basis of only half the instrument, it needs to be corrected to assess reliability for the whole. This is known as *stepped-up reliability*. The stepped-up reliability for the whole instrument is calculated by a formula called the Spearman–Brown formula (a statistical procedure).

Validity and reliability in qualitative research

One of the areas of difference between quantitative and qualitative research is in the use of and the importance given to the concepts of validity and reliability. The debate centres on whether or not, given the framework of qualitative research, these concepts can or even should be applied in qualitative research. As you know, validity in the broader sense refers to the ability of a research instrument to demonstrate that it is finding out what you designed it to and reliability refers to consistency in its findings when used repeatedly. In qualitative research, as answers to research questions are explored through multiple methods and procedures which are both flexible and evolving, to ensure standardisation of research tools as well as the processes becomes difficult. As a newcomer to research you may wonder how these concepts can be applied in qualitative research when it does not use standardised and structured methods and procedures which are the bases of testing validity and reliability as defined in quantitative research. You may ask how you can ascertain the ability of an instrument to measure what it is expected to and how consistent it is when the data collection questions are neither fixed nor structured.

However, there are some attempts to define and establish validity and reliability in qualitative research. In a chapter entitled 'Competing paradigms in qualitative research' (pp. 105–117) in the *Handbook of Qualitative Research*, edited by Denzin and Lincoln (1994), Guba and Lincoln have suggested a framework of four criteria as a part of the constructivism paradigm paralleling 'validity' and 'reliability' in quantitative research. According to them, there are two sets of criteria 'for judging the goodness or quality of an inquiry in constructivism paradigm' (1994: 114). These are: *'trustworthiness'* and *'authenticity'*. According to Guba and Lincoln, trustworthiness in a qualitative study is determined by four indicators – **credibility**, **transferability**,

dependability and **confirmability** – and it is these four indicators that reflect validity and reliability in qualitative research. 'The *trustworthiness* criteria of credibility (paralleling internal validity), transferability (paralleling external validity), dependability (paralleling reliability), and confirmability (paralleling objectivity)', according to Guba and Lincoln (1994: 114) closely relates to the concepts of validity and reliability.

Trochim and Donnelly (2007) compare the criteria proposed by Guba and Lincoln in the following table with validity and reliability as defined in quantitative research:

Traditional criteria for judging quantitative research	Alternative criteria for judging qualitative research
Internal Validity	Credibility
External Validity	Transferability
Reliability	Dependability
Objectivity	Confirmability

(Trochim and Donnelly 2007: 149)

- **Credibility** – According to Trochim and Donnelly (2007: 149), 'credibility involves establishing that the results of qualitative research are credible or believable from the perspective of the participant in the research'. As qualitative research studies explore perceptions, experiences, feelings and beliefs of the people, it is believed that the respondents are the best judge to determine whether or not the research findings have been able to reflect their opinions and feelings accurately. Hence, credibility, which is synonymous to validity in quantitative research, is judged by the extent of respondent concordance whereby you take your findings to those who participated in your research for confirmation, congruence, validation and approval. The higher the outcome of these, the higher the validity of the study.
- **Transferability** – This 'refers to the degree to which the results of qualitative research can be generalized or transferred to other contexts or settings' (2007: 149). Though it is very difficult to establish transferability primarily because of the approach you adopt in qualitative research, to some extent this can be achieved if you extensively and thoroughly describe the process you adopted for others to follow and replicate.
- **Dependability** – In the framework suggested by Guba and Lincoln this is very similar to the concept of reliability in quantitative research: 'It is concerned with whether we would obtain the same results if we could observe the same thing twice' (Trochim and Donnelly 2007: 149). Again, as qualitative research advocates flexibility and freedom, it may be difficult to establish unless you keep an extensive and detailed record of the process for others to replicate to ascertain the level of dependability.
- **Confirmability** – This 'refers to the degree to which the results could be confirmed or corroborated by others' (2007: 149). Confirmability is also similar to reliability in quantitative research. It is only possible if both researchers follow the process in an identical manner for the results to be compared.

To the author's mind, to some extent, it is possible to establish the 'validity' and 'reliability' of the findings in qualitative research in the form of the model suggested by Guba and Lincoln, but its success is mostly dependent upon the identical replication of the process and methods for data collection which may not be easy to achieve in qualitative research.

Summary

One of the differences in quantitative and qualitative research is in the use of and importance attached to the concepts of validity and reliability. These concepts, their use and methods of determination are more accepted and developed in quantitative than qualitative research. The concept of validity refers to a situation where the findings of your study are in accordance with what you designed it to find out. The notion of validity can be applied to any aspect of the research process. With respect to measurement procedures, it relates to whether a research instrument is measuring what it set out to measure. In quantitative research, there are two approaches used to establish the validity of an instrument: the establishment of a logical link between the objectives of a study and the questions used in an instrument, and the use of statistical analysis to demonstrate these links. There are three types of validity in quantitative research: face and content, concurrent and predictive, and construct validity. However, the use of the concept of validity in qualitative research is debatable and controversial. In qualitative research 'credibility' as described by Guba and Lincoln seems to be the only indicator of internal validity and is judged by the degree of respondent concordance with the findings. The methods used to establish 'validity' are different in quantitative and qualitative research.

The reliability of an instrument refers to its ability to produce consistent measurements each time. When we administer an instrument under the same or similar conditions to the same or similar population and obtain similar results, we say that the instrument is 'reliable' – the more similar the results, the greater the reliability. You can look at reliability from two sides: reliability (the extent of accuracy) and unreliability (the extent of inaccuracy). Ambiguity in the wording of questions, a change in the physical setting for data collection, a respondent's mood when providing information, the nature of the interaction between interviewer and interviewee, and the regressive effect of an instrument are factors that can affect the reliability of a research instrument. In qualitative research 'reliability' is measured through 'dependability' and 'confirmability' as suggested by Guba and Lincoln.

There are external and internal consistency procedures for determining reliability in quantitative research. Test/retest and parallel forms of the same test are the two procedures that determine the external reliability of a research instrument, whereas the split-half technique is classified under internal consistency procedures. There seem to be no set procedures for determining the various indicators of validity and reliability in qualitative research.

For You to Think About

▸ Refamiliarise yourself with the keywords listed at the beginning of this chapter and if you are uncertain about the meaning or application of any of them revisit these in the chapter before moving on.
▸ Explore how the concepts of reliability and validity are applicable to research in your academic field or profession.
▸ Consider what strategies or procedures you could put in place to limit the affect on reliability of the following factors:

   ▸ wording of questions;
   ▸ physical setting;
   ▸ respondent's mood;
   ▸ interviewer's mood;
   ▸ nature of interaction;
   ▸ regression effect of an instrument.

This operational step includes one chapter:

- Chapter 12:   Selecting a sample

STEP IV Selecting a Sample

CHAPTER 12
Selecting a Sample

In this chapter you will learn about:

- The differences between sampling in qualitative and quantitative research
- Definitions of sampling terminology
- The theoretical basis for sampling
- Factors affecting the inferences drawn from a sample
- Different types of sampling including:
  - Random/probability sampling designs
  - Non-random/non-probability sampling designs
  - The 'mixed' sampling design
- The calculation of sample size
- The concept of saturation point

Keywords: *accidental sampling, cluster sampling, data saturation point, disproportionate sampling, equal and independent, estimate, information-rich, judgemental sampling, multi-stage cluster sampling, non-random sample, population mean, population parameters, quota sampling, random numbers, random sample, sample statistics, sampling, sampling design, sampling element, sampling error, sampling frame, sampling population, sampling unit, sample size, sampling strategy, saturation point, snowball sampling, study population, stratified sampling, systematic sampling.*

The differences between sampling
in quantitative and qualitative research

The selection of a sample in quantitative and qualitative research is guided by two opposing philosophies. In quantitative research you attempt to select a sample in such a way that it is unbiased and represents the population from where it is selected. In qualitative research, number considerations may influence the selection of a sample such as: the ease in accessing the potential respondents; your judgement that the person has extensive knowledge about an episode, an event or a situation of interest to you; how typical the case is of a category of individuals or simply that it is totally different from the others. You make every effort to select either a case that is similar to the rest of the group or the one which is totally different. Such considerations are not acceptable in quantitative research.

The purpose of sampling in quantitative research is to draw inferences about the group from which you have selected the sample, whereas in qualitative research it is designed either to gain in-depth knowledge about a situation/event/episode or to know as much as possible about different aspects of an individual on the assumption that the individual is typical of the group and hence will provide insight into the group.

Similarly, the determination of sample size in quantitative and qualitative research is based upon the two different philosophies. In quantitative research you are guided by a predetermined sample size that is based upon a number of other considerations in addition to the resources available. However, in qualitative research you do not have a predetermined sample size but during the data collection phase you wait to reach a point of data saturation. When you are not getting new information or it is negligible, it is assumed you have reached a data saturation point and you stop collecting additional information.

Considerable importance is placed on the sample size in quantitative research, depending upon the type of study and the possible use of the findings. Studies which are designed to formulate policies, to test associations or relationships, or to establish impact assessments place a considerable emphasis on large sample size. This is based upon the principle that a larger sample size will ensure the inclusion of people with diverse backgrounds, thus making the sample representative of the study population. The sample size in qualitative research does not play any significant role as the purpose is to study only one or a few cases in order to identify the spread of diversity and not its magnitude. In such situations the data saturation stage during data collection determines the sample size.

In quantitative research, randomisation is used to avoid bias in the selection of a sample and is selected in such a way that it represents the study population. In qualitative research no such attempt is made in selecting a sample. You purposely select 'information-rich' respondents who will provide you with the information you need. In quantitative research, this is considered a biased sample.

Most of the sampling strategies, including some non-probability ones, described in this chapter can be used when undertaking a quantitative study provided it meets the requirements. However, when conducting a qualitative study only the non-probability sampling designs can be used.

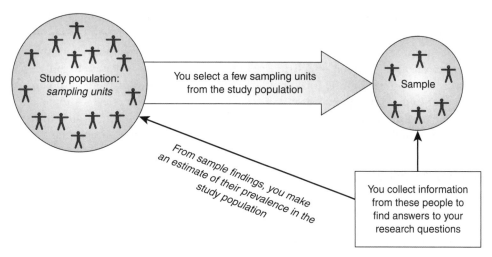

FIGURE 12.1 *The concept of sampling*

Sampling in quantitative research

The concept of sampling

Let us take a very simple example to explain the concept of sampling. Suppose you want to estimate the average age of the students in your class. There are two ways of doing this. The first method is to contact all students in the class, find out their ages, add them up and then divide this by the number of students (the procedure for calculating an average). The second method is to select a few students from the class, ask them their ages, add them up and then divide by the number of students you have asked. From this you can make an *estimate* of the average age of the class. Similarly, suppose you want to find out the average income of families living in a city. Imagine the amount of effort and resources required to go to every family in the city to find out their income! You could instead select a few families to become the basis of your enquiry and then, from what you have found out from the few families, make an estimate of the average income of families in the city. Similarly, election opinion polls can be used. These are based upon a very small group of people who are questioned about their voting preferences and, on the basis of these results, a *prediction* is made about the probable outcome of an election.

Sampling, therefore, is the process of selecting a few (a sample) from a bigger group (the **sampling population**) to become the basis for estimating or predicting the prevalence of an unknown piece of information, situation or outcome regarding the bigger group. A sample is a subgroup of the population you are interested in. See Figure 12.1.

This process of selecting a sample from the total population has advantages and disadvantages. The advantages are that it saves time as well as financial and human resources. However, the disadvantage is that you *do not find out the information* about the population's characteristics of interest to you but *only estimate* or *predict* them. Hence, the possibility of an error in your estimation exists.

Sampling, therefore, is a trade-off between certain benefits and disadvantages. While on the one hand you save time and resources, on the other hand you may compromise the level of accuracy in your findings. Through sampling you only make an estimate about the actual situation prevalent in the total population from which the sample is drawn. If you ascertain a piece of information from the total sampling population, and if your method of enquiry is correct, your findings should be reasonably accurate. However, if you select a sample and use this as the basis from which to estimate the situation in the total population, an error is possible. Tolerance of this possibility of error is an important consideration in selecting a sample.

Sampling terminology

Let us, again, consider the examples used above where our main aims are to find out the average age of the class, the average income of the families living in the city and the likely election outcome for a particular state or country. Let us assume that you adopt the sampling method – that is, you select a few students, families or electorates to achieve these aims. In this process there are a number of aspects:

- The class, families living in the city or electorates from which you select you select your sample are called the *population* or **study population**, and are usually denoted by the letter *N*.
- The small group of students, families or electors from whom you collect the required information to estimate the average age of the class, average income or the election outcome is called the **sample**.
- The number of students, families or electors from whom you obtain the required information is called the **sample size** and is usually denoted by the letter *n*.
- The way you select students, families or electors is called the **sampling design** or **sampling strategy**.
- Each student, family or elector that becomes the basis for selecting your sample is called the **sampling unit** or **sampling element**.
- A list identifying each student, family or elector in the study population is called the **sampling frame**. If all elements in a sampling population cannot be individually identified, you cannot have a sampling frame for that study population.
- Your findings based on the information obtained from your respondents (sample) are called **sample statistics.** Your sample statistics become the basis of estimating the prevalence of the above characteristics in the study population.
- Your main aim is to find answers to your research questions in the study population, not in the sample you collected information from. From sample statistics we make an estimate of the answers to our research questions in the study population. The estimates arrived at from sample statistics are called *population parameters* or the **population mean**.

Principles of sampling

The theory of sampling is guided by three principles. To effectively explain these, we will take an extremely simple example. Suppose there are four individuals A, B, C and D. Further suppose that A is 18 years of age, B is 20, C is 23 and D is 25. As you know their ages, you can *find out* (calculate) their average age by simply adding 18 + 20 + 23 + 25 = 86 and dividing by 4. This gives the average (mean) age of A, B, C and D as 21.5 years.

Now let us suppose that you want to select a sample of two individuals to make an *estimate* of the average age of the four individuals. To select an unbiased sample, we need to make sure that each unit has an equal and independent chance of selection in the sample. **Randomisation** is a process that enables you to achieve this. In order to achieve randomisation we use the theory of probability in forming pairs which will provide us with six possible combinations of two: A and B; A and C; A and D; B and C; B and D; and C and D. Let us take each of these pairs to calculate the average age of the sample:

1 A + B = 18 + 20 = 38/2 = 19.0 years;
2 A + C = 18 + 23 = 41/2 = 20.5 years;
3 A + D = 18 + 25 = 43/2 = 21.5 years;
4 B + C = 20 + 23 = 43/2 = 21.5 years;
5 B + D = 20 + 25 = 45/2 = 22.5 years;
6 C + D = 23 + 25 = 48/2 = 24.0 years.

Notice that in most cases the average age calculated on the basis of these samples of two (sample statistics) is different. Now compare these sample statistics with the average of all four individuals – the population mean (population parameter) of 21.5 years. Out of a total of six possible sample combinations, only in the case of two is there no difference between the sample statistics and the population mean. Where there is a difference, this is attributed to the sample and is known as **sampling error**. Again, the size of the sampling error varies markedly. Let us consider the difference in the sample statistics and the population mean for each of the six samples (Table 12.1).

TABLE 12.1 *The difference between sample statistics and the population mean*

Sample	Sample average (sample statistics) (1)	Population mean (population parameter) (2)	Difference between (1) and (2)
1	19.0	21.5	−2.5
2	20.5	21.5	−1.5
3	21.5	21.5	0.0
4	21.5	21.5	0.0
5	22.5	21.5	+1.0
6	24.0	21.5	+2.5

This analysis suggests a very important principle of sampling:

Principle 1 – in a majority of cases of sampling there will be a difference between the sample statistics and the true population mean, which is attributable to the selection of the units in the sample.

To understand the second principle, let us continue with the above example, but instead of a sample of two individuals we take a sample of three. There are four possible combinations of three that can be drawn:

1 A + B + C = 18 + 20 + 23 = 61/3 = 20.33 years;
2 A + B + D = 18 + 20 + 25 = 63/3 = 21.00 years;
3 A + C + D = 18 + 23 + 25 = 66/3 = 22.00 years;
4 B + C + D = 20 + 23 + 25 = 68/3 = 22.67 years.

Now, let us compare the difference between the sample statistics and the population mean (Table 12.2).

TABLE 12.2 *The difference between a sample and a population average*

Sample	Sample average (1)	Population average (2)	Difference between (1) and (2)
1	20.33	21.5	−1.17
2	21.00	21.5	−0.5
3	22.00	21.5	+0.5
4	22.67	21.5	+1.17

Compare the differences calculated in Table 12.1 and Table 12.2. In Table 12.1 the difference between the sample statistics and the population mean lies between −2.5 and +2.5 years, whereas in the second it is between −1.17 and +1.17 years. The gap between the sample statistics and the population mean is reduced in Table 12.2. This reduction is attributed to the increase in the sample size. This, therefore, leads to the second principle:

Principle 2 – the greater the sample size, the more accurate the estimate of the true population mean.

The third principle of sampling is particularly important as a number of sampling strategies, such as stratified and cluster sampling, are based on it. To understand this principle, let us continue with the same example but use slightly different data. Suppose the ages of four individuals are markedly different: A = 18, B = 26, C = 32 and D = 40. In other words, we are visualising a population where the individuals with respect to age – the variable we are interested in – are markedly different.

Let us follow the same procedure, selecting samples of two individuals at a time and then three. If we work through the same procedures (described above) we will find that the difference in the average age in the case of samples of two ranges between −7.00 and + 7.00 years and in the case of the sample of three ranges between −3.67 and +3.67. In both cases the range of the difference is greater than previously calculated. This is attributable to the greater difference in the ages of the four individuals – the sampling population. In other words, the sampling population is more heterogeneous (varied or diverse) in regard to age.

Principle 3 – the greater the difference in the variable under study in a population for a given sample size, the greater the difference between the sample statistics and the true population mean.

These principles are crucial to keep in mind when you are determining the sample size needed for a particular level of accuracy, and in selecting the sampling strategy best suited to your study.

Factors affecting the inferences drawn from a sample

The above principles suggest that two factors may influence the degree of certainty about the inferences drawn from a sample:

1 **The size of the sample** – Findings based upon larger samples have more certainty than those based on smaller ones. As a rule, *the larger the sample size, the more accurate the findings*.
2 **The extent of variation in the sampling population** – The greater the variation in the study population with respect to the characteristics under study, for a given sample size, the greater the uncertainty. (In technical terms, the greater the standard deviation, the higher the standard error for a given sample size in your estimates.) If a population is homogeneous (uniform or similar) with respect to the characteristics under study, a small sample can provide a reasonably good estimate, but if it is heterogeneous (dissimilar or diversified), you need to select a larger sample to obtain the same level of accuracy. Of course, if all the elements in a population are identical, then the selection of even one will provide an absolutely accurate estimate. As a rule, *the higher the variation with respect to the characteristics under study in the study population, the greater the uncertainty for a given sample size*.

Aims in selecting a sample

When you select a sample in quantitative studies you are primarily aiming to achieve maximum precision in your estimates within a given sample size, and avoid bias in the selection of your sample.

Bias in the selection of a sample can occur if:

- sampling is done by a non-random method – that is, if the selection is consciously or unconsciously influenced by human choice;
- the sampling frame – list, index or other population records – which serves as the basis of selection, does not cover the sampling population accurately and completely;
- a section of a sampling population is impossible to find or refuses to co-operate.

Types of sampling

The various sampling strategies in quantitative research can be categorised as follows (Figure 12.2):

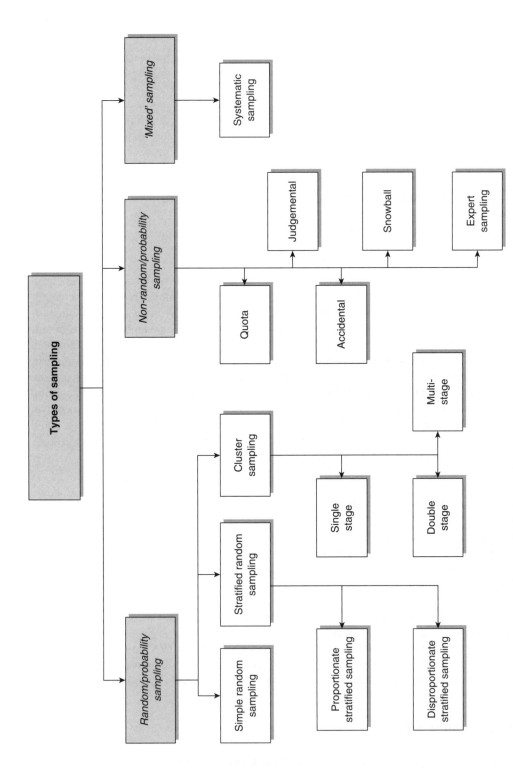

FIGURE 12.2   Types of sampling in quantitative research

- random/probability sampling designs;
- non-random/non-probability sampling designs selecting a predetermined sample size;
- 'mixed' sampling design.

To understand these designs, we will discuss each type individually.

Random/probability sampling designs

For a design to be called **random sampling** or **probability sampling**, it is imperative that each element in the population has an *equal* and *independent* chance of selection in the sample. Equal implies that the probability of selection of each element in the population is the same; that is, the choice of an element in the sample is not influenced by other considerations such as personal preference. The concept of independence means that the choice of one element is not dependent upon the choice of another element in the sampling; that is, the selection or rejection of one element does not affect the inclusion or exclusion of another. To explain these concepts let us return to our example of the class.

Suppose there are 80 students in the class. Assume 20 of these refuse to participate in your study. You want the entire population of 80 students in your study but, as 20 refuse to participate, you can only use a sample of 60 students. The 20 students who refuse to participate could have strong feelings about the issues you wish to explore, but your findings will not reflect their opinions. Their exclusion from your study means that each of the 80 students does not have an equal chance of selection. Therefore, your sample does not represent the total class.

The same could apply to a community. In a community, in addition to the refusal to participate, let us assume that you are unable to identify all the residents living in the community. If a significant proportion of people cannot be included in the sampling population because they either cannot be identified or refuse to participate, then any sample drawn will not give each element in the sampling population an equal chance of being selected in the sample. Hence, the sample will not be representative of the total community.

To understand the concept of an *independent chance of selection*, let us assume that there are five students in the class who are extremely close friends. If one of them is selected but refuses to participate because the other four are not chosen, and you are therefore forced to select either the five or none, then your sample will not be considered an independent sample since the selection of one is dependent upon the selection of others. The same could happen in the community where a small group says that either all of them or none of them will participate in the study. In these situations where you are forced either to include or to exclude a part of the sampling population, the sample is not considered to be independent, and hence is not representative of the sampling population. However, if the number of refusals is fairly small, in practical terms, it should not make the sample non-representative. In practice there are always some people who do not want to participate in the study but you only need to worry if the number is significantly large.

A sample can only be considered a random/probability sample (and therefore representative of the population under study) if both these conditions are met. Otherwise, bias can be introduced into the study.

There are two main advantages of random/probability samples:

1 As they represent the total sampling population, the inferences drawn from such samples can be generalised to the total sampling population.
2 Some statistical tests based upon the theory of probability can be applied only to data collected from random samples. Some of these tests are important for establishing conclusive correlations.

Methods of drawing a random sample

Of the methods that you can adopt to select a random sample the three most common are:

1 **The fishbowl draw** – if your total population is small, an easy procedure is to number each element using separate slips of paper for each element, put all the slips into a box and then pick them out one by one without looking, until the number of slips selected equals the sample size you decided upon. This method is used in some lotteries.
2 **Computer program** – there are a number of programs that can help you to select a random sample.
3 **A table of randomly generated numbers** – most books on research methodology and statistics include a table of randomly generated numbers in their appendices (see, e.g., Table 12.3). You can select your sample using these tables according to the procedure described in Figure 12.3.

The procedure for selecting a sample using a **table of random numbers** is as follows:

Let us take an example to illustrate the use of Table 12.3 for random numbers. Let us assume that your sampling population consists of 256 individuals. Number each individual from 1 to 256. Randomly select the starting page, set of column (1 to 10) or row from the table and then identify three columns or rows of numbers.

Suppose you identify the ninth column of numbers and the last three digits of this column (underlined). Assume that you are selecting 10 per cent of the total population as your sample (25 elements). Let us go through the numbers underlined in the ninth set of columns. The first number is 049 which is below 256 (total population); hence, the 49th element becomes a part of your sample. The second number, 319, is more than the total elements in your population (256); hence, you cannot accept the 319th element in the sample. The same applies to the next element, 758, and indeed the next five elements, 589, 507, 483, 487 and 540. After 540 is 232, and as this number is within the sampling frame, it can be accepted as a part of the sample. Similarly, if you follow down the same three digits in the same column, you select 052, 029, 065, 246 and 161, before you come to the element 029 again. As the 29th element has already been selected, go to the next number, and so on until 25 elements have been chosen. Once you have reached the end of a column, you can either move to the next set of columns or randomly select another one in order to continue the process of selection. For example, the 25 elements shown in Table 12.4 are selected from the ninth, tenth and second columns of Table 12.3.

TABLE 12.3 *Selecting a sample using a table for random numbers*

	1	2	3	4	5	6	7	8	9	10
1	48461	14952	72619	73689	52059	37086	60050	86192	67049	64739
2	76534	38149	49692	31366	52093	15422	20498	33901	10319	43397
3	70437	25861	38504	14752	23757	29660	67844	78815	23758	86814
4	59584	03370	42806	11393	71722	93804	09095	07856	55589	46820
5	04285	58554	16085	51555	27501	73883	33427	33343	45507	50063
6	77340	10412	69189	85171	29802	44785	86368	02583	96483	76553
7	59183	62687	91778	80354	23512	97219	65921	02035	59487	91403
8	91800	04281	39979	03927	82564	28777	59049	97532	54540	79472
9	12066	24817	81099	48940	69554	55925	48379	12866	41232	21580
10	69907	91751	53512	23748	65906	91385	84983	27915	48491	91068
11	80467	04873	54053	25955	48518	13815	37707	68687	15570	08890
12	78057	67835	28302	45048	56761	97725	58438	91529	24645	18544
13	05648	39387	78191	88415	60269	94880	58812	42931	71898	61534
14	22304	39246	01350	99451	61862	78688	30339	60222	74052	25740
15	61346	50269	67005	40442	33100	16742	61640	21046	31909	72641
16	56793	37696	27965	30459	91011	51426	31006	77468	61029	57108
17	56411	48609	36698	42453	85061	43769	39948	87031	30767	13953
18	62098	12825	81744	28882	27369	88185	65846	92545	09065	22653
19	68775	06261	54265	16203	23340	84750	16317	88686	86842	00879
20	52679	19599	13687	74872	89181	01939	18447	10787	76246	80072
21	84096	87152	20719	25215	04349	54434	72344	93008	83282	31670
22	83964	55937	21417	49944	38356	98404	14850	17994	17161	98981
23	31191	75131	72386	11689	95727	05414	88727	45583	22568	77700
24	30545	68523	29850	67833	05622	89975	79042	27142	99257	32349
25	52573	91001	52315	26430	54175	30122	31796	98842	37600	26025
26	16586	81842	01076	99414	31574	94719	34656	80018	86988	79234
27	81841	88481	61191	25013	30272	23388	22463	65774	10029	58376
28	43563	66829	72838	08074	57080	15446	11034	98143	74989	26885
29	19945	84193	57581	77252	85604	45412	43556	27518	90572	00563
30	79374	23796	16919	99691	80276	32818	62953	78831	54395	30705
31	48503	26615	43980	09810	38289	66679	73799	48418	12647	40044
32	32049	65541	37937	41105	70106	89706	40829	40789	59547	00783
33	18547	71562	95493	34112	76895	46766	96395	31718	48302	45893
34	03180	96742	61486	43305	84183	99605	67803	13491	09243	29557
35	94822	24738	67749	83748	59799	25210	31093	62925	72061	69991
36	04330	60599	85828	19152	68499	27977	35611	96240	62747	89529
37	43770	81537	59527	95674	76692	86420	69930	10020	72881	12532
38	56908	77192	50623	41215	14311	42834	80651	93750	59957	31211
39	32787	07189	80539	75927	75475	73965	11796	72140	48944	74156
40	52441	78392	11733	57703	29133	71164	55355	31006	25526	55790
41	22377	54723	18227	28449	04570	18882	00023	67101	06895	08915
42	18376	73460	88841	39602	34049	20589	05701	08249	74213	25220
43	53201	28610	87957	21497	64729	64983	71551	99016	87903	63875
44	34919	78801	59710	27396	02593	05665	11964	44134	00273	76358
45	33617	92159	21971	16901	57383	34262	41744	60891	57624	06962
46	70010	40964	98780	72418	52571	18415	64362	90637	38034	04909
47	19282	68447	35665	31530	59838	49181	21914	65742	89815	39231
48	91429	73328	13266	54898	68795	40948	80808	63887	89939	47938
49	97637	78393	33021	05867	86520	45363	43066	00988	64040	09803
50	95150	07625	05255	83254	93943	52325	93230	62668	79529	66964

Source: Statistical Tables, 3e, by F. James Rohlf and Robert R. Sokal. Copyright © 1969, 1981, 1994 by W.H. Freeman and Company. Used with permission.

Step 1	Identify the total number of elements in the study population, for example 50, 100, 430, 795 or 1265. The total number of elements in a study population may run up to four or more digits (if your total sampling population is 9 or less, it is one digit; if it is 99 or less, it is two digits; …).
Step 2	Number each element starting from 1.
Step 3	If the table for random numbers is on more than one page, choose the starting page by a random procedure. Again, select a column or row that will be your starting point with a random procedure and proceed from there in a predetermined direction.
Step 4	Corresponding to the number of digits to which the total population runs, select the same number, randomly, of columns or rows of digits from the table.
Step 5	Decide on your sample size.
Step 6	Select the required number of elements for your sample from the table. If you happen to select the same number twice, discard it and go to the next. This can happen as the table for random numbers is generated by sampling with replacement.

FIGURE 12.3   *The procedure for using a table of random numbers*

TABLE 12.4   *Selected elements using the table of random numbers*

Column in Table 12.3	Elements selected				
9	49 246 34	232 161 40	52 243	29 61	65 213
10	63 234 231	68 44	108 211	72 156	25 220
2	149	246			

Sampling with or without replacement

Random sampling can be selected using two different systems:

1 sampling without replacement;
2 sampling with replacement.

Suppose you want to select a sample of 20 students out of a total of 80. The first student is selected out of the total class, and so the probability of selection for the first student is 1/80. When you select the second student there are only 79 left in the class and the probability of selection for the second student is not 1/80 but 1/79. The probability of selecting the next student is 1/78. By the time you select the 20th student, the probability of his/her selection is 1/61. This type of sampling is called **sampling without replacement**. But this is contrary to our basic definition of randomisation; that is, each element has an equal and independent chance of selection. In the second system, called **sampling with replacement**, the selected

Step 1   Identify by a number all elements or sampling units in the population.

Step 2   Decide on the sample size *n*.

Step 3   Select *n* using the fishbowl draw, the table of random numbers or a computer program.

FIGURE 12.4   *The procedure for selecting a simple random sample*

element is replaced in the sampling population and if it is selected again, it is discarded and the next one is selected. If the sampling population is fairly large, the probability of selecting the same element twice is fairly remote.

Specific random/probability sampling designs

There are three commonly used types of random sampling design.

1 **Simple random sampling (SRS)** – The most commonly used method of selecting a probability sample. In line with the definition of randomisation, whereby each element in the population is given an equal and independent chance of selection, a simple random sample is selected by the procedure presented in Figure 12.4.

   To illustrate, let us again take our example of the class. There are 80 students in the class, and so the first step is to identify each student by a number from 1 to 80. Suppose you decide to select a sample of 20 using the simple random sampling technique. Use the fishbowl draw, the table for random numbers or a computer program to select the 20 students. These 20 students become the basis of your enquiry.

2 **Stratified random sampling** – As discussed, the accuracy of your estimate largely depends on the extent of variability or heterogeneity of the study population with respect to the characteristics that have a strong correlation with what you are trying to ascertain (Principle 3). It follows, therefore, that if the heterogeneity in the population can be reduced by some means for a given sample size you can achieve greater accuracy in your estimate. Stratified random sampling is based upon this logic.

   In stratified random sampling the researcher attempts to stratify the population in such a way that the population within a stratum is homogeneous with respect to the characteristic on the basis of which it is being stratified. It is important that the characteristics chosen as the basis of stratification are clearly identifiable in the study population. For example, it is much easier to stratify a population on the basis of gender than on the basis of age, income or attitude. It is also important for the characteristic that becomes the basis of stratification to be related to the main variable that you are exploring. Once the sampling population has been separated into non-overlapping groups, you select the required number of elements from each stratum, using the simple random sampling technique. There are two types of stratified sampling: **proportionate stratified sampling** and **disproportionate stratified sampling**. With proportionate stratified sampling, the number of elements from each stratum in relation to its proportion in the total population is selected, whereas in disproportionate stratified sampling, consideration is not given to the size of the stratum. The procedure for selecting a stratified sample is schematically presented in Figure 12.5.

FIGURE 12.5 *The procedure for selecting a stratified sample*

3 **Cluster sampling** – Simple random and stratified sampling techniques are based on a researcher's ability to identify each element in a population. It is easy to do this if the total sampling population is small, but if the population is large, as in the case of a city, state or country, it becomes difficult and expensive to identify each sampling unit. In such cases the use of cluster sampling is more appropriate.

Cluster sampling is based on the ability of the researcher to divide the sampling population into groups (based upon visible or easily identifiable characteristics), called clusters, and then to select elements within each cluster, using the SRS technique. Clusters can be formed on the basis of geographical proximity or a common characteristic that has a correlation with the main variable of the study (as in stratified sampling). Depending on the level of clustering, sometimes sampling may be done at different levels. These levels constitute the different stages (single, double or multiple) of clustering, which will be explained later.

Imagine you want to investigate the attitude of post-secondary students in Australia towards problems in higher education in the country. Higher education institutions are in

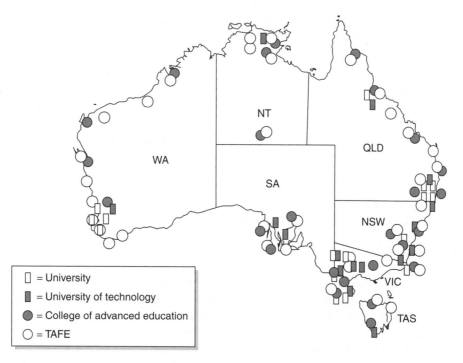

FIGURE 12.6   *The concept of cluster sampling*

every state and territory of Australia. In addition, there are different types of institutions, for example universities, universities of technology, colleges of advanced education and colleges of technical and further education (TAFE) (Figure 12.6). Within each institution various courses are offered at both undergraduate and postgraduate levels. Each academic course could take three to four years. You can imagine the magnitude of the task. In such situations cluster sampling is extremely useful in selecting a random sample.

The first level of cluster sampling could be at the state or territory level. Clusters could be grouped according to similar characteristics that ensure their comparability in terms of student population. If this is not easy, you may decide to select all the states and territories and then select a sample at the institutional level. For example, with a simple random technique, one institution from each category within each state could be selected (one university, one university of technology and one TAFE college). This is based upon the assumption that institutions within a category are fairly similar with regards to student profile. Then, within an institution on a random basis, one or more academic programmes could be selected, depending on resources. Within each study programme selected, students studying in a particular year could then be selected. Further, selection of a proportion of students studying in a particular year could then be made using the SRS technique. The process of selecting a sample in this manner is called *multi-stage cluster sampling*.

Non-random/non-probability sampling designs in quantitative research

Non-probability sampling designs do not follow the theory of probability in the choice of elements from the sampling population. Non-probability sampling designs are used when the number of elements in a population is either unknown or cannot be individually identified. In such situations the selection of elements is dependent upon other considerations. There are five commonly used non-random designs, each based on a different consideration, which are commonly used in both qualitative and quantitative research. These are:

1 **quota sampling;**
2 **accidental sampling;**
3 **judgemental sampling** or **purposive sampling;**
4 **expert sampling;**
5 **snowball sampling.**

What differentiates these designs being treated as quantitative or qualitative is the predetermined sample size. In quantitative research you use these designs to select a predetermined number of cases (sample size), whereas in qualitative research you do not decide the number of respondents in advance but continue to select additional cases till you reach the data saturation point. In addition, in qualitative research, you will predominantly use judgemental and accidental sampling strategies to select your respondents. Expert sampling is very similar to judgemental sampling except that in expert sampling the sampling population comprises experts in the field of enquiry. You can also use quota and snowball sampling in qualitative research but without having a predetermined number of cases in mind (sample size).

Quota sampling

The main consideration directing quota sampling is the researcher's ease of access to the sample population. In addition to convenience, you are guided by some visible characteristic, such as gender or race, of the study population that is of interest to you. The sample is selected from a location convenient to you as a researcher, and whenever a person with this visible relevant characteristic is seen that person is asked to participate in the study. The process continues until you have been able to contact the required number of respondents (quota).

Let us suppose that you want to select a sample of 20 male students in order to find out the average age of the male students in your class. You decide to stand at the entrance to the classroom, as this is convenient, and whenever a male student enters the classroom, you ask his age. This process continues until you have asked 20 students their age. Alternatively, you might want to find out about the attitudes of Aboriginal and Torres Strait Islander students towards the facilities provided to them in your university. You might stand at a convenient location and, whenever you see such a student, collect the required information through whatever method of data collection (such as interviewing, questionnaire) you have adopted for the study.

The advantages of using this design are: it is the least expensive way of selecting a sample; you do not need any information, such as a sampling frame, the total number of elements, their location, or other information about the sampling population; and it guarantees the inclusion of the type of people you need. The disadvantages are: as the resulting sample is not a probability one, the findings cannot be generalised to the total sampling population; and the most accessible individuals might have characteristics that are unique to them and hence might not be truly representative of the total sampling population. You can make your sample more representative of your study population by selecting it from various locations where people of interest to you are likely to be available.

Accidental sampling

Accidental sampling is also based upon convenience in accessing the sampling population. Whereas quota sampling attempts to include people possessing an obvious/visible characteristic, accidental sampling makes no such attempt. You stop collecting data when you reach the required number of respondents you decided to have in your sample.

This method of sampling is common among market research and newspaper reporters. It has more or less the same advantages and disadvantages as quota sampling but, in addition, as you are not guided by any obvious characteristics, some people contacted may not have the required information.

Judgemental or purposive sampling

The primary consideration in purposive sampling is your judgement as to who can provide the best information to achieve the objectives of your study. You as a researcher only go to those people who in your opinion are likely to have the required information and be willing to share it with you.

This type of sampling is extremely useful when you want to construct a historical reality, describe a phenomenon or develop something about which only a little is known. This sampling strategy is more common in qualitative research, but when you use it in quantitative research you select a predetermined number of people who, in your judgement, are best positioned to provide you the needed information for your study.

Expert sampling

The only difference between judgemental sampling and expert sampling is that in the case of the former it is entirely your judgement as to the ability of the respondents to contribute to the study. But in the case of expert sampling, your respondents must be known experts in the field of interest to you. This is again used in both types of research but more so in qualitative research studies. When you use it in qualitative research, the number of people you talk to is dependent upon the data saturation point whereas in quantitative research you decide on the number of experts to be contacted without considering the saturation point.

You first identify persons with demonstrated or known expertise in an area of interest to you, seek their consent for participation, and then collect the information either individually or collectively in the form of a group.

FIGURE 12.7   *Snowball sampling*

Snowball sampling

Snowball sampling is the process of selecting a sample using networks. To start with, a few individuals in a group or organisation are selected and the required information is collected from them. They are then asked to identify other people in the group or organisation, and the people selected by them become a part of the sample. Information is collected from them, and then these people are asked to identify other members of the group and, in turn, those identified become the basis of further data collection (Figure 12.7). This process is continued until the required number or a **saturation point** has been reached, in terms of the information being sought.

This sampling technique is useful if you know little about the group or organisation you wish to study, as you need only to make contact with a few individuals, who can then direct you to the other members of the group. This method of selecting a sample is useful for studying communication patterns, decision making or diffusion of knowledge within a group. There are disadvantages to this technique, however. The choice of the entire sample rests upon the choice of individuals at the first stage. If they belong to a particular faction or have strong biases, the study may be biased. Also, it is difficult to use this technique when the sample becomes fairly large.

Systematic sampling design: a 'mixed' design

Systematic sampling has been classified as a 'mixed' sampling design because it has the characteristics of both random and non-random sampling designs.

In systematic sampling the sampling frame is first divided into a number of segments called *intervals*. Then, from the first interval, using the SRS technique, one element is selected. The selection of subsequent elements from other intervals is dependent upon the order of the element selected in the first interval. If in the first interval it is the fifth element, the fifth element of each subsequent interval will be chosen. Notice that from the first interval the choice of an element is on a random basis, but the choice of the elements from subsequent intervals is dependent upon the choice from the first, and hence cannot be classified as a random sample. The procedure used in systematic sampling is presented in Figure 12.8.

Step 1   Prepare a list of all the elements in the study population (*N*).

Step 2   Decide on the sample size (*n*).

Step 3   Determine the *width of the interval* (*k*) = $\dfrac{\text{total population}}{\text{sample size}}$

Step 4   Using the SRS, select an element from the first interval (*n*th order).

Step 5   Select the same order element from each subsequent interval.

FIGURE 12.8   *The procedure for selecting a systematic sample*

Although the general procedure for selecting a sample by the systematic sampling technique is described above, you can deviate from it by selecting a different element from each interval with the SRS technique. By adopting this, systematic sampling can be classified under probability sampling designs.

To select a random sample you must have a sampling frame (Figure 12.9). Sometimes this is impossible, or obtaining one may be too expensive. However, in real life there are situations where a kind of sampling frame exists, for example records of clients in an agency, enrolment lists of students in a school or university, electoral lists of people living in an area, or records of the staff employed in an organisation. All these can be used as a sampling frame to select a sample with the systematic sampling technique. This convenience of having a 'ready-made' sampling frame may be at a price: in some cases it may not truly be a random listing. Mostly these lists are in alphabetical order, based upon a number assigned to a case, or arranged in a way that is convenient to the users of the records. If the 'width of an interval' is large, say, 1 in 30 cases, and if the cases are arranged in alphabetical order, you could preclude some whose surnames start with the same letter or some adjoining letter may not be included at all.

Suppose there are 50 students in a class and you want to select 10 students using the systematic sampling technique. The first step is to determine the width of the interval (50/10 = 5). This means that from every five you need to select one element. Using the SRS technique, from the first interval (1–5 elements), select one of the elements. Suppose you selected the third element. From the rest of the intervals you would select every third element.

The calculation of sample size

Students and others often ask: 'How big a sample should I select?', 'What should be my sample size?' and 'How many cases do I need?' Basically, it depends on what you want to

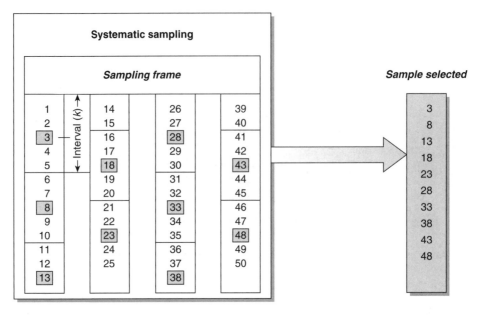

FIGURE 12.9   *Systematic sampling*

do with the findings and what type of relationships you want to establish. Your purpose in undertaking research is the main determinant of the level of accuracy required in the results, and this level of accuracy is an important determinant of sample size. However, in qualitative research, as the main focus is to explore or describe a situation, issue, process or phenomenon, the question of sample size is less important. You usually collect data till you think you have reached saturation point in terms of discovering new information. Once you think you are not getting much new data from your respondents, you stop collecting further information. Of course, the diversity or heterogeneity in what you are trying to find out about plays an important role in how fast you will reach saturation point. And remember: *the greater the heterogeneity or diversity in what you are trying to find out about, the greater the number of respondents you need to contact to reach saturation point.* In determining the size of your sample for quantitative studies and in particular for cause-and-effect studies, you need to consider the following:

- At what *level of confidence* do you want to test your results, findings or hypotheses?
- With what *degree of accuracy* do you wish to estimate the population parameters?
- What is the estimated *level of variation* (standard deviation), with respect to the main variable you are studying, in the study population?

Answering these questions is necessary regardless of whether you intend to determine the sample size yourself or have an expert do it for you. The size of the sample is important for testing a hypothesis or establishing an association, but for other studies the general rule is: *the larger the sample size, the more accurate your estimates.* In practice, your budget determines the size of your sample. Your skills in selecting a sample, within the constraints of your budget, lie in the way you select your elements so that they effectively and adequately represent your sampling population.

To illustrate this procedure let us take the example of a class. Suppose you want to find out the average age of the students within an accuracy of 0.5 of a year; that is, you can tolerate an error of half a year on either side of the true average age. Let us also assume that you want to find the average age within half a year of accuracy at the 95 per cent confidence level; that is, you want to be 95 per cent confident about your findings.

The formula (from statistics) for determining the confidence limits is

$$\hat{x} = \bar{x} \pm (t_{0.05}) \frac{\sigma}{\sqrt{\eta}}$$

where
$\hat{x}$ = estimated value of the population mean
$\bar{x}$ = average age calculated from the sample
$t_{0.05}$ = value of t at 95 per cent confidence level

$\sigma/\sqrt{\eta}$ = standard error
$\quad\sigma$ = standard deviation
$\quad\eta$ = sample size
$\quad\sqrt{}$ = square root
If we decide to tolerate an error of half a year, that means

$$\bar{x} \pm (t_{0.05}) \frac{\sigma}{\sqrt{\eta}}$$

$$= 0.5$$

$$= \bar{x} \pm 0.5$$

in other words we would like $\bar{x} \pm (t_{0.05}) \dfrac{\sigma}{\sqrt{\eta}}$

or (1.96★) $\sigma/\sqrt{\eta}$ = 0.5 (value of $t_{0.05}$ = 1.96)

$$\therefore \sqrt{\eta} = \frac{1.96 \times \sigma}{0.5}$$

★*t*-value from the following table

Level	0.02	0.10	0.05	0.02	0.01	0.001
t-value	1.282	1.645	1.960	2.326	2.576	3.291

There is only one unknown quantity in the above equation, that is σ.

Now the main problem is to find the value of σ without having to collect data. This is the biggest problem in estimating the sample size. Because of this it is important to know as much as possible about the study population.

The value of σ can be found by one of the following:

1   guessing;
2   consulting an expert;
3   obtaining the value of σ from previous comparable studies; or
4   carrying out a pilot study to calculate the value.

Let us assume that σ is 1 year. Then

$$\sqrt{\eta} = \frac{1.96 \times 1}{0.5} = 3.92$$

$$\therefore \eta = 15.37, \text{ say, } 16$$

Hence, to determine the average age of the class at a level of 95 per cent accuracy (assuming σ = 1 year) with half a year of error, a sample of at least 16 students is necessary.

Now assume that, instead of 95 per cent, you want to be 99 per cent confident about the estimated age, tolerating an error of half a year. Then

$$\sqrt{\eta} = \frac{2.576 \times 1}{0.5}$$

$$= 5.15$$

$$\therefore \eta = 26.54, \text{ say, } 27$$

Hence, if you want to be 99 per cent confident and are willing to tolerate an error of half a year, you need to select a sample of 27 students. Similarly, you can calculate the sample size with varying values of σ. Remember the golden rule: *the greater is the sample size, the more accurately your findings will reflect the 'true' picture.*

Sampling in qualitative research

As the main aim in qualitative enquiries is to explore the diversity, sample size and sampling strategy do not play a significant role in the selection of a sample. If selected carefully, diversity can be extensively and accurately described on the basis of information obtained even from one individual. All non-probability sampling designs – purposive, judgemental, expert, accidental and snowball – can also be used in qualitative research with two differences:

1   In quantitative studies you collect information from a predetermined number of people but, in qualitative research, you do not have a sample size in mind. Data collection based upon

a predetermined sample size and the saturation point distinguishes their use in quantitative and qualitative research.

2 In quantitative research you are guided by your desire to select a random sample, whereas in qualitative research you are guided by your judgement as to who is likely to provide you with the 'best' information.

The concept of saturation point in qualitative research

As you already know, in qualitative research data is usually collected to a point where you are not getting new information or it is negligible – the data saturation point. This stage determines the sample size.

It is important for you to keep in mind that the concept of data saturation point is highly subjective. It is you who are collecting the data and decide when you have attained the saturation point in your data collection. How soon you reach the saturation point depends upon how diverse is the situation or phenomenon that you are studying. The greater the diversity, the greater the number of people from whom you need to collect the information to reach the saturation point.

The concept of saturation point is more applicable to situations where you are collecting information on a one-to-one basis. Where the information is collected in a collective format such as focus groups, community forums or panel discussions, you strive to gather as diverse and as much information as possible. When no new information is emerging it is assumed that you have reached the saturation point.

Summary

In this chapter you have learnt about sampling, the process of selecting a few elements from a sampling population. Sampling, in a way, is a trade-off between accuracy and resources. Through sampling you *make an estimate* about the information of interest. You do not find the true population mean.

Two opposing philosophies underpin the selection of sampling units in quantitative and qualitative research. In quantitative studies a sample is supposed to be selected in such a way that it represents the study population, which is achieved through randomisation. However, the selection of a sample in qualitative research is guided by your judgement as to who is likely to provide you with complete and diverse information. This is a non-random process.

Sample size does not occupy a significant place in qualitative research and it is determined by the data saturation point while collecting data instead of being fixed in advance.

In quantitative research, sampling is guided by three principles, one of which is that the greater the sample size, the more accurate the estimate of the true population mean, given that everything else remains the same. The inferences drawn from a sample can be affected by both the size of the sample and the extent of variation in the sampling population.

Sampling designs can be classified as random/probability sampling designs, non-random/non-probability sampling designs and 'mixed' sampling designs. For a sample to be called a random sample, each element in the study population must have an equal and independent chance of selection. Three random designs were discussed: simple random sampling, stratified random sampling and cluster sampling. The procedures for selecting a sample using these designs were detailed step by step. The use of the fishbowl technique, the table of random numbers and specifically designed computer programs are three commonly used methods of selecting a probability sample.

There are five non-probability sampling designs: quota, accidental, judgemental, expert and snowball. Each is used for a different purpose and in different situations in both quantitative and qualitative studies. In quantitative studies their application is underpinned by the sample size whereas the data saturation point determines the 'sample size' in qualitative studies.

Systematic sampling is classified under the 'mixed' category as it has the properties of both probability and non-probability sampling designs.

The last section of the chapter described determinants of, and procedures for, calculating sample size. Although it might be slightly more difficult for the beginner, this was included to make you aware of the determinants involved as questions relating to this area are so commonly asked. In qualitative research, the question of sample size is less important, as your aim is to explore, not quantify, the extent of variation for which you are guided by reaching saturation point in terms of new findings.

For You to Think About

▶ Refamiliarise yourself with the keywords listed at the beginning of this chapter and if you are uncertain about the meaning or application of any of them revisit these in the chapter before moving on.

▶ Consider the implications of selecting a sample based upon your choice as a researcher and how you could make sure that you do not introduce bias.

▶ In the absence of a sampling frame for employees of a large organisation, which sampling design would you use to select a sample of 219 people? Explain why you would choose this design and the process you would undertake to ensure that the sample is representative.

▶ From your own area of interest, identify examples of where cluster sampling could be applied.

▶ What determines sample size in qualitative research?

▶ What is the data saturation point in qualitative studies?

This operational step includes one chapter:

- Chapter 13:   Writing a research proposal

STEP V Writing a Research Proposal

CHAPTER 13
How to Write a Research Proposal

In this chapter you will learn about:

- The purpose of a research proposal in quantitative and qualitative research
- How to structure a research proposal
- How to write a research proposal

Keywords: *conceptual framework, data analysis, data processing, hypothesis, limitations, literature review, research design, research problem, sampling, study design, study objectives, theoretical framework, time-frame.*

The research proposal in quantitative and qualitative research

All research endeavours, in both qualitative and quantitative research, in every academic and professional field are preceded by a research proposal. It informs your academic supervisor or potential research contract provider about your conceptualisation of the total research process that you propose to undertake so that they can examine its validity and appropriateness. In any academic field, your research proposal will go through a number of committees for approval. Unless it is approved by all of them, you will not be able to start your research. Hence, it is important for you to study closely what constitutes a research proposal.

You need to write a research proposal whether your research study is quantitative or qualitative and in both cases you use a similar structure. The main difference is in the proposed procedures and methodologies for undertaking the research endeavour. When providing details for different parts of the research proposal, for quantitative studies, you will detail quantitative methods, procedures and models and, for qualitative studies, your proposed process will be based upon methods and procedures that form the qualitative research methodology.

Certain requirements for a research proposal may vary from university to university, and from discipline to discipline within a university. What is outlined here will satisfy most requirements but you should be selective regarding what is needed in your situation.

A research proposal is an overall plan, scheme, structure and strategy designed to obtain answers to the research questions or problems that constitute your research project. A research proposal should outline the various tasks you plan to undertake to fulfil your research objectives, test hypotheses (if any) or obtain answers to your research questions. It should also state your reasons for undertaking the study. Broadly, a research proposal's main function is *to detail the operational plan for obtaining answers to your research questions. In doing so it ensures and reassures the reader of the validity of the methodology for obtaining answers to your research questions accurately and objectively.*

In order to achieve this function, a research proposal must tell you, your research supervisor and reviewers the following information about your study:

- *what* you are proposing to do;
- *how* you plan to find answers to *what* you are proposing;
- *why* you selected the proposed strategies of investigation.

Contents of a research proposal

A research proposal should contain the following information about your study:

- an introduction, including a brief *literature review*;
- *theoretical framework* that underpins your study;
- *conceptual framework* which constitutes the basis of your study;
- *objectives* or *research questions* of your study;
- *hypotheses* to be tested, if applicable;
- *study design* that you are proposing to adopt;
- *setting* for your study;
- *research instrument(s)* you are planning to use;
- *sampling design* and *sample size*;
- *ethical issues* involved and how you propose to deal with them;
- *data processing procedures*;
- *proposed chapters* of the report;
- *problems* and *limitations* of the study;
- proposed *time-frame* for the project.

A research proposal should communicate the above contents clearly and specifically in such a way that anyone going through it should be able to undertake all tasks in the same manner as you would have. It should also:

- enable you to return to the proposal for your own guidance in decision making at different stages of the research process;
- convince your research supervisor or a reviewer that your proposed methodology is meritorious, valid, appropriate and workable in terms of obtaining answers to your research questions or objectives.

Universities and other institutions may have differing requirements regarding the style and content of a research proposal. Requirements may also vary within an institution, from discipline to discipline or from supervisor to supervisor. (The guidelines set out in this chapter therefore provide a framework within which a research proposal should be written.)

Your proposal should follow the suggested guidelines and be written in an academic style. It must contain appropriate references in the body of the text and a bibliography at the end. Your survey of the relevant literature should cover major publications on the topic. The **theoretical framework** for your study must emerge from this literature review and must have its grounding in empirical evidence. As a rule, the literature review includes:

- a **conceptual framework**, and theoretical and empirical information about the main issues under study;
- some of the major research findings relating to your topic, research questions raised in the literature and gaps identified by previous researchers.

Your literature review should also raise issues relating to the methodology you are proposing. For example, it may examine how other studies operationalised the major variables of relevance to your study and may include a critique of methodology relevant to your study. The critiques of methods and procedures should be included under their respective headings. For example, a critique of the sampling design you adopt should be included under 'sampling' or a critique to the study design should be discussed under 'study design'.

Note that the suggested research proposal structure does not contain a section entitled 'survey of the literature' or 'literature review'. This is because references to the literature should be integrated with your arguments conceptually rather than chronologically and should become a part of all the aspects of your research report from problem conceptualisation to conclusions. The literature should be reviewed under main themes that emerge from your reading of the literature and should be included in the 'introduction' and 'the problem'. Issues identified in the literature to do with research methodology and problems pertinent to the various aspects of research procedures should be discussed under their respective headings. For example, issues pertaining to the study design under 'study design', issues relating to sampling under 'sampling' and the literature pertaining to the research instrument under the 'measurement procedure'.

In suggesting this format it is assumed that you are reasonably well acquainted with research methodology and an academic style of writing. That is, you know how to write a set of objectives or construct a hypothesis, you are familiar with the various study designs and you can construct a research instrument and cite a reference.

The pages that follow outline a framework for a research proposal. The contents under each heading may vary markedly from discipline to discipline, according to the academic level of the student (BA Hons, MA, PhD) and whether your study is predominantly quantitative or qualitative. For quantitative proposals you need to be very specific in proposing how you are going to undertake each step of the research journey, whereas for qualitative research proposals such details are not expected as your methodology is flexible and unstructured to accommodate in-depth search. However, you need to provide a broad approach to your enquiry as a part of your research proposal.

Each section of the proposed outline for a research proposal is divided into two parts:

1 a suggested title for the section and an outline of its contents;
2 examples outlining contents for the section – the same four examples of research projects, each taken from a different discipline, are used as illustrations in each section.

Preamble/introduction

The proposal should start with an introduction to include some of the information listed below. Remember that some of the contents suggested in this section may not be relevant to certain studies, so use your discretion in selecting only what is pertinent to your study. In writing this section, the literature review (see Chapter 3 on reviewing the literature) is of central importance as it serves two main functions:

1 It acquaints you with the available literature in the area of your study, thereby broadening your knowledge base.
2 It provides you with information on the methods and procedures other people have used in similar situations and tells you what works and what does not.

The type, extent and quality of a literature review are mostly dependent upon the academic level for which you are writing the proposal. The contents of this section may also vary greatly according to the subject area under study.

Start with a very broad perspective of the main subject area, before gradually narrowing the focus to the central problem under investigation. In doing so, cover the following aspects of your study area:

* an overview of the main area under study;
* a historical perspective (development, growth, etc.) pertinent to the study area;
* philosophical or ideological issues relating to the topic;
* trends in terms of prevalence, if appropriate;
* major theories, if any;
* the main issues, problems and advances in the subject area under study;
* important theoretical and practical issues relating to the central problem under study;
* the main findings relating to the core issue(s).

Four examples of possible topics for the preamble/introduction for a research proposal follow.

Example A

Suppose that you are conducting a study to investigate the impact of immigration on the family. The preamble/introduction should include a brief description of the following:

- The origins of migratory movements in the world.
- General theories developed to explain migratory behaviour.
- The reasons for migration.
- Current trends in migration (national and state).
- The impact of immigration on family roles and relationships (e.g. on husband and wife, on children and parents, on parental expectations of children, etc.).
- Occupational mobility.
- etc.

Example B

Suppose your research project is to conduct a study of the attitudes of foster carers towards foster payment in ... (name of the place/state/country). The preamble/introduction would include the following:

- The origins of foster placement, the philosophy of foster care, a historical overview of foster care and changes over the years.
- Reasons for foster care and changes over time.
- The origins of foster placement in ... (the country in which you are conducting your study).
- The effects of foster placement on children and parents.
- Policies with respect to foster care in ... (the region).
- The origins of foster care in ... (the region).
- Administrative procedures for foster care in ... (the region).
- The training of foster parents in ... (the region).
- The role and responsibility of foster parents.
- etc.

Example C

Suppose that you plan to study the relationship between academic achievement and social environment. The preamble/introduction would include the following:

- The role of education in our society.
- Major changes in the philosophy of education over time.

(Continued)

(Continued)

- Factors affecting attitudes towards education.
- The development of education in ... (country).
- Trends in education participation rates in ... (country) with particular reference to the region in which the study is being carried out.
- Changing educational values.
- Role of parents and peers in academic achievement.
- Impact of social environment on academic achievement.
- etc.

Example D

Suppose you are undertaking a qualitative study to find out what it means to have a child with ADHD in the family. The preamble/introduction should include your thoughts and arguments, and what the literature says around the following aspects of ADHD.

- Definitions and symptoms of ADHD.
- Causes of ADHD.
- Medical perspective on ADHD.
- Effects of ADHD on family life.
- Treatment for ADHD.
- Implications for a child if untreated.
- Management of ADHD.
- etc.

The problem

Having provided a broad introduction to the area under study, now focus on issues relating to its central theme, identifying some of the gaps in the existing body of knowledge. Identify some of the main unanswered questions. Here some of the main research questions that you would like to answer through your study should also be raised, and a rationale and relevance for each should be provided. Knowledge gained from other studies and the literature about the issues you are proposing to investigate should be an integral part of this section. Specifically, this section should:

- identify the issues that are the basis of your study;
- specify the various aspects of/perspectives on these issues;

- identify the main gaps in the existing body of knowledge;
- raise some of the main research questions that you want to answer through your study;
- identify what knowledge is available concerning your questions, specifying the differences of opinion in the literature regarding these questions if differences exist;
- develop a rationale for your study with particular reference to how your study will fill the identified gaps.

The following examples outline the topics about which the literature should be reviewed and included in the section entitled 'The problem'. Keep in mind that these are just suggestions and should serve only as examples for you to develop and change as you feel appropriate for your own study.

Example A

- What settlement process does a family go through after immigration?
- What adjustments do immigrants have to make?
- What types of change can occur in family members' attitudes? (Theory of acculturation etc.)
- What is the possible impact of settlement on family roles and relationships?
- In terms of impact, what specific questions do you want to answer through the study? What does the literature say about these questions? What are the different viewpoints on these issues? What are your own ideas about these questions?
- What do you think will be the relevance of the findings of your study to the existing body of knowledge and to your profession?
- How will the findings add to the body of knowledge and be useful to professionals in your field?
- etc.

Example B

- What are the broad issues, debates, arguments and counter-arguments regarding foster-care payment?
- What are the attitudes of foster parents to the amount, mode and form of payment and what does the literature say about these issues?
- What are the different viewpoints/perspectives regarding payment for foster care?
- What main questions will your study answer?
- How will your findings help in policy formulation and programme development?
- etc.

Example C

- What theories have been developed to explain the relationship between academic achievement and social environment?
- What is the relationship between educational achievement and social environment: what theoretical model will be the basis of your study?
- What do previous theories and researches have to say regarding the components of the theoretical model and academic achievement? For example, the relationship between academic achievement and:

  — the self-esteem and aspirations/motivation of a student;
  — peer group influence;
  — parental involvement and its relationship with their socioeconomic status;
  — the motivation and interest of students in the subject;
  — employment prospects;
  — relationship with a teacher;
  — etc.

Example D

- What are the effects on the family of having a child with ADHD in the family as identified in the literature?
- According to the literature, are there any differences between these effects and the type of family?
- What strategies have been used for the management of ADHD by a family?
- What effects, according to the literature, does ADHD have on sibling relationships?
- What are the perceptions of family members about the effects and management of ADHD?
- How do families cope when they have a child with ADHD in the family?
- etc.

Objectives of the study

In this section include a statement of both your study's main and subobjectives (see Chapter 4). Your main objective indicates the central thrust of your study whereas the subobjectives identify the specific issues you propose to examine.

The objectives of the study should be clearly stated and specific in nature. Each subobjective should delineate only one issue. Use action-oriented verbs such as 'to determine', 'to find out' and 'to ascertain' in formulating subobjectives, which should be numerically listed. If the objective is to test a hypothesis, you must follow the convention of hypothesis formulation in wording the specific objectives.

In qualitative studies the statement of objectives is not as precise as in quantitative studies. In qualitative studies you should simply mention an overall objective of the study as your aim is to explore as much as possible as you go along. As you know, the strength of qualitative research is in flexibility of approach and the ability to incorporate new ideas while collecting data. Having structured statements that bind you to a predetermined framework of exploration is not a preferred convention in qualitative research. Statements like to explore 'what does it mean to have a child with ADHD in the family?', 'how does it feel to be a victim of domestic violence?', 'how do people cope with racial discrimination?', 'the relationship between resilience and yoga' or 'reconstructing life after bushfire', are sufficient to communicate your intent of objectives in qualitative research. More detailed objectives, if need be, can be developed after a study is complete.

Example A

Main objective:

To ascertain the impact of immigration on the family.

Subobjectives:

1 To determine the impact of immigration on husband/wife roles as perceived by immigrants.
2 To find out the impact of immigration on marital relations.
3 To ascertain perceived changes in parental expectations of children's academic and professional achievement.
4 To determine perceived changes of attitude towards marriage in the study population.

Example B

Main objective:

To determine the opinion of foster carers about the form and extent of foster payment they feel they should receive for taking care of a foster child.

Subobjectives:

1 To determine the form and mode of payment for taking care of a foster child.
2 To identify the factors that foster parents believe should be the basis for determining the rate of payment for fostering a child.
3 To determine the relationship, if any, between the socioeconomic graphic characteristics of foster parents and their views on payment.

Example C

Main objective:

    To examine the relationship between academic achievement and social environment.

Subobjectives:

1 To find out the relationship, if any, between self-esteem and a student's academic achievement at school.
2 To ascertain the association between parental involvement in a student's studies and his/her academic achievement at school.
3 To examine the links between a student's peer group and academic achievement.
4 To explore the relationship between academic achievement and the attitude of a student towards teachers.

Example D

Main objective:

    To explore what it means to have a child with ADHD in the family.

Hypotheses to be tested

A hypothesis is a statement of your assumptions about the prevalence of a phenomenon or about a relationship between two variables that you plan to test within the framework of the study (see Chapter 6). If you are going to test hypotheses, list them in this section.

    When formulating a hypothesis you have an obligation to draw conclusions about it in the text of the report. Hypotheses have a particular style of formulation. You must be acquainted with the correct way of wording them. In a study you may have as many hypotheses as you want to test. However, it is *not* essential to have a hypothesis in order to undertake a study – you can conduct a perfectly satisfactory study without formulating a hypothesis.

Example A

H_1 = In most cases there will be a change in husband/wife roles after immigration.
H_2 = In a majority of cases there will be a change in parents' expectations of their children.
H_i = etc.

Example B

H_1 = Most people become foster parents because of their love of children.
H_2 = A majority of foster parents would like to be trained to care for foster children.
H_i = etc.

Example C

H_1 = A student's self-esteem and academic achievement at school are positively correlated.
H_2 = The greater the parental involvement in a student's studies, the higher the academic achievement.
H_3 = A student's attitude towards teachers is positively correlated with his/her academic achievement in that subject.
H_i = etc.

Example D

Hypotheses are not constructed in qualitative research.

Study design

Describe the study design (for details see Chapter 8) you plan to use to answer your research questions. (For example, say whether it is a case study, descriptive, cross-sectional, before-and-after, experimental or non-experimental design.) Identify the strengths and weaknesses of your study design.

Include details about the various logistical procedures you intend to follow while executing the study design. One characteristic of a good study design is that it explains the details with such clarity that, if someone else wants to follow the proposed procedure, s/he will be able to do exactly as you would have done. Your study design should include information about the following:

- Who makes up the study population?
- Can each element of the study population be identified? If yes, how?
- Will a sample or the total population be studied?
- How will you get in touch with the selected sample?
- How will the sample's consent to participate in the study be sought?
- How will the data be collected (e.g. by interview, questionnaire or observation)?
- In the case of a mailed questionnaire, to what address should the questionnaire be returned?

- Are you planning to send a reminder regarding the return of questionnaires?
- How will confidentiality be preserved?
- How and where can respondents contact you if they have queries?

Example A

The study is primarily designed to find out from a cross-section of immigrants from ..., ... and ... (names of the countries) the perceived impact of immigration on family roles. Initial contact with the ethnic associations for these countries will be made through the elected office bearers to obtain a list of members. Five immigrants will be selected from the list at random, and will be contacted by phone to explain the purpose of the study and its relevance, and to seek their agreement to participate in the study. Those who give their consent will be interviewed at their homes or any other convenient place. To select a further sample, a snowball sampling technique will be used until the desired sample size is obtained.

Example B

The study design is cross-sectional in nature, being designed to find out from a cross-section of foster parents their opinions about foster payment. All foster parents currently registered with the Department of ... (name of the office) constitute the study population. From the existing records of this department it seems that there are 457 foster parents in ... (name of the region). As it is impossible for the researcher, within the constraints of time and money, to collect information from all the foster parents, it is proposed to select a sample of 50 per cent of the study population with the proposed sampling strategy. The questionnaire, with a supporting letter from the department will be sent with a prepaid envelope. The respondents will be requested to return the questionnaire by ... (date). The letter from the researcher attached to the questionnaire will explain the objectives and relevance of the study, assure the respondents of anonymity and give them the option of not participating in the study if they wish. A contact number will be provided in case a respondent has any questions. In the case of a low response rate (less than 25 per cent), a reminder will be sent to respondents.

Example C

It is proposed that the study will be carried out in two government high schools in the metropolitan area. The principals of the schools most accessible to the researcher will be contacted to explain the purpose of the study and the help needed from the school, and to seek their permission for the students to participate in the study. As the constraints of time and resources do not permit the researcher to select more than two schools, negotiations with other schools will cease when two schools agree to participate in the study.

It is proposed to select Year 9 students as the academic achievement of students in Years 8 and 10 could be affected by factors unique to them. Year 8 students may be experiencing anxiety as a result of having just made the transition to a new system. The motivation of students in Year 10 could be affected by their being at the stage in their education where they must decide if they will stay on at school.

In order to control the variance attributable to the gender of a student it is proposed to select only male students.

Once the principal of a school agrees to allow the study to be carried out, the researcher will brief the teacher in charge about the study and its relevance, and will arrange a date and time for administering the questionnaire.

When the students are assembled, ready to participate in the study, the researcher will explain its purpose and relevance, and then distribute the questionnaire. The researcher will remain with the class to answer any questions the students might have.

Example D

The researcher is known to a family that has a child with ADHD and that belongs to an ADHD support group which meets every month. The researcher proposes to make initial contact with the group through the known family. The researcher will attend one of the monthly meetings and brief the group on the purpose and relevance of the study, criteria for inclusion in the study, what it entails to be involved in the study, and other aspects of the study. The respondents will also be assured of the anonymity of the information shared by them and its ethical use. The members of the group will be encouraged to ask questions about any aspect of the study. Having sought their consent, the researcher will seek opinions of some group members to decide who should participate in the study in light of the inclusion criteria.

It is proposed to select six families, three where both parents are involved in the treatment and management of an ADHD child and three from families where the mother is the sole carer. This is primarily to see if there are differences in looking after a child with ADHD among different types of family.

The potential respondents will be individually contacted by the researcher to seek their consent for participation in the study. Once consent has been obtained the place and timings for interviews will be fixed with each family. Depending upon the type of family, the issues will be discussed either collectively with the father and mother or with the mother only. Before starting an interview their permission to record the interview on a tape recorder will be sought. Having completed the interviews, the researcher will transcribe the responses and a copy will be given to the respondents for confirmation and validation.

The setting

Briefly describe the organisation, agency or community in which you will conduct your study. If the study is about a group of people, highlight some of the salient characteristics of the group (e.g. its history, size, composition and structure) and draw attention to any available relevant information.

If your research concerns an agency, office or organisation, include the following in your description:

- the main services provided by the agency, office or organisation;
- its administrative structure;
- the type of clients served;
- information about the issues that are central to your research.

If you are studying a community, briefly describe some of the main characteristics, such as:

- the size of the community;
- a brief social profile of the community (i.e. the composition of the various groups within it);
- issues of relevance to the central theme of your study.

Note that, due to the nature of the content, it would be difficult to provide examples.

Measurement procedures

This section should contain a discussion of your instrument (see Chapters 9 and 10) and the details of how you plan to operationalise your *major* variables (Chapter 5).

To start with, justify your choice of research tool, highlighting its strengths and pointing out its weaknesses. Then outline the major segments of your research tool and their relevance to the main objectives of the study. If you are using a standard instrument, briefly discuss the availability of evidence on its reliability and validity. If you adapt or modify it in any way, describe and explain the changes you have made.

You should also discuss how you are going to operationalise the major concepts. For example, if measuring effectiveness, specify how it will be measured. If you plan to measure the self-esteem of a group of people, mention the main indicators of self-esteem and the procedures for its measurement (e.g. the Likert or Thurstone scale, or any other procedure).

Ideally, for quantitative studies you should attach a copy of the research instrument to your proposal.

Note that, due to the nature of the content, it would be difficult to provide examples for this section.

Ethical issues

All academic institutions are particular about any ethical issues that research may have. To deal with them, all institutions have some form of policy on ethics. You need to be acquainted with your institution's policy. It is imperative that in your proposal you identify any ethical issues and describe how you propose to deal with them. You need to look at the ethical issues particularly from the viewpoint of your respondents and, in case of any potential 'harm', psychological or otherwise, you need to detail the mechanism in place to deal with it. Further information on ethical issues is provided in Chapter 14.

Sampling

Under this section of the proposal include the following (consult Chapter 12 on sampling):

- the size of the sampling population (if known) and from where and how this information will be obtained;
- the size of the sample you are planning to select and your reasons for choosing this size;
- an explanation of the sampling design you are planning to use in the selection of the sample (simple random sampling, stratified random sampling, quota sampling, etc.).

Example A

Because a lack of information as to the exact location of migrant families makes it difficult to use a probability sampling design, it is proposed that the researcher will employ a snowball sampling technique. The researcher will make initial contact with five families who have emigrated from ... (name of the country) during the past seven to ten years, who are either known to him/her or on the basis of information obtained from the office bearers of the formal associations representing the migrant groups. From each respondent the researcher will obtain names and addresses of other immigrants who have come from the same country during the same period. The respondents thus identified will then be interviewed and asked to identify other respondents for the researcher. This process will continue until the researcher has interviewed 70 respondents.

Example B

Because of the constraints of time and resources it is proposed to select 50 per cent of the foster parents currently registered (457) with the department using the systematic random sampling technique. Every other foster parent registered with the department will be selected, thus 229 individuals will constitute the sample for the study.

Example C

The selection of schools will be done primarily through quota sampling. Schools will be selected on the basis of their geographical proximity to the researcher. The researcher will prepare a list of schools, in rank order, of accessibility. Once two schools agree to participate in the study, negotiations with other schools will cease.

All Year 9 male students will constitute the study population. It is expected that the sample will not exceed 100 students.

Example D

It is proposed to use the judgemental/purposive sampling technique to select six families from the group, three where both parents look after an ADHD child and three where only the mother has the main responsibility (single parent families). On the basis of informal discussions with the group members, those families who are expected to be information rich in treating and managing a child with ADHD will be selected to be interviewed.

Analysis of data

In general terms, describe the strategy you intend to use for data analysis (Chapter 15). Specify whether the data will be analysed manually or by computer. For computer analysis, identify the program and where appropriate the statistical procedures you plan to perform on the data. For quantitative studies also identify the main variables for cross-tabulation.

For qualitative studies, describe how you plan to analyse your interviews or observation notes to draw meanings from what your respondents have said about issues discussed or observation notes made. One of the common techniques is to identify main themes, through analysing the contents of the information gathered by you in the field. You first need to decide whether you want to analyse this information manually or use a computer program for the purpose.

There are three ways to proceed with content analysis:

1 From your field notes develop a framework of your write-up and as you go through your notes directly integrate that information within the structure developed. If you adopt this method, you need to be reasonably clear about the structure. It does not mean that you cannot develop the structure as you go on analysing; still, a clear vision will be of immense help in slotting information gathered in the field by you into the write-up.
2 The second method is that you transcribe your field notes to be read by you over and over again to identify the main themes. These themes become the basis of your write-up.
3 There are computer programs such as NUD*IST, Ethnograph, NVivo specifically designed to handle descriptive data. You may prefer to use one of these programs. These programs are also based upon the principle of content analysis. The only difference is that instead of your searching manually, they identify where a particular text identifying the theme appears.

You need to specify which particular strategy you are proposing for data analysis for your study.

Example A

Frequency distributions in terms of:

- age;
- education;
- occupation;
- number of children;
- duration of immigration;
- etc.

Cross-tabulations:
Impact of husband/wife roles

- age;
- number of children;
- education;
- occupation;
- etc.

Example B

Frequency distributions in terms of:

- age;
- income;
- education;
- occupation;
- marital status;
- duration of foster care;
- number of foster children;
- etc.

Cross-tabulations:
Attitude towards foster payment

- age;
- number of children;
- education;

(Continued)

(Continued)

- occupation;
- etc.

Statistical tests to be applied:

- chi square;
- regression analysis;
- etc.

Example C

Frequency distributions in terms of:

- age;
- parents' occupation;
- parents' educational levels;
- students' occupational aspirations;
- parental involvement in students' studies;
- self-esteem;
- peer group influence;
- number of hours spent on studies;
- etc.

Cross-tabulations:
Academic achievement

- peer group influence;
- parental involvement in students' studies;
- self-esteem;
- occupational aspirations;
- attitude towards teachers;
- etc.

Example D

The in-depth interviews carried out with the families will be transcribed using Microsoft Word. These transcribed interviews will be closely studied to identify the main themes they communicate. These themes will be sorted by issues relating to management and treatment of a child with ADHD. The themes will then become part of the write-up.

Structure of the report

As clearly as possible, state how you intend to organise the final report (see Chapter 17). In organising your material for the report, the specific objectives of your study are of immense help. Plan to develop your chapters around the main themes of your study. The title of each chapter should clearly communicate the main thrust of its contents.

The first chapter, possibly entitled 'Introduction', should be an overall introduction to your study, covering most of your project proposal and pointing out deviations, if any, from the original plan.

The second chapter should provide some information about the study population itself – that is, some of its socioeconomic–demographic characteristics. The main aim of this chapter is to give readers some background on the population from which you collected the information. The second chapter, therefore, may be entitled, 'Socioeconomic–demographic characteristics of the study population' or 'The study population' or any other title that communicates this theme to readers. Titles for the rest of the chapters will vary from study to study but, as mentioned, each chapter should be written around a main theme. Although the wording of chapter titles is an individual choice, each must communicate the main theme of the chapter. In developing these themes the specific objectives of the study should be kept in the front of your mind.

If your study is qualitative, the main issues identified during data collection and analysis stages should become the basis of developing chapters. Having developed significant issues, the next step is to organise the main themes under each issue and develop a structure that you will follow to communicate your findings to your readers.

Example A

It is proposed that the report will be divided into the following chapters:

Chapter 1:   Introduction
Chapter 2:   The socioeconomic–demographic characteristics of the study population
Chapter 3:   The impact on husband/wife roles
Chapter 4:   The impact on marital relations
Chapter 5:   The impact on expectations of children
Chapter 6:   The impact on attitudes towards marriage
Chapter 7:   Summary, conclusions and recommendations

Example B

The dissertation will be divided into the following chapters:

Chapter 1:   Introduction
Chapter 2:   A profile of the study population

(Continued)

(Continued)

Chapter 3: Foster carers' perceptions of their role
Chapter 4: Attitudes of foster carers towards foster-care payment
Chapter 5: The preferred method of payment
Chapter 6: General comments made by respondents about foster care
Chapter 7: Summary, conclusions and recommendations

Example C

The report will have the following chapters:

Chapter 1: Introduction
Chapter 2: The study population
Chapter 3: Occupational aspirations, self-esteem and academic achievement
Chapter 4: The extent of parental involvement and academic achievement
Chapter 5: Peer group influence and academic achievement
Chapter 6: Academic achievement and student attitudes towards teachers
Chapter 7: Summary, conclusions and recommendations

Example D

It is proposed that the report will have the following chapters:

Chapter 1: ADHD: A theoretical perspective
Chapter 2: Issues and difficulties faced by family members in bringing up a child with ADHD
Chapter 3: ADHD and its perceived effects on the child
Chapter 4: ADHD and its perceived impact on sibling relationships
Chapter 5: Managing treatment
Chapter 6: Perceived effects of ADHD on schooling of the child
Chapter 7: Perceived effects of ADHD on relationships with other children
Chapter 8: A case history
Chapter 9: Summary and conclusions

Problems and limitations

This section should list any problems you think you might encounter concerning, for example, the availability of data, securing permission from the agency/organisation to carry out the study, obtaining the sample, or any other aspect of the study.

You will not have unlimited resources and as this may be primarily an academic exercise, you might have to do less than an ideal job. However, it is important to be aware of – and communicate – any limitations that could affect the validity of your conclusions and generalisations.

Here, *problems* refer to difficulties relating to logistical details, whereas *limitations* designate structural problems relating to methodological aspects of the study. In your opinion the study design you chose may not be the best but you might have had to adopt it for a number of reasons. This is classified as a limitation of the study. This is also true for sampling or measurement procedures. Such limitations should be communicated to readers.

Appendix

As an appendix, in the case of quantitative studies, attach your research instrument. Also, attach a list of references in the appendix of the proposal.

Work schedule

You must set yourself dates as you need to complete the research within a certain time-frame. List the various operational steps you need to undertake and indicate against each the date by which you aim to complete that task. Remember to keep some time towards the end as a 'cushion' in case the research process does not go as smoothly as planned. Develop a chart as shown in Table 13.1.

TABLE 13.1 *Developing a time-frame for your study*

	To be completed by (weeks or months)														
Tasks **(Any tasks which you** **consider important)**	**1**	**2**	**3**	**4**	**5**	**6**	**7**	**8**	**9**	**10**	**11**	**12**	**13**	**14**	**15**
Proposal writing															
Instrument construction															
Data collection															
Coding															
Data analysis															
Report/first															
Report/final															
Typing															

Summary

A research proposal details the operational plan for obtaining answers to research questions. It must tell your supervisor and others what you propose to do, how you plan to proceed and why the chosen strategy has been selected. It thus assures readers of the validity of the methodology used to obtain answers accurately and objectively.

The guidelines set out in this chapter provide only a framework within which a research proposal for both quantitative and qualitative studies should be written and assume that you are reasonably well acquainted with research methodology and an academic style of writing. The contents of your proposal are arranged under the following headings: preamble/introduction, the problem, objectives of the study, hypotheses to be tested, study design, setting, measurement procedures, sampling, analysis of data, structure of the report, and problems and limitations. The specifics, under each heading, will vary with the type of study you are proposing to undertake. The write-up for qualitative studies will be based upon qualitative methodology and quantitative methodology will determine the contents of quantitative studies.

The 'preamble' or 'introduction' introduces the main area of the study. To start with, the literature review is broad and then it gradually narrows to the specific problem you are investigating. The theoretical framework should be a part of this section. The next section, 'the problem', details the specific problem under study. The research questions for which you are planning to find answers are raised in this section. 'Objectives of the study' contains your main objectives and your subobjectives. Hypotheses, if any, should be listed in the section 'hypotheses to be tested'. The logistical procedures you intend to follow are detailed under 'study design'. 'The setting' consists of a description of the organisation or community in which you plan to conduct your study. The procedure for obtaining information and the measurement of major variables are explained in the 'measurement procedures' section. You need to write about ethical issues that your study might have and how you propose to deal with them. How you will select your sample is described under 'sampling'. The procedure for data analysis is discussed under 'analysis of data'. The way you plan to structure your report is outlined under 'structure of the report'. Anticipated problems in conducting the study and limitations with its design are described under 'problems and limitations'. As an appendix to your proposal attach a copy of the research instrument and a list of the references.

A work schedule provides a time-frame for your study.

For You to Think About

▸ Refamiliarise yourself with the keywords listed at the beginning of this chapter and if you are uncertain about the meaning or application of any of them revisit these in the chapter before moving on.
▸ Compare the research proposal contents suggested in this chapter with those recommended by your university or department. If they are different, what are the differences?
▸ Find out the process that a research proposal goes through in your university before approval is granted.

This operational step includes one chapter to make you aware of the ethical issues in research:

- Chapter 14: Considering ethical issues in data collection

STEP VI Collecting Data

CHAPTER 14

Considering Ethical Issues in Data Collection

In this chapter you will learn about:

- Ethics: the concept
- Stakeholders in research
- Ethical issues to consider concerning research participants
- Ethical issues to consider relating to the researcher
- Ethical issues to consider regarding the sponsoring organisation

Keywords: *bias, code of conduct, confidentiality, deprivation of treatment, ethos, harm, informed consent, principles of conduct, research participants, sensitive information, sponsoring organisations, stakeholders, subjectivity.*

Ethics: the concept

All professions are guided by a code of ethics that has evolved over the years to accommodate the changing ethos, values, needs and expectations of those who hold a stake in the professions. Some professions are more advanced than others in terms of the level of development of their code of ethics. Some have very strict guidelines, monitor conduct effectively and take appropriate steps against those who do not abide by the guidelines.

Most professions have an overall code of conduct that also governs the way they carry out research. In addition, many research bodies have evolved a code of ethics separately for research. Medicine, epidemiology, business, law, education, psychology and other social sciences have well-established codes of ethics for research.

Let us first examine what we mean by 'ethics' or 'ethical behaviour'. According to the *Collins Dictionary* (1979: 502), ethical means 'in accordance with principles of conduct that are considered correct, especially those of a given profession or group'. The keywords here, 'principles of conduct' and 'considered correct', raise certain questions:

- What are these principles of conduct?
- Who determines them?
- In whose judgement must they be considered correct?

Closely related questions are as follows:

- Are there universal principles of conduct that can be applied to all professions?
- Do these change with time?
- Should they?
- What happens when a professional does not abide by them?

The subject of ethics needs to be considered in light of these questions.

The way each profession serves society is continuously changing in accordance with society's needs and expectations and with the technology available for the delivery of a service. The ethical codes governing the manner in which a service is delivered also need to change. What has been considered ethical in the past may not be so judged at present, and what is ethical now may not remain so in the future. Any judgement about whether a particular practice is ethical is made on the basis of the code of conduct prevalent at that point in time.

As the service and its manner of delivery differ from profession to profession, no code of conduct can be uniformly applied across all professions. Each profession has its own code of ethics, though there are commonalities. If you want guidelines on ethical conduct for a particular profession, you need to consult the code of ethics adopted by that profession or discipline.

'What are these principles of conduct?' is the most important question as it addresses the issue of the contents of **ethical practice** in a profession. As the code of conduct varies from profession to profession, it is not possible to provide a universal answer to this question. However, in research, any dilemma stemming from a moral quandary is a basis of ethical conduct. There are certain behaviours in research – such as causing harm to individuals, breaching confidentiality, using information improperly and introducing bias – that are considered **unethical** in any profession.

The next question is: in whose judgement must a code of conduct be considered correct? Who decides whether a particular practice is wrong? If a procedure is carried out wrongly, what penalties should be imposed? It is the overall body of professionals or government organisations that collectively develops a professional code of conduct and forms a judgement as to whether or not it is being followed.

As mentioned, most professions have established an overall code of ethics and also a code of ethics for conducting research in their respective fields. As this book is designed for researchers in the social sciences, we will examine ethical issues relating to research in general and issues that are applicable to most social science disciplines.

Stakeholders in research

There are many **stakeholders in research**, whether it is quantitative or qualitative. It is important to look at ethical issues in relation to each of them. The various stakeholders in a research activity are:

1 the research participants or subjects;
2 the researcher;
3 the funding body.

Who should be considered as a research participant varies from profession to profession. Generally, all those with direct and indirect involvement in a research study are considered as research participants, hence stakeholders. In addition, those who are likely to be affected by the findings of a study are also considered as stakeholders. In the fields of medicine, public health, epidemiology and nursing, patients and non-patients who become part of a study and those who participate in an experiment to test the effectiveness of a drug or treatment are considered as research participants. Service providers, service managers and planners who are involved in either providing the service or collecting information relating to the study are also stakeholders in the research. In the social sciences, the participants include individuals, groups and communities providing information to help a researcher to gain understanding of a phenomenon, situation, issue or interaction. In social work and psychology, participants include clients as well as non-clients of an agency from whom information is collected to find out the magnitude of a problem, the needs of a community or the effectiveness of an intervention; and service providers, social workers and psychologists, when they provide information for a study. In marketing, consumers as well as non-consumers of a product provide information about consumption patterns and behaviour. In education, subjects include students, teachers and perhaps the community at large who participate in educational research activities. Similarly, in any discipline in which a research activity is undertaken, those from whom information is collected or those who are studied by a researcher become participants of the study.

Researchers constitute the second category of stakeholders. Anyone who collects information for the specific purpose of understanding, consolidation, enhancement and development of professional knowledge, adhering to the accepted code of conduct, is a researcher. S/he may represent any academic discipline.

Funding organisations responsible for financing a research activity fall into the third category of stakeholders. Most research is carried out using funds provided by business organisations, pharmaceutical companies, service institutions (government, semi-government or voluntary), research bodies and/or academic institutions. The funds are given for specific purposes.

Each category of stakeholders in a research activity may have different interests, perspectives, purposes, aims and motivations that could affect the way in which the research activity is carried out and the way results are communicated and used. Because of this, it is important to ensure that research is not affected by the self-interest of any party and is not carried out in a way that harms any party. It is therefore important to examine ethical conduct in research concerning different stakeholders under separate categories.

Ethical issues to consider concerning research participants

There are many ethical issues to consider in relation to the participants of a research activity.

Collecting information

One could ask: why should a respondent give any information to a researcher? What right does a researcher have to knock at someone's door or to send out a questionnaire? Is it ethical to disturb an individual, even if you ask permission before asking questions? Why should a person give you his/her time? Your request for information may create anxiety or put pressure on a respondent. Is this ethical?

But the above questions display a naive attitude. The author believes that if this attitude had been adopted, there would have been no progress in the world. Research is required in order to improve conditions. Provided any piece of research is likely to help society directly or indirectly, it is acceptable to ask questions, if you first obtain the respondents' **informed consent**. Before you begin collecting information, you must consider the relevance and usefulness of the research you are undertaking and be able to convince others of this also. If you cannot justify the relevance of the research you are conducting, you are wasting your respondents' time, which is unethical.

Seeking consent

In every discipline it is considered unethical to collect information without the knowledge of participants, and their expressed willingness and informed consent. Seeking informed consent 'is probably the most common method in medical and social research' (Bailey 1978: 384). Informed consent implies that subjects are made adequately aware of the type of information you want from them, why the information is being sought, what purpose it will be put to, how they are expected to participate in the study, and how it will directly or indirectly affect them. It is important that the consent should also be voluntary and without pressure of any kind. Schinke and Gilchrist write:

> Under standards set by the National Commission for the Protection of Human Subjects, all informed-consent procedures must meet three criteria: participants must be competent to give consent; sufficient information must be provided to allow for a reasoned decision; and consent must be voluntary and uncoerced. (1993: 83)

Competency, according to Schinke and Gilchrist, 'is concerned with the legal and mental capacities of participants to give permission' (1993: 83). For example, some very old people, those suffering from conditions that exclude them from making informed decisions, people in crisis, people who cannot speak the language in which the research is being carried out, people who are dependent upon you for a service and children are not considered to be competent.

Providing incentives

Is it ethical to provide incentives to respondents to share information with you? Some researchers provide incentives to participants for their participation in a study, feeling this to be quite proper as participants are giving their time. Others think that the offering of inducements is unethical.

In the author's experience most people do not participate in a study because of incentives, but because they realise the importance of the study. Therefore, giving a small gift after having obtained your information, as a token of appreciation, is in the author's opinion not unethical. However, giving a present before data collection is unethical.

Seeking sensitive information

Information sought can pose an ethical dilemma in research. Certain types of information can be regarded as sensitive or confidential by some people and thus an invasion of privacy. Asking for this information may upset or embarrass a respondent. However, if you do not ask for the information, it may not be possible to pursue your interest in the area and contribute to the existing body of knowledge.

For most people, questions on sexual behaviour, drug use and shoplifting are intrusive. Even questions on marital status, income and age may be considered to be an invasion of privacy by some. In collecting data you need to be careful about the sensitivities of your respondents.

The dilemma you face as a researcher is whether you should ask sensitive and intrusive questions. In the author's opinion it is not unethical to ask such questions provided that you clearly and frankly tell your respondents the type of information you are going to ask, and give them sufficient time to decide if they want to share the information with you, without any major inducement.

The possibility of causing harm to participants

Is the research going to harm participants in any way? Harm includes:

> not only hazardous medical experiments but also any social research that might involve such things as discomfort, anxiety, harassment, invasion of privacy, or demeaning or dehumanising procedures. (Bailey 1978: 384)

When you collect data from respondents or involve subjects in an experiment, you need to examine carefully whether their involvement is likely to harm them in any way. If it is, you must make sure that the risk is minimal. Minimum risk means that the extent of harm or discomfort in the research is not greater than that ordinarily encountered in daily life. It is unethical if the way you seek information creates anxiety or harassment, and if you think it may happen, you need to take steps to prevent this.

Maintaining confidentiality

Sharing information about a respondent with others for purposes other than research is unethical. Sometimes you need to identify your study population to put your findings into context. In such a situation you need to make sure that at least the information provided by respondents is kept anonymous. It is unethical to identify an individual respondent and the information provided by him/her. Therefore, you need to ensure that after the information has been collected, its source cannot be identified. In certain types of study you might need to visit respondents repeatedly, in which case you will have to identify them until the completion of your visits. In such situations you need to be extra careful that others do not have access to the information. It is unethical to be negligent in not protecting the confidentiality and anonymity of the information gathered from your respondents. If you are doing research for someone else, you need to make sure that confidentiality is maintained by this party as well.

Ethical issues to consider relating to the researcher

Avoiding bias

Bias on the part of the researcher is unethical. Bias is different from subjectivity. Subjectivity, as mentioned earlier, is related to your educational background, training and competence in research, and your philosophical perspective. Bias is a deliberate attempt either to hide what you have found in your study, or to highlight something disproportionately to its true existence. It is absolutely unethical to introduce bias into a research activity. If you are unable to control your bias, you should not be engaging in the research. Remember, it is the bias that is unethical and not the subjectivity.

Provision or deprivation of a treatment

Both the provision and deprivation of a treatment may pose an ethical dilemma for you as a researcher. When testing an intervention or a treatment, a researcher usually adopts a control experiment design. In such studies, is it ethical to provide a study population with an intervention or treatment that has not yet been conclusively proven effective or beneficial? But if you do not test a treatment/intervention, how can you prove or disprove its effectiveness or benefits? On the other hand, you are providing an intervention that may not be effective. Is this ethical? Is it ethical to deprive the control group of a treatment even if it may prove to be only slightly effective? And beyond the issue of control groups, is it ethical to deprive people who are struggling for life of the possible benefit, however small, which may be derived from a drug that is only under trial? As a researcher you need to be aware of these ethical issues. There are arguments and counter-arguments about these issues. However, it is usually accepted that deprivation of a trial treatment to a control group is not unethical as, in the absence of this, a study can never establish the effectiveness of a treatment which may deprive many others of its possible benefits. This deprivation of the possible benefits, on the other hand, is considered by some as unethical.

There are no simple answers to these dilemmas. Ensuring informed consent, 'minimum risk' and frank discussion as to the implications of participation in the study may help to resolve some of these ethical issues.

Using inappropriate research methodology

A researcher has an obligation to use appropriate methodology, within his/her knowledge base, in conducting a study. It is unethical to use deliberately a method or procedure you know to be inappropriate to prove or disprove something that you want to, such as by selecting a highly biased sample, using an invalid instrument or by drawing wrong conclusions.

Incorrect reporting

To report the findings in a way that changes or slants them to serve your own or someone else's interest is unethical. Correct and unbiased reporting of the findings are important characteristics of ethical research practice.

Inappropriate use of the information

How will the information obtained from respondents be used by the researcher? The use of information in a way that directly or indirectly affects respondents adversely is unethical. Can information be used adversely to affect the study population? If so, how can the study population be protected? As a researcher you need to consider and resolve these issues. Sometimes it is possible to harm individuals in the process of achieving benefits for organisations. An example would be a study to examine the feasibility of restructuring an organisation. Restructuring may be beneficial to the organisation as a whole but may be harmful to some individuals. Should you ask respondents for information that is likely to be used against them? If you do, the information may be used against them, and if you do not, the organisation may not be able to derive the benefits of restructuring. In the author's opinion, it is ethical to ask questions provided you tell respondents of the potential use of the information, including the possibility of its being used against some of them, and you let them decide if they want to participate. Some may participate for the betterment of the organisation even though it may harm them and others may decide against it. However, to identify either of them is unethical in research.

Ethical issues regarding the sponsoring organisation

Restrictions imposed by the sponsoring organisation

Most research in the social sciences is carried out using funds provided by sponsoring organisations for a specific purpose. The funds may be given to develop a programme or evaluate it;

to examine its effectiveness and efficiency; to study the impact of a policy; to test a product; to study the behaviour of a group or community; or to study a phenomenon, issue or attitude. Sometimes there may be direct or indirect controls exercised by sponsoring organisations. They may select the methodology, prohibit the publication of 'what was found' or impose other restrictions on the research that may stand in the way of obtaining and disseminating accurate information. Both the imposition and acceptance of these controls and restrictions are unethical, as they constitute interference and could amount to the sponsoring organisation tailoring research findings to meet its vested interests.

The misuse of information

How is the sponsoring body going to use the information? How is this likely to affect the study population? Sometimes sponsoring organisations use research as a pretext for obtaining management's agenda. It is unethical to let your research be used as a reason for justifying management decisions when the research findings do not support them. However, it is recognised that it may be extremely difficult or even impossible for a researcher to prevent this from happening.

Summary

This chapter is designed to make you aware of the ethical issues to be considered when conducting research. The ethical issues to be considered are the same in both quantitative and qualitative research. How you resolve them depends upon you, and the conditions under which you are working.

Being ethical means adhering to the code of conduct that has evolved over the years for an acceptable professional practice. Any deviation from this code of conduct is considered as unethical and the greater the deviation, the more serious the breach. For most professions ethical codes in research are an integral part of their overall ethics, though some research bodies have evolved their own codes.

Ethical issues in research can be looked at as they relate to research participants, researchers and sponsoring organisations. With regard to research participants, the following areas could pose ethical issues if not dealt with properly: collecting information; seeking consent; providing incentives; seeking sensitive information; the possibility of causing harm to participants; and maintaining confidentiality. It is important to examine these areas thoroughly for any unethical practice. With regard to the researcher, areas of ethical concern include the following: introducing bias; providing and depriving individuals of treatment; using unacceptable research methodology; inaccurate reporting; and the inappropriate use of information. Ethical considerations in relation to sponsoring organisations concern restrictions imposed on research designs and the possible use of findings. As a newcomer to research you should be aware of what constitutes unethical practice and be able to put appropriate strategies in place to deal with any harm that may done to any stakeholder.

For You to Think About

▸ Refamiliarise yourself with the keywords listed at the beginning of this chapter and if you are uncertain about the meaning or application of any of them revisit these in the chapter before moving on.

▸ Find a copy of your university's or department's code of ethics for research (or examples of codes of conduct for your chosen profession). Can you identify any areas of research or approaches that might come into conflict with these guidelines?

▸ Some might suggest that asking for any kind of information from an individual is unethical as it is an invasion of his/her privacy. Consider how you might argue for and against this suggestion.

▸ Ethical issues may arise at any point in the research process. Reflecting on the principles raised in this chapter, make a list of ethical issues that you think should be considered at each step in the eight-step model.

▸ Imagine you are planning to undertake a hypothetical research study in an area of interest to you. Identify the various stakeholder groups and list the possible ethical concerns you need to be aware of from the perspective of each one of the groups.

STEP VII Processing and Displaying Data

This operational step includes two chapters:

- Chapter 15: Processing data
- Chapter 16: Displaying data

CHAPTER 15
Processing Data

In this chapter you will learn about:

- Methods for processing data in quantitative studies
- How to edit data and prepare data for coding
- How to code data
- How to code qualitative data in quantitative studies
- Methods for processing data in qualitative studies
- Analysing data in qualitative and quantitative studies
- The role of computers in data analysis
- The role of statistics in research

Keywords: *analysis, closed questions, code book, coding, concepts, content analysis, cross-tabulation, data displaying, data processing, editing, frame of analysis, frequency distribution, multiple responses, open-ended questions, pre-test.*

If you were actually doing a research study, you would by now have reached a stage where you have either extracted or collected the required information. The next step is what to do with this information. How do you find the answers to your research questions? How do you make sense of the information collected? How do you prove or disprove your hypothesis if you had one? How should the information be analysed to achieve the objectives of your study? To answer these questions you need to subject your data to a number of procedures that constitute the core of data processing (Figure 15.1).

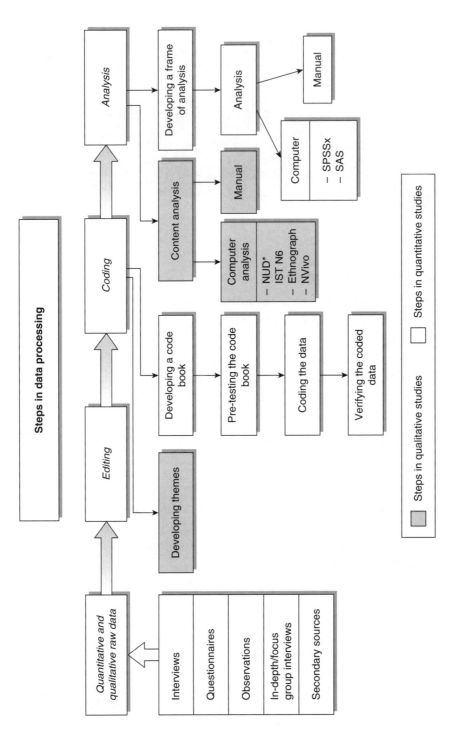

FIGURE 15.1 Steps in data processing

These procedures are the same whether your study is quantitative or qualitative, but what you do within each procedure is different. For both types of study you need to visualise how you are going to present your findings to your readership in light of its background and the purpose of the study. You need to decide what type of analysis would be appropriate for the readers of your report. It is in light of the purpose of your study and your impression about the level of understanding of your readership that you decide the type of analysis you should undertake. For example, there is no point in doing a sophisticated statistical analysis if your readers are not familiar with statistical procedures. In quantitative research the main emphasis in data analysis is to decide how you are going to analyse information obtained in response to each question that you asked of your respondents. In qualitative research the focus is on what should be the basis of analysis of the information obtained; that is, is it contents, discourse, narrative or event analysis? Because of the different techniques used in processing data in quantitative and qualitative research, this chapter is divided into two parts. Part One deals with data processing in quantitative studies and Part Two with qualitative.

Part one: Data processing in quantitative studies

Editing

Irrespective of the method of data collection, the information collected is called *raw data* or simply *data*. The first step in processing your data is to ensure that the data is 'clean' – that is, free from inconsistencies and incompleteness. This process of 'cleaning' is called **editing**.

Editing consists of scrutinising the completed research instruments to identify and minimise, as far as possible, errors, incompleteness, misclassification and gaps in the information obtained from the respondents. Sometimes even the best investigators can:

- forget to ask a question;
- forget to record a response;
- wrongly classify a response;
- write only half a response;
- write illegibly.

In the case of a questionnaire, similar problems can crop up. These problems to a great extent can be reduced simply by (1) checking the contents for completeness, and (2) checking the responses for internal consistency.

The way you check the contents for completeness depends upon the way the data has been collected. In the case of an interview, just checking the interview schedule for the above problems may improve the quality of the data. It is good practice for an interviewer to take a few moments to peruse responses for possible incompleteness and inconsistencies. In the case of a questionnaire, again, just by carefully checking the responses some of the problems may be reduced. There are several ways of minimising such problems:

- **By inference** – Certain questions in a research instrument may be related to one another and it might be possible to find out the answer to one question from the answer to another. Of course, you must be careful about making such inferences or you may introduce new errors into the data.
- **By recall** – If the data is collected by means of interviews, sometimes it might be possible for the interviewer to recall a respondent's answers. Again, you must be extremely careful.
- **By going back to the respondent** – If the data has been collected by means of interviews or the questionnaires contain some identifying information, it is possible to visit or phone a respondent to confirm or ascertain an answer. This is, of course, expensive and time consuming.

There are two ways of editing the data:

1 examine all the answers to one question or variable at a time;
2 examine all the responses given to all the questions by one respondent at a time.

The author prefers the second method as it provides a total picture of the responses, which also helps you to assess their internal consistency.

Coding

Having 'cleaned' the data, the next step is to code it. The method of **coding** is largely dictated by two considerations:

1 the way a variable has been measured (measurement scale) in your research instrument (e.g. if a response to a question is descriptive, categorical or quantitative);
2 the way you want to communicate the findings about a variable to your readers.

For coding, the first level of distinction is whether a set of data is qualitative or quantitative in nature. For qualitative data a further distinction is whether the information is descriptive in nature (e.g. a description of a service to a community, a case history) or is generated through discrete qualitative categories. For example, the following information about a respondent is in discrete qualitative categories: income – above average, average, below average; gender – male, female; religion – Christian, Hindu, Muslim, Buddhist, etc.; or attitude towards an issue – strongly favourable, favourable, uncertain, unfavourable, strongly unfavourable. Each of these variables is measured either on a **nominal scale** or an **ordinal scale**. Some of them could also have been measured on a **ratio scale** or an **interval scale**. For example, income can be measured in dollars (ratio scale), or an attitude towards an issue can be measured on an interval or a ratio scale. The way you proceed with the coding depends upon the measurement scale used in the measurement of a variable and whether a question is open-ended or closed.

In addition, the types of statistical procedures that can be applied to a set of information to a large extent depend upon the measurement scale on which a variable was measured in the research instrument. For example, you can find out different statistical descriptors such as mean, mode and median if income is measured on a ratio scale, but not if it is measured on an ordinal or a nominal scale. It is extremely important to understand that the way you are able to analyse a set of information is dependent upon the measurement scale used in the research instrument for measuring a variable. It is therefore important to visualise – particularly at the planning stage when constructing the research instrument – the way you are going to communicate your findings.

How you can analyse information obtained in response to a question depends upon how a question was asked, and how a respondent answered it. In other words, it depends upon the measurement scale on which a response can be measured/classified. If you study answers given by your respondents in reply to a question, you will realise that almost all responses can be classified into one of the following three categories:

1 quantitative responses;
2 categorical responses (which may be quantitative or qualitative);
3 descriptive responses (which are invariably qualitative – keep in mind that this is qualitative data collected as part of quantitative research and not the qualitative research).

For the purpose of analysis, quantitative and categorical responses need to be dealt with differently from descriptive ones. Both quantitative and categorical information go through a process that is primarily aimed at transforming the information into numerical values, called *codes*, so that the information can be easily analysed, either manually or by computers. On the other hand, descriptive information first goes through a process called *content analysis*, whereby you identify the main themes that emerge from the descriptions given by respondents in answer to questions. Having identified the main themes, there are three ways that you can deal with them: (1) you can examine verbatim responses and integrate them with the text of your report to either support or contradict your argument; (2) you can assign a code to each theme and count how frequently each has occurred; and (3) you can combine both methods to communicate your findings. This is your choice, and it is based on your impression of the preference of your readers.

For coding quantitative and qualitative data in quantitative studies you need to go through the following steps:

Step I developing a code book;
Step II pre-testing the code book;
Step III coding the data;
Step IV verifying the coded data.

Step I: Developing a code book

A **code book** provides a set of rules for assigning numerical values to answers obtained from respondents. Let us take an example. Figure 15.2 lists some questions taken from a questionnaire used in a survey conducted by the author to ascertain the impact of occupational redeployment on an individual. The questions selected should be sufficient to serve as a prototype for developing a code book, as they cover the various issues involved in the process.

1   Please indicate:

   (a) Your current age in completed years: _____

   (c) Your marital status: (Please tick)

      Currently married _____

      Living in a de facto relationship _____

      Separated _____

      Divorced _____

      Never married _____

2   (b) If tertiary/university, please specify the level achieved and area of study.

     (Please specify all postgraduate qualifications.)

Level of achievement	*Area of study: e.g. engineering, accounting*
Associate diploma	
Diploma	
Bachelor	
Graduate diploma	
Masters	
PhD	

11 What, in your opinion, are the main differences between your jobs prior to and after redeployment?

_____

_____

_____

12 We would like to know your perception of the two jobs *before* and *after* redeployment with respect to the following aspects of your job. Please rate them on a five-point scale using the following guide:

   5 = extremely satisfied, 4 = very satisfied, 3 = satisfied, 2 = dissatisfied, 1 = extremely dissatisfied

Before redeployment					*Areas*	*After redeployment*				
1	2	3	4	5		1	2	3	4	5
					Job status					
					Job satisfaction					
					Motivation to work					
					Interest in the job					
					Self-esteem					
					Professional competence					
					Peer interaction					
					Morale					
					Work environment					
					Social interaction					

FIGURE 15.2   *Example of questions from a survey*

There are two formats for data entry: 'fixed' and 'free'. In this chapter we will be using the fixed format to illustrate how to develop a code book. The fixed format stipulates that a piece of information obtained from a respondent is entered in a specific column. Each column has a number and the 'Col. no.' in the code book refers to the column in which a specific type of information is to be entered. The information about an individual is thus entered in a row(s) comprising these columns.

For a beginner it is important to understand the structure of a code book (Table 15.1), which is based on the responses given to the questions listed in Figure 15.2.

In Table 15.1, *column 1* refers to the columns in which a particular piece of information is to be entered. Allocation of columns in a fixed format is extremely important because, when you write a program, you need to specify the column in which a particular piece of information is entered so that the computer can perform the required procedures.

Column 2 identifies the question number in the research instrument for which the information is being coded. This is primarily to identify coding with the question number in the instrument.

Column 3 refers to the name of the variable. Each variable in a program is given a unique name so that the program can carry out the requested statistical procedures. Usually there are restrictions on the way you can name a variable (e.g. the number of characters you can use to name a variable and whether you use the alphabet or numerals). You need to check your program for this. It is advisable to name a variable in such a way that you can easily recognise it from its name.

Column 4 lists the responses to the various questions. Developing a response pattern for the questions is the most important, difficult and time-consuming part of developing a code book. The degree of difficulty in developing a response pattern differs with the types of questions in your research instrument (open ended or closed). If a question is closed, the response pattern has already been developed as part of the instrument construction and all you need to do at this stage is to assign a numerical value to each response category. In terms of analysis, this is one of the main advantages of closed questions. If a closed question includes 'other' as one of the response categories, to accommodate any response that you may not have listed when developing the instrument, you should analyse the responses and assign them to non-overlapping categories in the same way as you would do for open-ended questions. Add these to the already developed response categories and assign each a numerical value.

If the number of responses to a question is less than nine, you need only one column to code the responses, and if it is more than nine but less than 99, you need two columns (column 1 in the code book). But if a question asks respondents to give more than one response, the number of columns assigned should be in accordance with the number of responses to be coded. If there are, say, eight possible responses to a particular question and a respondent is asked to give three responses, you need three columns to code the responses to the question. Let us assume there are 12 possible responses to a question. To code each response you need two columns and, therefore, to code three responses you need six columns.

The coding of open-ended questions is more difficult. Coding of open-ended questions requires the response categories to be developed first through a process called content analysis. One of the easier ways of analysing open-ended questions is to select a number of interview schedules/questionnaires randomly from the total completed interview schedules or

TABLE 15.1 *An example of a code book*

Col. no. 1	Q. no. 2	Variable name 3	Response pattern 4	Code 5
1–3	S. no.	ID	Actual serial number	Code actual
4	Record no.	RNO	First record	1
			Second record	2
			Third record	3
5	1(a)	Age	20–24	1
			25–29	2
			30–34	3
			35–39	4
			40–44	5
			45–49	6
			No response	9
6	1(c)	MS	Currently married	1
			Living in a de facto relationship	2
			Separated	3
			Divorced	4
			Never married	5
			No response	9
	2(b)	TEDU	Assoc. Dip.	1
			Diploma	2
			Bachelors	3
			Grad. Dip.	4
			Masters	5
			PhD	6
			Not applicable	8
			No response	9
7		TEDU1	Same as in TEDU	Code
8		TEDU2	Same as in TEDU	as in
9		TEDU3	Same as in TEDU	TEDU
		STUDY	Behavioural Sciences	1
			Business	2
			Economics/Commerce	3
			Communication	4
			Engineering	5
			Geography	6
			History	7
			Graphics	8
			Librarianship	9
			Nursing	10
			Performing Arts	11
			Secretarial	12
			Social Work	13
			Psychology	14
			Education	15
			Chartered Acct.	16
			Zoology	17
			Anthropology	18
			Social Sciences	19
			Public/Health Admin.	20
			English	21
			Audio–visual Aids Education	22

(Continued)

TABLE 15.1 *(Continued)*

Col. no. 1	Q. no. 2	Variable name 3	Response pattern 4	Code 5
			Not applicable	88
			No response	99
10–11	2(b)	STUDY 1	Same as in STUDY	Code
12–13		STUDY 2	Same as in STUDY	as in
				STUDY
14–15		STUDY 3	Same as in STUDY	
	11	DIFWK	Lack of job satisfaction	
			– current job	01
			– previous job	02
			Less responsibility	
			– current job	03
			– previous job	04
			Low morale	
			– current job	05
			– previous job	06
			Lack of recognition of hard work	
			–current job	07
			– previous job	08
			Skills irrelevant	
			– current job	09
			– previous job	10
			Repetitious nature	
			–current job	11
			–previous job	12
			Job more segmented	
			–current job	13
			–previous job	14
			Reduction in occup. status	15
			Greater involvement in total process	
			– current job	16
			– previous job	17
			More restricted duties	
			– current job	18
			– previous job	19
			Less flexibility	
			– current job	20
			– previous job	21
			More people contact	
			– current job	22
			– previous job	23
			Less people contact	
			– current job	24
			– previous job	25
			More responsibility	
			– current job	26
			– previous job	27
			Better work environment	
			– current job	28

(Continued)

TABLE 15.1 *(Continued)*

Col. no. 1	Q. no. 2	Variable name 3	Response pattern 4	Code 5
			– previous job	29
			Better work morale	
			– current job	30
			– previous job	31
			Working in a team	
			– current job	32
			– previous job	33
			Work as an individual	
			– current job	34
			– previous job	35
			Lack of job security	
			– current job	36
			– previous job	37
			Current job full–time	38
			Better career prospects	
			– current job	39
			– previous job	40
			No commonality	41
			Different working conditions	42
			Change in occup. status (not specified)	43
			High occup. level	
			– current job	44
			– previous job	45
			More job security in present job	46
			More professional environment in	
			– current job	47
			– previous job	48
			Different skills to learn in current job	49
			Higher workload	
			– current job	50
			– previous job	51
			Less supervision in	
			– current job	52
			– previous job	53
			Current job more relevant to my training	54
			Current job more rewarding	55
			Better morale in current job	56
			Greater variety of duties in	
			– current job	57
			– previous job	58
			Current job more rewarding	59
			Better morale in	
			– current job	60
			Less variety of tasks	

(Continued)

TABLE 15.1 *(Continued)*

Col. no. 1	Q. no. 2	Variable name 3	Response pattern 4	Code 5
			in current job	61
			Fewer skills required in	
			– current job	62
			– previous job	63
			Change in job title	64
			Previous job very demanding	65
			Opportunity to use initiative in previous job	66
			Current job does not require initiative	67
			Different skills required in current job	68
			No career prospects	
			– current job	69
			– previous job	70
			More professional environment in current job	71
			Different skills to learn in current job	72
			Different working conditions	73
			Change in occup. status (change not specified)	74
			Change in job resp. (change not specified)	75
			Current job is more structured	76
			Now part of the team	77
			No change	78
			Irrelevant response	79
			Other	80
			Not applicable	88
			No response	99
16–17	11	DIFWK1	Same as in DIFWK	code as
18–19		DIFWK2	Same as in DIFWK	in
20–21		DIFWK3	Same as in DIFWK	DIFWK
22–23		DIFWK4		
24–25		DIFWK5		
			Extremely dissatisfied	1
			Dissatisfied	2
	12	BEAFTER	Satisfied	3
			Very satisfied	4
			Extremely satisfied	5
			Same as in BEAFTER	
	26	JOBSTA	Same as in BEAFTER	Code as
	27	JOBSTB	Same as in BEAFTER	in
				BEAFTER
	28	JOBSATA	Same as in BEAFTER	Code as in
	29	JOBSATB	Same as in BEAFTER and so on	BEAFTER

questionnaires received. Then select an open-ended question from one of these schedules or questionnaires and write down the response(s) on a sheet of paper. If the person has given more than one response, write them separately on the same sheet. Similarly, from the same questionnaire/schedule select another open-ended question and write down the responses given on a separate sheet. In the same way you can select other open-ended questions and write down the response(s). Remember that the response to each question should be written on a separate sheet. Now select another questionnaire/interview schedule and go through the same process, adding response(s) given for the same question on the sheet for that question. Continue the process until you feel that the responses are being repeated and you are getting no or very few new ones – that is, when you have reached a saturation point.

Now, one by one, examine the responses to each question to ascertain the similarities and differences. If two or more responses are similar in meaning though not necessarily in language, try to combine them under one category. Give a name to the category that is descriptive of the responses. Remember, when you code the data you code categories, *not* responses per se. It is advisable to write down the different responses under each category in the code book so that, while coding, you know the type of responses you have grouped under a category. In developing these categories there are three important considerations:

1   The categories should be *mutually* exclusive. Develop non-overlapping categories. A response should not be able to be placed within two categories.
2   The categories should be *exhaustive*; that is, almost every response should be able to be placed within one of the categories. If too many responses cannot be so categorised, it is an indication of ineffective categorisation. In such a situation you should examine your categories again.
3   The use of the '*other*' category, effectively a 'waste basket' for those odd responses that cannot be put into any category, must be kept to the absolute minimum because, as mentioned, it reflects the failure of the classification system. This category should not include more than 5 per cent of the total responses and should not contain any more responses than any other category.

Column 5 lists the actual codes of the code book that you decide to assign to a response. You can assign any numerical value to any response so long as you do not repeat it for another response within the same question. Two responses to questions are commonly repeated: 'not applicable' and 'no response'. You should select a number that can be used for these responses for all or most questions. For example, responses such as 'not applicable' and 'no response' could be given a code of 8 and 9 respectively, even though the responses to a question may be limited to only 2 or 3. In other words, suppose you want to code the gender of a respondent and you have decided to code female = 1 and male = 2. For 'no response', instead of assigning a code of 3, assign a code of 9. This suggestion helps in remembering codes, which will help to increase your speed in coding.

To explain how to code, let us take the questions listed in the example in Figure 15.2. We will take each question one by one to detail the process.

Question 1(a)

Your current age in completed years: _____

This is an open-ended quantitative question. In questions like this it is important to determine the range of responses – the respondent with the lowest and the respondent with the highest age. To do this, go through a number of questionnaires/interview schedules. Once the range is established, divide it into a number of categories. The categories developed are dependent upon a number of considerations such as the purpose of analysis, the way you want to communicate the findings of your study and whether the findings are going to be compared with those of another study. Let us assume that the range in the study is 23 to 49 years and assume that you develop the following categories to suit your purpose: 20–24, 25–29, 30–34, 35–39, 40–44 and 45–49. If your range is correct you should need no other categories. Let us assume that you decide to code 20–24 = 1, 25–29 = 2, 30–34 = 3, and so on. To accommodate 'no response' you decide to assign a code of 9. Let us assume you decided to code the responses to this question in column 5 of the code sheet.

Question 1(c)

Your marital status: (Please tick)
*Currently married*_____
*Living in a de facto relationship*_____
*Separated*_____
*Divorced*_____
*Never married*_____

This is a closed categorical question. That is, the response pattern is already provided. In these situations you just need to assign a numerical value to each category. For example, you may decide to code 'currently married' = 1, 'living in a de facto relationship' = 2, 'separated' = 3, 'divorced' = 4 and 'never married' = 5. You may add 'no response' as another category and assign it with a code of 9. The response to this question is coded in column 6 of the code sheet.

Question 2(b)

If tertiary/university, please specify the level achieved and the area of study. (Please specify all postgraduate qualifications.)

In this question a respondent is asked to indicate the area in which s/he has achieved a tertiary qualification. The question asks for two aspects: (1) level of achievement, which is categorical; and (2) area of study, which is open ended. Also, a person may have more than one qualification which makes it a multiple response question. In such questions both aspects of the question are to be coded. In this case, this means the level of achievement (e.g. associate diploma, diploma) and the area of study (e.g. engineering, accounting). When coding multiple responses, decide on the maximum possible number of responses to be coded. Let us assume you code a maximum number of three levels of tertiary education. (This would depend upon the maximum number of levels of achievement identified by the study population.) Firstly, code the levels of achievement TEDU (TEDU: T = tertiary and EDU = education; the naming of the variable – 'level of achievement' – in this manner is done for easy identification) and then the area of study, STUDY (the variable name given to the 'area of study' = STUDY). In the above example, let us assume that you decided to code three levels of achievement. To distinguish them from each other we call the first level TEDU1, the second TEDU2 and the third TEDU3, and decide to code them in columns, 7, 8 and 9 respectively. Similarly, the names given to the three areas of STUDY are STUDY1, STUDY2 and STUDY3 and we decide to code them in columns 10–11, 12–13 and 14–15. The codes (01 to 23) assigned to different qualifications are listed in the code book. If a respondent has only one qualification, the question of second and third qualification is not applicable and you need to decide a code for 'not applicable'. Assume you assigned a code of 88. 'No response' would then be assigned a code of 99 for this question.

Question 11

What, in your opinion, are the main differences between your jobs prior to and after redeployment?

_____

_____

_____

This is an open-ended question. To code this you need to go through the process of content analysis as explained earlier. Within the scope of this chapter it is not possible to explain the details, but response categories that have been listed are based upon the responses given by 109 respondents to the survey on occupational redeployment. In coding questions like this, on the one hand you need to keep the variation in the respondents' answers and, on the other, you want to break them up into meaningful categories to identify the commonalities. Because this question is asking respondents to identify the differences between their jobs before and after redeployment, for easy identification let us assume this variable was named DIFWK (DIF = difference and WK = work). Responses to this question are listed in Figure 15.3. These responses have been selected at random from the questionnaires returned.

A close examination of these responses reveals that a number of themes are common, for example: 'learning new skills in the new job'; 'challenging tasks are missing from the new position'; 'more secure in the present job'; 'more interaction in the present job'; 'less responsibility'; 'more variety'; 'no difference'; 'more satisfying'. There are many similar themes that hold for both the before and after jobs. Therefore, we developed these themes for 'current job' and 'previous job'.

One of the main differences between qualitative and quantitative research is the way responses are used in the report. In qualitative research the responses are normally used either verbatim or are organised under certain themes and the actual responses are provided to substantiate them.

In quantitative research the responses are examined, common themes are identified, the themes are named (or categories are developed) and the responses given by respondents are classified under these themes. The data then can also be analysed to determine the frequency of the themes if so desired. It is also possible to analyse the themes in relation to some other characteristics such as age, education and income of the study population.

Respondent 3

'Hours now FT: totally different skills required; deal with public; busier, more structured day and duties; now a part of the team instead of an independent worker.'

Respondent 20

'That I am happy and made to feel as though I am a valuable part of a team.'

Respondent 41

'This one is great, other one was lousy due to mismanagement, poor morale and feelings that dedication and hard work counted for nothing. Department of … is well managed and morale is good and the graphic design work is fun and I am supported by my supervisors and subordinates.'

Respondent 48

'Before	*After*
15 hours per week	*24 hours per week*
Monday to Friday	*Very satisfactory*
On the go the whole time	*Dealing with the public*
No sitting	*Dealing with severe psychiatric*
Dealings with the public	*patients can be very stressful.'*

Respondent 52

'No difference.'

Respondent 54

'My substantive position has been the same before and after the redeployment, but before the redeployment I was acting as Project Manager (level 5) and after being redeployed I was assigned to programming duties (level e).'

Respondent 63

'This position has more day-to-day administration (it includes corporate services, finance, PR, IT, etc).'

Respondent 69

'Had to find my own job.'

Respondent 72

'The job I was doing I looked after the needs of a workshop where in this job I process files and deliver them.'

Respondent 78

'Challenging tasks are missing from the new position now that I am familiar with it. Many routine activities (that I have been glad to learn in terms of career development) but that I am becoming bored with. My previous job was much more difficult and interesting than this one.'

Respondent 79

'I am more secure in my present job and it is better paid as I work longer hours now. I only worked 6 ½ hours as a tea attendant.'

Respondent 81

'My previous job required me to be involved in the whole area of government/community and non-government requiring assistance in relation to settlement needs of migrants. My current position does not provide job satisfaction, particularly in relation to the offenders that I currently deal with.'

Respondent 97

'Less responsibility, more specific job, restricted job.'

Respondent 105

'More variety, more flexibility, more responsibility in the present job, but less confidence, more caution and some resentment.'

FIGURE 15.3 *Some selected responses to the open-ended question (no. 11) in Figure 15.2*

The code book lists the themes developed on the basis of responses given. As you can see, many categories may result. The author's advice is not to worry about this as categories can always be combined later if required. The reverse is impossible unless you go back to the raw data.

Let us assume you want to code up to five responses to this question and that you have decided to name these five variables as DIFWK1, DIFWK2, DIFWK3, DIFWK4 and DIFWK5. Let us also assume that you have coded them in columns 16–17, 18–19, 20–21, 22–23 and 24–25 respectively.

Question 12

> We would like to know your level of satisfaction with the two jobs *before* and *after* redeployment with respect to the following aspects of your job. Please rate them on a five-point scale using the following guide:
>
> 5 = extremely satisfied, 4 = very satisfied, 3 = satisfied, 2 = dissatisfied, 1 = extremely dissatisfied

This is a highly structured question asking respondents to compare on a five-point ordinal scale their level of satisfaction with various areas of their job before and after redeployment. As we are gauging the level of satisfaction before and after redeployment, respondents are expected to give two responses to each area. In this example let us assume you have used the name JOBSTA for job status after redeployment (JOB = job, ST = status and A = after redeployment) and JOBSTB for before redeployment (JOB = job, ST = status and B = before redeployment). Similarly, for the second area, job satisfaction, you have decided that the variable name, JOBSATA (JOB = job, SAT = satisfaction and A = after), will stand for the level of job satisfaction after redeployment and JOBSATB will stand for the level before redeployment. Other variable names have been similarly assigned. In this example the variable, JOBSTA, is entered in column 26, JOBSTB in column 27, and so on.

Step II: Pre-testing the code book

Once a code book is designed, it is important to pre-test it for any problems before you code your data. A **pre-test** involves selecting a few questionnaires/interview schedules and actually coding the responses to ascertain any problems in coding. It is possible that you may not have provided for some responses and therefore will be unable to code them. Change your code book, if you need to, in light of the pre-test.

Step III: Coding the data

Once your code book is finalised, the next step is to code the raw data. There are three ways of doing this:

1 coding on the questionnaires/interview schedule itself, if space for coding was provided at the time of constructing the research instrument;

2 coding on separate code sheets that are available for purchase;
3 coding directly into the computer using a program such as SPSSx, SAS.

To explain the process of coding let us take the same questions that were used in developing the code book. We select three questionnaires at random from a total of 109 respondents (Figures 15.4, 15.5, 15.6). Using the code book as a guide, we code the information from these sheets onto the coding sheet (Figure 15.7). Let us examine the coding process by taking respondent 3 (Figure 15.4).

Respondent 3

The total number of respondents is more than 99 and this is the third questionnaire, so 003 was given as the identification number which is coded in columns 1–3 (Figure 15.7). Because it is the first record for this respondent, 1 was coded in column 4. This respondent is 49 years of age and falls in the category 45–49, which was coded as 6. As the information on age is entered in column 5, 6 was coded in this column of the code sheet. The marital status of this person is 'divorced', hence 4 was coded in column 6. This person has a Bachelors degree in librarianship. The code chosen for a Bachelors degree is 3, which was entered in column 7. Three tertiary qualifications have been provided for, and as this person does not have any other qualifications, TEDU2 and TEDU3 are not applicable, and therefore a code of 8 is entered in columns 8 and 9. This person's Bachelors degree is in librarianship for which code 09 was assigned and entered in columns 10–11. Since there is only one qualification, STUDY2 and STUDY3 are not applicable; therefore, a code of 88 was entered in columns 12–13 and 14–15. This person has given a number of responses to question no. 11 (DIFWK), which asks respondents to list the main differences between their jobs before and after redeployment. In coding such questions much caution is required.

Examine the responses named DIFWK1, DIFWK2, DIFWK3, DIFWK4 and DIFWK5, to identify the codes that can be assigned. A code of 22 (now deal with public) was assigned to one of the responses, which we enter in columns 16–17. The second difference, DIFWK2, was assigned a code of 69 (totally different skill required), which is coded in columns 18–19.

DIFWK3 was assigned a code of 77 (current job more structure) and coded in columns 20–21. Similarly, the fourth (DIFWK4) and the fifth (DIFWK5) difference in the jobs before and after redeployment are coded as 78 (now part of the team instead of independent worker) and 38 (hours – now full time), which are entered in columns 22–23 and 24–25 respectively. Question 12 is extremely simple to code. Each area of a job has two columns, one for before and the other for after. Job status (JOBST) is divided into two variables, JOBSTA for a respondent's level of satisfaction after redeployment and JOBSTB for his/her level before redeployment. JOBSTA is entered in column 26 and JOBSTB in column 27. For JOBSTA the code, 5 (as marked by the respondent), is entered in column 26 and the code for JOBSTB, 4, is entered in column 27. Other areas of the job before and after redeployment are similarly coded.

The other two examples are coded in the same manner. The coded data is shown in Figure 15.7. In the process of coding you might find some responses that do not fit your predetermined categories. If so, assign them a code and add these to your code book.

RESPONDENT = 3

1   Please indicate:
    (a) Your current age in completed years: ___49___
    (c) Your marital status: (Please tick)
        Currently married _____
        Living in a de facto relationship _____
        Seperated _____
        Divorced ___✓___
        Never married _____

2   (b) If teritiary/university, please specify the level achieved and area of study. (Please specify all postgraduate qualifications.)

Level of achievement	Area of study: e.g. engineering, accounting
Associate diploma	
Diploma	
Bachelor	Librarianship
Graduate diploma	
Masters	
PhD	

11 What, in your opinion, are the main differences between your jobs prior to and after redeployment?

'Hours-now F.T', 'Totally different skills required', 'Now deal with public',

'Busier, more structured day and duties', 'Now part of the team instead of independent worker'

12 We would like to know your perception of the two jobs *before* and *after* redeployment with respect to the following aspects of your job. Please rate them on a five-point scale, using the following guide:

5 = extremely satisfied, 4 = very satisfied, 3 = satisfied, 2 = dissatisfied, 1 = extremely dissatisfied

Before redeployment					Areas	After redeployment				
1	2	3	4	5		1	2	3	4	5
			✓		Job status					✓
			✓		Job satisfaction					✓
			✓		Motivation to work					✓
			✓		Interest in the job					✓
			✓		Self-esteem					✓
			✓		Professional competence				✓	
			✓		Peer interaction					✓
			✓		Morale				✓	
			✓		Work environment				✓	
				✓	Social interaction			✓		

FIGURE 15.4   *Some questions from a survey – respondent 3*

RESPONDENT = 59

1 Please indicate:

(a) Your current age in completed years: ___45___

(c) Your marital status: (Please tick)
Currently married __✓__
Living in a de facto relationship _____
Separated _____
Divorced _____
Never married _____

2 (b) If tertiary/university, please specify the level achieved and area of study.
(Please specify all postgraduate qualifications.)

Level of achievement	Area of study: e.g. engineering, accounting
Associate diploma	
Diploma	
Bachelor	*Behavioural Sciences*
Graduate diploma	
Masters	
PhD	

11 What, in your opinion, are the main differences between your jobs prior to and after redeployment?

'Less Responsibility', 'More specific jobs'

'Restricted scope'.

12 We would like to know your perception of the two jobs *before* and *after* redeployment with respect to the following aspects of your job. Please rate them on a five-point scale using the following guide:

5 = extremely satisfied, 4 = very satisfied, 3 = satisfied, 2 = dissatisfied, 1 = extremely dissatisfied

Before redeployment					Areas	After redeployment				
1	2	3	4	5		1	2	3	4	5
			✓		Job status		✓			
			✓		Job satisfaction			✓		
			✓		Motivation to work		✓			
				✓	Interest in the job			✓		
				✓	Self-esteem			✓		
				✓	Professional competence			✓		
				✓	peer interaction				✓	
				✓	Morale		✓			
				✓	Work environment			✓		
			✓		Social interaction				✓	

FIGURE 15.5   *Some questions from a survey – respondent 59*

RESPONDENT = 81

1 Please indicate:

   (a) Your current age in completed years:___42___

   (c) Your marital status: (Please tick)

      Currently married ___✓___
      Living in a de facto relationship _____
      Separated _____
      Divorced _____
      Never married

2 (b) If tertiary/university, please specify the level achieved and area of study.

      (Please specify all postgraduate qualifications.)

Level of achievement	Area of study: e.g. engineering, accounting
Associate diploma	
Diploma	
Bachelor	Social work
Graduate diploma	
Masters	
PhD	

11 What, in your opinion, are the main differences between your jobs prior to and after redeployment?

'My previous job required me to be involved in the whole area of government/community and non-government requiring assistance in relation to settlement needs of migrants. My current position does not provide job satisfaction particularly in relation to the offenders that I currently deal with.'

12 We would like to know your perception of the two jobs *before* and *after* redeployment with respect to the following aspects of your job. Please rate them on a five-point scale using the following guide:

   5 = extremely satisfied, 4 = very satisfied, 3 = satisfied, 2 = dissatisfied, 1 = extremely dissatisfied

Before redeployment					Areas	After redeployment				
1	2	3	4	5		1	2	3	4	5
		✓			Job status		✓			
			✓		Job satisfaction		✓			
				✓	Motivation to work			✓		
			✓		Interest in the job		✓			
			✓		Self-esteem		✓			
		✓			Professional competence		✓			
		✓			Peer interaction			✓		
			✓		Morale		✓			
			✓		Work environment		✓			
		✓			Social interaction		✓			

FIGURE 15.6   *Some questions from a survey – respondent 81*

Fortran S

1	2	3	4	5	6	7	8	9	10	11	12	13	14	15	16	17	18	19	20	21	22	23	24	25	26	27	28	29	30	31	32	33	34	35	36	37	38	39	40
	0	0	1	6	4	3	8	8	0	9	8	8	8	8	2	2	6	9	7	7	7	8	3	8	5	4	5	4	5	4	5	4	5	4					
	0	5	9	6	1	3	8	8	0	1	8	8	8	8	0	3	1	9	7	7	8	8	8	8	2	4	3	4	2	4	3	5	3	5					
	0	8	1	5	1	2	8	8	1	3	8	8	8	8	1	7	0	1	8	8	8	8	8	8	2	3	2	4	3	5	2	4	2	4					

Column group labels:
- Identification number
- Statement Number
- Cont.
- Marital status
- Study area
- Difference in work
- Level of satisfaction
- Fortran S

Record no. — Age — Achievement level

FIGURE 15.7   An example of coded data on a code sheet

Step IV: Verifying the coded data

Once the data is coded, select a few research instruments at random and record the responses to identify any discrepancies in coding. Continue to verify coding until you are sure that there are no discrepancies. If there are discrepancies, re-examine the coding.

Developing a frame of analysis

Although a framework of analysis needs to evolve continuously while writing your report, it is desirable to broadly develop it before analysing the data. A **frame of analysis** should specify:

- which variables you are planning to analyse;
- how they should be analysed;
- what cross-tabulations you need to work out;
- which variables you need to combine to construct your major concepts or to develop indices (in formulating a research problem concepts are changed to variables – at this stage change them back to concepts);
- which variables are to be subjected to which statistical procedures.

To illustrate, let us take the example from the survey used in this chapter.

Frequency distributions

A **frequency distribution** groups respondents into the subcategories into which a variable can be divided. Unless you are not planning to use answers to some of the questions, you should have a frequency distribution for all the variables. Each variable can be specified either separately or collectively in the frame of analysis. To illustrate, they are identified here separately by the names used in the code book. For example, frame of analysis should include frequency distribution for the following variables:

- AGE;
- MS;
- TEDU (TEDU1, TEDU2, TEDU3 – multiple responses, to be collectively analysed);
- STUDY (STUDY1, STUDY2, STUDY3 – multiple responses, to be collectively analysed);
- DIFWK (DIFWK1, DIFWK2, DIFWK3, DIFWK4, DIFWK5 – multiple responses, to be collectively analysed);
- JOBSTA, JOBSTB;
- JOBSATA, JOBSATB;
- MOTIVA, MOTIVB.
- etc.

Cross-tabulations

Cross-tabulations analyse two variables, usually independent and dependent or attribute and dependent, to determine if there is a relationship between them. The subcategories of both the variables are cross-tabulated to ascertain if a relationship exists between them. Usually, the absolute number of respondents, and the row and column percentages, give you a reasonably good idea as to the possible association.

In the study we cited as an example in this chapter, one of the main variables to be explained is the level of satisfaction with the 'before' and 'after' jobs after redeployment. We developed two indices of satisfaction:

1 satisfaction with the job before redeployment (SATINDB);
2 satisfaction with the job after redeployment (SATINDA).

Differences in the level of satisfaction can be affected by a number of personal attributes such as the age, education, training and marital status of the respondents. Cross-tabulations help to identify which attributes affect the levels of satisfaction. Theoretically, it is possible to correlate any variables, but it is advisable to be selective or an enormous number of tables will result. Normally only those variables that you think have an effect on the dependent variable should be correlated. The following cross-tabulations are an example of the basis of a frame of analysis. You can specify as many variables as you want.

SATINDA and SATINDB by:

- AGE;
- MS;
- TEDU;
- STUDY;
- DIFWK.

These determine whether job satisfaction before and after redeployment is affected by age, marital status, education, and so on.

- SATINDA by SATINDB.
- This ascertains whether there is a relationship between job satisfaction before and after redeployment.

Reconstructing the main concepts

There may be places in a research instrument where you look for answers through a number of questions about different aspects of the same issue, for example the level of satisfaction with jobs before and after redeployment (SATINDB and SATINDA). In the questionnaire there were 10 aspects of a job about which respondents were asked to identify their level of satisfaction before and after redeployment. The level of satisfaction may vary from aspect to aspect. Though it is important to know respondents' reactions to each aspect, it is equally important to gauge an overall index of their satisfaction. You must therefore ascertain, before you actually analyse data, how you will combine responses to different questions.

In this example the respondents indicated their level of satisfaction by selecting one of the five response categories. A satisfaction index was developed by assigning a numerical value – the greater the magnitude of the response category, the higher the numerical score – to the response given by a respondent. The numerical value corresponding to the category ticked was added to determine the satisfaction index. The satisfaction index score for a respondent varies between 10 and 50. The interpretation of the score is dependent upon the way the numerical values are assigned. In this example the higher the score, the higher the level of satisfaction.

Statistical procedures

In this section you should list the statistical procedures that you want to subject your data to. You should identify the procedures followed by the list of variables that will be subjected to those procedures. For example,

Regression analysis:

- SATINDA and SATINDB.

Multiple regression analysis:

- SATINDA with AGE, EDUCATION, MS.
- SATINDB with AGE, EDUCATION, MS.

Analysis of variance (ANOVA):

Similarly, it may be necessary to think about and specify the different variables to be subjected to the various statistical procedures. There are a number of user-friendly programs such as SPSSx and SAS that you can easily learn.

Analysing quantitative data manually

Coded data can be analysed manually or with the help of a computer. If the number of respondents is reasonably small, there are not many variables to analyse, and you are neither familiar with a relevant computer program nor wish to learn one, you can manually analyse the data. However, manual analysis is useful only for calculating frequencies and for simple cross-tabulations. If you have not entered data into a computer but want to carry out statistical tests, they will have to be calculated manually, which may become extremely difficult and time consuming. However, the use of statistics depends upon your expertise and desire/need to communicate the findings in a certain way.

Be aware that manual analysis is extremely time consuming. The easiest way to analyse data manually is to code it directly onto large graph paper in columns in the same way as you would enter it into a computer. On the graph paper you do not need to worry about the column number. Detailed headings can be used or question numbers can be written on each column to code information about the question (Figure 15.8).

To analyse data manually (frequency distributions), count various codes in a column and then decode them. For example, age from Figure 15.8, 5 = 1, 6 = 2. This shows that out of the three respondents, one was between 40 and 44 years of age and the other two were between 45 and 49. Similarly, responses for each variable can be analysed. For cross-tabulations two columns must be read simultaneously to analyse responses in relation to each other.

If you want to analyse data using a computer, you should be familiar with the appropriate program. You should know how to create a data file, how to use the procedures involved, what statistical tests to apply and how to interpret them. Obviously in this area knowledge of computers and statistics plays an important role.

ID	Age	MS	Education			Study area			Difference in work					Status		Satisfaction	
			1	2	3	1	2	3	1	2	3	4	5	Before	After	Before	After
03	6	4	3	8	8	09	88	88	22	69	77	78	38	5	4	5	4
59	6	1	3	8	8	01	88	88	03	18	77	88	88	2	4	3	4
81	5	1	2	8	8	13	88	88	17	01	88	88	88	2	3	2	4

FIGURE 15.8 *Manual analysis using graph paper*

Part two: Data processing in qualitative studies

How you process and analyse data in a qualitative study depends upon how you plan to communicate the findings. Broadly, there are three ways in which you can write about your findings in qualitative research: (1) developing a narrative to describe a situation, episode, event or instance; (2) identifying the main themes that emerge from your field notes or transcription of your in-depth interviews and writing about them, quoting extensively in verbatim format; and (3) in addition to (2) above, also quantify the main themes in order to provide their prevalence and thus significance.

Editing, as understood for quantitative studies, is inappropriate for qualitative research. However, it is possible that you may be able to go through your notes to identify if something does not make sense. In such an event, you may be able to recall the context and correct the contents, but be careful in doing so as inability to recall precisely may introduce inaccuracies (**recall error**) in your description. Another way of ensuring whether you are truly reflecting the situation is to transcribe the interviews or observational notes and share them with the respondents or research participants for confirmation and approval. Validation of the information by a respondent is an important aspect of ensuring the accuracy of data collected through unstructured interviews.

For writing in a narrative format there is no analysis per se, however, you need to think through the sequence in which you need or want to narrate. For the other two ways of writing about the findings, you need to go through content analysis, as mentioned earlier. Content analysis means analysing the contents of interviews or observational field notes in order to identify the main themes that emerge from the responses given by your respondents or the observation notes made by you. This process involves a number of steps:

Step 1   **Identify the main themes.** You need to go carefully through descriptive responses given by your respondents to each question in order to understand the *meaning* they communicate. From these responses you develop broad themes that reflect these meanings. You will notice that people use different words and language to express themselves. It is important for you to select the wording of your themes in a way that accurately represents the meaning of the responses categorised under a theme. These themes become the basis for analysing the text of unstructured interviews. Similarly, you need to go through your field notes to identify the main themes.

Step 2   **Assign codes to the main themes.** Whether or not you assign a code to a main theme is dependent upon whether or not you want to count the number of times a theme has occurred in an interview. If you decide to count these themes you should, at random, select a few responses to an open-ended question or from your observational or discussion notes and identify the main themes. You continue to identify these themes from the same question till you have reached saturation point. Write these themes and assign a code to each of them, using numbers or keywords, otherwise just identify the main themes.

Step 3   **Classify responses under the main themes.** Having identified the themes, the next step is to go through the transcripts of all your interviews or your notes and classify the responses or contents of the notes under the different themes. You can also use a computer program such as Ethnograph, NUD*IST N6, NVivo, XSight for undertaking this thematic analysis. You will benefit by learning one of these programs if your data is suitable for such analysis.

Step 4   **Integrate themes and responses into the text of your report.** Having identified responses that fall within different themes, the next step is to integrate them into the text of your report. How you integrate them into your report is mainly your choice. Some people, while discussing the main themes that emerged from their study, use verbatim responses to keep the 'feel' of the responses. There are others who count how frequently a theme has occurred, and then provide a sample of the responses. It entirely depends upon the way you want to communicate the findings to your readers.

Content analysis in qualitative research – an example

The above four-step process was applied to a study recently carried out by the author to develop an operational service model, based upon the principle of family engagement. The information was predominantly gathered through in-depth and focus group discussions with clients, service providers and service managers. After informal talks with a number of stakeholders, a list of possible issues was developed to form the basis of discussions in these in-depth interviews and group discussions. The list was merely a guiding framework and was open to inclusion of any new issue that emerged during the discussions. Out of the several issues that were identified to examine various aspects of the model, here the author has taken only one to show the process of identifying themes that emerged during the discussions. Note that these themes have not been quantified. They are substantiated as verbatim, which is one of the main differences between qualitative and quantitative research. The following example shows perceived strengths of the Family Engagement Model (FEM) as identified by the stakeholders during in-depth interviews and focus groups. Information provided in Figure 15.8 provides an example of the outcome of this process.

Example: Developing themes through content analysis

Perceived strengths of the model

The framework developed for the perceived strengths of the model is based upon the analysis of the information gathered, which suggested that the various themes that emerged during the data collection stage reflecting strengths of the model can be classified under four perspectives. The following diagram shows the framework that emerged from the analysis.

Different perspectives classifying perceived strengths of the model.

Perceived strengths from the perspective of the family

This section details the perceived strengths of the model from the perspective of the family. Keep in mind that the sequential order of the perceived strengths is random and does not reflect any order or preference. Also, the naming of these themes is that of the author, which to the best of his knowledge captured the 'meanings' of the intention of the research participants.

Empowerment of families

Almost everyone expressed the opinion that one of the main strengths of the model is that it empowers families and clients to deal with their own problems. The model provides an opportunity to families to express their feelings about issues of concern to them and, to some extent, to take control of their situations themselves. It seems that in 'preparing a plan for a child under this model, the family of the child will play an extremely important role in deciding about the future of the child, which is the greatest strength of the model'. One of the respondents expressed his/her opinion as follows:

> Oh, the Family Engagement model actually gives the power back to the family but with the bottom line in place, like the Department's bottom lines, they have to meet them. Oh ... the old model would have been black and white; kids remain in Mum's care, he (the father) would have supervised contacts with kids and it all would have been set up ... the Family Engagement model was about pulling them in the whole family then coming up with the solutions as long as they reach the Department's bottom line. They actually have to come up and nominate what they were willing to do ... He (father) returned home, which was much better ... If they have relapse we bring them back in and we talk about it, get them back on track, make sure they were engaging with the services ... In the old method, kids just would have been removed and kids would have gone into the Department's care ... It is more empowering to the family, and it is much easier to work with the family at that level than you are standing over and telling them that you have to do this and this, and holding it against them that if you do not do, well, the kids are out. It is much, much better for the families. You've got more opportunity to work with the family at that level, rather than being on the outside dictating.

Another participant said:

> I think this model empowers the family a lot more ... you are having meetings all the time. You give them the bottom line, and they develop their own strategy ... I think it empowers the family when they come back ... because they are developing their plan, they are using their own network and resources ... I think it is empowering.

Yet, according to another respondent: 'It allows them to feel that they can make some decisions ... They are able to work with the Department and that their voices or views are as valid as the Department's.'

Building of capacity of families

Another advantage that came out of the discussions is that the process adopted as a part of the FEM makes clients aware of community resources which, in turn, help them to build their capacity to deal with a situation effectively and independently. As one participant pointed out:

They know that, ok, if something goes wrong in this aspect of their life, they know they can go there for support, they do not need to be calling us ... they may have resolved their own issues ... that is really empowering.

Another participant said: 'Under this model, a family has taken a much stronger role in bringing about change as compared to the case conference approach.'

Acknowledgement of positives in families

One of the strengths of the approach is that it acknowledges the strengths of families. The model is primarily based upon designing interventions based on the strengths and positives of a situation rather than on the negatives. 'In the old model the strengths were not acknowledged to a large degree and certainly not of the parents.' During one of the focus groups, a participant expressed the views that:

The Family Engagement model starts with the strengths of the family, so bringing the family in at an earlier stage, and trying to get them to help make decisions about what is going to happen to children who are in crisis ... so ... it is involving more people, their extended family, and getting them to come up with a plan.

In another focus group, a respondent said:

It is only because you actually do work with that strength-based approach and you acknowledge it. It is a huge part of what happens. You can actually say to somebody that you are doing so well, it is great to see the change in you, and even though you personally have nothing to do with those changes, you say, well done ... it is so good to see you looking so well ... You get to a point in a process where you are no longer seen as an outsider, you are no longer seen as a prescriptive organisation, but you are seen as a supportive organisation which is actually assisting that person in the process ... This Department has not been good in acknowledging change, we have not been.

Collaborative decision making and solutions

Another strength pointed out by many is that solutions pertaining to a child are now developed in close collaboration with the family, extended family and other appropriate stakeholders, which makes them (decisions and solutions) more acceptable and workable. In one of the focus group interviews a participant expressed this strength of the model as follows:

They come up with answers, they got it. You are up front with the family. It gives the family a very clear idea what exactly is expected of them ... this is what they have done, what are the

(Continued)

(Continued)

> *concerns of the Department ... So by having family support meetings, you are telling the family this is what we feel is happening with the child and these are the things that cannot happen to your children, what we intend to do about it in the future to be able to have them back or to improve their environment ... it is straight in front of them, not behind their back ... Previously I know of a case where a family was not involved in any of the discussions and they did not understand why their children were removed from them.*

Many participants felt very positive about this collaborative approach. They felt that, 'having a family support meeting clearly tells them what has happened, what are the intentions of the Department, and how the Department is going to work with them'. Another participant in one of the focus group discussions added:

> *There are differences between how the meetings are held but, I guess, oh, sometimes to get the family to develop, and remind them of the bottom line, rather than us saying, 'This is what I want to happen.' I mean, obviously in the discussion of the general situation, you make things clear, but you let the family take the responsibility to develop their own plan.*

A respondent in an in-depth interview expressed the opinion that, now, 'We are identifying the members of the extended family. Once upon-a-time we just had parents; now you have to go around and search and get them all together to make a decision.'

Yet another respondent, talking about the strengths of the model, said, 'Now we approach very differently.' According to him/her:

> *We inform you, we advise you, that the children are at risk ... whatever with the children, we want to sit down and work with you. Throughout this process we want to work with you, and also, plans have been set up. We want you to be a part of that.*

It appears that, under this model, decisions are made not by a single individual, but by all those involved. According to one respondent, 'You are sharing responsibility with other agencies and family members; it is not only your decision, it is the decision of everybody.'

Keeps families intact

Some respondents also felt, that in certain cases, 'The children may not even be taken from the family so quickly.' It seems there is a greater attempt to keep the children in the family. One participant said: 'I am actually working with quite a few kids where they are trying to keep the family together.' Another participant added that, 'The apprehension rate has come down substantially.'

Perceived strengths from the perspective of the child

A greater focus on children

Many family workers as well as team leaders felt that the whole approach is a lot more focused on children. The approach is child centred and, at every step, concerns for children form the core of an intervention: 'It is a lot more child-focused as well. Rather than focusing on the parents, it is focusing on how we are going to make this child safe, and how we are going to achieve that.'

Returns children to their parents quicker

Some respondents felt that the new approach helped children to get back to their parents quicker. In one of the focus group discussions, one participant said:

I think it gets the children back to their parents quicker because at the meeting it identifies strong people in the family that can support the parents to keep their kids. So what I found in the office is that some of the kids get back to their parents quicker than through the Case Conference. The Case Conference is every year ... what the families have to jump through by the end of the twelve months at the next meeting ... here it is none of that. It is a strong person, how you are going to support the Mum to keep getting the kids back ... what you do need ... sometimes the kids go back, just like that.

Prevention of removal of children

Some respondents felt that the model actually prevented kids from being removed from their families. According to one participant, 'that is the big advantage of this model; to prevent kids from being removed'.

Perceived strengths from the perspective of service providers

Greater job satisfaction

Almost every service provider said that their work after the introduction of the model had become 'much more satisfying' because 'it is enabling workers and clients'.

Easier for the workers to work under the model

Many respondents felt that 'initially it is more work for a worker but, in the long run, it is less work because of the shared responsibility'. According to one participant:

As a case worker, I remember the days when I had to really work so hard to meet so many people and do so many things individually and all the responsibility was on my shoulders ... but now there is a shared responsibility ... you have to do the ground work but when it is done the long term engagement is easier because there are more people involved and they in part make the decisions.

Decline in hostility towards the Department

Another advantage that some respondents pointed out was a decline in hostility among families towards the Department. It was pointed out that though it depended upon the

(Continued)

(Continued)

circumstances, there was a feeling that, on the whole, hostility among clients towards the Department had declined. They also felt that though, in the beginning, there might have been hostility, working under the new model, in most situations, made that hostility disappear. In some situations, an increase in hostility was possibly attributable to a situation such as the apprehension of a child. Most respondents were of the opinion that, as compared to the Case Management model, they had experienced far less hostility towards them while working under the new approach.

Increased trust in the staff by clients

Another advantage some workers saw in the new approach was that they felt that clients had started trusting them a lot more. A participant in one of the focus groups described his/her feelings as follows:

> They call us now, I do not have to go and look for them. They are calling me now and asking what is this? ... which means they are taking an interest. They are not sitting back and saying, oh well, they are going to tell us or not tell us.

Better rapport with families

Because of the increased number of contacts, it appears that staff were able to build more congenial and trusting relationships with families. In a focus group, one of the respondents said, 'I think the relationship is more respectful and trustful'. Another respondent said:

> Family relationships are a little bit better, and a family also understands that a DCD worker is not someone who goes to homes and removes their children ... how horrible people we are, but, by interacting with them they actually understand that we are people at work, and that we are not going to do these things, that is the old way of doing. We are not going to remove a child without saying anything. We have communication with them.

Develops better understanding by workers of the family dynamics

'One of the strengths that I have seen is that it allows the social worker to feel the family dynamics, to think about the dynamics and it allows the families to participate in whatever they want to', said a participant of a focus group.

Fewer aggressive clients

Another obvious difference between the two models, according to some respondents, was fewer aggressive clients. One respondent said,

> There are far less aggressive clients here as compared to other places. I think it is partly because of the approach. Here you very rarely see people who get agitated, it is much more controlled, and it is a calmer atmosphere.

(Continued)

(Continued)

Develops a sense of ownership of a case

One of the advantages of the FEM as pointed out by various respondents was that under the model, 'you feel the case belongs to you; you "own" a child'. Because of this, according to some participants, there was a greater affiliation between the family worker and the child.

Greater community interaction

Another advantage pointed out by family workers was that the model resulted in their having a greater interaction with community agencies and, consequently, had more knowledge of their community and the services available in it. This was primarily because of restructuring under the Family Engagement model whereby family workers were allocated particular geographical areas, called, 'patch': 'You also develop really nice working relations with those people. You are working together collaboratively towards the goals, and I think, that is really a great benefit', said one participant. There was 'a lot more linking with other agencies' under the model. Not only was the interaction between community agencies increased but, it appears, clients had also started making more use of community agencies.

Greater knowledge about community members

Another benefit of working under the FEM and within a 'patch' was that family workers got to know a lot more community members. According to one respondent, 'The relationship with people in your community is much stronger and widespread.' Another respondent said:

> After a certain time you get to know who lives on what street, family links between people, especially, when you are working with Aboriginal families. Family links are so important, and knowing who is dealing with whom ... knowing who is in the area, what resources you have, makes your job a lot more effective.

Greater control over personal values by workers

Another advantage identified by some respondents was that, with the new model, 'case workers own values and morals cannot be imposed'.

Perceived strengths from the perspective of the service delivery manner

An open, honest and transparent process

The whole process is open to all stakeholders. 'All the cards are on the table', said one participant, and another expressed the opinion that: 'The case worker may be honest, but, I guess, the process, how it was done, was not.' One respondent said that one of the good things about this model was that 'everyone knows what is going on'. According to a respondent:

(Continued)

(Continued)

> *Another good thing about these family meetings is that there is the parents, there is the family. The parents might have been telling us one thing or a part of the story and Jaime, another part of the story, not telling Uncle Jimmy ... so it is good in a way that everyone knows what is going on. The whole information is there for everyone that is there. So they cannot push it to us and push it to the family. That is another good thing: they all get the same information, and we get and give the same information to them ... and it is amazing the plan they want to come up with ... it is based upon the information given to them.*

Another respondent in a focus group said:

> *And you are actually fighting the parents about the guardianship of the child: at the end of the day that is what you are doing, and, I think, just to have the transparent working relationship within the Family Engagement model actually makes that process a lot easier because everything is out in the open and when it comes up in the court, they are not going to be surprised.*

Greater informality in meetings

Family meetings under the FEM are far less formal: 'The family members and others are encouraged to say whatever they want to. They can interrupt and stop the chairperson any time, if they disagree. They can even come back later.' 'What is important is that the minutes are written up, and the family gets a copy of the minutes so that they can go back home and read the minutes. They can come back to us.'

More frequent review of cases

Many people felt that the model provided an opportunity to review cases more frequently which helped them to achieve goals more quickly and, if an intervention was not working, it helped them to change the intervention. As one participant pointed out, 'Changes in the plan to reflect the changes in the family dynamics are undertaken frequently.' Hence, under the model, 'The plan for a child is continually being reviewed.' There seemed to be a lot more flexibility in terms of changing a plan under the model.

Increased honesty, transparency and accountability

Some respondents also felt that, because of the transparency and accountability of the process, simply working within the parameters of the model had helped to keep workers honest and accountable. According to one participant, 'From a practice viewpoint, it allows the social worker to be honest, accountable and to be transparent.'

A fairer approach

Many respondents felt that the FEM was fairer, as it was open, participatory and empowered a family.

Goals set for clients are more attainable and workable

According to one of the participants of a focus group: 'I think the plan of Family Engagement meetings is more attainable and more workable ... what they are actually capable of doing. We are not setting what they are not going to achieve, so they are not going to fail.' In addition, it seems, because families were involved in developing a plan, they had a feeling of ownership, and hence they attained the tasks set out in it. Another participant was of the opinion that: 'If you are a part of the solution, then you actually have an investment in making the change.'

Equality in relation to expression of opinion

Some respondents felt that the model provided freedom of expression to parties. All involved were free to express their opinions, and they were encouraged to share their views. As long as the bottom line was met, their opinions were taken into consideration in developing a strategy.

A less chaotic process

As one participant observed: 'It is far less chaotic, just the perception of what was going on. They [referring to workers in the CMM] felt a bit chaotic because work was coming in all the time and they were holding on to cases. Here it is more organised', one participant observed. With the old structure, 'case workers were very stressed; they were not operating particularly well'.

A less stressful approach

Many participants felt that the new approach was less stressful because of its many benefits. It was less stressful for them, and for families, as well as children. In one of the focus groups, a participant expressed his/her feeling in the following words:

> You do not feel that I hate to go to this home ... how are they going to react, what are they going to say to me, or how should I leave or how should I protect myself? You do not have to have those stresses now; it is a calmer situation, it is a happier situation and that is good for the kids, not only for us, but for the kids ... it is actually the kids who also benefit from the approach.

Fewer conflicts with families

Many respondents felt that ongoing conflicts with families were far fewer after the introduction of the new model.

Equality regarding choice of a facilitator for meetings

Another strength was that some participants thought that under the new model facilitation work was not only confined to case managers. Under the model, anyone could become a facilitator.

Increased reflection on practice

Some people also felt that the model provided an opportunity to reflect on practice thus helping them to improve it.

Total responsibility for cases

Some also pointed out that workers have the total responsibility for cases which seemed to be much better from a number of viewpoints. As pointed out by one person, 'Under the model, a field worker is responsible for the total intervention, from A to Z. You do everything in a patch.'

(Continued)

(Continued)

Compliance with government's child placement policy

One of the participants pointed out that the model actually complied with the government's legislative obligation to place Aboriginal and Torres Strait Islander children with their families. According to this participant:

The model actually meets, for Aboriginal and Torres Strait Islanders child placement principle which is now enshrined in our legislation, where it actually states that children will be placed with family, extended family, immediate community and extended community and a non-Aboriginal person is a last resort … So this model actually meets that.

The role of statistics in research

The role of statistics in research is sometimes exaggerated. Statistics have a role only when you have collected the required information, adhering to the requirements of each operational step of the research process. Once data is collected you encounter two questions:

1 How do I organise this data to understand it?
2 What does the data mean?

In a way, the answer to the first question forms the basis for the second. Statistics can play a very important role in answering your research questions in such a manner that you are able to quantify, measure, place a level of confidence on the findings, make an assessment of the contribution each variable has made in bringing out change, measure the association and relationship between various variables, and help predict what is likely to happen in the light of current trends.

From individual responses, particularly if there are many, it becomes extremely difficult to understand the patterns in the data, so it is important for the data to be summarised. Some simple statistical measures such as percentages, means, standard deviations and coefficients of correlation can reduce the volume of data, making it easier to understand. In computing summary measures, certain information is lost and therefore misinterpretation is possible. Hence, caution is required when interpreting data.

Statistics play a vital role in understanding the relationship between variables, particularly when there are more than two. With experience, it is easy to 'read' the relationship between two variables from a table, but not to quantify this relationship. Statistics help you to ascertain the strength of a relationship. They confirm or contradict what you read from a piece of information, and provide an indication of the strength of the relationship and the level of confidence that can be placed in findings. When there are more than two variables, statistics are also helpful in understanding the interdependence between them and their contribution to a phenomenon or event.

Indirectly, knowledge of statistics helps you at each step of the research process. Knowledge of the problems associated with data analysis, the types of statistical test that can be applied to certain types of variable, and the calculation of summary statistics in relation to the measurement scale used plays an important role in a research endeavour. However, you can also carry out a perfectly valid study without using any statistical procedures. This depends upon the objectives of your study.

Summary

In this chapter you have learnt about processing data. Irrespective of the method of data collection, qualitative or quantitative, the information is called 'raw data' or simply 'data'. The processing of data includes all operations undertaken from when a set of data is collected until it is ready to be analysed either manually or by a computer. Data processing in quantitative studies starts with data editing, which is basically 'cleaning' your data. This is followed by the coding of data, which entails developing a code book, pre-testing it, coding per se and verifying the coded data. In this chapter we have provided a prototype for developing a code book, detailing descriptions of how to develop codes for open-ended and closed questions, and a step-by-step guide to coding data, taking an example from a survey. The chapter also includes detailed information about content analysis and how to treat data for narrative and thematic styles of writing, and an extended example from a qualitative study is provided.

Though the development of a frame of analysis continues until you have finished the report, it helps immensely in data analysis to develop this before you begin analysing data. In the frame of analysis the type of analysis to be undertaken (e.g. frequency distribution, cross-tabulation, content analysis), and the statistical procedures to be applied, should be specified.

Computers primarily help by saving labour associated with analysing data manually. Their application in handling complicated statistical and mathematical procedures, word processing, displaying and graphic presentation of the analysed data saves time and increase speed. Statistics are desirable but not essential for a study. The extent of their application depends upon the purpose of the study. Statistics primarily help you to make sense of data, 'read' the data, explore relationships and the interdependence between variables, ascertain the magnitude of an existing relationship or interdependence and place confidence in your findings.

For You to Think About

▸ Refamiliarise yourself with the keywords listed at the beginning of this chapter and if you are uncertain about the meaning or application of any of them revisit these in the chapter before moving on.
▸ What procedures can you set in place to ensure the accuracy of the information obtained in both quantitative and qualitative studies?
▸ Thinking of examples from your own area of study, consider the advantages and disadvantages of having used open-ended or closed questions when you come to process your data.
▸ Assess the role of statistics for a study in your area of interest.

CHAPTER 16
Displaying Data

In this chapter you will learn about:

- Methods of communicating and displaying analysed data in quantitative and qualitative research
- How to present your data in tables
- Different types of graphs and how to use them to represent your data

Keywords: *area chart, bar diagram, bivariate, cumulative frequency polygon, data display, frequency graph, line diagram, pie chart, polygon, polyvariate, scattergram, table, univariate.*

Methods of communicating and displaying analysed data

Having analysed the data that you collected through either quantitative or qualitative method(s), the next task is to present your findings to your readers. The main purpose of using data display techniques is to make the findings easy and clear to understand, and to provide extensive and comprehensive information in a succinct and effective way. There are many ways of presenting information. The choice of a particular method should be determined primarily by your impressions/knowledge of your likely readership's familiarity with the topic and with the research methodology and statistical procedures. If your readers are likely to be familiar with 'reading' data, you can use complicated methods of data display; if not, it is wise to keep to simple techniques. Although there are many ways of displaying data, this chapter is limited to the more commonly used ones. There are many computer programs that can help you with this task.

Broadly, there are four ways of communicating and displaying the analysed data. These are:

1 text;
2 tables;
3 graphs; and
4 statistical measures.

Because of the nature and purpose of investigation in qualitative research, text becomes the dominant and usually the sole mode of communication. In quantitative studies the text is very commonly combined with other forms of data display methods, the extent of which depends upon your familiarity with them, the purpose of the study and what you think would make it easier for your readership to understand the content and sustain their interest in it. Hence as a researcher it is entirely up to you to decide the best way of communicating your findings to your readers.

Text

Text, by far, is the most common method of communication in both quantitative and qualitative research studies and, perhaps, the only method in the latter. It is, therefore, essential that you know how to communicate effectively, keeping in view the level of understanding, interest in the topic and need for academic and scientific rigour of those for whom you are writing. Your style should be such that it strikes a balance between academic and scientific rigour and the level that attracts and sustains the interest of your readers. Of course, it goes without saying that a reasonable command of the language and clarity of thought are imperative for good communication.

Your writing should be thematic: that is, written around various themes of your report; findings should be integrated into the literature citing references using an acceptable system of citation; your writing should follow a logical progression of thought; and the layout should be attractive and pleasing to the eye. Language, in terms of clarity and flow, plays an important role in communication. According to the Commonwealth of Australia *Style Manual* (2002: 49):

> The language of well-written documents helps to communicate information effectively. Language is also the means by which writers create the tone or register of a publication and establish relationships with their readers. For these relationships to be productive, the language the writer uses must take full account of the diversity of knowledge, interests and sensitivities within the audience.

Tables

Structure

Other than text, **tables** are the most common method of presenting analysed data. According to *The Chicago Manual of Style* (1993: 21), 'Tables offer a useful means of presenting large amounts of detailed information in a small space.' According to the Commonwealth of Australia *Style Manual* (2002: 46), 'tables can be a boon for readers. They can dramatically clarify text, provide visual relief, and serve as quick point of reference.' It is, therefore, essential for beginners to know about their structure and types. Figure 16.1 shows the structure of a table.

A table has five parts:

1 **Title** – This normally indicates the table number and describes the type of data the table contains. It is important to give each table its own number as you will need to refer to the tables when interpreting and discussing the data. The tables should be numbered sequentially as they appear in the text. The procedure for numbering tables is a personal choice. If you are writing an article, simply identifying tables by number is sufficient. In the case of a dissertation or a report, one way to identify a table is by the chapter number followed by the sequential number of the table in the chapter – the procedure adopted in this book. The main advantage of this procedure is that if it becomes necessary to add or delete a table when revising the report, the table numbers for that chapter only, rather than for the whole report, will need to be changed.

   The description accompanying the table number must clearly specify the contents of that table. In the description identify the variables about which information is contained in the table, for example 'Respondents by age' or 'Attitudes towards uranium mining'. If a table contains information about two variables, the dependent variable should be identified first in the title, for example 'Attitudes towards uranium mining [dependent variable] by gender [independent variable]'.

2 **Stub** – The subcategories of a variable, listed along the *y*-axis (the left-hand column of the table). According to *The McGraw-Hill Style Manual* (Long year 1983: 97), 'The stub, usually the first column on the left, lists the items about which information is provided in the horizontal rows to the right.' *The Chicago Manual of Style* (1993: 331) describes the stub as: 'a vertical listing of categories or individuals about which information is given in the columns of the table'.

3 **Column headings** – The subcategories of a variable, listed along the *x*-axis (the top of the table). In univariate tables (tables displaying information about one variable) the column heading is usually the 'number of respondents' and/or the 'percentage of respondents' (Tables 16.1 and 16.2). In bivariate tables (tables displaying information about two variables) it is the subcategories of one of the variables displayed in the column headings (Table 16.3).

4 **Body** – The cells housing the analysed data.

5 **Supplementary notes or footnotes** – There are four types of footnote: source notes; other general notes; notes on specific parts of the table; and notes on the level of probability (*The Chicago Manual of Style* 1993: 333). If the data is taken from another source, you have an obligation to acknowledge this. The source should be identified at the bottom of the table, and labelled by the word 'Source:' as in Figure 16.1. Similarly, other explanatory notes should be added at the bottom of a table.

Types of tables

Depending upon the number of variables about which information is displayed, tables can be categorised as:

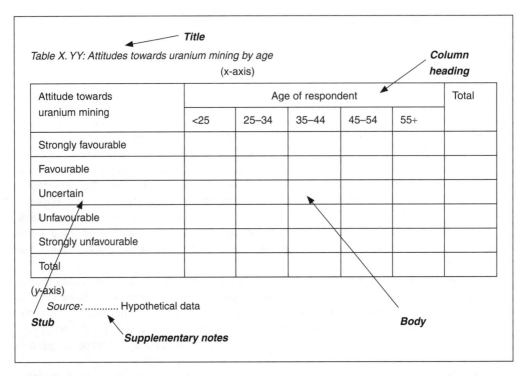

FIGURE 16.1   *The structure of a table*

TABLE 16.1   *Respondents by age (frequency table for one population – hypothetical data)*

Age	No. of respondents
<20 years	2 (2.0)
20–24	12 (12.0)
25–29	22 (22.0)
30–34	14 (14.0)
35–39	17 (17.0)
40–44	10 (10.0)
45–49	11 (11.0)
50–54	9 (9.0)
55+00	3 (3.0)
Total	100 (100.0)

Note: Figures in parentheses are percentages.

- univariate (also known as frequency tables) – containing information about one variable, for example Tables 16.1 and 16.2;
- bivariate (also known as cross-tabulations) – containing information about two variables, for example Table 16.3; and
- polyvariate or multivariate – containing information about more than two variables, for example Table 16.4.

TABLE 16.2   *Respondents by age (frequency table comparing two populations – hypothetical data)*

Age	Population A	Population B
<20	2 (2.0)	1 (0.6)
20–24	12 (12.0)	17 (10.9)
25–29	22 (22.0)	23 (14.7)
30–34	14 (14.0)	18 (11.5)
35–39	17 (17.0)	26 (16.7)
40–44	10 (10.0)	16 (10.3)
45–49	11 (11.0)	18 (11.5)
50–54	9 (9.0)	27 (17.3)
55+00	3 (3.0)	10 (6.4)
No response	0 (0.0)	0 (0.0)
Total	100 (100.0)	156 (99.9*)

Note: Figures in parentheses are percentages (*rounding error).

TABLE 16.3   *Respondents by attitude towards uranium mining and age (cross-tabulation – hypothetical data)*

Attitude towards uranium mining	Age					Total
	<25	25–34	35–44	45–54	55+	
	(0.0)*	(5.5)	(14.8)	(35.0)	(100.0)	
Strongly favourable	0	2	4	7	3	16
	(0.0)@	(12.5)@	(25.0)@	(43.6)@	(18.6)@	(100.0)@
	(0.0)*	(8.3)	(18.5)	(20.0)	(0.0)	
Favourable	0	3	5	4	0	12
	(0.0)	(25.0)	(41.7)	(33.3)	(0.0)	(100.0)
	(0.0)*	(0.0)	(7.4)	(20.0)	(0.0)	
Uncertain	0	0	2	4	0	6
	(0.0)	(0.0)	(33.3)	(66.7)	(0.0)	(100.0)
	(14.3)*	(19.4)	(3.7)	(0.0)	(0.0)	
Unfavourable	2	7	1	0	0	10
	(20.0)	(70.0)	(10.0)	(0.0)	(0.0)	(100.0)
	(85.7)*	(66.7)	(55.6)	(25.0)	(0.0)	
Strongly unfavourable	12	24	15	5	0	56
	(21.4)	(42.9)	(26.8)	(8.9)	(0.0)	(100.0)
	(100.0)*	(100.0)	(100.0)	(100.0)	(100.0)	(100.0)
Total	14	36	27	20	3	100

* = Column percentage; @ = Row percentage.

Types of percentages

The abilities to interpret data accurately and to communicate findings effectively are important skills for a researcher. For accurate and effective interpretation of data, you may need to calculate measures such as percentages, cumulative percentages or ratios. It is also sometimes important to apply other statistical procedures to data. The use of percentages is a common procedure in the interpretation of data. There are three types of percentage: 'row', 'column'

TABLE 16.4 *Attitude towards uranium mining by age and gender (hypothetical data)*

Attitude towards uranium mining	Number of respondents												
	<25		25–34		35–44		45–54		55+		Total		
	F	M	F	M	F	M	F	M	F	M	F	M	T
Strongly favourable	0	0	1	1	3	1	5	2	3	–	12	4	16
Favourable	0	0	1	2	3	2	3	1	0	0	7	5	12
Uncertain	0	0	0	0	1	1	2	2	0	0	3	3	6
Unfavourable	1	1	4	3	1	0	0	0	0	0	6	4	10
Strongly unfavourable	4	8	17	7	8	7	2	3	0	0	31	25	56
Total	5	9	23	13	16	11	12	8	3	0	59	41	100

and 'total'. It is important to understand the relevance, interpretation and significance of each. Let us take some examples.

Tables 16.1 and 16.2 are univariate or frequency tables. In any univariate table, percentages calculate the magnitude of each subcategory of the variable out of a constant number (100). Such a table shows what would have been the expected number of respondents in each subcategory had there been 100 respondents. Percentages in a univariate table play a more important role when two or more samples or populations are being compared (Table 16.2). As the total number of respondents in each sample or population group normally varies, percentages enable you to standardise them against a fixed number (100). This standardisation against 100 enables you to compare the magnitude of the two populations within the different subcategories of a variable.

In a cross-tabulation such as in Table 16.3, the subcategories of both variables are examined in relation to each other. To make this table less congested, we have collapsed the age categories shown in Table 16.1. For such tables you can calculate three different types of percentage, row, column and total, as follows:

- **Row percentage** – Calculated from the total of *all* the subcategories of one variable that are displayed along a row in different columns, in relation to only *one* subcategory of the other variable. For example, in Table 16.3 figures in parentheses marked with @ are the row percentages calculated out of *the total* (16) of all age subcategories of the variable age in relation to only one subcategory of the second variable (i.e. those who hold a strongly favourable attitude towards uranium mining) – in other words, one subcategory of a variable displayed on the stub by all the subcategories of the variable displayed on the column heading of a table. Out of those who hold a strongly unfavourable attitude towards uranium mining, 21.4 per cent are under the age of 25 years, none is above the age of 55 and the majority (42.9 per cent) are between 25 and 34 years of age (Table 16.3). This row percentage has thus given you the variation in terms of age among those who hold a strongly unfavourable attitude towards uranium mining. It has shown how the 56 respondents who hold a strongly unfavourable attitude towards uranium mining differ in age from one another. Similarly, you can select any other subcategory of the variable (attitude towards uranium mining) to examine its variation in relation to the other variable, age.

- **Column percentage** – In the same way, you can hold age at a constant level and examine variations in attitude. For example, suppose you want to find out differences in attitude among 25–34-year-olds towards uranium mining. The age category 25–34 (column) shows that of the 36 respondents, 24 (66.7 per cent) hold a strongly unfavourable attitude while only two (5.5 per cent) hold a strongly favourable attitude towards uranium mining. You can do the same by taking any subcategory of the variable age, to examine differences with respect to the different subcategories of the other variable (attitudes towards uranium mining).
- **Total percentage** – This standardises the magnitude of each cell; that is, it gives the percentage of respondents who are classified in the subcategories of one variable in relation to the subcategories of the other variable. For example, what percentage do those who are under the age of 25 years, and hold a strongly unfavourable attitude towards uranium mining, constitute of the total population?

It is possible to sort data for three variables. Table 16.4 (percentages not shown) examines respondents' attitudes in relation to their age and gender. As you add more variables to a table it becomes more complicated to read and more difficult to interpret, but the procedure for interpreting it is the same.

The introduction of the third variable, gender, helps you to find out how the observed association between the two subcategories of the two variables, age and attitude, is distributed in relation to gender. In other words, it helps you to find out how many males and females constitute a particular cell showing the association between the other two variables. For example, Table 16.4 shows that of those who have a strongly unfavourable attitude towards uranium mining, 24 (42.9 per cent) are 25–34 years of age. This group comprises 17 (70.8 per cent) females and 7 (29.2 per cent) males. Hence, the table shows that a greater proportion of female than male respondents between the ages of 25 and 34 hold a strongly unfavourable attitude towards uranium mining. Similarly, you can take any two subcategories of age and attitude and relate these to either subcategory (male/female) of the third variable, gender.

Graphs

Graphic presentations constitute the third way of communicating analysed data. Graphic presentations can make analysed data easier to understand and effectively communicate what it is supposed to show. One of the choices you need to make is whether a set of information is best presented as a table, a graph or as text. The main objective of a graph is to present data in a way that is easy to understand and interpret, and interesting to look at. Your decision to use a graph should be based mainly on this consideration: 'A graph is based entirely on the tabled data and therefore can tell no story that cannot be learnt by inspecting a table. However, graphic representation often makes it easier to see the pertinent features of a set of data' (Minium 1978: 45).

Graphs can be constructed for every type of data – quantitative and qualitative – and for any type of variable (measured on a nominal, ordinal, interval or ratio scale). There are different types of graph, and your decision to use a particular type should be made on the basis of the measurement scale used in the measurement of a variable. It is equally important to keep in mind the measurement scale when it comes to interpretation. It is not uncommon to find people misinterpreting a graph and drawing wrong conclusions simply because they have overlooked the measurement scale used in the measurement of a variable. The type of graph you choose depends upon the type of data you are displaying. For categorical variables you can construct only bar charts, histograms or pie charts, whereas for continuous variables, in addition to the above, line or trend graphs can also be constructed. The number of variables shown in a graph are also important in determining the type of graph you can construct.

When constructing a graph of any type it is important to be acquainted with the following points:

- A graphic presentation is constructed in relation to two axes: horizontal and vertical. The horizontal axis is called the 'abscissa' or, more commonly, the x-axis, and the vertical axis is called the 'ordinate' or, more commonly, the y-axis (Minium 1978: 45).
- If a graph is designed to display only one variable, it is customary, but not essential, to represent the subcategories of the variable along the x-axis and the frequency or count of that subcategory along the y-axis. The point where the axes intersect is considered as the zero point for the y-axis. When a graph presents two variables, one is displayed on each axis and the point where they intersect is considered as the starting or zero point.
- A graph, like a table, should have a title that describes its contents. The axes should be labelled also.
- A graph should be drawn to an appropriate scale. It is important to choose a scale that enables your graph to be neither too small nor too large, and your choice of scale for each axis should result in the spread of axes being roughly proportionate to one another. Sometimes, to fit the spread of the scale (when it is too spread out) on one or both axes, it is necessary to break the scale and alert readers by introducing a break (usually two slanting parallel lines) in the axes.

The histogram

A **histogram** consists of a series of rectangles drawn next to each other without any space between them, each representing the frequency of a category or subcategory (Figures, 16.2a,b,c). Their height is in proportion to the frequency they represent. The height of the rectangles may represent the absolute or proportional frequency or the percentage of the total. As mentioned, a histogram can be drawn for both categorical and continuous variables. When interpreting a histogram you need to take into account whether it is representing categorical or continuous variables. Figures 16.2a, b and c provide three examples of histograms using data from Tables 16.1 and 16.4. The second histogram is effectively the same as the first but is presented in a three-dimensional style.

The bar chart

The **bar chart** or diagram is used for displaying categorical data (Figure 16.3). A bar chart is identical to a histogram, except that in a bar chart the rectangles representing the various frequencies are spaced, thus indicating that the data is categorical. The bar chart is used for variables measured on nominal or ordinal scales. The discrete categories are usually displayed

FIGURE 16.2a   *Two-dimensional histogram*

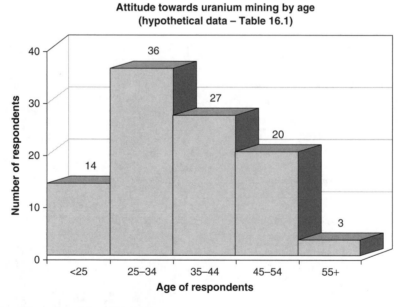

FIGURE 16.2b   *Three-dimensional histogram*

along the *x*-axis and the number or percentage of respondents on the *y*-axis. However, as illustrated, it is possible to display the discrete categories along the *y*-axis. The bar chart is an effective way of visually displaying the magnitude of each subcategory of a variable.

RESEARCH METHODOLOGY

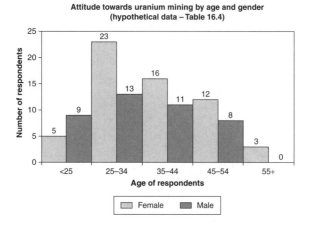

FIGURE 16.2c   *Two-dimensional histogram with two variables*

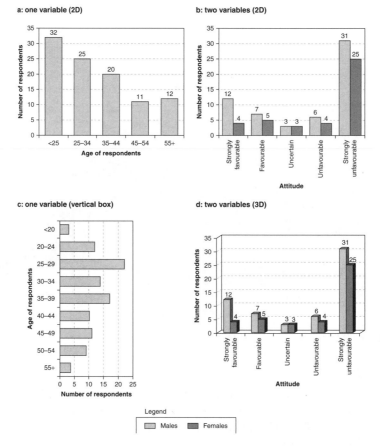

FIGURE 16.3   *Bar charts*

The stacked bar chart

A **stacked bar chart** is similar to a bar chart except that in the former each bar shows information about two or more variables stacked onto each other vertically (Figure 16.4). The sections of a bar show the proportion of the variables they represent in relation to one another. The stacked bars can be drawn only for categorical data.

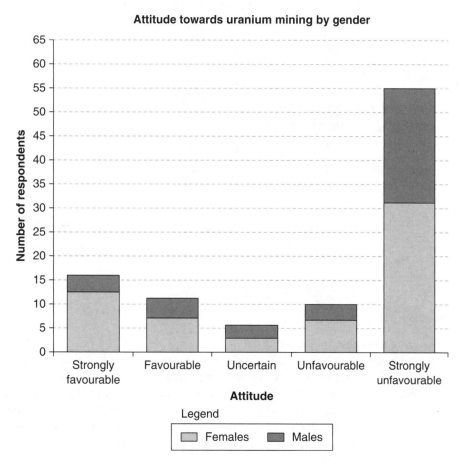

FIGURE 16.4   *The stacked bar chart*

The 100 per cent bar chart

The **100 per cent bar chart** (Figure 16.5) is very similar to the stacked bar chart. In this case, the subcategories of a variable are converted into percentages of the total population. Each bar, which totals 100, is sliced into portions relative to the percentage of each subcategory of the variable.

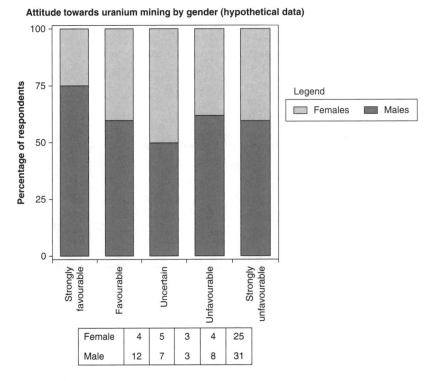

FIGURE 16.5   *The 100 per cent bar chart*

The frequency polygon

The **frequency polygon** is very similar to a histogram. A frequency polygon is drawn by joining the midpoint of each rectangle at a height commensurate with the frequency of that interval (Figure 16.6). One problem in constructing a frequency polygon is what to do with the two categories at either extreme. To bring the polygon line back to the *x*-axis, imagine that the two extreme categories have an interval similar to the rest and assume the frequency in these categories to be zero. From the midpoint of these intervals, you extend the polygon line to meet the *x*-axis at both ends. A frequency polygon can be drawn using either absolute or proportionate frequencies.

The cumulative frequency polygon

The **cumulative frequency polygon** or cumulative frequency curve (Figure 16.7) is drawn on the basis of cumulative frequencies. The main difference between a frequency polygon and a cumulative frequency polygon is that the former is drawn by joining the midpoints

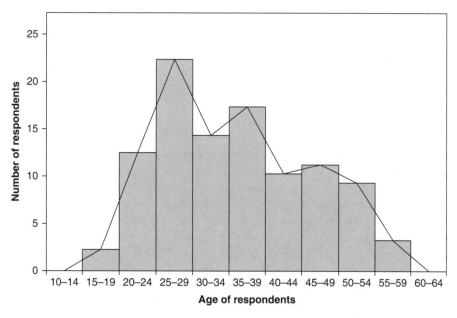

FIGURE 16.6   *The frequency polygon*

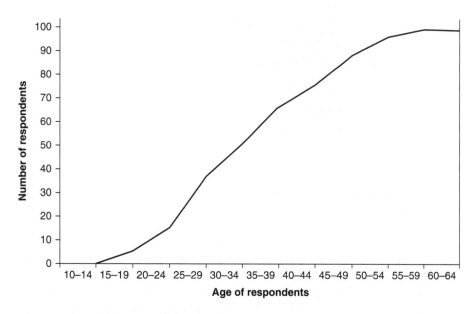

FIGURE 16.7   *The cumulative frequency polygon*

of the intervals, whereas the latter is drawn by joining the end points of the intervals because cumulative frequencies interpret data in relation to the upper limit of an interval. As a cumulative frequency distribution tells you the number of observations less than a given value and is usually based upon grouped data, to interpret a frequency distribution the upper limit needs to be taken.

The stem-and-leaf display

The **stem-and-leaf display** is an effective, quick and simple way of displaying a frequency distribution (Figure 16.8). The stem-and-leaf diagram for a frequency distribution running into two digits is plotted by displaying digits 0 to 9 on the left of the *y*-axis, representing the tens of a frequency. The figures representing the units of a frequency (i.e. the right-hand figure of a two-digit frequency) are displayed on the right of the *y*-axis. Note that the stem-and-leaf display does not use grouped data but absolute frequencies. If the display is rotated 90 degrees in an anti-clockwise direction, it effectively becomes a histogram. With this technique some of the descriptive statistics relating to the frequency distribution, such as the mean, the mode and the median, can easily be ascertained; however, the procedure for their calculation is beyond the scope of this book. Stem-and-leaf displays are also possible for frequencies running into three and four digits (hundreds and thousands).

1	89
2	000111222222334455555666677777788899
3	001112223333334455556666777777889
4	112223333444555566779
5	000113355667

FIGURE 16.8   *The stem-and-leaf display*

The pie chart

The **pie chart** is another way of representing data graphically (Figure 16.9), this time as a circle. There are 360 degrees in a circle, and so the full circle can be used to represent 100 per cent, or the total population. The circle or pie is divided into sections in accordance with the magnitude of each subcategory, and so each slice is in proportion to the size of each subcategory of a frequency distribution. The proportions may be shown either as absolute numbers or as percentages. Manually, pie charts are more difficult to draw than other types of graph because of the difficulty in measuring the degrees of the pie/circle. They can be drawn for both qualitative data and variables measured on a continuous scale but grouped into categories.

Respondents by age
Attitude towards uranium mining (hypothetical data)

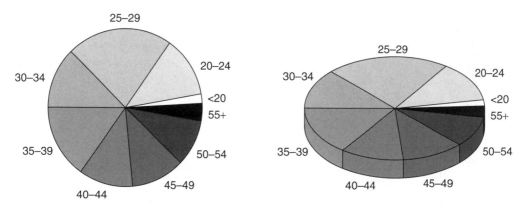

FIGURE 16.9   *Two- and three-dimensional pie charts*

The line diagram or trend curve

A set of data measured on a continuous interval or a ratio scale can be displayed using a line diagram or **trend curve**. A trend line can be drawn for data pertaining to both a specific time (e.g. 1995, 1996, 1997) or a period (e.g. 1985–1989, 1990–1994, 1995–). If it relates to a period, the midpoint of each interval at a height commensurate with each frequency – as in the case of a frequency polygon – is marked as a dot. These dots are then connected with straight lines to examine trends in a phenomenon. If the data pertains to exact time, a point is plotted at a height commensurate with the frequency. These points are then connected with straight lines. A line diagram is a useful way of visually conveying the changes when long-term trends in a phenomenon or situation need to be studied, or the changes in the subcategory of a variable are measured on an interval or a ratio scale (Figure 16.10). Trends plotted as a line diagram are more clearly visible than in a table. For example, a line diagram would be useful for illustrating trends in birth or death rates and changes in population size.

The area chart

For variables measured on an interval or a ratio scale, information about the subcategories of a variable can also be presented in the form of an **area chart**. This is plotted in the same way as a line diagram but with the area under each line shaded to highlight the total magnitude of the subcategory in relation to other subcategories. For example, Figure 16.11 shows the number of male and female respondents by age.

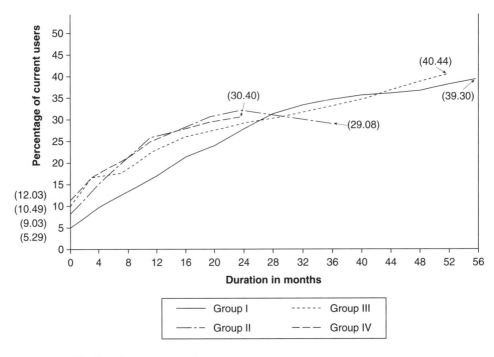

FIGURE 16.10　*The line diagram or trend curve*

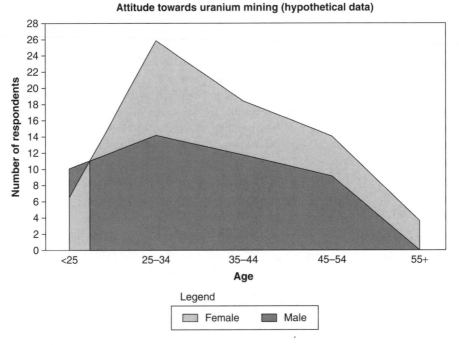

FIGURE 16.11　*The area chart*

The scattergram

When you want to show visually how one variable changes in relation to a change in the other variable, a **scattergram** is extremely effective.

For a scattergram, both the variables must be measured either on interval or ratio scales and the data on both the variables needs to be available in absolute values for each observation – you cannot develop a scattergram for categorical variables. Data for both variables is taken in pairs and displayed as dots in relation to their values on both axes. Let us take the data on age and income for 10 respondents of a hypothetical study in Table 16.5. The relationship between age and income based upon hypothetical data is shown in Figure 16.12.

TABLE 16.5   *Age and income data*

Respondent	Income	Age
A	25 500	24
B	46 000	50
C	30 500	36
D	55 000	45
E	27 000	29
F	35 000	38
G	40 000	37
H	52 000	48
I	47 000	41
J	38 000	47

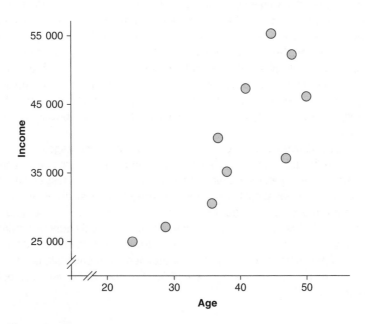

FIGURE 16.12   *The scattergram*

Statistical measures

Statistical measures are extremely effective in communicating the findings in a precise and succinct manner. Their use in certain situations is desirable and in some it is essential, however, you can conduct a perfectly valid study without using any statistical measure.

There are many statistical measures ranging from very simple to extremely complicated. On one end of the spectrum you have simple descriptive measures such as mean, mode, median and, on the other; there are inferential statistical measures like analysis of variance, factorial analysis, multiple regressions.

Because of its vastness, statistics is considered a separate academic discipline and before you are able to use these measures, you need to learn about them.

Use of statistical measures is dependent upon the type of data collected, your knowledge of statistics, the purpose of communicating the findings, and the knowledge base in statistics of your readership.

Before using statistical measures, make sure the data lends itself to the application of statistical measures, you have sufficient knowledge about them, and your readership can understand them.

Summary

Research findings in both quantitative and qualitative research are usually conveyed to readers through text. In qualitative research this is more or less the sole method of communication. However, in quantitative studies, though text is still the dominant method of communicating research findings, it is often combined with other forms such as tables, graphs and statistical measures. These can make communication better, clearer, more effective and easier to understand. What you use should be determined by what you feel comfortable with, what you think will be easiest for readers to understand and what you think will enhance the understanding of your writing. Tables have the advantage of containing a great deal of information in a small space, while graphs make it easy for readers to absorb information at a glance.

Usually, a table will have five parts: title, stub, column headings, body and supplementary notes or footnotes. Depending upon the number of variables about which information in a table is stored, there are three types of table: univariate (frequency), bivariate (cross-tabulation) and polyvariate.

To interpret a table, simple arithmetic procedures such as percentages, cumulative frequencies or ratios can be used. You can also calculate simple descriptive statistical procedures such as the mean, the mode, the median, the chi-square test, the *t*-test and the coefficient of correlation. If you have statistical knowledge, advanced statistics can be applied.

While there are many types of graphs, the common ones are: the histogram, the bar diagram, the stacked bar chart, the 100 per cent bar chart, the frequency polygon, the stem-and-leaf display, the pie chart, the line or trend diagram, the area chart and the scattergram. Which is used depends upon your purpose and the measurement scale used to measure the variable(s) being displayed. Some graphs are difficult to draw but several computer programs are capable of this.

For You to Think About

▸ Refamiliarise yourself with the keywords listed at the beginning of this chapter and if you are uncertain about the meaning or application of any of them revisit these in the chapter before moving on.

▸ Identify two specific examples where you could use a table rather than just text to communicate findings and two examples where graphs would be better.

▸ Construct a hypothetical bivariate table, within the context of an area of interest. Calculate different types of percentages and interpret the data.

This operational step includes one chapter:

- Chapter 17:   Writing a research report

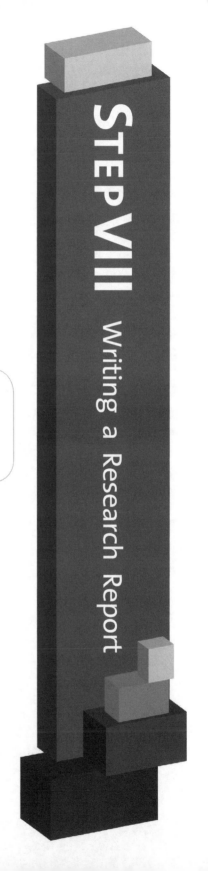

STEP VIII   Writing a Research Report

CHAPTER 17

Writing a Research Report

In this chapter you will learn about:

- How to write a research report
- How to develop an outline for your research report
- Writing about a variable
- Different referencing systems
- How to write a bibliography

Keywords: association, bibliography, intellectual rigour, non-spurious, outline, referencing, spurious, variable, verifiability.

Writing a research report

The last step in the research process is writing the research report. Each step of the process is important for a valid study, as negligence at any stage will affect the quality of not just that part but the whole study. In a way, this last step is the most crucial as it is through the report that the findings of the study and their implications are communicated to your supervisor and readers. Most people will not be aware of the amount and quality of work that has gone into your study. While much hard work and care may have been put into every stage of the research, all readers see is the report. Therefore, the whole enterprise can be spoiled if the report is not well written. As Burns writes, 'extremely valuable and interesting practical work may be spoiled at the last minute by a student who is not able to communicate the results easily' (1997: 229).

In addition to your understanding of research methodology, the quality of the report depends upon such things as your written communication skills and clarity of thought, your ability to express thoughts in a logical and sequential manner, and your knowledge base of the subject area. Another important determinant is your experience in research writing: the more experience you acquire, the more effective you will become in writing a research report. The use of statistical procedures will reinforce the validity of your conclusions and arguments as they enable you to establish if an observed association is due to chance or otherwise (i.e. whether a relationship is spurious or non-spurious) and indicate the strength of an association so readers can place confidence in your findings. The use of graphs to present the findings, though not essential, will make the information more easily understood by readers. As stated in the previous chapter, whether or not graphs are used depends upon the purpose for which the findings are to be used.

The main difference between research and other writing is in the degree of control, rigorousness and caution required. Research writing is controlled in the sense that you need to be extremely careful about what you write, the words you choose, the way ideas are expressed, and the validity and verifiability of the bases for the conclusions you draw. What most distinguishes research writing from other writing is the high degree of intellectual rigour required. Research writing must be absolutely accurate, clear, free of ambiguity, logical and concise. Your writing should not be based upon assumptions about knowledge of your readers about the study. Bear in mind that you must be able to defend whatever you write should anyone challenge it. Do not use ornamental and superficial language. Even the best researchers make a number of drafts before writing up their final one, so be prepared to undertake this task.

The way findings are communicated differs in quantitative and qualitative research. As mentioned earlier, in qualitative research the findings are mostly communicated in descriptive or narrative format written around the major themes, events or discourses that emerge from your findings. The main purpose is to describe the variation in a phenomenon, situation, event or episode without making an attempt to quantify the variation. One of the ways of writing a qualitative report is described in Chapter 15 as a part of the content analysis process. On the other hand, the writing in quantitative research, in addition to being descriptive, also includes its quantification. Depending upon the purpose of the study, statistical measures and tests can also become a part of the research writing to support the findings.

Developing an outline

Before you start writing your report, it is good practice to develop an outline ('chapterisation'). This means deciding how you are going to divide your report into different chapters and planning what will be written in each one. In developing chapterisation, the subobjectives of your study or the major significant themes that emerged from content analysis can provide immense guidance. Develop the chapters around the significant subobjectives or themes of your study. Depending upon the importance of a theme or a subobjective, either devote a complete chapter to it or combine it with related themes to form one chapter. The title of each chapter should be descriptive of the main theme, communicate its main thrust and be clear and concise. This is applicable to both types of research.

The following approach is applicable to both qualitative and quantitative types of research but keep in mind that it is merely suggestive and may be of help if you have no idea where to start. Feel free to change the suggested format in any way you like or if you prefer a different one, follow that.

The first chapter of your report, possibly entitled 'Introduction', should be a general introduction to the study, covering most of your project proposal and pointing out the deviations, if any, from the original plan. This chapter covers all the preparatory tasks undertaken prior to conducting the study, such as the literature review, the theoretical framework, the objectives of the study, study design, the sampling strategy and the measurement procedures.

To illustrate this, two examples are provided below for projects referred to previously in this book: the study on foster-care payments and the Family Engagement model. The first chapters of these reports could be written around the subheadings below. The subsequent structure of these reports is quite different. Keeping in view the purpose for which Family Engagement evaluation was commissioned, the report was divided into three parts: the Introduction, the perceived model, and conclusions and recommendation.

Attitudes towards foster-care payments: suggested contents of chapter 1

Chapter I   Introduction

- Introduction
- The development of foster care
- Foster care in Australia
- Foster care in Western Australia
- The Department of Community Services
- The out-of-home and community care programme
- Current trends in foster-care placement in Western Australia
- Becoming a foster carer
- Foster-care subsidies
- Issues regarding foster-care payment
- Rationale for the study
- Objectives of the study
- Study design
- Sampling
- Measurement procedure
- Problems and limitations
- Working definitions

The Family Engagement – A service delivery model: suggested contents of chapter 1
Part One: Introduction

- Background: The origin of the Family Engagement idea
- Historical perspective
- The perceived model

    – Conceptual framework
    – Philosophical perspective underpinning the model
    – Indented outcomes

- Objectives of the evaluation
- Evaluation methodology

(Note: In this section, the conceptual framework of the model, its philosophical basis, perceived outcomes as identified by the person(s) responsible for initiating the idea, and what was available in the literature, were included. It also included details about evaluation objectives and evaluation methodology.)

The second chapter in quantitative research reports should provide information about the study population. Here, the relevant social, economic and demographic characteristics of the study population should be described. This chapter serves two purposes:

1 It provides readers with some background information about the population from which you collected the information so they can relate the findings to the type of population studied.
2 It helps to identify the variance within a group; for example, you may want to examine how the level of satisfaction of the consumers of a service changes with their age, gender or education.

The second chapter in a quantitative research report, therefore, could be entitled 'Socioeconomic–demographic characteristics of the study population' or just 'The study population'. This chapter could be written around the subheadings below which are illustrated by taking the example of the foster-care payment study.

As qualitative studies are mostly based upon a limited number of in-depth interviews or observations, you may find it very difficult to write about the study population.

Attitude towards foster–care payments: suggested contents of chapter II
Chapter II   The study population

- Introduction
- Respondents by age (Information obtained in response to the question on age should be presented here. Consult 'Writing about a variable', the next section of this chapter.)
- Respondents by gender (Follow the suggestions made under 'Writing about a variable' (see below) for the rest of the variables.)
- Marital status of the study population
- Ethnicity of respondents

(Continued)

(Continued)

- Study population by number of children
- Annual average income of the study population
- Study population by type of dwelling
- etc.

The title and contents of subsequent chapters depend upon what you have attempted to describe, explore, examine, establish or prove in your study. As the content of each project is different, these chapters will be different. As indicated earlier, the title of each chapter should reflect the main thrust of its contents.

The outline should specify the subsections of the chapter. These subsections should be developed around the different aspects of the theme being discussed in the chapter. If you plan to correlate the information obtained from one variable with another, specify the variables. Plan the sequence for discussion of the variables. In deciding this, keep in mind the linkage and logical progression between the sections. This does not mean that the proposed outline cannot be changed when writing the report – it is possible for it to be significantly changed. However, an outline, even if extremely rough, will be of immense help to you. Again, let us take the study on foster–care payment and the Family Engagement model as examples:

Attitudes towards foster-care payments: suggested contents of chapter III
Chapter III　　Attitudes towards the present level of payment for foster care

- Introduction
- Attitudes towards adequacy of payment for foster care (Responses to questions on the adequacy of foster-care payment should be presented here.)

  - adequacy by age (Cross-tabulation, i.e. responses to the question on adequacy of foster-care payment, is examined in relation to the responses to questions on age.)
  - adequacy by marital status (Cross-tabulation, i.e. responses to the question on adequacy of foster-care payment, is examined in relation to the responses to questions on marital status.)
  - adequacy by income of the family (Cross-tabulation, i.e. responses to the question on adequacy of foster-care payment, is examined in relation to the responses to questions on income.)

- Aspects of foster care not covered by the payment
- Major costs borne by foster carers
- Effects of the current level of payment on the family
- Reasons for increasing the payment
- Proposed level of payment

  - proposed level by income of the family

- Conclusions

(Note: Cross-tabulations can be included for any variable where appropriate.)

Family Engagement model: suggested contents of chapter II
Part Two: The perceived model

- The philosophy underpinning the model
- Development of the model
- The model in practice
- Perceived differences in practice before and after the introduction of the model
- Perceived strengths of the model
- Perceived weaknesses of the model
- Skills required for effective functioning under the model
- Replication of the model
- Reasons for change to the new model
- Training

    – How should staff be trained?
    – Training provided

- Name of the model
- Determinants of successful implementation of the model
- Indicators of success of the model
- What could have been done differently?
- What needs to be done to improve the model?
- Role of Community Development Funding Officers
- Advantages and disadvantages of the Case Management model
- Satisfaction of staff with the model
- The model and departmental vision, philosophy, ethos, principles
- Attitude of clients towards the model
- Attitude of community agencies towards the model
- The model and changes in the selected indicators

(Note: In this section, findings about different aspects of the model as identified through in-depth interviews and focus group discussions were detailed.)

Family Engagement model: suggested contents of chapter III
Part Three: Conclusions and recommendations

- Conclusions

    A: General
    B: Specific to the model

- Recommendations

    A: General
    B: Specific to the ... office

This type of outline provides direction in your writing. As mentioned earlier, as you start writing you will certainly change it, but nevertheless you will find it very helpful in your write-up.

Writing about a variable

Having developed a chapter outline, the next step is to start writing. Though the way researchers organise their writing is extremely individualised, the following guidelines and format may prove helpful for beginners.

When writing about the information obtained in response to a question (variable), write as if you were providing answers to the following questions:

- Why did you think it important to study the variable? What effects, in your opinion, may this variable have on the main variable you are explaining? (*This is where you provide your own rationale for studying the variable.*)
- In the case of a cross-tabulation, what relationships have other studies found between the variables you are analysing? (*This is where the literature review is integrated into the findings of the study.*)
- What did you expect to find out in terms of the relationship between the two variables? (*If you have formulated a hypothesis, state it here.*)
- What has your study found out? (*Provide the hard data from your study here, as tables, graphs or text.*)
- What does the data show? (*Interpret the findings of your analysis.*)
- What conclusions can you draw? How do the conclusions drawn from your study compare with those from similar studies in the past? Does your study support or contradict them?
- What explanation can you provide for the findings of your study?

The above is only a suggested format for ordering your thoughts, not a list of subheadings. You may wish to change the suggested order to make the reading more interesting. Below is an example of writing about a variable, 'Adequacy of payment for foster care', from Chapter 13:

- Why did you think it important to find out if foster-care payments are adequate? What effects, in your opinion, could the adequacy or otherwise of payment for foster care have on the quality of foster care?
- What have other studies in your literature review said about the adequacy of foster-care payments?
- What did you expect to find out from your study population in terms of if its feelings about the adequacy of foster-care payments? If you formulated a hypothesis, you should specify that here. For example, H_i = *Most foster parents would consider the current level of foster-care payments to be adequate.*
- What did you find out about the adequacy of foster-care payments? What proportion of the study population said they were adequate? What proportion said they were inadequate?

Provide a table or graph showing the distribution of respondents by their response to the question regarding the adequacy of foster-care payments.

- What does your data show about the adequacy of foster-care payments? What are the main findings of your study? How do these findings compare with those of other studies you found in your literature review? Does your study support or contradict them?
- What conclusions can you draw about the adequacy of the amount of payment for foster care?
- What explanation can you provide for the observed findings? Why do you think those who said that foster payments are either adequate or inadequate feel that way?

In the suggested format in writing about information obtained from questions, notice that the literature review is integrated with the findings and conclusions. The extent of the integration of the literature with findings mostly depends upon the level at which you are writing your dissertation (Honours, Masters or PhD) – the higher the level, the more extensive the literature review, the greater its integration with your findings, and the more careful and confident you need to be about your conclusions.

Writing in qualitative research is more descriptive and narrative than analytical, hence you need to use your imagination in terms of placement of information, linkage between the thoughts and flow of language to make the writing interesting to read and meaningful in conveying the findings.

The suggested format is organised around the main themes of the study. There are other formats. Some researchers write everything under one heading, 'The findings'. This format is appropriate for a research paper, because it is short, but not for a research report or dissertation. Other writers follow the same order as in the research instrument; for example, findings are discussed under each question. The reader needs to refer continuously to the instrument for each question. It is segmental, lacks linkage and integration, and does not place findings into perspective.

Referencing

The report should follow an academic style of referencing. According to Butcher (1981: 226), there are four referencing systems from which to choose:

1 the short-title system;
2 the author–date system;
3 the reference by number system;
4 the author–number system.

You need to adopt the one that is acceptable to your university and academic discipline: 'The first of these is used in most general books, the second mainly in science and social science books; the third and fourth less frequently' (Butcher 1981: 167).

Writing a bibliography

Again, there are several well-established systems for writing a bibliography and your choice is dependent upon the preference of the discipline and university. In the social sciences some of the most commonly used ones are (Longyear 1983: 83):

- the Harvard system;
- the American Psychological Association system;
- the American Medical Association system;
- the McGraw-Hill system;
- the Modern Languages Association system;
- the footnote system.

To learn about these systems and styles, consult the references provided at the end of this book or consult your library.

Summary

In a way, writing your report is the most crucial step in the research process as it communicates the findings to your research supervisor and readers. A badly written report can spoil all the hard work you have put into your research study.

Styles of research writing vary markedly among researchers but all research reports must be written clearly and concisely. Furthermore, scientific writing requires intellectual rigour and there are certain obligations in terms of accuracy and objectivity. Reports can be written in different formats and this chapter has suggested one that research students have found to be helpful.

Writing in quantitative and qualitative research differs to the extent that in qualitative research your style is descriptive and narrative, whereas in quantitative research, in addition to being descriptive, it is also analytical and every assertion is supported by empirical evidence gathered through the investigation.

There are different ways of referencing and of writing a bibliography. You need to select the system that is acceptable to your discipline and university.

Before you start writing the research report, develop an outline of the different chapters and their contents. The chapters should be written around the main themes of the study and for this your subobjectives are of immense help. When providing specific information about a variable, the write-up should integrate the rationale for studying the variable; the literature review; the hypothesis, if any; findings; conclusions drawn; and possible explanations for the findings.

The suggested format can be described as **thematic writing** – writing organised around the significant themes of your study. Within a theme the information is provided in an integrated manner following a logical progression of thought.

For You to Think About

▶ Refamiliarise yourself with the keywords listed at the beginning of this chapter and if you are uncertain about the meaning or application of any of them revisit these in the chapter before moving on.

▶ A literature review is an integral part of research writing. Reflecting on examples from your own area of interest, explore how you might be able to integrate your research findings with your literature review when it comes to writing your report.

▶ Can you think of three ways in which report writing in qualitative and quantitative research differs?

CHAPTER 18

Research Methodology and Practice Evaluation

In this chapter you will learn about:

- What evaluation is and why it is done
- The process for using evaluation to develop an intervention
- The two different perspectives in the classification of evaluation studies
- Types of evaluation from a *focus* perspective
- Types of evaluation from a *philosophical* perspective
- The process of undertaking an evaluation
- The importance of involving stakeholders in evaluation
- Ethics in evaluation

Keywords: *client-centred evaluation, cost–benefit evaluation, cost-effectiveness evaluation, ethics, evaluation, evaluation process, goal-centred, holistic evaluation, illuminative evaluation, impact evaluation, improvement-oriented evaluation, indicators, intervention, monitoring, objective-oriented evaluation, outcome evaluation, perspectives, process evaluation, stakeholders.*

Research methodology and practice evaluation are integrally related. Practice evaluation relies very heavily on the techniques, methods and skills of research methodology. For an evaluator it is imperative to be a good researcher. As this book is primarily written for newcomers to research and for practitioners in human services who are increasingly being asked to provide evidence of the effectiveness of their practice, it is only appropriate that this book includes a chapter that briefly outlines evaluation research and its relationship with research methodology.

Over the past few decades evaluation research has gained greater prominence and has developed rapidly, in both its applications and methodology. Scarcity of resources, emergence of a need to be accountable for effective and efficient delivery of services, realisation that consumers have the right to know about the quality of the service they are receiving, and the onset of an era of economic rationalism have all contributed to this rapid development. Though it relies very heavily on the contents of research methodology per se, evaluation research is now considered to be a self-defined discipline in its own right, with its own literature, techniques and skills. Methods and models of evaluation have now been applied to almost every field of knowledge in our society. Evaluators are being engaged to evaluate many social, economic, health, education and political programmes.

The very first question that may come to your mind, as a beginner, is: what is evaluation research? **Evaluation** may have a different meaning in different situations and, also, it may be understood differently by different people. It is, therefore, important for you to understand the various perspectives on and aspects of evaluation, so that when you come upon it you can define its meaning for your situation.

What is evaluation?

If you go through the literature on evaluation research, you will come across many different definitions. Below are some definitions that have been selected to highlight the various dimensions of evaluation. According to Rossi, Freeman and Lipsey (1999: 4): 'Program evaluation is the use of social research procedures to systematically investigate the effectiveness of social interventions programs.'

As quoted by Stufflebeam and Shinkfield (1985: 3), the definition of the Joint Committee on Standards for Education Evaluation is: 'Evaluation is the systematic assessment of the worth and merit of some objects.'

According to Alkin and Solomon (1983: 14):

Evaluation is a process of ascertaining the decision areas of concern, selecting appropriate information, and collecting and analysing information in order to report summary data useful to decision makers in selecting among alternatives.

According to Rutman (1980: 17), 'Program evaluation refers to the use of research methods to measure the effectiveness of operative programs.' In another book, edited by Rutman (1977: 16), he also uses the following definition:

Evaluation research is, first and foremost, a process of applying scientific procedures to accumulate reliable and valid evidence in the manner and the extent to which specific activities produce particular effects or outcomes.

If you critically examine these definitions, you will notice that in the evaluation process (as in research methodology) there are certain properties such as validity, reliability and thoroughness.

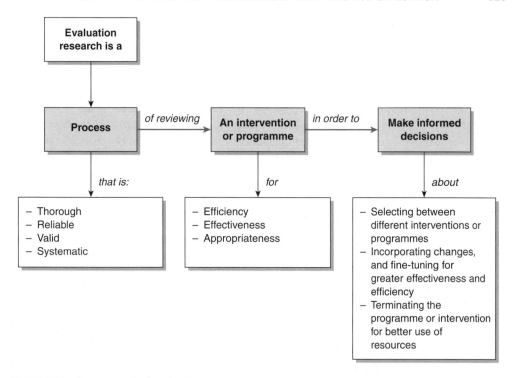

FIGURE 18.1   *The concept of evaluation*

And both processes are designed to collect and analyse information in order to answer research questions. In evaluation research, research questions mainly revolve around various aspects of an intervention, programme or practice, whereas in general research they may relate to any aspect or issue of concern or significance. Evaluation research, therefore, is primarily concerned with a critical examination of such aspects as the appropriateness, effectiveness and efficiency of an intervention. Issues relating to efficiency and effectiveness in relation to the costs and benefits of an intervention are also an integral part of evaluation studies. See Figure 18.1.

Why evaluation?

Suppose you are working in a human service agency. At some point in the course of your work, questions may come to your mind about the appropriateness of your service, its effectiveness, why some people like or benefit from it and others do not, how it can be improved, what sort of workload a service provider can carry and what the cost of delivering the service is. Consumers and administrators of your service may ask you similar questions. You can obtain answers to these questions in a number of ways, ranging from gathering anecdotal evidence to undertaking a systematic study, adhering to the principles of scientific enquiry.

Evaluation methodology, which (as mentioned) is based upon research methodology, is one way of finding answers to such questions.

You may come across professionals with differing attitudes towards evaluation. Some attach immense importance to it, while others consider it to be not as important because they think of themselves as solely the providers of a service. Whether or not you become involved in evaluating your practice is dependent upon your interest in examining the practice and upon the demands placed on you by others. However, as a beginner in research methodology, you need to be aware of the importance of evaluation and of the links between it and research methodology. Also, you need to appreciate the significance of evaluation in critically examining a practice for greater efficiency and effectiveness. Even as a service provider you need to be familiar with how your clinical skills can benefit from evaluation processes. Specifically:

- You have a professional and ethical responsibility to provide a good quality of service to your clients. To ensure its effectiveness and efficiency, you need to assess your practice. Knowledge of evaluation research will help you to assess your practice objectively or help you to communicate with an evaluator knowledgeably and professionally about evaluation issues.
- While you, as a professional, have an obligation to provide an effective service to your clients, your clients, on the other hand, have a right to know the quality of the service they are receiving from you. In this age of consumerism, your clients can demand evidence of the quality of your service. In the modern era of consumerism, the emphasis is not only on providing a service but also on how well it is delivered to consumers. In most service professions the concept of so-called evidence-based practice is growing at a very rapid rate. (See also the section on evidence-based practice in Chapter 1.)
- When you are dependent upon outside funding for providing a service, you usually need to provide evidence of the effectiveness of your service for renewal of funding. Nowadays almost every funding body uses evaluation reports as the basis of funding decisions. Quite often an evaluation report from an independent evaluator is required. For effective communication with an outside evaluator, knowledge of evaluation will go a long way.
- Because of the paucity of resources and a greater emphasis on economic rationalism nowadays, there is a growing demand on service providers to demonstrate that the service they are providing is worth the expenditure, and people are getting value for money. Critical examination through evaluation of your service will help you to demonstrate the worth and value of your service.
- How do consumers view your service? What do the consumers of your service feel about it? What do they see as the positive aspects of your service? What, in their opinion, are the negative aspects? How can your service be improved? Is your service really helping those for whom it was designed? Is it achieving its objectives? In what ways is it benefiting your clients? To answer such questions you need to evaluate your practice.
- How expensive is your service? What is the cost of providing the service to clients? Is this cost justified? Is the money being well spent?

In the final two points above are some of the questions that you need to answer as a service provider. Skills in evaluation research can help you to answer these questions with greater confidence, objectivity and validity.

Intervention–development–evaluation process

To understand the evaluation process for an intervention, it is important that you also know how it is linked to the development of an intervention. **The intervention–development–evaluation process** is divided into four phases (Figure 18.2):

1 needs assessment;
2 intervention/programme development;
3 intervention/programme execution;
4 intervention/programme evaluation.

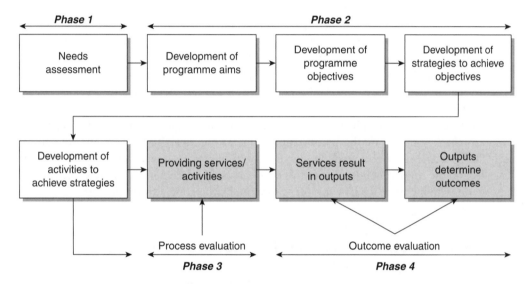

FIGURE 18.2   *The intervention–development–evaluation model*

The development of an intervention usually starts with an assessment of the needs of a community, group or people living in a geographical area (phase 1). Based upon the needs, the aims and objectives for a programme are developed to meet these needs, which in turn become the basis of developing a conceptual intervention programme. This conceptual construction is primarily based on previous experiences, understanding of the problem area, knowledge about how others have dealt with the problem in other places and/or opinion of experts in the area. In the development of this conceptual model, particular attention is given to the formulation of strategies to achieve the objectives of the programme. Next, the precise activities needed to achieve these strategies are identified. Procedures for undertaking these activities are then drawn up. These activities and procedures constitute the contents of a programme (phase 2). Of course, they may need to be streamlined, modified or otherwise changed in the light of experience. Sometimes, a conceptual–intervention model is first 'tested' out as a feasibility study to identify problems and modifications before launching on a full scale. Having fine-tuned the intervention contents, it is executed in accordance with the proposed plan (phase 3). Services/activities constitute programme *inputs*, which result in intervention *outputs*, which in turn produce *outcomes/impacts*. Outputs are the direct products of a programme's activities and are usually measured in terms of volume of tasks accomplished. Outcomes are benefits or changes in individuals or populations that can be attributed to the inputs of a programme. They may manifest as cognitive and/or non-cognitive changes. These may relate to values, attitudes, knowledge, behaviour, change in a situation or any other aspect that came about in an individual following the introduction of a programme. Though some evaluations are focused on the process by which a service is delivered (phase 3), the majority of evaluations are around either outputs or outcomes (phase 4).

Let us take an example: random breath testing (RBT). In RBT the outputs include the number of people tested; the number of awareness campaigns organised; the number of newspaper and television advertisements placed; the number of community forums held; and the number of police officers employed for the task of breath testing. The desired outcomes – the changes sought in people's behaviour and the situation – may include a reduction in alcohol-related road accidents and deaths, and a reduction in the number of people caught driving under the influence of alcohol.

Let us take another example: the counselling service for couples with marital problems. In this example the outputs are the number of sessions with couples and the number of couples seen. The outcomes might be a reduction in the conflicts; greater marital stability with a beneficial effect on the couple's children; a positive effect on work, productivity and income; increased satisfaction with life in general; or smooth separation by the couple from each other.

Perspectives in the classification of evaluation studies

The various types of evaluation can be looked at from two perspectives:

- the *focus of the evaluation;*
- the *philosophical base* that underpins an evaluation.

It is important to remember that these perspectives are *not* mutually exclusive. All evaluations categorised from the viewpoint of focus of evaluation have a philosophical base underpinning them, and so can be classified from within this perspective as well.

For example, an *impact/outcome evaluation* from the focus-of-evaluation point of view can *also* be classified as a *goal-centred evaluation* from the philosophical perspective. In an *outcome evaluation* (classified from the focus-of-evaluation perspective), you can either explore the way an intervention has impacted on the study population, or seek to determine outcomes by establishing whether or not the programme has achieved its intended objective. If the evaluation is from the focus perspective, it is classified as an impact/outcome evaluation, and if the focus is from the philosophical perspective, it is also classified as a goal-centred evaluation. Again, if you determine the impact of a programme/intervention by asking what clients/consumers

FIGURE 18.3   *Perspectives in the classification of evaluation studies*

perceive its effects to have been on them, this is also classified as a *client-centred evaluation* from a philosophical perspective. If you examine every aspect of a programme with regard to its outcome, process and any other aspect, this is categorised as a *holistic evaluation*. Finally, every type of evaluation, process or outcome can be classified as an *improvement-oriented evaluation* from the philosophical perspective as the ultimate aim of any evaluation is to improve an intervention/programme. To avoid confusion between the two perspectives, an integrated picture is provided in Figure 18.3.

Types of evaluation from a *focus* perspective

From the perspective of the focus of evaluation there are four types of evaluation: *programme/ intervention planning*, *process/monitoring*, *impact/outcome* and *cost–benefit/cost-effectiveness*. Each type addresses a main and significantly different issue. **Evaluation for planning** addresses the issue of establishing the need for a programme or intervention; **process evaluation** emphasises the evaluation of the process in order to enhance the efficiency of the delivery system;

the measurement of outcomes is the focus of an **outcome evaluation**; and the central aim of a cost–benefit evaluation is to put a price tag on an intervention in relation to its benefits. Hence, from this perspective, the classification of an evaluation is primarily dependent upon its focus.

It is important for you to understand the different evaluation questions that each is designed to answer. Table 18.1 will help you to understand the application of each type of evaluation.

Evaluation for programme/intervention planning

In many situations it is desirable to examine the feasibility of starting a programme/ intervention by evaluating the nature and extent of a chosen problem. Actually, this type of study evaluates the problem per se: its nature, extent and distribution. Specifically, **programme planning evaluation** includes:

- estimating the extent of the problem – in other words, estimating how many people are likely to need the intervention;
- delineating the characteristics of the people and groups who are likely to require the intervention;
- identifying the likely benefits to be derived from the intervention;
- developing a method of delivering the intervention;
- developing programme contents: services, activities and procedures;
- identifying training needs for service delivery and developing training material;
- estimating the financial requirements of the intervention;
- developing evaluation indicators for the success or failure of the intervention and fixing a time-line for evaluation.

There are a number of methods for evaluating the extent and nature of a problem, and for devising a service delivery manner. The choice of a particular method should depend upon the financial resources available, the time at your disposal and the level of accuracy required in your estimates. Some of the methods are:

- **Community need-assessment surveys** – Need-assessment surveys are quite prevalent to determine the extent of a problem. You use your research skills to undertake a survey in the relevant community to ascertain the number of people who will require a particular service. The number of people requiring a particular service can be extrapolated using demographic information about the community and results from your community sample survey. If done properly, a need-assessment survey can give you a reasonably accurate estimate of the needs of a community or the need for a particular type of service. However, you must keep in mind that surveys are not cheap to undertake.
- **Community forums** – Conducting **community discussion forums** is another method used to find out the extent of the need for a particular service. However, it is important to keep in mind that community forums suffer from a problem in that participants are self-selected; hence, the picture provided may not be accurate. In a community forum not everyone will participate and those who do may have a vested interest for or against the service. If, somehow, you can make sure that all interest groups are represented in a community forum, it can provide a

TABLE 18.1 *Types of evaluation from the perspective of its focus and the questions they are designed to answer*

Type of evaluation	Focus of evaluation	Main issue for evaluation	Questions to be answered
Programme/intervention planning evaluation	Planning for programme/ intervention	*Need for a programme/ intervention*	– Is there a need for the proposed programme/ intervention? – If yes, what is its extent? – Who is eligible to receive the service? – What services should be provided and how? – Who should provide the service(s)? – What is the geographical distribution of the target population? – How should the success or failure of the programme/ intervention be assessed? – Where should the services be located? – What are the training needs?
Process/monitoring evaluation	Service delivery	*Efficiency of the service delivery*	– What are the problems with the way the service is being delivered? – How can service delivery be improved? – How satisfied are clients with the way the service is being delivered? – Do staff need additional training? – How satisfied are service providers with the service delivery manner?
Impact/outcome evaluation	Outcomes/ effectiveness	*Effectiveness of a programme/intervention*	– What are the outputs of the programme? – What are the outcomes, both direct and indirect, of the programme? – How has the programme affected clients? – To what extent has the programme achieved the objectives set out at the planning stage? – How satisfied are clients with the benefits from the service? – How satisfied are service providers with the intervention outcomes?
Cost–benefit/ cost-effectiveness evaluation	Cost- effectiveness	*Cost of delivering the service*	– What is the cost of delivering the service? – Do the effects justify the cost? – Do benefits justify the cost? – As compared to others, what is the cost of per unit of service?

reasonable picture of the demand for a service. Community forums are comparatively cheap to undertake but you need to examine the usefulness of the information for your purpose. With community forums you cannot ascertain the number of people who may need a particular service, but you can get some indication of the demand for a service and different prevalent community perspectives with respect to the service.

- **Social indicators** – Making use of social indicators, in conjunction with other demographic data, if you have information about them, is another method. However, you have to be careful that these indicators have a high correlation with the problem/need and are accurately recorded. Otherwise, the accuracy of the estimates will be affected.
- **Service records** – There are times when you may be able to use existing service records to identify the unmet needs for a service. For example, if an agency is keeping a record of the cases where it has not been able to provide a service for lack of resources, you may be able to use it to estimate the number of people who are likely to need that service.
- **Focus groups of potential service consumers, service providers and experts** – You can also use focus groups made up of consumers, service providers and experts to establish the need for a service.

Community surveys and social indicators tend to be quantitative, whereas the others tend to be qualitative. Thus they give you different types of information. Service records provide an indication of the gap in service and are not reflective of its need.

It is important to remember that all these methods, except the community needs survey, provide only an indication of the demand for a service in a community. You have to determine how accurately you need to estimate the potential number of users to start a service. A community survey will provide you with the most accurate figures but it could put a strain on the resources. Also, keep in mind that use of multiple methods will produce more accurate estimates.

Process/monitoring evaluation

Process evaluation, also known as monitoring evaluation, focuses on the manner of delivery of a service in order to identify issues and problems concerning delivery. It also identifies ways of improving service delivery procedures for a better and more efficient service. Specifically, process evaluation is used for:

- determining whether or not the delivery of a service is consistent with the original design specifications and, if not, for identifying the reasons and justifications for non-compliance;
- identifying changes needed in the delivery manner for greater coverage and efficiency;
- ascertaining, when an intervention has no impact, whether this is because of the intervention itself or the manner in which it is being delivered;
- determining whether or not an intervention is reaching the appropriate target population.

Process evaluation includes evaluating the:

- extent of participation of the target population;
- delivery manner of a programme/intervention.

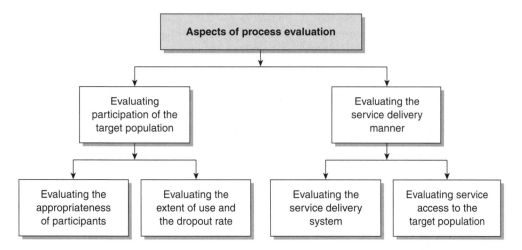

FIGURE 18.4   *Aspects of process evaluation*

Evaluating the participation of the target population in turn involves: (1) ascertaining the appropriateness of the clients for the service in question; and (2) establishing the total number of clients and the dropout rate among them. Evaluating the service delivery manner, in the same way, includes two tasks: (1) examining the procedures used in providing the service; and (2) examining the issues relating to the accessibility of the service to potential clients (Figure 18.4).

Evaluating participation of the target population

In an evaluation study designed to examine the process of delivering an intervention, it is important to examine the appropriateness of the users of the service because, sometimes, some people use a service even though they do not strictly fall within the inclusion criteria. In other words, in evaluation studies it is important to determine not just the number of users, but whether or not they are eligible users. Determining the appropriate use of an intervention is an integral part of an evaluation.

It is also important to ascertain the total number of users of a programme/intervention because it provides an indication of the need for a service, and to find out the number of dropouts because this establishes the extent of the rejection of the service for any reason. There are a number of procedures for evaluating the participation of a target population in an intervention:

- **Percentage of users** – The acceptance of a programme by the target population is one of the important indicators of a need for it: the higher the acceptance, the greater the need for the intervention. Some judge the desirability of a programme by the number of users alone. Hence, as an evaluator, you can examine the total number of users and, if possible, calculate this as a percentage of the total target population. However, you should be careful using the percentage of users in isolation as an indicator of the popularity of a programme. People may be unhappy and dissatisfied with a service, yet use it simply because there is no other option available to them. If used with other indicators, such as consumer satisfaction or in relation to evidence of the effectiveness of a programme, it can provide a better indication of its acceptance.

- **Percentage of eligible users of a service** – Service records usually contain information on service users that may include data on their eligibility for the service. An analysis of this information will provide you with a percentage of eligible users of the service: the higher the percentage of eligible users, the more positive the evaluation. That is,

$$\frac{\text{no. of eligible users} \times 100}{\text{no. of total users}} = \text{percentage of eligible users}$$

You can also undertake a survey of the consumers of a service in order to ascertain the percentage of eligible users.

- **Percentage of dropouts** – The dropout rate from a service is reflective of the satisfaction level of consumers with the programme. A higher rate indicates either inappropriate service content or flaws in the way the service is being delivered: it does not establish whether the problem is with the delivery manner or the intervention content. However, the figure will provide you with an overall indication of the level of satisfaction of consumers with the service: the higher the dropout rate, the higher the level of dissatisfaction, either with the contents of a service (its relevance to the needs of the population) or the way it is being delivered.

$$\frac{\text{no. of dropouts from a programme} \times 100}{\text{no. of total programme acceptors*}} = \text{dropout rate}$$

*Acceptors are ever-users of a service.

- **Survey of the consumers of a service** – If service records do not include data regarding client eligibility for a service, you can undertake a survey of ever-users/acceptors of the service to ascertain their eligibility for the service. From the ever-users surveyed, you can also determine the dropout rate among them. In addition, you can find out many other aspects of the evaluation, such as client satisfaction, problems and issues with the service, or how to improve its efficiency and effectiveness. How well you do this survey is dependent upon your knowledge of research methodology and availability of resources.
- **Survey of the target population** – Target population surveys, in addition to providing information about the extent of appropriate use of a service, also provide data on the extent of acceptance of a service among those for whom it was designed. The proportion of people who have accepted an intervention can be calculated as follows:

$$\frac{\text{no. of ever-users of the service} \times 100}{\text{no. of eligible individuals surveyed}} = \text{acceptance of a service}$$

- **Survey of dropouts** – Dropouts are an extremely useful source of information for identifying ways of improving an intervention. These are the people who have gone through an intervention, have experienced both positives and negatives, and have then decided to withdraw. Talking to them can provide you with their first-hand experience of the programme. They are the people who can provide you with information on possible problems, either with the content of an intervention or with the way it has been delivered. They are also an excellent source of suggestions on how to improve a service. A survey, focus group discussion or in-depth interviews can provide valuable information about the strengths as well as weaknesses of a programme. Issues raised by them and suggestions made may become the basis for improving that intervention.
- **Survey of non-users of a service** – Whereas a group of dropouts can provide extremely useful information about the problems with an intervention, non-users are important in understanding why some, for whom the programme was designed, have not accepted it. Choose any method, quantitative or qualitative, to collect information from them. Of course it could be a problem to identify the non-users in a community.

Evaluating service delivery manner

There are situations when a programme may not have achieved its intended goals. In such situations, there are two possible causes: the content of the intervention and the way it is being delivered. It is to make sure that an intervention is being delivered effectively that you undertake process evaluation. It involves identifying problems with the way a service is being delivered to consumers or finding ways of improving the delivery system. Evaluating the delivery manner of a programme is a very important aspect of process evaluation. There are a number of issues in delivering a service that may impact upon its delivery manner and process evaluation considers them. Some of the issues are:

- the delivery manner per se;
- the contents of the service and its relevance to the needs of consumers;
- the adequacy and quality of training imparted to service providers to enable them to undertake various tasks;
- staff morale, motivation and interest in the programme, and ways of enhancing these;
- the expectations of consumers;
- resources available and their management;
- issues relating to access to services by the target population;
- ways of further improving the delivery of a service.

A process evaluation aims at studying some or all of these issues. There are a number of strategies that are used in process evaluation. The purpose for which you are going to use the findings should determine whether you adopt a quantitative or qualitative approach. Considerations that determine the use of qualitative or quantitative methods in general also apply in evaluation studies. Methods that can be used in undertaking a process evaluation are:

- **Opinion of consumers** – One of the best indicators of the quality of a service is how the consumers of that service feel about it. They are best placed to identify problems in the delivery manner, to point out its strengths and weaknesses, and to tell you how the service can be improved to meet their needs. Simply by gathering the experiences of consumers with respect to utilisation of a service you can gain valuable information about its strengths and weaknesses. Consumer surveys give you an insight into what the consumers of a service like and do not like about a service. In the present age of consumerism it is important to take their opinions into consideration when designing, delivering or changing a service.

  If you want to adopt a qualitative approach to evaluation, you can use in-depth interviewing, focus group discussions and/or target population forums as ways of collecting information about the issues mentioned above. If you prefer to use a quantitative approach you can undertake a survey, giving consideration to all the aspects of quantitative research methodology including sample size and its selection, and methods of data collection. Keep in mind that qualitative methods will provide you with a diversity of opinions and issues but will not tell you the extent of that diversity. If you need to determine the extent of these issues, you should combine qualitative and quantitative approaches.

- **Opinions of service providers** – Equally important in process evaluation studies are the opinions of those engaged in providing a service. Service providers are fully aware of the strengths and weaknesses of the way in which a programme is being delivered. They are also well informed about what could be done to improve inadequacies. As an evaluator, you will find invaluable information from service providers for improving the efficiency of a service. Again, you can use qualitative or quantitative methods for data collection and analysis.

- **Time-and-motion studies** – Time-and-motion studies, both quantitative and qualitative, can provide important information about the delivery process of a service. The dominant technique involves observing the users of a service as they go through the process of using it. You, as an evaluator, passively observe each interaction and then draw inferences about the strengths and weaknesses of service delivery.

  In a qualitative approach to evaluation you mainly use observation as a method of data collection, whereas in a quantitative approach you develop more structured tools for data collection (even for observation) and subject the data to appropriate statistical analysis in order to make inferences.

- **Functional analysis studies** – Analysis of the functions performed by service providers is another approach people use in the search for increased efficiency in service delivery. An observer, with expertise in programme content and the process of delivering a service, follows a client as s/he goes through the process of receiving it. The observer keeps note of all the activities undertaken by the service provider, with the time spent on each of them. Such observations become the basis for judging the desirability of an activity as well as the justification for the time spent on it, which then becomes the basis of identifying 'waste' in the process.

Again, you can use qualitative or quantitative methods of data collection. You can adopt very flexible methods of data collection or highly structured ones. You should be aware that observations can be very structured or unstructured. The author was involved in a functional analysis study which involved two-minute observations of activities of health workers in a community health programme.

- **Panel of experts** – Another method that is used to study the delivery process of a service is to ask experts in the area of that service to make recommendations about the process. These experts may use various methods (quantitative or qualitative) to gather information, and supplement it with their own knowledge. They then share their experiences and assessments with each other in order to come up with recommendations.

The use of multiple methods may provide more detailed and possibly better information but would depend upon the resources at your disposal and the purpose of your evaluation. Your skills as an evaluator lie in selecting a method (or methods) that best suits the purpose of evaluation within the given resources.

Impact/outcome evaluation

Impact or outcome evaluation is one of the most widely practised types of evaluation. It is used to assess what changes can be attributed to the introduction of a particular intervention, programme or policy. It establishes causality between an intervention and its impact, and estimates the magnitude of this change(s). It plays a central role in decision making by practitioners, managers, administrators and planners who wish to determine whether or not an intervention has achieved its desired objectives in order to make an informed decision about its continuation, termination or alteration. Many funding organisations base their decisions about further funding for programmes on impact evaluations. Specifically, an outcome evaluation is for the purpose of:

- establishing causal links between intervention inputs and outcomes;
- measuring the magnitude of these outcomes;
- determining whether a programme or intervention has achieved its intended goals;
- finding out the unintended effects, if any, of an intervention;
- comparing the impacts of an intervention with an alternative one in order to choose the more effective of the two.

As you are aware, in any cause-and-effect relationship, in addition to the cause there are many other factors that can affect the relationship. (For details see Chapter 7.) Just to refresh your memory:

In relation to a programme or intervention, this is

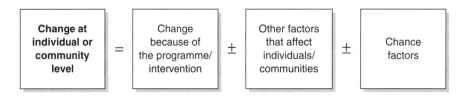

This **theory of causality** is of particular relevance to impact assessment studies. In determining the impact of an intervention, it is important to realise that the changes produced by an intervention may not be solely because of the intervention. Sometimes, other factors (extraneous variables) may play a more important role than the intervention in bringing about changes in the dependent variable. When you evaluate the effectiveness of an intervention, without comparing it to that of a control group, your findings will include the effects of extraneous variables. If you want to separate out the respective contributions of extraneous variables and the intervention, you need to use a control study design.

There are many designs from which you can choose in conducting an **impact assessment evaluation**. Impact assessment studies range from descriptive ones – in which you describe people's experiences and perceptions of the effectiveness of an intervention – to random–control–blind experiments. Again, your choice of a particular design is dependent upon the purpose of the evaluation and resources available. Some of the commonly used designs are:

- **After-only design** – Though technically inappropriate, **after-only design** is a commonly used design in evaluation studies. It measures the impact of a programme or intervention (after it has occurred) without having a baseline. The effectiveness of the intervention is judged on the basis of the current picture of the state of evaluation indicators. It relies on indicators such as:

  - number of users of the service;
  - number of dropouts from the service;
  - satisfaction of clients with the service;
  - stories/experiences of clients that changed them;
  - assessment made by experts in the area;
  - the opinions of service providers.

  It is on the basis of findings about these outcome indicators that a decision about continuation, termination or alterations in an intervention is made. One of the major drawbacks of this design is that it does not measure change that can be attributed to the intervention as such, since (as mentioned) it has neither a baseline nor a control group to compare results with. However, it provides the current picture in relation to the outcome indicators. This design is therefore inappropriate when you are interested in studying the impact of an intervention per se.

- **Before-and-after design** – The **before-and-after design** is technically sound and appropriate for measuring the impact of an intervention. There are two ways of establishing the baseline. One way is where the baseline is determined before the introduction of an intervention, which requires advance planning; and the other is where the baseline is established retrospectively, either from previous service records or through recall by clients of their situation before the introduction of the intervention. Retrospective construction of the baseline may produce less accurate data than after the data collection and hence may not be comparable. However, in the absence of anything better, it does provide some basis of comparison.

    As you may recall, one of the drawbacks of this design is that the change measured includes change brought about by extraneous and change variables. Hence, this design, though acceptable and better than the after-only design, still has a technical problem in terms of evaluation studies. Also, it is more expensive than the after-only design.
- **Experimental–control design** – The before-and-after study, with a control group, is probably the closest to a technically correct design for impact assessment of an intervention. One of the biggest strengths of this design is that it enables you to isolate the impact of independent and extraneous variables. However, it adds the problem of comparability between control and experimental groups. Sometimes this problem of comparability can be overcome by forming the groups through randomisation. Unfortunately, complexity in its execution and increased cost restrict the use of this design for the average evaluation study. Also, in many situations it may not be possible to find or construct a suitable control group.
- **Comparative study design** – The **comparative study design** is used when evaluating two or more interventions. For comparative studies you can follow any of the above designs; that is, you can have a comparative study using *after-only*, *before-and-after* or *experimental–control* design.
- **Reflexive control design** – To overcome the problem of comparability in different groups, sometimes researchers treat data collected during the non-intervention period to represent a control group, and information collected after the introduction of the intervention as if it pertained to an experimental group (Figure 18.5).

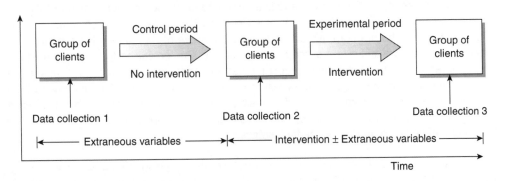

FIGURE 18.5   *Reflexive control design*

In the **reflexive control design**, comparison between *data collection 2* and *data collection 1* provides information for the control group, while comparison between *data collection 3* and *data collection 2* provides data for the experimental group. One of the main advantages of this design is that you do not need to ensure the comparability of two groups. However, if there are rapid changes in the study population over time, and if the outcome variables are likely to be affected significantly, use of this design could be problematic.

- **Interrupted time-series design** – In the **interrupted time-series design** you study a group of people before and after the introduction of an intervention. It is like the before-and-after design, except that you have multiple data collections at different time intervals to constitute an aggregated before-and-after picture (Figure 18.6). The design is based upon the assumption that one set of data is not sufficient to establish, with a reasonable degree of certainty and accuracy, the before-and-after situations.

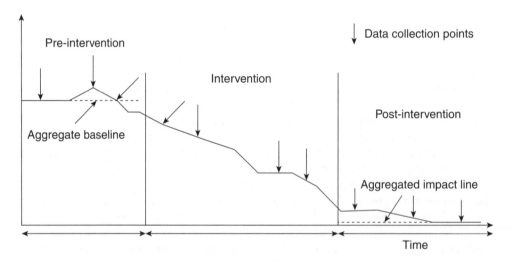

FIGURE 18.6   *Interrupted time-series design*

- **Replicated cross-sectional design** – The **replicated cross-sectional design** studies clients at different stages of an intervention, and is appropriate for those interventions that take new clients on a continuous or periodic basis. See Figure 18.7. This design is based on the assumption that those who are currently at the termination stage of an intervention are similar in terms of the nature and extent of the problem to those who are currently at the intake stage.

  In order to ascertain the change that can be attributed to an intervention, a sample at the intake and termination stages of the programme is selected, so that information can be collected pertaining to pre-situations and post-situations with respect to the problem for which the intervention is being sought. To evaluate the pattern of impact, sometimes researchers collect data at one or more intermediary stages.

These designs vary in sophistication and so do the evaluation instruments. Choice of design is difficult and (as mentioned earlier) it depends upon the purpose and resources available.

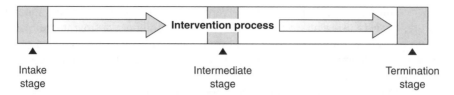

You select a sample from different stages of an intervention

FIGURE 18.7   *Replicated cross-sectional design*

Another difficulty is to decide when, during the intervention process, to undertake the evaluation. How do you know that the intervention has made its impact? One major difficulty in evaluating social programmes revolves around the question: was the change a product of the intervention or did it come from a consumer's relationship with a service provider? Many social programmes are accepted because of the confidence consumers develop in a service provider. In evaluation studies you need to keep in mind the importance of a service provider in bringing about change in individuals.

Cost–benefit/cost-effectiveness evaluation

While knowledge about the process of service delivery and its outcomes is highly useful for an efficient and effective programme, in some cases it is critical to be informed about how intervention costs compare with outcomes. In today's world, which is characterised by scarce resources and economic rationalism, it is important to justify a programme in relation to its cost. Cost–benefit analysis provides a framework for relating costs to benefits in terms of a common unit of measurement, monetary or otherwise. Specifically, cost–benefit analysis or **cost-effectiveness evaluation** is important because it helps to:

- put limited resources to optimal use;
- decide which of two equally effective interventions to replicate on a larger scale.

Cost–benefit analysis follows an input/output model, the quality of which depends upon the ability to identify accurately and measure all intervention inputs and outputs. Compared with technical interventions, such as those within engineering, social interventions are more difficult to subject to cost–benefit analysis. This is primarily because of the difficulties in accurately identifying and measuring inputs and outputs, and then converting them to a common monetary unit. Some of the problems in applying cost–benefit analysis to social programmes are outlined below:

- What constitutes an input for an intervention? There are direct and indirect inputs. Identifying these can sometimes be very difficult. Even if you have been able to identify them, the next problem is putting a price tag on each of them.

- Similarly, the outputs or benefits of an intervention need to be identified and measured. Like inputs, benefits can also be direct and indirect. In addition, a programme may have short-term as well as long-term benefits. How do you cost the various benefits of a programme? Another complexity is the need to consider benefits from the perspectives of different stakeholders.
- The main problem in cost–benefit analysis is the difficulty in converting inputs as well as outputs to a common unit. In social programmes, it often becomes difficult even to identify outputs, let alone measure and then convert them to a common unit of measurement.

Types of evaluation from a *philosophical* perspective

From a philosophical perspective, there are no specific models for or methods of evaluation. You use the same methods and models but the required information is gathered from different people or aspects depending upon the philosophy that you subscribe to. Stufflebeam and Shinkfield's book *Systematic Evaluation: A Self-Instructional Guide to Theory and Practice* is an excellent source to acquaint you with these perspectives. Types of evaluation categorised on the basis of philosophies, mentioned below, are dealt with in greater detail in their book and it is highly recommended that you refer to that if you want to gain a better appreciation of these perspectives. On the basis of these perspectives, there are four types of evaluation. Again, you should keep in mind that this classification and the classification developed on the basis of the *focus of evaluation* are not mutually exclusive.

Goal-centred/objective-oriented evaluation

This approach is based upon the philosophy that the success or failure of an intervention should be based upon the extent of congruence between the objectives of an intervention and its actual outcomes. This approach studies outcomes to determine the achievement of objectives, and congruence between the two is regarded as the sole determinant of success or failure. One of the main criticisms of **objective-oriented evaluation** is that it assesses the effectiveness of a programme without explaining the reasons for it.

Basically, the process of evaluation involves, firstly, identification of the desired goals of an intervention and, secondly, the use of a process to measure their success or failure. Again, you can use either qualitative or quantitative methods to achieve this.

Consumer-oriented/client-centred evaluation

The core of this philosophy rests on the assumption that assessment of the value or merit of an intervention – including its effectiveness, outcomes, impact and relevance – should be judged from the perspective of the consumer. Consumers, according to the philosophy of **consumer-oriented evaluation**, are the best judges of a programme.

Client-centred evaluations, again, may use qualitative or quantitative methods to find out how clients feel about various aspects of an intervention. You can even use a mix of the two to find out consumers' perceptions and opinions.

Improvement-oriented evaluation

The basic philosophy behind improvement-oriented evaluation is that an evaluation should foster improvement. 'Not to prove but to improve' seems to be the central theme of such evaluations. The focus is to study the context in order to help improve an intervention content – the process rather than outcomes.

Again, a multiplicity of methods can be used to undertake such evaluation.

Holistic/illuminative evaluation

The primary concern of **holistic research** or **illuminative evaluation** is description and interpretation, rather than measurement and prediction. It fits with the social–anthropological paradigm, acknowledging as it does historical, cultural and social factors when evaluating an intervention. The aim is to study a programme in all its aspects: how it operates, how it is influenced by various contexts, how it is applied, how those directly involved view its strengths and weaknesses, and what the experiences are of those who are affected by it. In summary, it tries to illuminate a complex array of questions, issues and factors, and to identify procedures that give both desirable and undesirable results. So a holistic/illuminative evaluation tries to understand issues relating to an intervention from many perspectives: it seeks to view the performance of a programme in its totality.

An evaluation can be conducted from any one of the above philosophical perspectives. To us, these are perspectives rather than evaluation models, but some use them as types of evaluation. The aim of this section has been to acquaint you with some of these perspectives.

Undertaking an evaluation: the process

Like the research methodology model, which forms the basis of this book, the evaluation process is also based upon certain operational steps. It is important for you to remember that the order in the write-up of these steps is primarily to make it easier for you to understand the process. Once you are familiar with these steps, their order can be changed.

Step 1: Determining the purpose of evaluation

In a research study you formulate your research problem before developing a methodology. In an evaluation study too, you need to identify the purpose of undertaking it and develop your objectives before venturing into it. It is important to seek answers to questions such as: 'Why do I want to do this evaluation?' and 'For what purpose would I use the findings?' Specifically, you need to consider the following matters, and to identify their relevance and application to your situation. Is the evaluation being undertaken to do the following?

- Identify and solve problems in the delivery process of a service.
- Increase efficiency of the service delivery manner.
- Determine the impacts of the intervention.
- Train staff for better performance.
- Work out an optimal workload for staff.
- Find out about client satisfaction with the service.
- Seek further funding.
- Justify continuation of the programme.
- Resolve issues so as to improve the quality of the service.
- Test out different intervention strategies.
- Choose between the interventions.
- Estimate the cost of providing the service.

It is important that you identify the purpose of your evaluation and find answers to your reasons for undertaking it with the active involvement and participation of the various stakeholders. It is also important that all stakeholders – clients, service providers, service managers, funding organisations and you, as an evaluator – agree with the aims of the evaluation. Make sure that all stakeholders also agree that the findings of the evaluation will not be used for any purpose other than those agreed upon. This agreement is important in ensuring that the findings will be acceptable to all, and for developing confidence among those who are to provide the required information do so freely. If your respondents are sceptical about the evaluation, you will not obtain reliable information from them.

Having decided on the purpose of your evaluation, the next step is to develop a set of objectives that will guide it.

Step 2: Developing objectives or evaluation questions

As in a research project, you need to develop evaluation questions, which will become the foundation for the evaluation. Well-articulated objectives bring clarity and focus to the whole evaluation process. They also reduce the chances of disagreement later among various parties.

Some organisations may simply ask you 'to evaluate the programme', whereas others may be much more specific. The same may be the situation if you are involved in evaluating your own intervention. If you have been given specific objectives or you are in a situation where you are clear about the objectives, you do not need to go through this step. However, if the brief is broad, or you are not clear about the objectives in your own situation, you need to construct for yourself and others a 'meaning' of *evaluation*.

As you know, evaluation can mean different things to different people. To serve the purpose of evaluation from the perspectives of different stakeholders, it is important to *involve all stakeholders in the development of evaluation objectives and to seek their agreement with them.* You need to follow the same process as for a research study (Chapter 4). The examples in Figure 18.8 may help you to understand more about objective formulation.

Example: Developing evaluation objectives: examples

Recently the author was asked to undertake two evaluations. For one, the brief was 'To evaluate the principle of community responsiveness in the delivery of health in ... (name of the state)', and for the other it was 'To evaluate ... (name of the model) service delivery model in ... (name of the region)'.

Evaluating a programme: Example One

For the first evaluation, after having initial discussions with various stakeholders, it was discovered that understanding of the principle of 'community responsiveness' was extremely vague and varied among different people. Also, there were neither any instructions about how to achieve community responsiveness nor any training programme for the purpose. A few people, responsible for ensuring the implementation of the principle, had no idea about its implementation. Our first question was: 'Can we evaluate something about which those responsible for implementation are not clear, and for which there is no specific strategy in place?' The obvious answer was 'no'. We discussed with the sponsors of the evaluation what questions they had in mind when asking us for the evaluation. On the basis of our discussion with them and our understanding of their reasons for requesting the evaluation, we proposed that the evaluation be carried out in two phases. For the first phase, the aim of the evaluation should be to define 'community responsiveness', identify/develop/ explore operational strategies to achieve it, and identify the indicators of its success or otherwise. During the second phase, an evaluation to measure the impact of implementation of the community responsiveness strategies was proposed. Our proposal was accepted. We developed the following objectives in consultation with the various stakeholders.

Evaluation of the principle of community responsiveness in health
Phase One

Main objective:
To develop a model for implementing the principle of community responsiveness in the delivery of health care in ... (name of the state).

Specific objectives:

1 To find out how the principle of community responsiveness is understood by health planners, administrators, managers, service providers and consumers, and to develop an operational definition of the term for the department.

(Continued)

(Continued)

2 To identify, with the participation of stakeholders, strategies to implement the concept of community responsiveness in the delivery of health services.
3 To develop a set of indicators to evaluate the effectiveness of the strategies used to achieve community responsiveness.
4 To identify appropriate methodologies that are acceptable to stakeholders for measuring effectiveness indicators.

Phase Two

Main objective:
To evaluate the effectiveness of the strategies used to achieve the principle of community responsiveness in the delivery of health services.

Subobjectives:

1 To determine the impact of community responsiveness strategies on community participation in decision making about health issues affecting the community.
2 To find out the opinions of the various stakeholders on the degree to which the provision of community responsiveness in the delivery of health services has been/is being observed.
3 To find out the extent of involvement of the community in decision making in issues concerning the community and its attitude towards involvement.

Evaluating a programme: Example Two

Now let us take the second study. In this case the service delivery model was well developed and the evaluation brief was clear in terms of its expectations; that is, the objective was to evaluate the model's effectiveness. Before starting the evaluation, the following objectives were developed in consultation with the steering committee, which had representatives from all stakeholder groups.

Remember, it is important that your objectives be unambiguous, clear and specific, and that they are written using verbs that express your operational intentions.

The ... Model

Main objective:

To evaluate the effectiveness of the ... (name of the model) developed by ... (name of the office).

Subobjectives:

1 To identify the strengths and weaknesses of the model as perceived by various stakeholders.
2 To find out the attitudes of consumers, service providers and managers, and relevant community agencies towards the model.

3 To determine the extent of reduction, if any, in the number of children in the care of the department since the introduction of the model.

4 To determine the impact of the model on the number of Child Concern Reports and Child Maltreatment Allegations.

5 To assess the ability of the model to build the capacity of consumers and service providers to deal with problems in the area of child protection.

6 To recommend strategies to overcome problems, if any, with the model.

7 To estimate the cost of delivering services in accordance with the model to a family.

Step 3: Converting concepts into indicators into variables

In evaluation, as well as in other research studies, often we use concepts to describe our intentions. For example, we say that we are seeking to evaluate outcomes, effectiveness, impact or satisfaction. The meaning ascribed to such words may be clear to you but may differ markedly from the understanding of others. This is because these terms involve subjective impressions. They need operational definitions in terms of their measurement in order to develop a uniform understanding. When you use concepts, the next problem you need to deal with is the development of a 'meaning' for each concept that describes them appropriately for the contexts in which they are being applied. The meaning of a concept in a specific situation is arrived at by developing **indicators**. To develop indicators, you must answer questions such as: 'What does this concept mean?', 'When can I say that the programme is effective, or has brought about a change, or consumers or service providers are satisfied?' and 'On what basis should I conclude that an intervention has been effective?' Answers to such questions become your indicators and their measurement and assessment become the basis of judgement about effectiveness, impact or satisfaction. Indicators are specific, observable, measurable characteristics or changes that can be attributed to the programme or intervention.

A critical challenge to an evaluator in outcome measurement is identifying and deciding what indicators to use in order to assess how well the programme being evaluated has done regarding an outcome. Remember that not all changes or impacts of a programme may be reflected by one indicator. In many situations you need to have multiple indicators to make an assessment of the success or failure of a programme. Figure 18.9 shows the process of converting concepts into questions that you ask of your respondents.

Some indicators are easy to measure, whereas others may be difficult. For example, an indicator such as the number of programme users is easy to measure, whereas a programme's impact on self-esteem is more difficult to measure.

In order to assess the impact of an intervention, different types of effectiveness indicators can be used. These indicators may be either qualitative or quantitative, and their measurement may range from subjective–descriptive impressions to objective–measurable–discrete changes. If you are inclined more towards qualitative studies, you may use in-depth interviewing, observation or focus groups to establish whether or not there have been changes in perceptions, attitudes or behaviour among the recipients of a programme with respect to

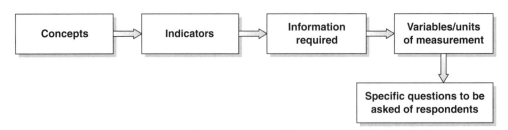

FIGURE 18.8   *Converting concepts into indicators into variables*

these indicators. In this case, changes are as perceived by your respondents: there is, as such, no measurement involved. On the other hand, if you prefer a quantitative approach, you may use various methods to measure change in the indicators using *interval* or *ratio* scales. In all the designs that we have discussed above in outcome evaluation, you may use qualitative or quantitative indicators to measure outcomes.

Now let us take an example to illustrate the process of converting concepts to questions. Suppose you are working in a department concerned with protection of children and are test-ing a new model of service delivery. Let us further assume that your model is to achieve greater participation and involvement of children, their families and non-statutory organisations work-ing in the community in decision making about children. Your assumption is that with their involvement and participation in developing the proposed intervention strategies, higher com-pliance will result, which, in turn, will result in the achievement of the desired goals.

As part of your evaluation of the model, you may choose a number of indicators such as the impact on the:

- number of children under the care of the department/agency;
- number of children returned to the family or the community for care;
- number of reported cases of 'Child Maltreatment Allegations';
- number of reported cases of 'Child Concern Reports';
- extent of involvement of the family and community agencies in the decision-making process about a child.

You may also choose indicators such as the attitude of:

- children, where appropriate, and family members towards their involvement in the decision-making process;
- service providers and service managers towards the usefulness of the model;
- non-statutory organisations towards their participation in the decision-making process;
- various stakeholders towards the ability of the model to build the capacity of consumers of the service for self-management;
- family members towards their involvement in the decision-making process.

The scales used in the measurement determine whether an indicator will be consid-ered as 'soft' or 'hard'. Attitude towards an issue can be measured using well-advanced

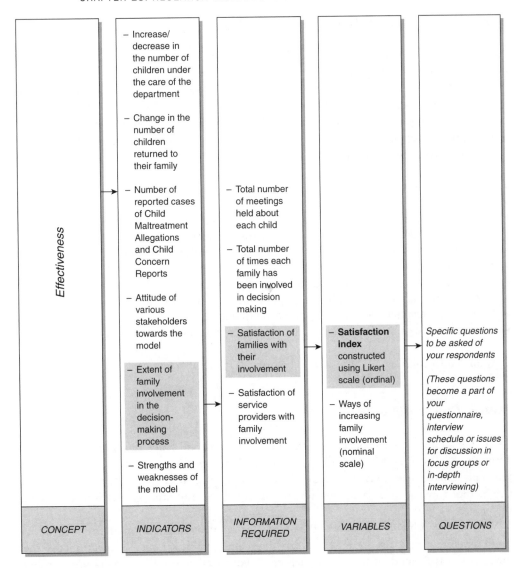

FIGURE 18.9 *An example of converting concepts into questions*

attitudinal scales or by simply asking a respondent to give his/her opinion. The first method will yield a hard indicator while the second will provide a soft one. Similarly, a change in the number of children, if asked as an opinion question, will be treated as a soft indicator.

Figure 18.10 summarises the process of converting concepts into questions, using the example described above. Once you have understood the logic behind this operationalisation, you will find it easier to apply in other similar situations.

Step 4: Developing evaluation methodology

As with a non-evaluative study, you need to identify the design that best suits the objectives of your evaluation, keeping in mind the resources at your disposal. In most evaluation studies the emphasis is on 'constructing' a comparative picture, before and after the introduction of an intervention, in relation to the indicators you have selected. On the basis of your knowledge about study designs and the designs discussed in this chapter, you propose one that is most suitable for your situation. Also, as part of evaluation methodology, do not forget to consider other aspects of the process such as:

- From whom will you collect the required information?
- How will you identify your respondents?
- Are you going to select a sample of respondents? If yes, how and how large will it be?
- How will you make initial contact with your potential respondents?
- How will you seek the informed consent of your respondents for their participation in the evaluation?
- How will the needed information be collected?
- How will you take care of the ethical issues confronting your evaluation?
- How will you maintain the anonymity of the information obtained?
- What is the relevance of the evaluation for your respondents or others in a similar situation?

You need to consider all these aspects before you start collecting data.

Step 5: Collecting data

As in a research study, data collection is the most important and time-consuming phase. As you know, the quality of evaluation findings is entirely dependent upon the data collected. Hence, the importance of data collection cannot be overemphasised. Whether quantitative or qualitative methods are used for data collection, it is essential to ensure that quality is maintained in the process.

You can have a highly structured evaluation, placing great emphasis on indicators and their measurement, or you can opt for an unstructured and flexible enquiry: as mentioned earlier, the decision is dependent upon the purpose of your evaluation. For exploratory purposes, flexibility and a lack of structure are an asset, whereas, if the purpose is to formulate a policy, measure the impact of an intervention or to work out the cost of an intervention, a greater structure and standardisation and less flexibility are important.

Step 6: Analysing data

As with research in general, the way you can analyse the data depends upon the way it was collected and the purpose for which you are going to use the findings. For policy decisions and decisions about programme termination or continuation, you need to ascertain the magnitude of change, based on a reasonable sample size. Hence, your data needs to be subjected to a statistical framework of analysis. However, if you are evaluating a process or procedure, you can use an interpretive frame of analysis.

Step 7: Writing an evaluation report

As previously stated, the quality of your work and the impact of your findings are greatly dependent upon how well you communicate them to your readers. Your report is the only basis of judgement for an average reader. Hence, you need to pay extra attention to your writing.

As for a research report, there are different writing styles. In the author's opinion you should communicate your findings under headings that reflect the objectives of your evaluation. It is also suggested that the findings be accompanied by recommendations pertaining to them. Your report should also have an executive summary of your findings and recommendations.

Step 8: Sharing findings with stakeholders

A very important aspect of any evaluation is sharing the findings with the various groups of stakeholders. It is a good idea to convene a group comprising all stakeholders to communicate what your evaluation has found. Be open about your findings and resist pressure from any interest group. Objectively and honestly communicate what your evaluation has found. It is of utmost importance that you adhere to ethical principles and the professional code of conduct.

As you have seen, the process of a research study and that of an evaluation is almost the same. The only difference is the use of certain models in the measurement of the effectiveness of an intervention. It is therefore important for you to know about research methodology before undertaking an evaluation.

Involving stakeholders in evaluation

Most evaluations have a number of stakeholders, ranging from consumers to experts in the area, including service providers and managers. It is important that all categories of stakeholder be involved at all stages of an evaluation. Failure to involve any group may hinder success in completion of the evaluation and seriously affect confidence in your findings. It is therefore important that you identify all stakeholders and seek their involvement and participation in the evaluation. This ensures that they feel a part of the evaluation process, which, in turn, markedly enhances the probability of their accepting the findings. The following steps outline a process for involving stakeholders in an evaluation study.

Step 1   **Identifying stakeholders.** First of all, talk with managers, planners, programme administrators, service providers and the consumers of the programme either individually or collectively, and identify who they think are the direct and indirect stakeholders. Having collected this information, share it with all groups of stakeholders to see if anyone has been left out. Prepare a list of all stakeholders making sure it is acceptable to all significant ones. If there are any disagreements, it is important to resolve them.

Step 2   **Involving stakeholders.** In order to develop a common perspective with respect to various aspects of the evaluation, it is important that different categories of stakeholder be actively involved in the whole process of evaluation from the identification of their concerns to the sharing of its findings. In particular, it is important to involve them in developing a framework for evaluation, selecting the evaluation indicators, and developing procedures and tools for their measurement.

Step 3   **Developing a common perspective among stakeholders towards the evaluation.** Different stakeholders may have different understandings of the word 'evaluation'. Some may have a very definite opinion about it and how it should be carried out while others may not have any conception. Different stakeholders may also have different opinions about the relevance of a particular piece of information for answering an evaluation question. Or they may have different interests. To make evaluation meaningful to the majority of stakeholders, it is important that their perspectives and understandings of evaluation be understood and that a common perspective on the evaluation be arrived at during the planning stage.

Step 4   **Resolving conflicts of interest.** As an evaluator, if you find that stakeholders have strong opinions and there is a conflict of interest among them with respect to any aspect of the evaluation, it is extremely important to resolve it. However, you have to be very careful in resolving differences and must not give the impression that you are favouring any particular subgroup.

Step 5   **Identifying the information stakeholders need from the proposed evaluation.** Identify, from each group of stakeholders, the information they think is important to meet their needs and the objectives of the evaluation.

Step 6   **Forming a steering committee.** For routine consultation, the sharing of ideas and day-to-day decision making, it is important that you ask the stakeholders to elect a steering committee with whom you, as the evaluator, can consult and interact. In addition to providing you with a forum for consultation and guidance, such a committee gives stakeholders a continuous sense of involvement in the evaluation.

Ethics in evaluation

Being ethical is the core requirement of an evaluation. If for some reason you cannot be ethical, do not undertake the evaluation, as you will end up doing harm to others, and that is unethical. Although, as a good evaluator, you may have involved all the stakeholders in the planning and conduct of the evaluation, it is possible that sometimes, when findings are not in someone's interest, a stakeholder will challenge you. It is of the utmost importance that you stand firm on the findings and do not surrender to any pressure from anyone. Surrendering to such pressure is unethical.

Summary

In this chapter some of the aspects of evaluation research are discussed, in brief, in order to make you aware of them, rather than to provide you with a detailed knowledge base. It is highly recommended that you read some books on evaluation research. This chapter highlights the relationship between research methodology per se and its application to evaluation in practice. Evaluation skills are built on the knowledge and skills of research methodology: an evaluator has to be a good researcher.

In this chapter we looked at some of the definitions of 'evaluation', identified its characteristics and examined the reasons for undertaking an evaluation. The intervention–development–evaluation process is discussed in detail, exploring the relationship between programme development and its evaluation. Evaluation studies are classified from two perspectives: the *focus of evaluation* and the *philosophical basis* that underpins them. The typology of evaluation studies is developed from these perspectives. There are four different types of evaluation from the perspective of their focus: *programme/intervention planning evaluation*, *process/monitoring evaluation*, *impact/outcome evaluation* and *cost–benefit/cost-effectiveness evaluation*. From the perspective of the philosophies that underpin these evaluations, again, four types of evaluation are identified: *goal-centred/objective evaluation*, *consumer-oriented/client-centred evaluation*, *improvement-oriented evaluation* and *holistic evaluation*. The evaluation process was outlined step by step with considerable discussion centred on how to convert concepts into indicators into variables, enabling the formulation of questions for respondents that will elicit the required information. How to involve stakeholders in an evaluation process was also discussed using a step-by-step guide. Finally, the readers are alerted to some of the ethical issues in evaluation.

For You to Think About

▸ Refamiliarise yourself with the keywords listed at the beginning of this chapter and if you are uncertain about the meaning or application of any of them revisit these in the chapter before moving on.

▸ Imagine that you have been asked to evaluate a service offered by the organisation you work for. Consider how you would go about this process taking into account any ethical dilemmas that may arise and the practical problems that you may face.

▸ Taking an example of an evaluation study from your own area of interest or profession, identify the stakeholders and consider why it is important to involve them in the process.

▸ Why, as a service provider, is it important that you evaluate your own practice?

APPENDIX
Developing a research project: a set of exercises for beginners

Application is the essence of knowledge. However, there always remains a gap between theoretical knowledge and its application. It is only with practice that this gap can be narrowed. A beginner attempting to apply theoretical knowledge needs direction and guidance. This set of exercises has been developed with this belief. There is an exercise for almost each operational step of the proposed research process. Working through them will help you to develop a research project.

The main aim of these exercises is to provide you with a broad framework that is central to the operationalisation of each step of the research process. In most cases, a separate exercise is provided for quantitative and qualitative studies so it is important that you know before you start which approach you are going to take. Within each exercise, there are brief reminders of some of the key issues relating to the process and a series of questions to help you to think through procedures and provide a framework for the development of your study.

Answers to these questions and awareness of the issues that the exercises outline will put you in a position to complete the framework suggested for writing a research proposal (Chapter 13), and therefore these will also constitute the core of your research proposal.

It is important for a beginner to work through these exercises with considerable thought and care.

Exercise I: Formulation of a research problem

Quantitative studies

Now that you have gone through all the chapters that constitute Step I of the research process, this exercise provides you with an opportunity to apply that knowledge to formulate a research problem that is of interest to you. As you know, selecting a research problem is one of the most important aspects of social research, so this exercise will, therefore, help you in formulating your research problem by raising questions and issues that will guide you to examine critically various facets and implications of what you are proposing to study. The exercise is designed to provide a directional framework that guides you through the problem formulation path. Keep in mind that the questions and issues raised in this exercise are not prescriptive but indicative and directional, hence you need to be critical and innovative while working through them. Thinking through a research problem with care can prevent a tremendous wastage of human and financial resources.

A research problem should be clearly stated and be specific in nature. The feasibility of the study in terms of the availability of technical expertise, finances and time, and in terms of its relevance, should be considered thoroughly at the problem-formulation stage. In studies that attempt to establish a causal relationship or an association, the accuracy of the measurement of independent (cause) and dependent (effect) variables is of crucial importance and, hence, should be given serious consideration. If you have already selected a problem, you need not go through this process.

Start by identifying a broad area you are interested in. For example, a health, education or treatment programme; migration; patient care; community health; community needs; foster care; or the relationship between unemployment and street crime. Chapter 4 of this book will help you to work through this exercise.

Step I   Select a broad area of study that interests you from within your academic discipline.

Having selected an area, the next step is to 'dissect' it in order to identify its various aspects and subareas. For example, say your broad area of interest is migration. Some aspects or subareas of migration are:

- a socioeconomic–demographic profile of immigrants;
- reasons for immigration;
- problems of immigrants;
- services provided to immigrants;
- attitudes of immigrants towards migration;

- attitudes of host communities towards immigrants;
- the extent of acculturation and assimilation;
- racial discrimination in the host country.

Or perhaps you are interested in studying a public health programme. Dissect it as finely as possible in order to identify the aspects that could be studied. List them as they come to you. For example:

- a socioeconomic–demographic profile of the target group;
- the morbidity and mortality patterns in a community;
- the extent and nature of programme utilisation;
- the effects of a programme on a community;
- the effectiveness of a particular health promotion strategy.

Or your interest may be in studying delinquents. Some aspects of delinquency are:

- delinquency as related to unemployment, broken homes or urbanisation;
- a profile of delinquents;
- reasons for delinquency;
- various therapeutic strategies.

Step II   'Dissect' the broad area that you selected in Step I into subareas as discretely and finely as possible. Have a one-person (with yourself) brainstorming session.

1 _____

2 _____

3 _____

4 _____

5 _____

To investigate all these subareas is neither advisable nor feasible. Select only those subareas that would be possible for you to study within the constraints of time, finance and expertise at your disposal. One way to select your subarea is to start with a process of elimination: delete those areas you are not very interested in. Towards the end it may become difficult but you need to keep eliminating until you have selected a subarea(s) that can be managed within your constraints. Even one subarea can provide you with a valid and exhaustive study.

Step III   From the above subareas, select a subarea or subareas in which you would like to conduct your study.

1 _____

2 _____

3 _____

Step IV   Within each chosen subarea, what research questions do you hope to answer? (Be as specific as possible. You can select one or as many subareas as you want.)

Subarea Specific research questions to be answered

1   (a) _____

    (b) _____

    (c) _____

    (d) _____

    (e) _____

Subarea Specific research questions to be answered

2   (a) _____

    (b) _____

    (c) _____

    (d) _____

    (e) _____

3   (a) _____

    (b) _____

    (c) _____

    (d) _____

    (e) _____

The research questions to be answered through the study become the basis of your objectives. Use action-oriented words in the formulation of objectives. The main difference between research questions and objectives is the way they are written. Questions are worded in question form and objectives are statements referring to the achievement of a task.

Your main objective should indicate the overall focus of your study and the subobjectives, its specific aspects. Subobjectives should be listed numerically. They should be worded clearly and unambiguously. Make sure each objective contains only one aspect of the study.

Step V   On the basis of your research questions, formulate the main objective and the subobjectives of your study.

Main objective (the main focus of your study):

_____

_____

_____

Subobjectives (specific aspects of your study):

1 _____

2 _____

3 _____

4 _____

5 _____

Step VI   Carefully consider the following aspects of your study.

Task	What is involved	Time needed	Approx. cost	Technical expertise needed	Gaps in knowledge and skills
Literature review					
Instrument construction					
Data collection					
Data analysis					
Draft report					
Final report					

Now you have developed the objectives of your study. Take some time to think about them. Be clear about what tasks are involved, what time is realistically required and what skills you need to develop in order to conduct your study. Consider these areas carefully again.

Step VII   Double-check:

- Are you really interested in the study?

  Yes ☐   No ☐   Uncertain ☐

- Do you agree with the objectives of the study?

  Yes ☐   No ☐   Uncertain ☐

- Are you certain you want to pursue the study?

  Yes ☐ No ☐ Uncertain ☐

- Do you have adequate resources?

  Yes ☐ No ☐ Uncertain ☐

- Do you have access to an appropriate study population?

  Yes ☐ No ☐ Uncertain ☐

If your answer to any of these questions is either 'no' or 'uncertain', re-examine the selected aspects carefully and make the appropriate changes in your objectives.

What, in your opinion, is the relevance of this study to theory and practice? How will your study contribute to the existing body of knowledge, help the practitioners in your profession and assist in programme development and policy formulation?

Relevance to theory:_____

_____

_____

_____

Relevance to practice:_____

_____

_____

_____

_____

Now that you have formulated your research problem it is important to examine your objective, research questions and hypotheses to identify if you have used any concepts in their formulation. When you convert concepts into variables an understanding about variables plays a very important role. Concepts are highly subjective as their understanding varies from person to person and, as such, they may not be measurable. Any concept, perception or imagination that can be measured on any one of the four measurement scales (*nominal*, *ordinal*, *internal* or *ratio*) is called a variable. It is important for concepts used in a study to be operationalised in measurable terms so that the extent of variation in a study population's understanding of them is reduced, if not eliminated.

At this stage, when you have formulated your objectives, it is important for you to think how you will operationalise any concepts used in the objectives, research questions or hypotheses formulated: what are their indicators and how will they be measured?

The following table suggests how you might operationalise the concept of 'effectiveness', in relation to a health education programme on AIDS. It lists the indicators of effectiveness (you can have other indicators) sets out the variables that measure the indicators and describes the unit of measurement for the variables.

Concept	Indicator	Variable(s)	Unit of measurement
Effectiveness	*Awareness* of AIDS	Extent of change in:	Change in the *proportion* of the population, before and after the health education programme, with respect to:
	Knowledge about AIDS	Awareness Knowledge Practice	Awareness of, and knowledge about, different aspects of AIDS
	Use of contraceptives (*practice*)		Use of contraceptives for safe sex

This part of the exercise is designed to help you operationalise the major concepts used in your study. Refer to Chapter 5 for additional information on variables.

Step VIII   Operationalise your concepts.

Objectives/research questions/hypotheses	Major concepts	Indicators	Variables	Unit of measurement

It is essential to develop a working or operational definition of your study population. For example, who would you consider to be a patient, an immigrant, a youth, a psychologist, a teacher, a delinquent or a Christian? Working definitions play a crucial role in avoiding ambiguities in the selection of a sample and help you to narrow your study population.

Step IX   Operationally define your study population.

_____

_____

_____

_____

_____

As discussed, some believe that one must have a hypothesis to undertake an investigation; however, in the author's opinion, hypotheses, although they bring clarity, specificity and focus to a research problem, are not essential for a study. You can conduct a valid investigation without constructing a single formal hypothesis. On the other hand, you can construct as many hypotheses as you think appropriate. In epidemiological studies, to narrow the field of investigation, one must construct a hypothesis as to the probable cause of the condition to be investigated.

A hypothesis is a hunch, assumption, suspicion, assertion or idea about a phenomenon, relationship or situation, which you intend to investigate in order to find out if you are right. If it proves to be right, your assumption was correct; hence, you prove that your hypothesis was true. Otherwise, you conclude your hypothesis to be false.

Disproving a hypothesis is as important as, or more important than, proving it. As a hypothesis is usually constructed on the basis of what is commonly believed to be right, your disproving it might lead to something new that has been ignored by previous researchers.

A hypothesis should be conceptually simple, clear and specific, and be capable of verification and being expressed operationally.

There is a specific way of writing a hypothesis, with which you need to be familiar (refer to Chapter 6).

Step X   Construct your hypothesis or hypotheses for each subobjective/research question.

Objectives/research questions	Hypotheses to be tested
	1
	2
	3
	1
	2
	3
	1
	2
	3

For qualitative studies

As mentioned earlier, the difference in qualitative and quantitative research studies starts with the way you think about and formulate your research problem. In qualitative studies, the research problem is preferred to be broad, flexible and continuously formulated as the information is collected. In the process of data collection, if you find something interesting relating to your broad area of study, you add the aspect(s) and change the focus to accommodate the new vision.

This flexibility is an important strength of qualitative research but it is also important that you develop a conceptual framework of issue and questions for your study, as non-specificity about what you want to find out can often create problems for your respondents. Many do not feel comfortable or are not in a position to articulate the multiple aspects of an area without being prompted. For situations like this it is important that you are fully prepared with a framework in mind for your enquiry. No doubt you can develop this framework during data collection, while talking to your respondents, but this may create a problem in terms of completeness and comparability with the information obtained during the early phase of the study. You can minimise some of these problems by developing a conceptual framework in advance. It is also important that you communicate with respondents in specific terms without bias or influencing their thinking.

Remember, these are not the questions that you will ask of your respondents. These are just reminders for raising issues or questions if nothing much is forthcoming from a respondent.

In qualitative research the following would be considered as broad areas of interest:

- What does it mean to have a child with ADHD in the family?
- How resilient is this community?
- What is community responsiveness?
- Living with HIV/AIDS.
- How has a community coped after a major bush fire or tsunami?

Step I   Select a broad area of study that interests you or a question that you want to find answers to through the research study.

_____

_____

Step II   Having selected your main research question or broad area of study, list all questions that you want to find answers to. Also list all issues that you want to discuss with your respondents. Your literature review, discussions with others and consultation with potential respondents will be of immense help at this stage.

Questions: _____

_____

_____

_____

_____

_____

_____

_____

_____

_____

Issues: _____

_____

_____

_____

_____

_____

_____

_____

_____

_____

_____

Exercise II: Conceptualising a study design

Quantitative studies

Exercise I has been developed to help you to decide what you want to find out about. The next step is to decide how to go about it. This includes deciding on an overall plan and selecting procedures and methods that you propose to use during your research journey. The details of your plan, procedures and methods become the core of your study design.

A study design describes the design per se, that is the type of study design you propose to adopt; for example, whether the proposed study is cross-sectional, correlational or experimental. It should also provide details of the logistical procedures required for gathering information from the study population. This exercise helps you to put forward your arguments to justify the selection of the design you are proposing for your study, critically examining its strengths and weaknesses, and thus enabling you to select the best and workable study design. The exercise also challenges you to think through other logistical procedures such as outlining the process of identifying and contacting your study population and your plan to obtain the required information from your potential respondents, thus helping you to develop the roadmap for your journey.

For qualitative studies the process is the same though it varies in content.

The issues raised in this exercise will help you to conceptualise your study design. Chapter 8 details the various types of study design in both quantitative and qualitative research for you to refer to while working through this exercise.

A: Answers to the following questions will help you to develop your study design (Step II).

1 Is the design that you propose to adopt to conduct your study cross-sectional, longitudinal, experimental or comparative in nature? If possible draw a diagram depicting the design.

_____

_____

_____

2 Why did you select this design?

_____

_____

_____

3 What, in your opinion, are the strengths of this design?

_____

_____

_____

4 What are the weaknesses and limitations of this design?
   Weaknesses:

_____

_____

_____

   Limitations:

_____

_____

_____

5 Who constitutes your study population?

_____

_____

_____

6 Will you be able to identify each respondent in your study population?

   Yes ☐   No ☐

6(a) If yes, how will they be identified?

_____

_____

_____

6(b) If no, how do you plan to get in touch with them?

_____

_____

_____

7   Do you plan to select a sample?

Yes ☐   No ☐

7(a) In either case, explain the reasons for your decision.

_____

_____

_____

8   How will you collect data from your respondents (e.g. interview, questionnaire)?

_____

_____

_____

8(a) Why did you select this method of data collection?

_____

_____

_____

8(b) What, in your opinion, are its strengths and weaknesses?

Strengths:

_____

_____

_____

Weaknesses:

_____

_____

_____

8(c) If you are interviewing, where will the interviews be held?

_____

_____

_____

8(d) If you are using mailed questionnaires:

    (i) From where will you obtain the addresses of potential respondents?

_____

_____

_____

    (ii) Are you planning to enclose a self-addressed stamped envelope with the questionnaires?

Yes ☐   No ☐

    (iii) In the case of a low response rate, will you send a reminder?

Yes ☐   No ☐

    (iv) If there are queries, how should respondents get in touch with you?

_____

_____

_____

B: On the basis of the above information, describe your study design. (For further guidance, consult Chapter 8.)

For qualitative studies

A: Answers to the following questions will help you in developing a roadmap for your research journey.

1 In which geographical area, community, group or population group would you like to undertake your study?

_____

_____

_____

_____

2 How do you plan to get entry into the area, community or group? Which network, if any, are you planning to use?

_____

_____

_____

_____

3 Why did you select this group?

_____

_____

_____

_____

4 From whom will you gather the required information? (Who will be your respondents?)

_____

_____

_____

_____

5 If you are gathering information from secondary sources, have you checked their availability?

Yes ☐   No ☐   Not applicable ☐

6 Have you checked the availability of the required information in them?

Yes ☐   No ☐   Not applicable ☐

7 If you are gathering information from individuals, how many will you contact?

_____

_____

8 What will be the basis of selection of these individuals?

_____

_____

_____

_____

9 How will you collect the required information? List all methods that you plan to use.

_____

_____

_____

_____

Exercise III: Developing a research instrument

The construction of a research instrument is the first practical step in operationalising your study. It is an important aspect of your research as it constitutes the input; the quality of your output (the findings and conclusions) is entirely dependent upon the quality and appropriateness of your input – the research instrument. Items in a research instrument are questions asked of respondents. Responses to these questions become the raw data that is processed to find answers to your research questions. The famous saying about computers, 'garbage in, garbage out', also equally applies to the research instrument. To a large extent, the validity of the findings depends upon the quality of the raw data which, in turn, depends upon the research instrument you have used. If the latter is valid and reliable, the findings should also be valid and reliable.

The quality of a research instrument largely depends upon your experience in research. It is important for a beginner to follow the suggested steps outlined in Chapter 9.

For quantitative studies

Quantitative research is structured and predetermined in terms of what you want to find out about and how. As a part of this operational step, you need to decide what questions to ask of your respondents, the wording you are going to use and the order in which the questions will be asked. This exercise is designed to help to develop skills in constructing an instrument.

One of the ways to formulate the questions that are going to constitute your research instrument is by examining each subobjective/research question/hypothesis you have developed for your study, specifying for each the information you require, identifying the variables that are needed, and then by formulating questions to be asked of your respondents.

The wording of your questions should be simple and without ambiguities. Do not ask leading questions or questions based upon presumptions. Double-barrelled questions should be avoided.

The pre-test of a research instrument is an integral part of instrument construction. As a rule, the pre-test should not be carried out on your sample but on a similar population.

Step I   On a separate piece of paper, draw a table as shown below, then list all your sub-objectives/research questions/hypotheses in the first column and work through the other columns listing the required information.

Specific objectives/ research questions/ hypotheses	Specifically, what information do you require?	Identify the required variables	Formulate questions★ (on a separate piece of paper)

Step II   Formulate the questions,★ preferably on a separate piece of paper, giving particular attention to their wording and order. In your own mind you must examine the relevance and justification of each question in relation to the objectives of your study. If you cannot relate the relevance and justification of a question to the objectives of your study, it should be discarded.

Step III If you are developing a questionnaire, incorporate interactive statements at appropriate places.

Step IV   After developing the first draft of your research instrument, answer the questions yourself; that is, interview yourself or complete the questionnaire. You need to imagine that you are a member of the study population who will be asked these questions or requested to complete the questionnaire. If you find it difficult to answer a question, re-examine it.

Step V   Once you are satisfied with the research instrument, pre-test it with a few respondents from a population similar to the one you are going to study. The purpose of the pre-test/field test is not to obtain information but to uncover problems with the instrument. If the instrument is an interview schedule, interview the pre-test respondents to find out if they understand the questions. If a question is not understood, find out what the respondent did not understand. If the same problem is identified by more than one respondent, change the wording. If your instrument is a questionnaire, ask the pre-test respondents to go through the questions with the aim of identifying any questions that are difficult to understand. Discuss the problems that they had in understanding or interpreting a question. In light of these discussions, if necessary, change the wording of questions with which pre-test respondents have difficulties.

Step VI   Having pre-tested and, if necessary, amended the instrument, take a piece of paper and draw a table with two columns. In the first column write each subobjective, research question and hypothesis separately, and in the other, write the question number(s) that provide information for these objectives, research questions or hypotheses. In other words, make each question match the objective for which it provides information. If a question cannot be linked to a specific objective, research question or hypothesis, examine why it was included.

Step VII   Prepare the final draft of your research instrument. If you plan to use a computer for data analysis, you may provide space on the research instrument for coding the data.

For qualitative studies

If you are doing a qualitative study, you do not need to develop a list of questions. However, it is important that you construct a framework of the issues that you think you should cover to achieve the objectives of your study. This interview guide or conceptual framework will help you to continue with your interviews if nothing much is forthcoming from your respondents. Your aim is to let a respondent bring out the issues, but this framework is ready in case that does not happen. Consult Chapter 9 for developing a conceptual framework.

Write, in a point form, the issues that you think you want to discuss with your respondents. Most of it you have already done as a part of Exercise I.

_____

_____

_____

_____

_____

_____

_____

_____
_____
_____
_____

Exercise IV: Selecting a sample

The accuracy of what you find through your research endeavour, in addition to many other things, depends upon the way you select your sample.

The underlying premise in sampling is that a small number of units, if selected correctly, can provide, to a sufficiently high degree of probability, reasonably accurate insight into what is happening in the study population.

For details on sampling designs, refer to Chapter 12.

For quantitative studies

The basic objective of a sampling design in quantitative research is to minimise, within the limitation of cost, any difference between the values and estimates obtained from your sample and those prevalent in the study population. Sampling theory, in quantitative research, is thus guided by two principles:

1 the avoidance of bias in the selection of a sample;
2 the attainment of maximum precision for a given outlay of resources.

In quantitative research you can select any of the probability or a non-probability sample design. Both have advantages and disadvantages and both are appropriate for certain situations. But whatever sampling design you choose, make sure you take steps to avoid introducing your bias. When selecting a sample in quantitative studies you need to decide on two things: the sample size you plan to select; and how to select the required sampling units. You also need to think about your reasons for deciding the size and choosing the sampling strategy.

This exercise is designed for you to think through the issues which are important in helping you to develop your sampling strategy.

Step I Answer the following about your sampling design.

1 What is the total size of your study population?
_____Unknown ☐

2 Do you want to select a sample?

Yes ☐ No ☐

2(a) If yes, what will your sample size be?

2(b)   What are your reasons for choosing this sample size? _____

_____

_____

_____

_____

3   How will you select your sample? (What sampling design are you proposing?)
4   Why did you select this sampling design? (What are its strengths?)
5   What are the limitations of this design?

Step II   On the basis of the answers to the above questions, write about your sampling design, detailing the process and your justification for using it.

_____

_____

_____

_____

_____

_____

For qualitative studies

In qualitative research your aim is not to select a random or unbiased sample but one which can provide you, as far as possible, with the detailed, accurate and complete information that you are looking for. Hence, you are dominantly guided by your judgement in the selection of your respondents.

In qualitative research you can only use non-probability designs but you are not guided by the sample size. The numbers of people you are going to contact depend upon the attainment of the data saturation point during the data collection process.

You also need to decide who are going to be your respondents and how they are going to be identified. You need to think about the determinants on which you are going to base your judgement as to the suitability of your respondents.

Answers to the following questions will help you to think through the issues you are likely to face while developing a sampling strategy for your study.

A: What factors would you keep in mind when selecting a respondent?

_____

_____

_____

_____

_____

_____

_____

B: How would you identify your potential respondents?

_____

Exercise V: Developing a frame of analysis

For both quantitative and qualitative studies in general terms describe the strategy you plan to use for data analysis. Decide whether the data will be analysed manually or by computer. For computer analysis you need to identify the program you plan to use. Refer to Chapter 15 for details.

For quantitative studies

You should also specify the type of analysis you plan to carry out – that is, frequency distributions, cross-tabulations, regression analysis or analysis of variance. It is also important to plan which variables will be subjected to which type of statistical procedure.

If you have used certain concepts in your study, how will these concepts be operationalised? For example, if you were measuring the effectiveness of a health programme, how would the responses to the various questions, designed to find out the effectiveness, be combined to ascertain effectiveness? Keep in mind that when you actually carry out data analysis, it is only natural that you will develop new ideas on how to improve the analysis of data. You should feel free to change the frame of analysis when actually analysing data if you so desire. This exercise is a rough guide for you to start thinking about analysing your raw data.

Think through the following issues:

1 If you are planning to use a computer for data analysis, what software will you use?

_____

2 Which variables will you subject to frequency distribution analysis?

_____

3 Which variables will be cross-tabulated?

_____

_____

_____

_____

4   What variables will be subjected to which statistical procedures (e.g. regression analysis, ANOVA, factor analysis)?

_____

_____

_____

_____

_____

5   How do you plan to operationalise or construct the main concepts through combining responses to different questions (e.g. satisfaction index, effectiveness)?

_____

_____

_____

_____

For qualitative studies

> For qualitative studies it is also important for you to specify the type of analysis you are going to have. If it is a description or narration of an event, episode, situation or instance, you should outline how it is going to be structured. If you are going to identify the main themes, you should specify how you are planning to analyse the contents to identify them. Keep in mind that as you go through the analysis you will get many new ideas which you will need to incorporate.

1   If you are planning to use a computer for data analysis, what software will you use?

_____

_____

2   How are you going to identify the main themes that emerged from your field notes, in-depth interviews or any other source that you used?

_____

_____

_____

_____

_____

3   Are you going to quantify these themes? If yes, how?

_____
_____
_____
_____
_____

Exercise VI: Developing an outline of the chapters

Although each operational step is important, in a way writing the report is the most crucial as it tells others about the outcome of your study: it is the outcome of the hard work you have put into your study and is the only thing visible to readers. Hence, even the most valuable work could be lost if your report is not well written.

The quality of your report depends upon many things: your writing skills; the clarity of your thoughts and their logical expression; your knowledge of the subject; and your experience in research writing.

Developing an outline for the structure of the report is extremely useful. As a beginner it is important that you think through carefully the contents of your report, organise them around the main themes of your study, and ensure that the various aspects of a theme are well integrated and follow a logical progression.

This exercise is designed to help you to organise your thoughts with respect to writing your research report whether your study is quantitative or qualitative. You should, as far as possible, attempt to place the various aspects of your report under chapter headings, even if these are very tentative. For this exercise develop headings for your chapters and then list their tentative contents. Keep in mind that these are likely to change as you start writing the actual report. Though they can sometimes completely change, this exercise will still be very rewarding and may provide you with valuable guidance in organising your thoughts and writing. Consult Chapter 17 for more details.

1 What are the main themes of your study?

_____
_____
_____
_____
_____

2 Develop chapter headings under which the above themes will be organised in writing your report.

_____
_____
_____
_____

_____

_____

_____

3 Develop an outline of each chapter which briefly describes what you are going to write within each chapter.

_____

_____

_____

_____

_____

_____

Glossary

100 per cent bar chart: The 100 per cent bar chart is very similar to the stacked bar chart. The only difference is that in the former the subcategories of a variable for a particular bar total 100 per cent and each bar is sliced into portions in relation to their proportion out of 100.

Accidental sampling, as quota sampling, is based upon your convenience in accessing the sampling population. Whereas quota sampling attempts to include people possessing an obvious/visible characteristic, accidental sampling makes no such attempt. Any person that you come across can be contacted for participation in your study. You stop collecting data when you reach the required number of respondents you decided to have in your sample.

Action research, in common with participatory research and collaborative enquiry, is based upon a philosophy of community development that seeks the involvement of community members in planning, undertaking, developing and implementing research and programme agendas. Research is a means to action to deal with a problem or an issue confronting a group or community. It follows a cyclical process that is used to identify the issues, develop strategies and implement the programmes to deal with them and then again assessing strategies in light of the issues.

Active variable: In studies that seek to establish causality or association there are variables that can be changed, controlled and manipulated either by a researcher or by someone else. Such variables are called active variables.

After-only design: In an after-only design the researcher knows that a population is being, or has been, exposed to an intervention and wishes to study its impact on the population. In this design, baseline information (pre-test or before observation) is usually 'constructed' either on the basis of respondents' recall of the situation before the intervention, or from information available in existing records, i.e. secondary sources.

Alternate hypothesis: The formulation of an alternate hypothesis is a convention in scientific circles. Its main function is to specify explicitly the relationship that will be considered as true in case the research hypothesis proves to be wrong. In a way, an alternate hypothesis is the opposite of the research hypothesis.

Ambiguous question: An ambiguous question is one that contains more than one meaning and that can be interpreted differently by different respondents.

Applied research: Most research in the social sciences is applied in nature. Applied research is one where research techniques, procedures and methods that form the body of research methodology are applied to collect information about various aspects of a situation, issue, problem or phenomenon so that the information gathered can be utilised for other purposes such as policy formulation, programme development, programme modification and evaluation, enhancement of the understanding about a phenomenon, establishing causality and outcomes, identifying needs and developing strategies.

Area chart: For variables measured on an interval or a ratio scale, information about the subcategories of a variable can also be presented in the form of an area chart. It is plotted in the same way as a line diagram with the area under each line shaded to highlight the magnitude of the subcategory in relation to other subcategories. Thus an area chart displays the area under the curve in relation to the subcategories of a variable.

Attitudinal scales: Those scales that are designed to measure attitudes towards an issue are called attitudinal scales. In the social sciences there are three types of scale: the summated rating scale (Likert scale), the equal–appearing interval scale (Thurstone scale) and the cumulative scale (Guttman scale).

Attitudinal score: A number that you calculate having assigned a numerical value to the response given by a respondent to an attitudinal statement or question. Different attitude scales have different ways of calculating the attitudinal score.

Attitudinal value: An attitudinal scale comprises many statements reflecting attitudes towards an issue. The extent to which each statement reflects this attitude varies from statement to statement. Some statements are more important in determining the attitude than others. The attitudinal value of a statement refers to the weight calculated or given to a statement to reflect its significance in reflecting the attitude: the greater the significance or extent, the greater the attitudinal value or weight.

Attribute variables: Those variables that cannot be manipulated, changed or controlled, and that reflect the characteristics of the study population. For example, age, gender, education and income.

Bar chart: The bar chart or diagram is one of the ways of graphically displaying categorical data. A bar chart is identical to a histogram, except that in a bar chart the rectangles representing the various frequencies are spaced, thus indicating that the data is categorical. The bar diagram is used for variables measured on nominal or ordinal scales.

Before-and-after studies: A before-and-after design can be described as two sets of cross-sectional data collection points on the same population to find out the change in a phenomenon or variable(s) between two points in time. The change is measured by comparing the difference in the phenomenon or variable(s) between before and after observations.

Bias is a deliberate attempt either to conceal or highlight something that you found in your research or to use deliberately a procedure or method that you know is not appropriate but will provide information that you are looking for because you have a vested interest in it.

Blind studies: In a blind study, the study population does not know whether it is getting real or fake treatment or which treatment modality in the case of comparative studies. The main objective of designing a blind study is to isolate the placebo effect.

Case study: The case study design is based upon the assumption that the case being studied is atypical of cases of a certain type and therefore a single case can provide insight into the events and situations prevalent in a group from where the case has been drawn. In a case study design the 'case' you select becomes the basis of a thorough, holistic and in-depth exploration of the aspect(s) that you want to find out about. It is an approach in which a particular instance or a few carefully selected cases are studied intensively. To be called a case study it is important to treat the total study population as one entity. It is one of the important study designs in qualitative research.

Categorical variables are those where the unit of measurement is in the form of categories. On the basis of presence or absence of a characteristic, a variable is placed in a category. There is no measurement of the characteristics as such. In terms of measurement scales such variables are measured on nominal or ordinal scales. Rich/poor, high/low, hot/cold are examples of categorical variables.

Chance variable: In studying causality or association there are times when the mood of a respondent or the wording of a question can affect the reply given by the respondent when asked again in the post-test. There is no systematic pattern in terms of this change. Such variables are called chance or random variables.

Closed question: In a closed question the possible answers are set out in the questionnaire or interview schedule and the respondent or the investigator ticks the category that best describe a respondent's answer.

Cluster sampling: Cluster sampling is based on the ability of the researcher to divide a sampling population into groups (based upon a visible or easily identifiable characteristics), called clusters, and then select elements from each cluster using the SRS technique. Clusters can be formed on the basis of geographical proximity or a common characteristic that has a correlation with the main variable of the study (as in stratified sampling). Depending on the level of clustering, sometimes sampling may be done at different levels. These levels constitute the different stages (single, double or multiple) of clustering.

Code: The numerical value that is assigned to a response at the time of analysing the data.

Code book: A listing of a set of numerical values (set of rules) that you decided to assign to answers obtained from respondents in response to each question is called a code book.

Coding: The process of assigning numerical values to different categories of responses to a question for the purpose of analysing them is called coding.

Cohort studies are based upon the existence of a common characteristic such as year of birth, graduation or marriage, within a subgroup of a population that you want to study. People with the common characteristics are studied over a period of time to collect the information of interest to you. Studies could cover fertility behaviour of women born in 1986 or career paths of 1990 graduates from a medical school, for instance. Cohort studies look at the trends over a long period of time and collect data from the same group of people.

Collaborative enquiry is another name for participatory research that advocates a close collaboration between the researcher and the research participants.

Column percentages are calculated from the total of all the subcategories of one variable that are displayed along a column in different rows.

Community discussion forum: A community discussion forum is a qualitative strategy designed to find opinions, attitudes, ideas of a community with regard to community issues and problems. It is one of the very common ways of seeking a community's participation in deciding about issues of concern to it.

Comparative study design: Sometimes you seek to compare the effectiveness of different treatment modalities. In such situations a comparative design is used. With a comparative design, as with most other designs, a study can be carried out either as an experiment or non-experiment. In the comparative experimental design, the study population is divided into the same number of groups as the number of treatments to be tested. For each group the baseline with respect to the dependent variable is established. The different treatment modalities are then introduced to the different groups. After a certain period, when it is assumed that the treatment models have had their effect, the 'after' observation is carried out to ascertain changes in the dependent variable.

Concept: In defining a research problem or the study population you may use certain words that as such are difficult to measure and/or the understanding of which may vary from person to person. These words are called concepts. In order to measure them they need to be converted into indicators (not always) and then variables. Words like satisfaction, impact, young, old, happy are concepts as their understanding would vary from person to person.

Conceptual framework: A conceptual framework stems from the theoretical framework and concentrates, usually, on one section of that theoretical framework which becomes the basis of your study. The latter consists of the theories or issues in which your study is embedded, whereas the former describes the aspects you selected from the theoretical framework to become the basis of your research enquiry. The conceptual framework is the basis of your research problem.

Concurrent validity: When you investigate how good a research instrument is by comparing it with some observable criterion or credible findings, this is called concurrent validity. It is comparing the findings of your instrument with those found by another which is well accepted. Concurrent validity is judged by how well an instrument compares with a second assessment done concurrently.

Conditioning effect: This describes a situation where, if the same respondents are contacted frequently, they begin to know what is expected of them and may respond to questions without thought, or they may lose interest in the enquiry, with the same result. This situation's effect on the quality of the answers is known as the conditioning effect.

Confirmability refers to the degree to which the results obtained through qualitative research could be confirmed or corroborated by others. Confirmability in qualitative research is similar to reliability in quantitative research.

Constant variable: When a variable can have only one category or value, for example taxi, tree and water, it is known as a constant variable.

Construct validity is a more sophisticated technique for establishing the validity of an instrument. Construct validity is based upon statistical procedures. It is determined by ascertaining the contribution of each construct to the total variance observed in a phenomenon.

Consumer-oriented evaluation: The core philosophy of this evaluation rests on the assumption that assessment of the value or merit of an intervention – including its effectiveness, outcomes, impact and relevance – should be judged from the perspective of the consumer. Consumers, according to this philosophy, are the best people to make a judgement on these aspects. An evaluation done within the framework of this philosophy is known as consumer-oriented evaluation or client-centred evaluation.

Content analysis is one of the main methods of analysing qualitative data. It is the process of analysing the contents of interviews or observational field notes in order to identify the main themes that emerge from the responses given by your respondents or the observation notes made by you as a researcher.

Content validity: In addition to linking each question with the objectives of a study as a part of establishing the face validity, it is also important to examine whether the questions or items have covered all the areas you wanted to cover in the study. Examining questions of a research instrument to establish the extent of coverage of areas under study is called content validity of the instrument.

Continuous variables have continuity in their unit of measurement; for example age, income and attitude score. They can take on any value of the scale on which they are measured. Age can be measured in years, months and days. Similarly, income can be measured in dollars and cents.

Control design: In experimental studies that aim to measure the impact of an intervention, it is important to measure the change in the dependent variable that is attributed to the extraneous and chance variables. To quantify the impact of these sets of variables another comparable group is selected that is not subjected to the intervention. Study designs where you have a control group to isolate the impact of extraneous and change variables are called control design studies.

Control group: The group in an experimental study which is not exposed to the experimental intervention is called a control group. The sole purpose of the control group is to measure the impact of extraneous and chance variables on the dependent variable.

Correlational studies: Studies which are primarily designed to investigate whether or not there is a relationship between two or more variables are called correlational studies.

Cost–benefit evaluation: The central aim of a cost–benefit evaluation is to put a price tag on an intervention in relation to its benefits.

Cost-effectiveness evaluation: The central aim of a cost-effectiveness evaluation is to put a price tag on an intervention in relation to its effectiveness.

Credibility in qualitative research is parallel to internal validity in quantitative research and refers to a situation where the results obtained through qualitative research are agreeable to the participants of the research. It is judged by the extent of respondent concordance whereby you take your findings to those who participated in your research for confirmation, congruence, validation and approval: the higher the outcome of these, the higher the credibility (validity) of the study.

Cross–over comparative experimental design: In the cross-over design, also called the ABAB design, two groups are formed, the intervention is introduced to one of them and, after a certain period, the impact of this intervention is measured. Then the interventions are 'crossed over'; that is, the experimental group becomes the control and vice versa.

Cross-sectional studies, also known as one-shot or status studies, are the most commonly used design in the social sciences. This design is best suited to studies aimed at finding out the prevalence of a phenomenon, situation, problem, attitude or issue, by taking a cross-section of the population. They are useful in obtaining an overall 'picture' as it stands at the time of the study.

Cross-tabulation is a statistical procedure that analyses two variables, usually independent and dependent or attribute and dependent, to determine if there is a relationship between them. The subcategories of both the variables are cross-tabulated to ascertain if a relationship exists between them.

Cumulative frequency polygon: The cumulative frequency polygon or cumulative frequency curve is drawn on the basis of cumulative frequencies. The main difference between a frequency polygon and a cumulative frequency polygon is that the former is drawn by joining the midpoints of the intervals, whereas the latter is drawn by joining the end points of the intervals because cumulative frequencies interpret data in relation to the upper limit of an interval.

Dependability in qualitative research is very similar to the concept of reliability in quantitative research. It is concerned with whether we would obtain the same results if we could observe the same thing twice: the greater the similarity in two results, the greater the dependability.

Dependent variable: When establishing causality through a study, the variable assumed to be the cause is called an independent variable and the variables in which it produces changes are called the dependent variables. A dependent variable is dependent upon the independent variable and it is assumed to be because of the changes.

Descriptive studies: A study in which the main focus is on description, rather than examining relationships or associations, is classified as a descriptive study. A descriptive study attempts systematically to describe a situation, problem, phenomenon, service or programme, or provides information about, say, the living conditions of a community, or describes attitudes towards an issue.

Dichotomous variable: When a variable can have only two categories as in male/female, yes/no, good/bad, head/tail, up/down and rich/poor, it is known as a dichotomous variable.

Disproportionate stratified sampling: When selecting a stratified sample if you select an equal number of elements from each stratum without giving any consideration to its size in the study population, the process is called disproportionate stratified sampling.

Double-barrelled question: A double-barrelled question is a question within a question.

Double-blind studies: The concept of a double-blind study is very similar to that of a blind study except that it also tries to eliminate researcher bias by not disclosing to the researcher the identities of experimental, comparative and placebo groups. In a double-blind study neither the researcher nor the study participants know which study participants are receiving real, placebo or other forms of interventions. This prevents the possibility of introducing bias by the researcher.

Double-control studies: Although the control group design helps you to quantify the impact that can be attributed to extraneous variables, it does not separate out other effects that may be due to the research instrument (such as the reactive effect) or respondents (such as the maturation or regression effects, or placebo effect). When you need to identify and separate out these effects, a double-control design is required. In a double-control study, you have two control groups instead of one. To quantify, say, the reactive effect of an instrument, you exclude one of the control groups from the 'before' observation.

Editing consists of scrutinising the completed research instruments to identify and minimise, as far as possible, errors, incompleteness, misclassification and gaps in the information obtained from respondents.

Elevation effect: Some observers when using a scale to record an observation may prefer to use certain section(s) of the scale in the same way that some teachers are strict markers and others are not. When observers have a tendency to use a particular part(s) of a scale in recording an interaction, this phenomenon is known as the elevation effect.

Error of central tendency: When using scales in assessments or observations, unless an observer is extremely confident of his/her ability to assess an interaction, s/he may tend to avoid the extreme positions on the scale, using mostly the central part. The error this tendency creates is called the error of central tendency.

Ethical practice: Professional practice undertaken in accordance with the principles of accepted codes of conduct for a given profession or group.

Evaluation is a process that is guided by research principles for reviewing an intervention or programme in order to make informed decisions about its desirability and/or identifying changes to enhance its efficiency and effectiveness.

Evaluation for planning addresses the issue of establishing the need for a programme or intervention.

Evidence-based practice: A service delivery system that is based upon research evidence as to its effectiveness; a service provider's clinical judgement as to its suitability and appropriateness for a client; and a client's preference as to its acceptance.

Experimental group: An experimental group is one that is exposed to the intervention being tested to study its effects.

Experimental studies: In studying causality, when a researcher or someone else introduces the intervention that is assumed to be the 'cause' of change and waits until it has produced – or has been given sufficient time to produce – the change, then in studies like this a researcher starts with the cause and waits to observe its effects. Such types of studies are called experimental studies.

Expert sampling is the selection of people with demonstrated or known expertise in the area of interest to you to become the basis of data collection. Your sample is a group of experts from whom you seek the required information. It is like purposive sampling where the sample comprises experts only.

Explanatory research: In an explanatory study the main emphasis is to clarify why and how there is a relationship between two aspects of a situation or phenomenon.

Exploratory research: This is when a study is undertaken with the objective either to explore an area where little is known or to investigate the possibilities of undertaking a particular research study. When a study is carried out to determine its feasibility it is also called a feasibility or pilot study.

Extraneous variables: In studying causality, the dependent variable is the consequence of the change brought about by the independent variable. In everyday life there are many other variables that can affect the relationship between independent and dependent variables. These variables are called extraneous variables.

Face validity: When you justify the inclusion of a question or item in a research instrument by linking it with the objectives of the study, thus providing a justification for its inclusion in the instrument, the process is called face validity.

Feasibility study: When the purpose of a study is to investigate the possibility of undertaking it on a larger scale and to streamlining methods and procedures for the main study, the study is called a feasibility study.

Feminist research: Like action research, feminist research is more a philosophy than design. Feminist concerns and theory act as the guiding framework for this research. A focus on the viewpoints of women, the aim to reduce power imbalance between researcher and respondents, and attempts to change social inequality between men and women are the main characteristics of feminist research.

Fishbowl draw: This is one of the methods of selecting a random sample and is useful particularly when N is not very large. It entails writing each element number on a small slip of paper, folded and put into a bowl, shuffling thoroughly, and then taking one out till the required sample size is obtained.

Focus group: The focus group is a form of strategy in qualitative research in which attitudes, opinions or perceptions towards an issue, product, service or programme are explored through a free and open discussion between members of a group and the researcher. The focus group is a facilitated group discussion in which a researcher raises issues or asks questions that stimulate discussion among members of the group. Issues, questions and different perspectives on them and any significant points arising during these discussions provide data to draw conclusions and inferences. It is like collectively interviewing a group of respondents.

Frame of analysis: The proposed plan of the way you want to analyse your data, how you are going to analyse the data to operationalise your major concepts and what statistical procedures you are planning to use, all form parts of the frame of analysis.

Frequency distribution: The frequency distribution is a statistical procedure in quantitative research that can be applied to any variable that is measured on any one of the four measurement scales. It groups respondents into the subcategories in which a variable has been measured or coded.

Frequency polygon: The frequency polygon is very similar to a histogram. A frequency polygon is drawn by joining the midpoint of each rectangle at a height commensurate with the frequency of that interval.

Group interview: A group interview is both a method of data collection and a qualitative study design. The interaction is between the researcher and the group with the aim of collecting information from the group collectively rather than individually from members.

Guttman scale: The Guttman scale is one of the three attitudinal scales and is devised in such a way that the statements or items reflecting attitude are arranged in perfect cumulative order. Arranging statements or items to have a cumulative relation between them is the most difficult aspect of constructing this scale.

Halo effect: When making an observation, some observers may be influenced to rate an individual on one aspect of the interaction by the way s/he was rated on another. This is similar to something that can happen in teaching when a teacher's assessment of the performance of a student in one subject may influence his/her rating of that student's performance in another. This type of effect is known as the halo effect.

Hawthorne effect: When individuals or groups become aware that they are being observed, they may change their behaviour. Depending upon the situation, this change could be positive or negative – it may increase or decrease, for example, their productivity – and may occur for a number of reasons. When a change in the behaviour of persons or groups is attributed to their being observed, it is known as the Hawthorne effect.

Histogram: A histogram is a graphic presentation of analysed data presented in the form of a series of rectangles drawn next to each other without any space between them, each representing the frequency of a category or subcategory.

Holistic research is more a philosophy than a study design. The design is based upon the philosophy that as a multiplicity of factors interacts in our lives, we cannot understand a phenomenon from one or two perspectives only. To understand a situation or phenomenon we need to look at it in its totality or entirety; that is, holistically from every perspective. A research study done with this philosophical perspective in mind is called holistic research.

Hypothesis: A hypothesis is a hunch, assumption, suspicion, assertion or an idea about a phenomenon, relationship or situation, the reality or truth of which you do not know and you set up your study to find this truth. A researcher refers to these assumptions, assertions, statements or hunches as hypotheses and they become the basis of an enquiry. In most studies the hypothesis will be based either upon previous studies or on your own or someone else's observations.

Hypothesis of association: When as a researcher you have sufficient knowledge about a situation or phenomenon and are in a position to stipulate the extent of the relationship between two variables and formulate a hunch that reflects the magnitude of the relationship, such a type of hypothesis formulation is known as hypothesis of association.

Hypothesis of difference: A hypothesis in which a researcher stipulates that there will be a difference but does not specify its magnitude is called a hypothesis of difference.

Hypothesis of point-prevalence: There are times when a researcher has enough knowledge about a phenomenon that he/she is studying and is confident about speculating almost the exact prevalence of the situation or the outcome in quantitative units. This type of hypothesis is known as a hypothesis of point-prevalence.

Illuminative evaluation: The primary concern of illuminative or holistic evaluation is description and interpretation rather than measurement and prediction of the totality of a phenomenon. It fits with the social–anthropological paradigm. The aim is to study a programme in all its aspects: how it operates, how it is influenced by various contexts, how it is applied, how those directly involved view its strengths and weaknesses, and what the experiences are of those who are affected by it. In summary, it tries to illuminate an array of questions and issues relating to the contents, and processes, and procedures that give both desirable and undesirable results.

Impact assessment evaluation: Impact or outcome evaluation is one of the most widely practised evaluations. It is used to assess what changes can be attributed to the introduction of a particular intervention, programme or policy. It establishes causality between an intervention and its impact, and estimates the magnitude of this change(s).

Independent variable: When examining causality in a study, there are four sets of variables that can operate. One of them is a variable that is responsible for bringing about change. This variable which is the cause of the changes in a phenomenon is called an independent variable. In the study of causality, the independent variable is the cause variable which is responsible for bringing about change in a phenomenon.

In-depth interviewing is an extremely useful method of data collection that provides complete freedom in terms of content and structure. As a researcher you are free to order these in whatever sequence you wish, keeping in mind the context. You also have complete freedom in terms of what questions you ask of your respondents, the wording you use and the way you explain them to your respondents. You usually formulate questions and raise issues on the spur of the moment, depending upon what occurs to you in the context of the discussion.

Indicators: An image, perception or concept is sometimes incapable of direct measurement. In such situations a concept is 'measured' through other means which are logically 'reflective' of the concept. These logical reflectors are called indicators.

Informed consent implies that respondents are made adequately and accurately aware of the type of information you want from them, why the information is being sought, what purpose it will be put to, how they are expected to participate in the study, and how it will directly or indirectly affect them. It is important that the consent should also be voluntary and without pressure of any kind. The consent given by respondents after being adequately and accurately made aware of or informed about all aspects of a study is called informed consent.

Interrupted time-series design: In this design you study a group of people before and after the introduction of an intervention. It is like the before-and-after design, except that you have multiple data collections at different time intervals to constitute an aggregated before-and-after picture. The design is based upon the assumption that one set of data is not sufficient to establish, with a reasonable degree of certainty and accuracy, the before-and-after situations.

Interval scale: The interval scale is one of the measurement scales in the social sciences where the scale is divided into a number of intervals or units. An interval scale has all the characteristics of an ordinal scale. In addition, it has a unit of measurement that enables individuals or responses to be placed at equally spaced intervals in relation to the spread of the scale. This scale has a starting and a terminating point and is divided into equally spaced units/intervals. The starting and terminating points and the number of units/intervals between them are arbitrary and vary from scale to scale as it does not have a fixed zero point.

Intervening variables link the independent and dependent variables. In certain situations the relationship between an independent and a dependent variable does not eventuate till the intervention of another variable – the intervening variable. The cause variable will have the assumed effect only in the presence of an intervening variable.

Intervention–development–evaluation process: This is a cyclical process of continuous assessment of needs, intervention and evaluation. You make an assessment of the needs of a group or community, develop intervention strategies to meet these needs, implement the interventions and then evaluate them for making informed decisions to incorporate changes to enhance their relevance, efficiency and effectiveness. Reassess the needs and follow the same process for intervention–development–evaluation.

Interview guide: A list of issues, topics or discussion points that you want to cover in an in-depth interview is called an interview guide. Note that these points are not questions. It is basically a list to remind an interviewer of the areas to be covered in an interview.

Interview schedule: An interview schedule is a written list of questions, open ended or closed, prepared for use by an interviewer in a person-to-person interaction (this may be face to face, by telephone or by other electronic media). Note that an interview schedule is a research tool/ instrument for collecting data, whereas interviewing is a method of data collection.

Interviewing is one of the commonly used methods of data collection in the social sciences. Any person-to-person interaction, either face to face or otherwise, between two or more individuals with a specific purpose in mind is called an interview. It involves asking questions of respondents and recording their answers. Interviewing spans a wide spectrum in terms of its structure. On the one hand, it could be highly structured and, on the other, extremely flexible, and in between it could acquire any form.

Judgemental sampling: The primary consideration in this sampling design is your judgement as to who can provide the best information to achieve the objectives of your study. You as a researcher only go to those people who in your opinion are likely to have the required information and are willing to share it with you. This design is also called purposive sampling.

Leading question: A leading question is one which, by its contents, structure or wording, leads a respondent to answer in a certain direction.

Likert scale: The Likert scale, also known as the summated rating scale, is one of the attitudinal scales designed to measure attitudes. This scale is based upon the assumption that each statement/item on the scale has equal attitudinal 'value', 'importance' or 'weight' in terms of reflecting attitude towards the issue in question. Comparatively it is the easiest to construct.

Literature review: This is the process of searching the existing literature relating to your research problem to develop theoretical and conceptual frameworks for your study and to integrate your research findings with what the literature says about them. It places your study in perspective to what others have investigated about the issues. In addition the process helps you to improve your methodology.

Longitudinal study: In longitudinal studies the study population is visited a number of times at regular intervals, usually over a long period, to collect the required information. These intervals are not fixed so their length may vary from study to study. Intervals might be as short as a week or longer than a year. Irrespective of the size of the interval, the information gathered each time is identical.

Matching is a technique that is used to form two groups of patients to set up an experiment–control study to test the effectiveness of a drug. From a pool of patients, two patients with identical predetermined attributes, characteristics or conditions are matched and then randomly placed in either the experimental or control group. The process is called matching. The matching continues for the rest of the pool. The two groups thus formed through the matching process are supposed to be comparable thus ensuring uniform impact of different sets of variables on the patients.

Maturation effect: If the study population is very young and if there is a significant time lapse between the before-and-after sets of data collection, the study population may change simply because it is growing older. This is particularly true when you are studying young children. The effect of this maturation, if it is significantly correlated with the dependent variable, is reflected at the 'after' observation and is known as the maturation effect.

Maxmincon principle of variance: When studying causality between two variables there are three sets of variable that impact upon the dependent variable. Since your aim as a researcher is to determine the change that can be attributed to the independent variable, you need to design your study to ensure that the independent variable has the maximum opportunity to have its full impact on the dependent variable, while the effects that are attributed to extraneous and chance variables are minimised. Setting up a study to achieve the above is known as adhering to the maxmincon principle of variance.

Narratives: The narrative technique of gathering information has even less structure than the focus group. Narratives have almost no predetermined contents except that the researcher seeks to hear the personal experience of a person with an incident or happening in his/her life. Essentially, the person tells his/her story about an incident or situation and you, as the researcher, listen passively, occasionally encouraging the respondent.

Nominal scale: The nominal scale is one of the ways of measuring a variable in the social sciences. It enables the classification of individuals, objects or responses based on a common/shared property or characteristic. These people, objects or responses are divided into a number of subgroups in such a way that each member of the subgroup has the common characteristic.

Non–experimental studies: There are times when, in studying causality, a researcher observes an outcome and wishes to investigate its causation. From the outcomes the researcher starts linking causes with them. Such studies are called non-experimental studies. In a non-experimental study you neither introduce nor control/manipulate the cause variable. You start with the effects and try to link them with the causes.

Non-participant observation: When you, as a researcher, do not get involved in the activities of the group but remain a passive observer, watching and listening to its activities and interactions and drawing conclusions from them, this is called non-participant observation.

Non-probability sampling designs do not follow the theory of probability in the selection of elements from the sampling population. Non-probability sampling designs are used when the number of elements in a population is either unknown or cannot be individually identified. In such situations the selection of elements is dependent upon other considerations. Non-probability sampling designs are commonly used in both quantitative and qualitative research.

Null hypothesis: When you construct a hypothesis stipulating that there is no difference between two situations, groups, outcomes, or the prevalence of a condition or phenomenon, this is called a null hypothesis and is usually written as H_0.

Objective-oriented evaluation: This is when an evaluation is designed to ascertain whether or not a programme or a service is achieving its objectives or goals.

Observation is one of the methods for collecting primary data. It is a purposeful, systematic and selective way of watching and listening to an interaction or phenomenon as it takes place. Though dominantly used in qualitative research, it is also used in quantitative research.

Open-ended questions: In an open-ended question the possible responses are not given. In the case of a questionnaire, a respondent writes down the answers in his/her words, whereas in the case of an interview schedule the investigator records the answers either verbatim or in a summary describing a respondent's answer.

Operational definition: When you define concepts used by you either in your research problem or in the study population in a measurable form, they are called working or operational definitions. It is important for you to understand that the working definitions that you develop are only for the purpose of your study.

Oral history is more a method of data collection than a study design; however, in qualitative research, it has become an approach to study a historical event or episode that took place in the past or for gaining information about a culture, custom or story that has been passed on from generation to generation. It is a picture of something in someone's own words. Oral histories, like narratives, involve the use of both passive and active listening. Oral histories, however, are more commonly used for learning about cultural, social or historical events whereas narratives are more about a person's own experiences.

Ordinal scale: An ordinal scale has all the properties of a nominal scale plus one of its own. Besides categorising individuals, objects, responses or a property into subgroups on the basis of a common characteristic, it ranks the subgroups in a certain order. They are arranged in either ascending or descending order according to the extent that a subcategory reflects the magnitude of variation in the variable.

Outcome evaluation: The focus of an outcome evaluation is to find out the effects, impacts, changes or outcomes that the programme has produced in the target population.

Panel studies are prospective in nature and are designed to collect information from the same respondents over a period of time. The selected group of individuals becomes a panel that provides the required information. In a panel study the period of data collection can range from once only to repeated data collections over a long period.

Participant observation is when you, as a researcher, participate in the activities of the group being observed in the same manner as its members, with or without their knowing that they are being observed. Participant observation is principally used in qualitative research and is usually done by developing a close interaction with members of a group or 'living' in with the situation which is being studied.

Participatory research: Both participatory research and collaborative enquiry are not study designs per se but signify a philosophical perspective that advocates an active involvement of research participants in the research process. Participatory research is based upon the principle of minimising the 'gap' between the researcher and the research participants. The most important feature is the involvement and participation of the community or research participants in the research process to make the research findings more relevant to their needs.

Pie chart: The pie chart is another way of representing data graphically. As there are 360 degrees in a circle, the full circle can be used to represent 100 per cent or the total population. The circle or pie is divided into sections in accordance with the magnitude of each subcategory comprising the total population. Hence each slice of the pie is in proportion to the size of each subcategory of a frequency distribution.

Pilot study: *See* **Feasibility study**

Placebo effect: A patient's belief that s/he is receiving the treatment plays an important role in his/her recovery even though the treatment is fake or ineffective. The change occurs because a patient believes that s/he is receiving the treatment. This psychological effect that helps a patient to recover is known as the placebo effect.

Placebo study: A study that attempts to determine the extent of a placebo effect is called a placebo study. A placebo study is based upon a comparative study design that involves two or more groups, depending on whether or not you want to have a control group to isolate the impact of extraneous variables or other treatment modalities to determine their relative effectiveness.

Polytomous variable: When a variable can be divided into more than two categories, for example religion (Christian, Muslim, Hindu), political parties (Labor, Liberal, Democrat), and attitudes (strongly favourable, favourable, uncertain, unfavourable, strongly unfavourable), it is called a polytomous variable.

Population mean: From what you find out from your sample (sample statistics) you make an estimate of the prevalence of these characteristics for the total study population. The estimates about the total study population made from sample statistics are called population parameters or the population mean.

Predictive validity is judged by the degree to which an instrument can correctly forecast an outcome: the higher the correctness in the forecasts, the higher the predictive validity of the instrument.

Pre-test: In quantitative research, pre-testing is a practice whereby you test something that you developed before its actual use to ascertain the likely problems with it. Mostly, the pre-test is done on a research instrument or on a code book. The pre-test of a research instrument entails a critical examination of each question as to its clarity, understanding, wording and meaning as understood by potential respondents with a view to removing possible problems with the question. It ensures that a respondent's understanding of each question is in accordance with your intentions. The pre-test of an instrument is only done in structured studies. Pre-testing a code book entails actually coding a few questionnaires/interview schedules to identify any problems with the code book before coding the data.

Primary data: Information collected for the specific purpose of a study either by the researcher or by someone else is called primary data.

Primary sources: Sources that provide primary data such as interviews, observations, and questionnaires are called primary sources.

Probability sampling: When selecting a sample, if you adhere to the theory of probability, that is you select the sample in such a way that each element in the study population has an equal and independent chance of selection in the sample, the process is called probability sampling.

Process evaluation: The main emphasis of process evaluation is on evaluating the manner in which a service or programme is being delivered in order to identify ways of enhancing the efficiency of the delivery system.

Programme planning evaluation: Before starting a large-scale programme it is desirable to investigate the extent and nature of the problem for which the programme is being developed.

When an evaluation is undertaken with the purpose of investigating the nature and extent of the problem itself, it is called programme planning evaluation.

Proportionate stratified sampling: In proportionate stratified sampling, the number of elements selected in the sample from each stratum is in relation to its proportion in the total population. A sample thus selected is called a proportionate stratified sample.

Prospective studies refer to the likely prevalence of a phenomenon, situation, problem, attitude or outcome in the future. Such studies attempt to establish the outcome of an event or what is likely to happen. Experiments are usually classified as prospective studies because the researcher must wait for an intervention to register its effect on the study population.

Pure research is concerned with the development, examination, verification and refinement of research methods, procedures, techniques and tools that form the body of research methodology.

Purposive sampling: *See* **Judgemental sampling**

Qualitative research: In the social sciences there are two broad approaches to enquiry: qualitative and quantitative or unstructured and structured approaches. Qualitative research is based upon the philosophy of empiricism, follows an unstructured, flexible and open approach to enquiry, aims to describe than measure, believes in in-depth understanding and small samples, and explores perceptions and feelings than facts and figures.

Quantitative research is a second approach to enquiry in the social sciences that is rooted in rationalism, follows a structured, rigid, predetermined methodology, believes in having a narrow focus, emphasises greater sample size, aims to quantify the variation in a phenomenon, and tries to make generalisations to the total population.

Quasi-experiments: Studies which have the attributes of both experimental and non-experimental studies are called quasi- or semi-experiments. A part of the study could be experimental and the other non-experimental.

Questionnaire: A questionnaire is a written list of questions, the answers to which are recorded by respondents. In a questionnaire respondents read the questions, interpret what is expected and then write down the answers. The only difference between an interview schedule and a questionnaire is that in the former it is the interviewer who asks the questions (and, if necessary, explains them) and records the respondent's replies on an interview schedule, while in the latter replies are recorded by the respondents themselves.

Quota sampling: The main consideration directing quota sampling is the researcher's ease of access to the sample population. In addition to convenience, a researcher is guided by some visible characteristic of interest, such as gender or race, of the study population. The sample is selected from a location convenient to you as a researcher, and whenever a person with this visible relevant characteristic is seen, that person is asked to participate in the study. The process continues until you have been able to contact the required number of respondents (quota).

Random design: In a random design, the study population groups as well as the experimental treatments are not predetermined but randomly assigned to become control or experimental groups. Random assignment in experiments means that any individual or unit of the study population has an equal and independent chance of becoming a part of the experimental or control group or, in the case of multiple treatment modalities, any treatment has an equal and independent chance of being assigned to any of the population groups. It is important to note that the concept of randomisation can be applied to any of the experimental designs.

Random sampling: For a design to be called random or probability sampling, it is imperative that each element in the study population has an equal and independent chance of selection in the sample. Equal implies that the probability of selection of each element in the study population is the same. The concept of independence means that the choice of one element is not dependent upon the choice of another element in the sampling.

Random variable: When collecting information from respondents, there are times when the mood of a respondent or the wording of a question can affect the way a respondent replies. There is no systematic pattern in terms of this change. Such shifts in responses are said to be caused by random or chance variables.

Randomisation: In experimental and comparative studies, you often need to study two or more groups of people. In forming these groups it is important that they are comparable with respect to the dependent variable and other variables that affect it so that the effects of independent and extraneous variables are uniform across groups. Randomisation is a process that ensures that each and every person in a group is given an equal and independent chance of being in any of the groups, thereby making groups comparable.

Ratio scale: A ratio scale has all the properties of nominal, ordinal and interval scales plus its own property; the zero point of a ratio scale is fixed, which means it has a fixed starting point. Therefore, it is an absolute scale. As the difference between the intervals is always measured from a zero point, arithmetical operations can be performed on the scores.

Reactive effect: Sometimes the way a question is worded informs respondents of the existence or prevalence of something that the study is trying to find out about as an outcome of an intervention. This effect is known as reactive effect of the instrument

Recall error: Error that can be introduced in a response because of a respondent's inability to recall correctly its various aspects when replying.

Regression effect: Sometimes people who place themselves on the extreme positions of a measurement scale at the pre-test stage may, for a number of reasons, shift towards the mean at the post-test stage. They might feel that they have been too negative or too positive at the pre-test stage. Therefore, the mere expression of the attitude in response to a questionnaire or interview has caused them to think about and alter their attitude towards the mean at the time of the post-test. This type of effect is known as the regression effect.

Reflective journal log: Basically this is a method of data collection in qualitative research that entails keeping a log of your thoughts as a researcher whenever you notice anything, talk to someone, participate in an activity or observe something that helps you understand or add to whatever you are trying to find out about. This log becomes the basis of your research findings.

Reflexive control design: In experimental studies, to overcome the problem of comparability in different groups, sometimes researchers study only one population and treat data collected during the non-intervention period as representing a control group, and information collected after the introduction of the intervention as if it pertained to an experimental group. It is the periods of non-intervention and intervention that constitute control and experimental groups.

Reliability is the ability of a research instrument to provide similar results when used repeatedly under similar conditions. Reliability indicates accuracy, stability and predictability of a research instrument: the higher the reliability, the higher the accuracy; or the higher the accuracy of an instrument, the higher its reliability.

Replicated cross-sectional design: This study design is based upon the assumption that participants at different stages of a programme are similar in terms of their socioeconomic–demographic characteristics and the problem for which they are seeking intervention. Assessment of the effectiveness of an intervention is done by taking a sample of clients who are at different stages of the intervention. The difference in the dependent variable among clients at the intake and termination stage is considered to be the impact of the intervention.

Research is one of the ways of finding answers to your professional and practice questions. However, it is characterised by the use of tested procedures and methods and an unbiased and objective attitude in the process of exploration.

Research design: A research design is a procedural plan that is adopted by the researcher to answer questions validly, objectively, accurately and economically. A research design therefore answers questions that would determine the path you are proposing to take for your research journey. Through a research design you decide for yourself and communicate to others your decisions regarding what study design you propose to use, how you are going to collect information from your respondents, how you are going to select your respondents, how the information you are going to collect is to be analysed and how you are going to communicate your findings.

Research objectives are specific statements of goals that you set out to be achieved at the end of your research journey.

Research problem: Any issue, problem or question that becomes the basis of your enquiry is called a research problem. It is what you want to find out about during your research endeavour.

Research questions: Questions that you would like to find answers to through your research, like 'What does it mean to have a child with ADHD in a family?' or 'What is the impact of immigration on family roles?' Research questions become the basis of research objectives. The main difference between research questions and research objectives is the way they are worded. Research questions take the form of questions whereas research objectives are statements of achievements expressed using action-oriented words.

Retrospective study: A retrospective study investigates a phenomenon, situation, problem or issue that has happened in the past. Such studies are usually conducted either on the basis of the data available for that period or on the basis of respondents' recall of the situation.

Retrospective–prospective study: A retrospective–prospective study focuses on past trends in a phenomenon and studies it into the future. A study where you measure the impact of an intervention without having a control group by 'constructing' a previous baseline from either respondents' recall or secondary sources, then introducing the intervention to study its effect, is considered a retrospective–prospective study. In fact, most before-and-after studies, if carried out without having a control – where the baseline is constructed from the same population before introducing the intervention – will be classified as retrospective–prospective studies.

Row percentages are calculated from the total of all the subcategories of one variable that are displayed along a row in different columns.

Sample: A sample is a subgroup of the population which is the focus of your research enquiry and is selected in such a way that it represents the study population. A sample is composed of a few individuals from whom you collect the required information. It is done to save time, money and other resources.

Sample size: The number of individuals from whom you obtain the required information is called the sample size and is usually denoted by the letter n.

Sample statistics: Findings based on the information obtained from your respondents (sample) are called sample statistics.

Sampling is the process of selecting a few respondents (a sample) from a bigger group (the sampling population) to become the basis for estimating the prevalence of information of interest to you.

Sampling design: The way you select the required sampling units from a sampling population for identifying your sample is called the sampling design or sampling strategy. There are many sampling strategies in both quantitative and qualitative research.

Sampling element: Anything that becomes the basis of selecting your sample such as an individual, family, household, members of an organisation, residents of an area, is called a sampling unit or element.

Sampling error: The difference in the findings (sample statistics) that is due to the selection of elements in the sample is known as sampling error.

Sampling frame: When you are in a position to identify all elements of a study population, the list of all the elements is called a sampling frame.

Sampling population: The bigger group, such as families living in an area, clients of an agency, residents of a community, members of a group, people belonging to an organisation about whom you want to find out about through your research endeavour, is called the sampling population or study population.

Sampling strategy: *See* **Sampling design**

Sampling unit: *See* **Sampling element**

Sampling with replacement: When you select a sample in such a way that each selected element in the sample is replaced back into the sampling population before selecting the next, this is called sampling with replacement. Theoretically, this is done to provide an equal chance of selection to each element so as to adhere to the theory of probability to ensure randomisation of the sample. In case an element is selected again, it is discarded and the next one is selected. If the sampling population is fairly large, the probability of selecting the same element twice is fairly remote.

Sampling without replacement: When you select a sample in such a way that an element, once selected to become a part of your sample, is not replaced back into the study population, this is called sampling without replacement.

Saturation point: The concept of saturation point refers to the stage in data collection where you, as a researcher, are discovering no or very little new information from your respondents. In qualitative research this is considered an indication of the adequacy of the sample size.

Scale: This is a method of measurement and/or classification of respondents on the basis of their responses to questions you ask of them in a study. A scale could be continuous or categorical. It helps you to classify a study population in subgroups or as a spread that is reflective on the scale.

Scattergram: When you want to show graphically how one variable changes in relation to a change in the other, a scattergram is extremely effective. For a scattergram, both the variables must be measured either on an interval or ratio scale and the data on both the variables needs to be available in absolute values for each observation. Data for both variables is taken in pairs and displayed as dots in relation to their values on both axes. The resulting graph is known as a scattergram.

Secondary data: Sometimes the information required is already available in other sources such as journals, previous reports, censuses and you extract that information for the specific purpose of your study. This type of data which already exists but you extract for the purpose of your study is called secondary data.

Secondary sources: Sources that provide secondary data are called secondary sources. Sources such as books, journals, previous research studies, records of an agency, client or patient information already collected and routine service delivery records all form secondary sources.

Semi-experimental studies: A semi-experimental design has the properties of both experimental and non-experimental studies; part of the study may be non-experimental and the other part experimental.

Simple random sampling: This is the most commonly used method of selecting a random sample. It is a process of selecting the required sample size from the sampling population, providing each element with an equal and independent chance of selection by any method designed to select a random sample.

Snowball sampling is a process of selecting a sample using networks. To start with, a few individuals in a group or organisation are selected using purposive, random or network sampling to collect the required information from them. They are then asked to identify other people in the group or organisation who could be contacted to obtain the same information. The people selected by them become a part of the sample. The process continues till you reach the saturation point in terms of information being collected.

Stacked bar chart: A stacked bar chart is similar to a bar chart except that in the former each bar shows information about two or more variables stacked onto each other vertically. The sections of a bar show the proportion of the variables they represent in relation to one another. The stacked bars can be drawn only for categorical data.

Stakeholders in research: Those people or groups who are likely to be affected by a research activity or its findings. In research there are three stakeholders: the research participants, the researcher and the funding body.

Stem-and-leaf display: The stem-and-leaf display is an effective, quick and simple way of displaying a frequency distribution. The stem and leaf for a frequency distribution running into two digits is plotted by displaying digits 0 to 9 on the left of the *y*-axis, representing the tens of a frequency. The figures representing the units of a frequency (i.e. the right-hand figure of a two-digit frequency) are displayed on the right of the *y*-axis.

Stratified random sampling is one of the probability sampling designs in which the total study population is first classified into different subgroups based upon a characteristic that makes each subgroup more homogeneous in terms of the classificatory variable. The sample is then selected from each subgroup either by selecting an equal number of elements from each subgroup or selecting elements from each subgroup equal to its proportion in the total population.

Stub is a part of the table structure. It is the subcategories of a variable, listed along the *y*-axis (the left-hand column of the table). The stub, usually the first column on the left, lists the items about which information is provided in the horizontal rows to the right. It is the vertical listing of categories or individuals about which information is given in the columns of the table.

Study design: The term study design is used to describe the type of design you are going to adopt to undertake your study; that is, if it is going to be experimental, correlational, descriptive or before and after. Each study design has a specific format and attributes.

Study population: Every study in the social sciences has two aspects: study population and study area (subject area). People who you want to find out about are collectively known as the study population or simply population and are usually denoted by the letter *N*. It could be a group of people living in an area, employees of an organisation, a community, a group of people with special issues, etc. The people from whom you gather information, known as the sample *n*, are selected from the study population.

Subject area: Any academic or practice field in which you are conducting your study is called the subject or study area. It could be health or other needs of a community, attitudes of people towards an issue, occupational mobility in a community, coping strategies, depression, domestic violence, etc.

Subjectivity is an integral part of your way of thinking that is 'conditioned' by your educational background, discipline, philosophy, experience and skills. Bias is a deliberate attempt to change or highlight something which in reality is not there but you do it because of your vested interest. Subjectivity is not deliberate, it is the way you understand or interpret something.

Summated rating scale: *See* **Likert scale**

Systematic sampling is a way of selecting a sample where the sampling frame, depending upon the sample size, is first divided into a number of segments called intervals. Then, from the first interval, using the SRS technique, one element is selected. The selection of subsequent elements from other intervals is dependent upon the order of the element selected in the first interval. If in the first interval it is the fifth element, the fifth element of each subsequent interval will be chosen.

Table of random numbers: Most books on research methodology and statistics have tables that contain randomly generated numbers. There is a specific way of selecting a random sample using these tables.

Tables offer a useful way of presenting analysed data in a small space that brings clarity to the text and serves as a quick point of reference. There are different types of tables housing data pertaining to one, two or more variables.

Thematic writing: A style of writing which is written around main themes.

Theoretical framework: As you start reading the literature, you will soon discover that the problem you wish to investigate has its roots in a number of theories that have been developed from different perspectives. The information obtained from different sources needs to be sorted under the main themes and theories, highlighting agreements and disagreements among the authors. This process of structuring a 'network' of these theories that directly or indirectly has a bearing on your research topic is called the theoretical framework.

Theory of causality: The theory of causality advocates that in studying cause and effect there are three sets of variables that are responsible for the change. These are: cause or independent variable, extraneous variables and change variables. It is the combination of all three that produces change in a phenomenon.

Thurstone scale: The Thurstone scale is one of the scales designed to measure attitudes in the social sciences. Attitude through this scale is measured by means of a set of statements, the 'attitudinal value' of which has been determined by a group of judges. A respondent's agreement with the statement assigns a score equivalent to the 'attitudinal value' of the statement. The total score of all statements is the attitudinal score for a respondent.

Transferability: The concept of transferability refers to the degree to which the results of qualitative research can be generalised or transferred to other contexts or settings.

Trend curve: A set of data measured on an interval or a ratio scale can be displayed using a line diagram or trend curve. A trend line can be drawn for data pertaining to both a specific time and a period. If it relates to a period, the midpoint of each interval at a height commensurate with each frequency is marked as a dot. These dots are then connected with straight lines to examine trends in a phenomenon. If the data pertains to an exact time, a point is plotted at a height commensurate with the frequency and a line is then drawn to examine the trend.

Trend studies: These studies involve selecting a number of data observation points in the past, together with a picture of the present or immediate past with respect to the phenomenon under study, and then making certain assumptions as to the likely future trends. In a way you are compiling a cross-sectional picture of the trends being observed at different points in time over the past, present and future. From these cross-sectional observations you draw conclusions about the pattern of change.

Type I error: In testing a hypothesis, many reasons you may sometimes commit a mistake and draw the wrong conclusion with respect to the validity of your hypothesis. If you reject a null hypothesis when it is true and you should not have rejected it, this is called a Type I error.

Type II Error: In testing a hypothesis, for many reasons you may sometimes commit a mistake and draw the wrong conclusion in terms of the validity of your hypothesis. If you accept a null hypothesis when it is false and you should not have accepted it this is called a Type II error.

Unethical: Any professional activity that is not in accordance with the accepted code of conduct for that profession is considered unethical.

Validity: The concept of validity can be applied to every aspect of the research process. In its simplest form, validity refers to the appropriateness of each step in finding out what you set out to. However, the concept of validity is more associated with measurement procedures. In terms of the measurement procedure, validity is the ability of an instrument to measure what it is designed to measure.

Variable: An image, perception or concept that is capable of measurement – hence capable of taking on different values – is called a variable. In other words, a concept that can be measured is called a variable. A variable is a property that takes on different values. It is a rational unit of measurement that can assume any one of a number of designated sets of values.

Working definition: *See* **Operational definition**

Bibliography

Ackroyd, Stephen & John Hughes, 1992, *Data Collection in Context*, New York, Longman.

Alkin, Marvin C. & Lewis C. Solomon (eds), 1983, *The Costs of Evaluation*, Beverly Hills, CA, Sage.

Alwin, Duane F. (eds), 1978, *Survey Design and Analysis: Current Issues*, Beverly Hills, CA, Sage.

Babbie, Earl, 1989, *Survey Research Methods* (2nd edn), Belmont, CA, Wadsworth.

Babbie, Earl, 2007, *The Practice of Social Research* (11th edn), Belmont, CA, Wadsworth.

Bailey, Kenneth D., 1978, *Methods of Social Research* (3rd edn), New York, Free Press.

Barton, Ruth, 1988, *Understanding Social Statistics: An Introduction to Descriptive Statistics*, Perth Editorial/Publication Unit, Division of Arts, Education and Social Sciences, Curtin University of Technology.

Bernard, H. Russell, 1994, *Research Methods in Anthropology: Qualitative and Quantitative Approaches* (2nd edn), Thousand Oaks, CA, Sage.

Bernard, H. Russell, 2000, *Social Research Methods: Qualitative and Quantitative Approaches*, Thousand Oaks, CA, Sage.

Bilson, Andy (ed.), 2005, *Evidence-based Practice in Social Work*, London, Whiting & Birch.

Black, James A. & Dean J. Champion, 1976, *Methods and Issues in Social Research*, New York, Wiley.

Blaikie, Norman, 2007, *Approaches to Social Enquiry* (2nd edn), Cambridge, Polity Press.

Bogdan, Robert & Sari Knopp Biklen, 1992, *Qualitative Research for Education: An Introduction to Theory and Methods* (2nd edn), Boston, Allyn & Bacon.

Bradburn, M. Norman & Seymour Sudman, 1979, *Improving Interview Method and Questionnaire Design*, London, Jossey-Bass.

Brinberg, David & Joseph E. McGreth, 1985, *Validity and the Research Process*, Beverly Hills, CA, Sage.

Bulmer, Martin (eds), 1977, *Sociological Research Methods: An Introduction*, London, Macmillan.

Burns, Robert B., 1997, *Introduction to Research Methods* (2nd edn), Melbourne, Longman Cheshire.

Butcher, Judith, 1981, *Copy-Editing: The Cambridge Handbook for Editors, Authors and Publishers* (2nd edn), Cambridge, Cambridge University Press.

Carr, Wilfred & Steven Kemmis, 1986, *Becoming Critical: Education, Knowledge and Action Research*, Melbourne, Deakin University.

Cherry, Nita, 2002, *Action Research: A Pathway to Action, Knowledge and Learning*, Melbourne, RMIT Publishing.

The Chicago Manual of Style (14th edn), 1993, Chicago and London, University of Chicago Press.

Cohen, Morris R. & Ernest Nagel, 1966, *An Introduction to Logic and Scientific Methods*, London, Routledge & Kegan Paul.

Collins Dictionary of the English Language, 1979, Sydney, Collins.

Commonwealth of Australia, 2002, *Style Manual* (6th edn), Milton, Wiley Australia.

Cozby, C. Paul, 1985, *Methods in Behavioral Research*, London, Mayfield.

Crano, William D. & Marilynne B. Brewer, 2002, *Principle and Methods of Social Research* (2nd edn), London, Lawrence Erlbaum.

Creswell, John W., 2003, *Research Design: Qualitative, Quantitative and Mixed Methods Approaches* (2nd edn), Thousand Oaks, CA, Sage.

Creswell, John W., 2007, *Qualitative Inquiry and Research Design: Choosing among Five Approaches* (2nd edn), Thousand Oaks, CA, Sage.

Crotty, Michael, 1998, *The Foundations of Social Research*, St Leonards, NSW, Allen & Unwin.

Cunningham, J. Barton, 1993, *Action Research and Organizational Development*, London, Praeger.

de Vaus, David, 2002, *Surveys in Social Research* (5th edn), St Leonards, NSW, Allen & Unwin.

Denzin, Norman K. & Yvonna S. Lincoln (eds), 1994, *Handbook of Qualitative Research*, Thousand Oaks, CA, Sage.

Denzin, Norman K. & Yvonna S. Lincoln (eds), 1998, *Collecting and Interpreting Qualitative Materials*, Thousand Oaks, CA, Sage.

Denzin, Norman K. & Yvonna S. Lincoln (eds), 1998, *Strategies of Qualitative Inquiry*, Thousand Oaks, CA, Sage.

Denzin, Norman K. & Yvonna S. Lincoln (eds), 2005, *The Sage Handbook of Qualitative Research* (3rd edn), Thousand Oaks, CA, Sage.

Denzin, Norman K. & Yvonna S. Lincoln, 2008, *The Landscape of Qualitative Research* (3rd edn), Los Angeles, Sage.

Dixon, Beverly & Gary Bouma, 1984, *The Research Process*, Melbourne, Oxford University Press.

Duncan, Otis Dudley, 1984, *Notes on Social Measurement: Historical and Critical*, New York, Russell Sage Foundation.

Elliott, Jane, 2005, *Using Narrative in Social Research*, London, Sage.

Foreman, E. K., 1991, *Survey Sampling Principles*, New York, Marcel Dekker.

Festinger, Leon & Daniel Katz (eds), 1966, *Research Methods in Behavioral Sciences*, New York, Holt, Rinehart and Winston.

Gilbert, Nigel (ed.), 2008, *Researching Social Life* (3rd edn), London, Sage.

Gray, Mel, Debbie Plath & Stephen Webb, 2009, *Evidence-based Social Work*, London, Routledge.

Grinnell, Richard Jr (ed.), 1981, *Social Work Research and Evaluation*, Itasca, IL, F.E. Peacock.

Grinnell, Richard Jr (ed.), 1988, *Social Work Research and Evaluation* (3rd edn), Itasca, IL, F.E. Peacock.

Grinnell, Richard Jr (eds), 1993, *Social Work Research and Evaluation* (4th edn), Itasca, IL, F.E. Peacock.

Hakim, Catherine, 1987, *Research Design: Strategies and Choices in the Design of Social Research*, London, Allen & Unwin.

Hall, Irene & David Hall, 2004, *Evaluation and Social Research: Introducing Small Scale Practice*, Basingstoke, Palgrave Macmillan.

Hawe, Penelope, Deirdre Degeling & Jane Hall, 1992, *Evaluating Health Promotion*, Sydney, Maclennan+Petty.

Hessler, Richard M., 1992, *Social Research Methods*, New York, West Publishing.

Kaplan, David (eds), 2004, *The Sage Handbook of Quantitative Methodology for the Social Sciences*, Thousand Oaks, CA, Sage.

Kazdin, Alan, 1982, *Single-case Research Designs*, New York, Oxford University Press.

Kerlinger, Fred N., 1973, *Foundations of Behavioral Research* (2nd edn), New York, Holt, Rinehart and Winston.

Kerlinger, Fred N., 1979, *Behavioral Research: A Conceptual Approach*, Sydney, Holt, Rinehart and Winston.

Kerlinger, Fred N., 1986, *Foundations of Behavioral Research* (3rd edn), New York, Holt, Rinehart and Winston.

Kirk, Jerome & Marc L. Miller, 1986, *Reliability and Validity in Qualitative Research*, Newbury Park, CA, Sage.

Krueger, Richard & Mary Anne Casey, 2000, *Focus Groups: A Practical Guide for Applied Research* (4th edn), Thousand Oaks, CA, Sage.

Kvale, Steinar & Svend Brinkmann, 2009, *Interviews* (2nd edn), Thousand Oaks, CA, Sage.

Leary, Mark R., 1995, *Introduction to Behavioral Research Methods* (2nd edn), Pacific Grove, CA, Brooks/Cole.

Longyear, Marie (eds), 1983, *The McGraw-Hill Style Manual, A Concise Guide for Writers and Editors*, New York, McGraw-Hill.

Lundberg, George A., 1942, *Social Research: A Study in Methods of Gathering Data* (2nd edn), New York, Longmans, Green.

Marshall, Catherine & Gretchen B. Rossman, 2006, *Designing Qualitative Research*, Thousand Oaks, CA, Sage.

Martin, David W., 1985, *Doing Psychological Experiments* (2nd edn), Monterey, CA, Brooks/Cole.

May, Tim, 1997, *Social Research: Issues, Methods and Process* (2nd edn), Buckingham, Open University Press.

Minium, Edward W., 1978, *Statistical Reasoning in Psychology and Education* (2nd edn), New York, Wiley.

Monette, Duane R., Thomas J. Sullivan & Cornell R. DeJong, 1986, *Applied Social Research: Tools for the Human Services*, Forth Worth, TX, Holt, Rinehart, and Winston.

Moser, Claus A. & Graham Kalton, 1989, *Survey Methods in Social Investigation* (2nd edn), Aldershot, Gower.

Nachmias, David & Clara Nachmias, 1987, *Research Methods in Social Sciences*, New York, St Martin's Press.

Padgett, Deborah K., 2008, *Qualitative Methods in Social Work Research* (2nd edn), Thousand Oaks, CA, Sage.

Patton, Michael Quinn, 1990, *Qualitative Evaluation and Research Methods*, Newbury Park, CA, Sage.

Plano Clark, Vicki L. & John W. Creswell, 2009, *Understanding Research: A Consumer's Guide*, Melbourne, Pearson (Merrill).

Poincaré, 1952, *Science and Hypothesis*, New York, Dover.

Powers, Gerald T., Thomas M. Meenaghan & Beverley G. Twoomey, 1985, *Practice Focused Research: Integrating Human Practice and Research*, Englewood Cliffs, NJ, Prentice Hall.

Ritchie, Donald A., 2003, *Doing Oral History: A Practical Guide*, Oxford, Oxford University Press.

Robson, Colin, 2002, *Real World Research* (2nd edn), Oxford, Blackwell.

Rohlf, F. James & Robert R. Sokal, 1969, *Statistical Tables*, San Francisco, CA, W.H. Freeman.

Rossi, Peter H. & Howard E. Freeman, 1993, *Evaluation: A Systematic Approach*, Newbury Park, CA, Sage.

Rossi, Peter H., Howard E. Freeman & Mark W. Lipsey, 1999, *Evaluation: A Systematic Approach* (6th edn), Thousand Oaks, CA, Sage.

Rutman, Leonard (eds), 1977, *Evaluation Research Methods: A Basic Guide*, Beverly Hills, CA, Sage.

Rutman, Leonard, 1980, *Planning Useful Evaluations: Availability Assessment*, Beverly Hills, CA, Sage.

Rutman, Leonard, 1984, *Evaluation Research Methods: A Basic Guide* (2nd edn), Beverly Hills, CA, Sage.

Sandefur, Gary D., Howard E. Freeman & Peter H. Rossi, 1986, *Workbook for Evaluation: A Systematic Approach* (3rd edn), Beverly Hills, CA, Sage.

Sarantakos, S., 2005, *Social Research* (3rd edn), New York, Palgrave Macmillan.

Schinke, Steven P. & Lewayne Gilchrist, 1993, 'Ethics in research', in R. M. Grinnell (eds), *Social Work, Research and Evaluation* (4th edn), Itasca, IL, F.E. Peacock.

Selltiz, Jahoda, Morton Deutsch & Stuart Cook, 1962, *Research Methods in Social Relations* (rev. edn), New York, Holt, Rinehart and Winston.

Siegel, Sidney, 1956, *Nonparametric Statistics for the Behavioral Sciences*, Sydney, McGraw-Hill.

Silverman, David, 2004, *Qualitative Research: Theory, Methods and Practice* (2nd edn), London, Sage.

Silverman, David, 2005, *Doing Qualitative Research* (2nd edn), London, Sage.

Simon, Julian L., 1969, *Basic Research Methods in Social Sciences: The Art of Empirical Investigation*, New York, Random House.

Smith, Herman W., 1991, *Strategies of Social Research* (3rd edn), Orlando, FL, Holt, Rinehart and Winston.

Somekh, Bridget and Cathy Lewin (eds), 2005, *Research Methods in the Social Sciences*, Los Angeles, CA, Sage.

Stake, Robert E., 1995, *The Art of Case Study Research*, Thousand Oaks, CA, Sage.

Stevens, Stanley Smith, 1951, 'Mathematics, measurement, and psychophysics', in S. S. Stevens (ed.), *Handbook of Experimental Psychology*, New York, Wiley.

Stufflebeam, Daniel L. & Anthony J. Shinkfield, 1985, *Systematic Evaluation: A Self-Instructional Guide to Theory and Practice*, Boston, MA, Kluwer–Nizhoff.

Tashakkori, Abbas & Charles Teddue (eds), 2003, *Handbook of Mixed Methods in Social & Behavioral Research*, Thousand Oaks, CA, Sage.

Taylor, Steven J. & Robert Bogdan, 1998, *Introduction to Qualitative Research Methods: A Guidebook and Resource* (3rd edn), New York, Wiley.

Thyer, Bruce A., 1993, 'Single-systems research design', in R. M. Grinnell (eds), *Social Work Research and Evaluation* (4th edn), Itasca, IL, F.E. Peacock, pp. 94–117.

Trochim, William M. K. & James Donnelly, 2007, *The Research Methods Knowledge Base* (3rd edn), Mason, OH, Thomson Custom Publishing.

Walter, Maggie (eds), 2006, *Social Research Methods: An Australian Perspective*, Melbourne, Oxford University Press.

Webster's Third New International Dictionary, 1976, G. & C. Company, Springfield, MA.

Yegidis, Bonnie & Robert Weinback, 1991, *Research Methods for Social Workers*, New York, Longman.

Young, Pauline V., 1966, *Scientific Social Survey Research* (4th edn), Englewood Cliffs, NJ, Prentice Hall.

Index

Research Methods
Books from SAGE

INTERPRETING QUALITATIVE DATA THIRD EDITION

DAVID SILVERMAN

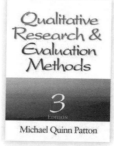

Qualitative Research & Evaluation Methods

3 EDITION

Michael Quinn Patton

Constructing Grounded Theory

A Practical Guide through Qualitative Analysis

Kathy Charmaz

EVALUATION
A Systematic Approach
SEVENTH EDITION

PETER H. ROSSI
MARK W. LIPSEY
HOWARD E. FREEMAN

SECOND EDITION
INTRODUCTION TO SOCIAL RESEARCH
QUANTITATIVE AND QUALITATIVE APPROACHES
KEITH F PUNCH

NIGEL GILBERT
RESEARCHING SOCIAL LIFE
THIRD EDITION

Sixth Edition
INVESTIGATING THE
Social World
THE PROCESS AND PRACTICE OF RESEARCH

Russell K. Schutt

AN INTRODUCTION TO
QUALITATIVE RESEARCH
UWE FLICK
EDITION 4

DEVELOPING
EFFECTIVE
RESEARCH
PROPOSALS
Keith F Punch
SECOND EDITION

www.sagepub.co.uk

SAGE